The West Country

CRUISING COMPANION

A yachtsman's pilot and cruising guide to ports and harbours from
Portland Bill to Padstow, including the Isles of Scilly

Mark Fishwick

WILEY ✦ NAUTICAL

Photographs © 2008 Mark Fishwick

Aerial photography ©Patrick Roach and Sealand Aerial Photography (pages 21, 31, 46, 54, 91, 104,
107, 133, 150, 158, 169, 191, 199, 211, 218, 227)

Additional photography:
Page 3 ©Sue Fishwick; Page 97 ©Plymouth Yacht Haven; Page 102 (bottom) ©Mayflower Marina;
Page 115 (bottom) ©Weir Quay Boatyard; Page 148 (bottom) ©Falmouth Premier Marina

For Wiley Nautical
Executive Editor: David Palmer
Project Editor: Brett Wells
Assistant Editor: Drew Kennerley

For Nautical Data
Cartography: Jamie Russell
Art Direction: Vanessa Bird and Jamie Russell
Cruising Companion series editors: Vanessa Bird and Lucinda Roch

ISBN-13: 978-0-470-98569-4

IMPORTANT NOTICE

This Companion is intended as an aid to navigation only. The information contained within should not solely
be relied on for navigational use, rather it should be used in conjunction with official hydrographic data.
Whilst every care has been taken in compiling the information contained in this Companion, the publishers,
author, editors and their agents accept no responsibility for any errors or omissions, or for any accidents
or mishaps which may arise from its use.

Neither the publisher nor the author can accept responsibility for errors, omissions or alterations in this book.
They will be grateful for any information from readers to assist in the update and accuracy of the publication.

Readers are advised at all times to refer to official charts, publications and notices.
The charts contained in this book are sketch plans and are not to be used for navigation.
Some details are omitted for the sake of clarity and the scales have been chosen
to allow best coverage in relation to page size.

Correctional supplements are available at www.wileynautical.com and on request from the publishers.

Printed by SNP Leefung Printers Ltd, China

PREFACE

In January 1970 the age of majority was reduced to 18, but for those of us born well before that date it will always remain as 21, and with this seventh edition the *West Country Cruising Companion* truly comes of age! A satisfying milestone, yes, but yet again, I reflect with some dismay how much water has passed under the keel since the book first appeared in 1987.

Thumbing through that first edition, how primitive it now looks – just a few colour pictures and the rest in black and white! The ports, facilities and our expectations have since seen much change, boats have become ever larger and more sophisticated, but so too have the charges! But most of all, it is the technological advances that have since changed the face of cruising so dramatically.

When I was researching the first edition, the only electronics on *Temptress* were a softly whirring Seafarer echo sounder and a Sestrel radio direction finder to home in on all the marine and aerial beacons. Communication with the shore meant waiting your turn to get a link call through to the local VHF coast radio station, and a conversation that anyone else with their ears pressed against a VHF could cheerfully enjoy. What a difference GPS and mobile phones have made, the only trouble now is that so much time seems to be taken up with staying in touch!

Computers on board, WiFi internet access, websites for just about everything, digital charts, electronic chart plotters, where, I wonder will it all be going next? I never imagined that one day the Port Guides would include something called internet access among all the other essentials. . .

Cyberspace apart, change continues apace in the real world, too; no major marinas or facilities have emerged during the four years since the last edition of the book but Dart Marina and Noss Marina are now separate entities, the regeneration of Torquay continues apace with much increased visitor berthing, and the once thriving china clay port of Par has closed. The next few years promise to be interesting, with the large Port Falmouth Marina due to open in Falmouth Docks in 2008, and other major marina projects under consideration in Mount's Bay and on the Dart.

For those who know the area, a few landmark changes have included the prohibition of anchoring in St Mary's harbour, Scilly, and within the inner reaches of the Helford River. I have noticed, too, a sinister trend in a number of ports increasing visitor berthing charges during the peak season!

Navigationally, one of the most important changes to note is the entrance channel to the River Exe, where encroaching sands have created a significant alteration to the status quo, and a new approach channel has emerged.

On the human side, this edition sees the largest flood tide of new harbourmasters to date, 10 no less, at Padstow, Newquay, St Mary's, Mousehole, St Mawes, Looe, Salcombe, Dartmouth, Teignmouth and West Bay. Marina managers, too, have been on the move with new faces at Mylor, Sutton Marina and Queen Anne's Battery! A notable loss to the boating community, though, was someone I had known since my boyhood on the Exe, Daniel Trout, who slipped his mooring in March 2007 after 93 busy years on the river. Joining his father's boatbuilding business at the age of 14, he later became quay master and eventually created Trout's Boatyard in the 1960s. One of Topsham's last real waterfront characters, his wry humour was legendary, he was a great raconteur, and a gentleman in the truest sense of the word.

There's also been change, too, close to home – eagle eyed devotees will have spotted a new publisher, Wiley Nautical, a larger format and, for the first time ever, a hardback cover.

I've not changed that much, hair's even greyer, and the brain cells, too: apologies if I seem to have trouble remembering your name! As always I have done my absolute best to ensure accuracy but apologise in advance for any mistakes or omissions that have crept in. Changes are continual and any assistance to keep this book up to date will always be much appreciated. Suggestions for improvements are also always welcome and, wherever possible, acted upon. A quick email to mfishwick@aol.com is all I would request, and my thanks to all those who have responded in the past and who will hopefully continue to do so.

That's it! Enough! Relax and enjoy your West Country cruising . . .

Mark Fishwick,
Lympstone, February 2008

THE AUTHOR

Born in Exeter and brought up on the River Exe, Mark Fishwick began sailing at an early age and soon ventured further to explore the rivers, creeks and harbours of the West Country in his parents' 18ft 6in Alacrity sloop *Vallette*. He moved to Cornwall in 1973 soon after buying his present boat, the 34ft 1910 gaff yawl *Temptress*, and since then has enjoyed a varied nautical life encompassing commercial fishing, charter skippering in the West Indies, yacht delivery, boatyard work, writing, photography and just occasionally sailing for fun! He has now returned to his roots and lives within sight of the River Exe, close to Lympstone.

Helford Pool looking west

ACKNOWLEDGEMENTS

The continuing accuracy of a book of this sort cannot be achieved without a large amount of assistance from others, now too numerous to mention by name, but my heartfelt thanks again to all the harbourmasters, marina managers, yacht club secretaries, readers and other diverse individuals who have generously helped with my requests for information and suggestions to keep this book up to date. My thanks also to Wiley Nautical, my new publisher, to Lucy Roch and Jamie Russell for the production, and last, but definitely not least, to my wife Sue for her tireless support and encouragement and for coping with Bosun while I was afloat for many weeks during 2007 researching this new edition. Increasingly grumpy, in spite of his salty name, our dog no longer goes happily to sea!

Temptress, Old Grimsby, Tresco, Scilly

CONTENTS

CONTENTS

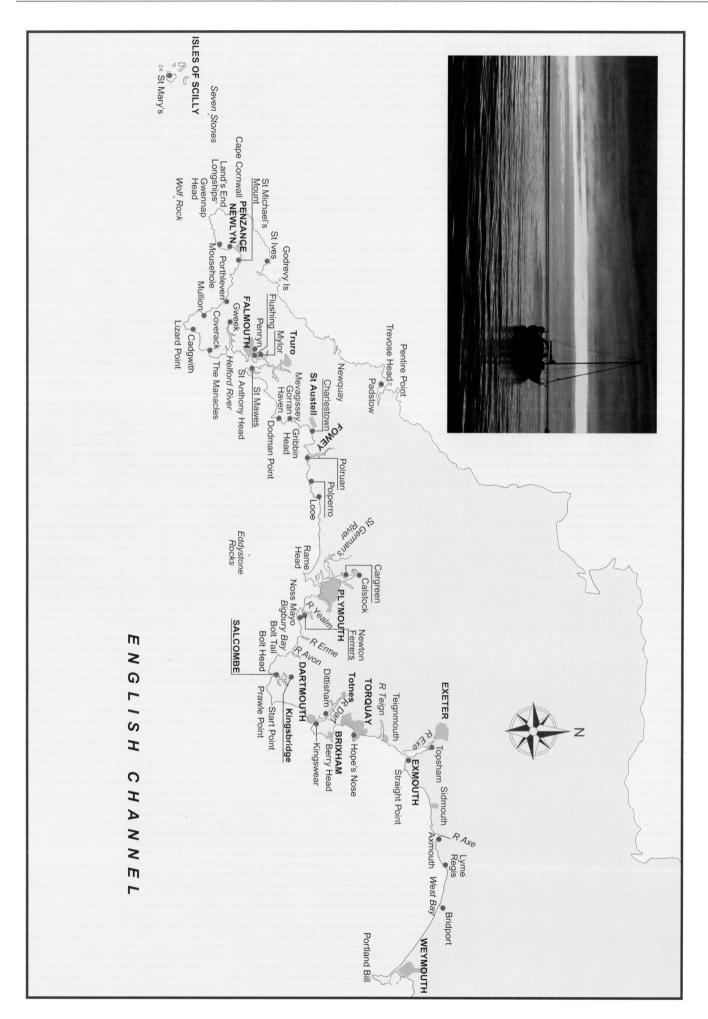

Promise of a perfect day, River Yealm

Introduction

If I were given a brief to design a perfect cruising ground the West Country would not fall too far short of it, and I would be little inclined to make many changes. Year after year the magnificent coastline of Devon and Cornwall has attracted more and more visiting yachts to its ports and rivers – deep and mostly of easy access – and its rock bound coast, steep-to with few off-lying dangers.

If there could be one major change that we would all agree on it would inevitably have to be the weather, but what would English cruising be without its unpredictability? Generally speaking, well in the track of the prevailing southwesterly air stream and its accompanying depressions, the early summer can often provide some of the better spells of weather, and we can also be lucky in the early autumn. There does, however, seem to be a tendency for far more unsettled weather, often a blow or two, in August; not in itself a great problem once the long haul across Lyme Bay is astern, for a whole variety of harbours and safe anchorages abound, all within an easy day's sail of each other, and deep-wooded rivers like the Dart and the Fal thread far inland to provide days of absorbing exploration in themselves.

Way back in 1957, *Yachting Monthly* produced a

slim little book called *West Country Rivers*, written by D J Pooley, and it proved invaluable throughout my early explorations of my home waters back in the 1960s. Long since out of print, it was a very pleasant surprise when *Yachting Monthly* invited me to revamp the book in 1987 and my researches then soon confirmed that in those 30 years much had changed 'down west'; sailing, at one time the pursuit of the select few, had become a big leisure business, and the changes reflected it. Once forgotten backwaters and creeks – the haunt of rotting hulks, whispering mud and seaweedy smells – had been cleared and dredged, and marinas had blossomed forth; anchorages that were easy of access under sail were diminishing fast and, as moorings encroached into every available space, a reliable auxiliary was no longer a luxury but a real necessity.

To my delight the resulting book, *West Country Cruising*, soon established itself as the definitive cruising guide for the area, growing with each new edition and evolving in 2001 into the *West Country Cruising Companion*. But (and how sobering is this), another 20 years have now elapsed, the changes continue apace, and more and more boats head west to visit these shores.

In spite of it all, the inherent beauty and atmosphere

of the West Country continues to survive the onslaught well, and the sailing is as good as ever. Ashore, the varied and colourful villages and towns provide all the facilities a cruising yacht might need, from essentials like good ale and launderettes, to engineers and riggers. There is much of historical interest, and with vast areas fortunately preserved by the National Trust, many lovely walks.

There can be few visitors to these waters who sail away disappointed – hopefully this latest edition of the *West Country Cruising Companion* will help to make your cruise just that little bit more enjoyable. . .

GENERAL INFORMATION

EMERGENCIES

Rescue services within the coastal and sea area covered by this book are coordinated by Portland Coastguard, Tel: 01305 760439 – as far west as Topsham (River Exe), Brixham Coastguard, Tel: 01803 882704 – Topsham to Dodman Point, and Falmouth Coastguard, Tel: 01326 317575 – Dodman Point to Bude, north Cornwall. All maintain a 24-hour loudspeaker listening watch on VHF Channel 16 and normally work on VHF Channels 67 (Small Craft Safety), 10, 23, 73, 84 and 86 (Maritime Safety Information – MSI).

In emergencies only, VHF direction finding facilities can be activated by the Coastguard to locate a vessel in distress from Grove Point on Portland Bill, Berry Head, Prawle Point, Rame Head, The Lizard, Land's End, St Mary's and Trevose Head.

With the implementation of the Global Maritime Distress and Safety System (GMDSS) Portland, Brixham and Falmouth Coastguards all have VHF Channel 70 Digital Selective Calling (DSC) and a distress signal on this channel will be automatically received and recorded once the distress button has been activated on the shipboard VHF set, including the vessel's MMSI (Maritime Mobile Service Identity) identification number. Each Coastguard station also has its own MMSI: Portland 002320012, Brixham 002320013 and Falmouth 002320014.

All of the UK is an A1 GMDSS sea area – which means that throughout it there are Coast Radio Stations with DSC receiver/transmitters within 40 miles of each other.

NATIONAL COASTWATCH INSTITUTION (NCI)

Formed in 1994, with its Headquarters in Fowey, Tel: 0870 7872147; email: info@nci.org; www.nci.org. uk, the NCI is a charity that maintains Visual Watch Stations around the UK coast, many of which are located in former Coastguard Lookouts. They are manned by volunteer watchkeepers who monitor VHF Channel 16 and provide a visual and verbal link with

the Coastguard and RNLI during search and rescue operations. Passing small craft traffic is routinely logged, they can provide local weather information by telephone and in poor visibility some stations keep a radar watch up to 20M offshore. Increasingly on the individual station websites, webcams and live weather stations are also being added, usually thanks to the generosity of local sponsors.

West Country NCI stations operational in 2008 are:
Portland Bill, Tel: 01305 860178, (Radar) www.nci-portlandbill.org.uk
Exmouth, Tel: 01395 222492, (Radar/webcam) www.nciexmouth.org.uk
Teignmouth, Tel: 01626 772377
Froward Point, Tel: 07976 505649, (Radar) www.nci-frowardpoint.org.uk
Prawle Point, Tel: 01584 511259, (Radar) www.prawlepoint.org.uk
Rame Head, Tel: 01752 823706, (Radar) www.nci-ramehead.org.uk
Polruan, Tel: 01726 870291, www.polruan-nci.org.uk
Charlestown, Tel: 01726 817068, (Radar)
Portscatho, Tel: 01872 580180
Nare Point, Tel: 01326 231113
Bass Point, Tel: 01326 290212, (Radar) www.nci-basspoint.co.uk
Penzance, Tel: 01736 367063
Gwennap Head, Tel: 01736 871351, (Radar) www.nci-gwennaphead.co.uk
Cape Cornwall, Tel: 01736 787890, (Radar)
St Ives, Tel: 01736 799398, www.nci-stives.org (webcam/weather)
Stepper Point, Tel: 07810 898041, (Radar) www.stepper-point.co.uk
Boscastle, Tel: 01840 250965

New stations are currently planned for St Anthony's Head, Falmouth, and St Mary's, Isles of Scilly.

PASSAGE PLANNING

Since July 2002, Regulation 34 of the Safety of Life at Sea (SOLAS) Convention makes voyage planning on all vessels that go to sea a legal requirement. This is not really as onerous as it might at first seem as most sensible people afloat have doubtless long been doing this as a matter of common sense. Nevertheless, given that any passage, however short, must now be pre-planned, even in familiar waters, you should at the very least adhere to a simple check list covering the following areas:

1)   Log the times of High and Low Water at relevant ports, and particularly those which might affect arrival and departure where there are tidal restrictions such as drying harbours, crossing bars or access into tidal locks.

2)   Note the times of favourable and contrary tidal streams, with special regard to tidal gates.

3)   Ensure that you have relevant charts and almanac and pilots to cover the intended route and alternative options should the passage plan need to be amended en route.

3)   With recourse to the chart, note down potential hazards to navigation and assess safe distances to clear them by.

4)   Note down relevant pilotage detail – lights, buoyage etc – that will be encountered along your route, with particular attention to entering unfamiliar harbours.

5)   Obtain and record the latest available weather forecast and outlook.

6)   Take into due account the competence and strength of your crew.

7)   Ensure that someone ashore is aware of your intended plan. The voluntary Coastguard Identification scheme enables you to register your vessel's details for free on a CG66 form which can be downloaded from www.mcga.gov.uk, and you can relay your passage plan by VHF to the appropriate CG station on departure.

BUOYAGE

All buoyage within the area of this cruising companion falls into IALA system A.

LATERAL MARKS, defining extremities of channels, are red cans with a square red topmark and red light – to be left to port. Green or black conical buoys with triangular topmark and green light are to be left to starboard, in both cases when proceeding in the direction of the main FLOOD stream.

CARDINAL MARKS are used in conjunction with the compass, placed north, south, east or west of a hazard. They are usually pillar buoys coloured with a combination of black and yellow (see abbreviations), with quick flashing white lights, the significant feature being the double cone topmark. Two black cones pointing upwards mean the best water lies to the north (ie 'go north'); two cones pointing down mean pass to the south; points up and down (like Elevator buttons) indicate safe water to the east, and two points together (Wineglass) likewise to the west.

Other marks likely to be encountered include ISOLATED DANGERS, black double spheres topmark, as on Black Rock, Falmouth. SPECIAL MARKS, yellow buoys, often with a yellow 'X' topmark (Fl Y), often 2, 5 or 10sec, mark the limits of danger areas such as the Naval firing ranges off Dodman Point. SAFE WATER MARKS, spherical, spar or pillar buoys with red and white vertical stripes, indicate that there is navigable water all round, typically to show a landfall, prior to entering a buoyed channel, (LFL 10s or Morse 'A' · —).

More unusual marks include PREFERRED CHANNEL MARKS, at the junction of two channels. A lateral red port hand buoy with green horizontal band (Fl (2+1) R) indicates preferred channel lies to starboard of the mark and the alternative channel lies on the other side; green starboard hand buoy with red horizontal band (Fl (2+1) G) indicates preferred channel lies to port. Introduced in 2006, a new style of temporary wreck marking buoy for use in the initial emergency, either a pillar or spar, sports an equal number of vertical blue and yellow stripes and an alternating blue and yellow flashing light.

Note that in the upper reaches of some of the rivers, buoys are privately maintained and do not necessarily conform to these shapes or colourings. A variety of beacons from simple poles or stakes in the mud to

Dawn departure, River Dart. West Rock buoy and the Mewstone

complicated perches with wire stays and topmarks can mark narrower creeks.

And finally, something you are not likely to encounter anywhere else in the UK – the approach fairway to Paignton harbour (Tor Bay) is marked by a unique seasonal red port hand buoy flying International Code Flag N (chequered white and blue) to indicate that vessels must keep to the port hand side of the channel when entering, rather than the conventional starboard side!

DEPTHS
Depths mentioned in the text (eg least depth 2m, or Polca Rock 1.2m) are all in metres and 10ths of metres reduced to Chart Datum, the level of the LOWEST ASTRONOMICAL TIDE – LAT. This effectively gives the minimum depth you are likely to encounter but it should always be remembered that predicted tidal heights and depths can be much affected by the weather. Very low atmospheric pressure and strong winds may occasionally increase the predicted height by as much as 1m; conversely very high atmospheric pressure can have the opposite effect and a predicted height may be much less than anticipated. Remember too, to make due allowance for sea and swell, a rock or bar with 1.5m LAT will have considerably less water over it in the bottom of a 1m trough.

Heights above sea level (eg Ham Stone, an isolated rock [11m]) are in metres and 10ths of metres above Mean High Water Springs, MHWS.

Drying heights (eg dries 1.5m) are in metres and 10ths of metres above LAT.

DISTANCES
These are in nautical miles (2,000yds/1.852km), cables (200yds/185m) or metres.

CHARTLETS
Are of necessity simplified to show the main basics a visitor will require and should always be used with caution. Green shading = dries LAT. Dark Blue = up to 5m LAT. Pale Blue = over 5m LAT. Soundings are shown in metres and tenths of metres showing depth of water above LAT. Underlined soundings show drying heights above LAT in metres and tenths of metres.

A back up of current/corrected Admiralty Charts is essential, or the Admiralty Small Craft Folios, which represent particularly good value.
Small Craft Folio SC5601 (East Devon and Dorset Coast, Exmouth to Christchurch), has various passage charts covering the coast between Start Point and the Needles and harbour plans for Christchurch, Poole, Swanage, Portland, Weymouth, Bridport, Lyme Regis and the River Exe.
Small Craft Folio SC 5602 (The West Country, Falmouth to Teignmouth) has passage charts covering the coast between Teignmouth and the Lizard and harbour plans for Teignmouth, Torquay, Brixham, Dartmouth, Salcombe, Plymouth, Polperro, Fowey, Par, Charlestown and Falmouth, including charts of the tidal upper reaches of the rivers.

Small Craft Folio SC5603 (Falmouth to Padstow, including the Isles of Scilly) incorporates passage charts and harbour plans for Helford, Cadgwith, Coverack, Porthallow, Porthoustock, Mullion Cove, Porthleven, Penzance, Newlyn, Mousehole, Isles of Scilly, St Ives, Newquay, Padstow and Port Isaac.

Corrections for Admiralty Charts and SC Folios can be obtained from the Hydrographic Office, www.hydro.gov.uk.

Imray 'C' series charts give good coastal coverage for passage making and also include plans. C5 Bill of Portland to Salcombe Harbour (Bridport, Lyme Regis, Exmouth,Teignmouth,Torquay, Brixham,Tor Bay, Dartmouth). C6 = Salcombe Harbour to Lizard Point (Salcombe, Plymouth Sound, Looe, Polperro, Fowey and approaches, Charlestown, Mevagissey, Falmouth). C7 Falmouth to Isles of Scilly & Trevose Head (Mullion Cove, Porthleven, St Michael's Mount, Penzance, Newlyn, Mousehole, St Mary's Road, Hugh Town, St Ives, Newquay Bay).

Imray also produces a West Country Pack (WCP), No 2400 in its '2000 Series' of smaller format charts. Covering the West Country from the Exe to Land's End, it comprises 13 harbour and passage charts for the area.

Stanfords Chart Packs, CP 22 (The South Devon Coast, Plymouth to Exmouth) and CP 23 (The West Country, Lizard to Rame Head), are another alternative. The company is also producing a new series of local charts (L) designed for smaller craft, with an increasing number being introduced for the West Country. L13 Plymouth Harbour, L14 Salcombe Harbour, L15 Dartmouth Harbour, L16 Falmouth Harbour. Stanfords Chart 2 is useful for passage making as it covers the English Channel western part.

Corrections for Imray and Stanfords Charts and Chart packs can be obtained from www.imray.com.

Electronic charts include: Arcs (Skipper): S-Folio 2 England South-West Coast.

Maptech: BACD01 England SW Coast, Land's End to Portland including Isles of Scilly.

C-map Local, Max M-EW-MO19, or NT+ M-EW-CO 19 English Channel Western, Portland to Lizard. Max M-EW-MO 17 or NT+ M-EW-CO 17 Falmouth to Lundy including Isles of Scilly.

Imray Digital Chart ID4 Western Channel, Isle of Wight to Scilly includes C4, 5, 6, 7, 10, 14 and Y58, as well as harbour and port plans.

BEARINGS
Are True from seaward except otherwise stated. Magnetic variation should be applied as shown on

current Admiralty charts. Variation in the West Country (2008) ranges roughly between 4°10′W (Scilly) and 3°20′W (Lyme Bay), decreasing about 8′ to 10′ annually.

WAYPOINTS
Waypoints, particularly when used with GPS, should be regarded with due caution and at all times a regular plot of your position – course, speed, set and leeway – should be maintained at hourly intervals in case of electronic failure. Particular care should be taken to avoid mistakes when loading lat/long coordinates into your GPS memory and, although accuracy is supposed to be within 20–25m, it is probably safest to assume 50m. It is essential that you plot waypoints derived from published sources on the chart to check their accuracy before loading them, and if planning a route for a passage it will avoid setting a course that might also cross areas of potential danger.

Throughout this book GPS waypoints are referenced to WGS84 datum, now that all of the Admiralty charts for the West Country have been converted to this datum. Remember though, if using any Admiralty charts published before 2003, that they were based on the OSGB36 datum and a small correction – WGS shift – as indicated on the chart under a Satellite Derived Position Note, will have to be applied before plotting your GPS (WGS84) position to achieve full accuracy. If this is not applied, errors of up to 175m can be expected. The range of WGS shift in the West Country varies between 0′.03S, 0′.09E in the east and 0′.04S and 0′.06E in the west (0.05′ approximates to 100m).

Although navigation in good visibility poses no problem, in close quarters situations and low visibility, great care should be taken and any other traditional back up, particularly soundings, needs to be taken into account when confirming your GPS position.

It should be noted that all lat/long positions used in this book are in degrees, minutes and hundreths of a minute – the last two figures adjoining the N or W notation, eg: 50°36′.45N 04°17′.88W to enable easy input into a GPS receiver.

TIDES
The maximum rate at Springs is used throughout this book to give an indication of the worst, or if you're going with it, the best rate you will encounter.

Generally, along the coast of the West Country, streams run parallel to the shore, but set in and out of the bays, and allowance should be made for this when crossing them. Within the bays, and inshore, streams are generally weak but increase considerably in the vicinity of headlands where overfalls are often found. Streams are also much stronger within the confines of the rivers, and here it should be remembered that these are fed by the large gathering basins of the inland moors, Dartmoor, Exmoor and Bodmin, and after any

period of rain, the amount of flooding fresh water can noticeably increase the rate of streams by up to two knots, particularly in the upper reaches. Explore upper reaches of rivers only on a rising tide and do not push your luck too close to High Water at Springs or you risk being neaped!

Spring tides occur a day or so after the full and new moon, approximately every 15/16 days. High Water is usually 50 minutes later each day; Low Water approximately six hours after High Water.

High Water at Springs occurs early morning and evenings, at Neaps High Water occurs towards the middle of the day.

Rise and fall of the tide is not at a constant rate, and the old 'rule of twelfths' is always a good guide:
Rise or fall during the 1st hour: 1/12 of range
Rise or fall during the 2nd hour: 2/12 of range
Rise or fall during the 3rd hour: 3/12 of range
Rise or fall during the 4th hour: 3/12 of range
Rise or fall during the 5th hour: 2/12 of range
Rise or fall during the 6th hour: 1/12 of range

WEST COUNTRY WEATHER
Global warming or not, as in most places in the British Isles, the weather in the West Country remains very changeable and can deteriorate fast, although with comprehensive forecasting and ports within easy reach of one another, there is little excuse for getting caught out.

However, in such an eventuality it is worth remembering that the exposed nature of much of the coastline and prevailing ground swell will produce seas considerably larger than elsewhere in the Channel, particularly with wind against tide. Remember, too, when negotiating the major headlands such as Portland Bill, Start Point, the Dodman and the Lizard, if the wind is forward of the beam a fair tide will also create a noticeable and sudden increase in its apparent strength.

Unpredictability is the keyword, but if it is remotely possible to generalise, May and June can often provide a fine spell giving rise to all sorts of hopeful predictions that we're in for a long hot summer. July, alas, has a tendency to dispel such promise and can often be very mixed, or as in 2007 downright miserable as one of the wettest on record in the West Country! Although summer gales are rare, August often serves up at least one bad blow, such as the Fastnet disaster in 1979, and the tail end of Hurricane Charley in 1986. However, for once it surpassed itself in 2003, with record breaking temperatures in the high 30s and a surfeit of sun! September, too, can be very unsettled, although occasionally the much vaunted Indian Summer does occur, as it finally did in 2007; little compensation though for the earlier miserable weather!

The prevailing southwesterly air stream and the warmer waters of the Gulf Stream which embrace the

High summer – Low Tide at Green Bay, Bryher

far west create the dominant feature of the weather – depressions which usually pass to the north of the area with associated trailing warm and cold fronts creating an unsettled but at least predictable sequence of wind and accompanying rain.

When the Azores High manages to push far enough north to keep these depressions at bay it should result in fine weather. Frequently it does – ashore – but the easterly airstream that usually results has a tendency to be unpredictable in its strength and is often fresh at sea, creating very hazy conditions, blowing hard during the day and easing at night.

As most of the West Country ports evolved to provide shelter from the prevailing westerlies, many can be very uncomfortable in easterlies – Falmouth inner harbour can be spectacularly rough in an easterly gale, while the Helford is a very miserable place to be – with justification borne of long experience, the 'beastly easterly' is a wind little loved by locals in west country havens.

The topography of the rivers creates its own localised effects, particularly those bounded by high steep shores like the Dart, Fowey and the Yealm, where baffling breezes are not only encountered in the entrance but also in the upper reaches, where frustratingly fluky winds often follow the river's course. The upper Fal is a classic example – a breeze will be dead ahead in one reach, you can then follow the next bend through 90 degrees and, instead of the expected freeing, you'll find it still doggedly on the nose!

In gales these same high shores, seemingly so protective, can often produce powerful, williwaw-like downdrafts that are very unpredictable in their direction – I recall one very restless night, anchored just below the Anchor Stone on the Dart, ranging wildly across the full scope of our chain as gusts hit us from every quarter, and on another occasion, tucked away in the perfect landlocked shelter of Yealm Pool during a southwesterly gale, the boat was laid over

almost on her beam ends on several occasions!

Many places, and in particular Fowey and Salcombe, can become doubly uncomfortable in strong winds blowing contrary to the tide, but at least the misery only has to be endured for a few hours at a time!

In settled spells of fine weather land and sea breezes can be encountered anywhere, but one particular localised phenomenon I have often encountered, notably in the approaches to the Fal, Plymouth, Salcombe and also the Exe, is a fresh catabatic breeze funnelling seawards in the late afternoon, making for an interesting final thrash into port.

Fog, fortunately, is not overly frequent this far west, but in fine weather banks of low-lying sea mist can occur without warning, often towards the end of a fine warm day. In settled weather, usually when high pressure prevails, early morning mist in rivers will often be surprisingly thick, but soon burns off as the sun rises. Poor visibility associated with the passage of fronts is far more frequent in the soft misty rain, known to the Cornish as 'mizzle'.

Thunderstorms do not occur particularly frequently, as they tend to generate over the continent and drift across the channel further to the east. And, having woken on many a depressing morning to the sound of steady rain on the coachroof, let us not forget the old adage: 'Rain at seven, fine by eleven.' It's remarkable how often it turns out to be true!

WEATHER FORECASTS

These can be obtained from a variety of sources: BBC RADIO 4 (LW198kHz, MW 756kHz, FM 92.4 – 96.1,103.5, 104.9MHz,) Shipping forecasts, weekdays, at local time 0048 and 0520 (LW, MW and FM, Gale warnings, full shipping forecast, inshore waters forecast and weather reports from Coastal Stations); 1201 (LW Shipping forecast only, no inshore water forecast or coastal station reports); 1754 (LW Shipping forecast only, also on FM Sat/Sun).

Portland, Plymouth, Sole, Lundy and Fastnet are the most relevent sea areas to the cruising grounds covered by this book. The inshore waters forecast areas are Selsey Bill to Lyme Regis, Lyme Regis to Land's End, including the Isles of Scilly, and Land's End to St David's Head, including the Bristol Channel.

BBC Local Radio Stations also issue Coastal Waters forecasts, but the times are subject to annual change.
BBC Radio Devon broadcasts on:
FM 95.8, 990kHz (Exeter area)
FM 103.4, 1458kHz (Torbay area)
FM 103.4, 855kHz (Plymouth area)
BBC Radio Cornwall broadcasts on:
FM 95.2, 657kHz (north and east)
FM103.9, 630kHz (mid and west)
FM 96.0 (Isles of Scilly)

In before the squall, visitors' pontoon, Yealm Pool

HM COASTGUARD MSI BROADCASTS

Major improvements were made to the HM Coastguard Maritime Safety Information (MSI) broadcasts on 1 February 2007. The broadcasts are now made in LOCAL ('clock') TIME every three hours, and the content is one of three different schedules: (A) involves a full MSI broadcast including the latest Gale Warnings, Shipping Forecast, Inshore Forecast navigational warnings, gunfacts and subfacts; (B) New Inshore Forecast, previous outlook and gale warnings; (C) Repetition of Inshore Forecast and gale warnings.

Broadcast times and schedule:
Solent/Portland   0130B, 0430C, 0730A, 1030C, 1330B, 1630C, 1930A, 2230C
Brixham/ Falmouth   0110B, 0410C, 0710A, 1010C, 1310B, 1610C, 1910A, 2210C
In addition, new gale or strong wind warnings are broadcast on receipt.

In all cases it should be noted that the timing of these broadcasts can be affected if there is an ongoing emergency. Following an initial announcement on VHF Channel 16, you will be advised to listen on one of the following channels: 10, 23, 73, 84 or 86. For specific details, see the *Safety information and weather* section in the introduction to each chapter.

The Coastguard will normally repeat the latest forecast on VHF request, but this facility should not be abused.

NAVTEX

The West Country is covered by Niton navtex station which transmits weather information on 518 kHz at 0840 and 2040 UT, with an extended outlook at 0040 UT. Inshore waters forecasts are transmitted on 490 kHz at 0520 and 1720 UT.

INTERNET

There are several good online sites where you can download free forecasts including the Met Office, www.metoffice.gov.uk/marine, and the BBC www.bbc.co.uk/weather/coast. Both include synoptic pressure charts, current shipping and inshore forecasts, outlook forecasts for the next five days and other goodies like current and recent conditions at weather buoys and additional sources of data.

WILEY NAUTICAL WEATHER APPLICATIONS

Wiley Nautical has launched two new programs that let you get detailed forecasts to your mobile or laptop while you are on the move. Both the mobile and desktop program include forecasts for inshore, offshore and mainland locations throughout the UK and surrounding waters. Forecasts are updated four times daily, cover out to seven days ahead, with a detailed breakdown for each three hour period. It's good to eventually see this quality of graphical forecasts available cheaply to sailors on the go.

Get it on your mobile: Text the 'WEATHER WILEY' to 60030 or visit **www.wileynautical.com/weather**. Your first three forecasts are free, future requests will be charged to you through your normal mobile bill. Latest rates and discounts are shown on the above site. Usual network operator charges for SMS text messages and downloads apply.

Get it on your computer: Visit **www.wileynautical.com/weather**. All forecasts are provided free through the desktop application.

OTHER SOURCES OF WEATHER INFORMATION

Nearly all the marinas, harbour authorities and yacht clubs within the area covered by this book display a daily forecast, three to five day outlook and synoptic weather charts.

YACHT CLUBS

The once stuffy image of many yacht clubs has fortunately changed dramatically in recent years and most West Country clubs now welcome genuine cruising crews to use their facilities on a temporary basis. It is, however, a privilege that visitors should not abuse, and on arrival at any new Club immediately introduce yourself to the steward, secretary or a member, ascertain if you are indeed welcome and ask for the visitors' book, which should be signed not only by yourself but also your crew. For two or three nights, this will be sufficient, but should you wish to use the club's facilities for a longer period, check with the secretary as to the arrangements for temporary membership, which is often available. Remember at all times, you are their guest and should behave and dress accordingly.

CUSTOMS

As long as you are only moving between countries within the European Union (EU) there is no longer any need to make declarations to the Customs on departure from or re-entry into the UK, although Customs Officers do retain the power to search any boat at any time. However, if you are departing to or arriving from any port outside the EU, AND THIS INCLUDES THE CHANNEL ISLANDS, you will have to obtain a copy of HM Customs form C1331, either from your nearest Customs Office, by phoning the National Advice Service (Tel: 0845 010 0900 0800 – 2000 Mon – Fri), or via its website www.hmrc.gov.uk. Copies can also usually be found at local yacht clubs and marinas. Part one of C1331 must be returned to the Customs prior to departure and part two retained for completion as soon as you re-enter UK 12 mile territorial waters when a Q flag must also be flown until all formalities are complete. On arrival contact the Customs immediately on its 24-hour Yachtline, Tel: 0845 7231110, for clearance, which can be usually effected over the phone.

Sadly, drug-smuggling has been increasing along the British coast and the West Country is no exception. Any suspicious activity, items being unloaded from boats in isolated bays, or small craft alongside each other at sea should be reported immediately to the Customs. Dial 0800 595000 and ask for DRUG SMUGGLING ACTION LINE.

As increasing numbers of pleasure boats are being used in this insidious trade, ultimately it can only bring the name of genuine cruising crews into suspicion and disrepute, so it is very much in our interests to do anything we can to help assist in stamping it out. It may be irksome at times to be asked who you are and where you have come from by Customs patrols; try not to forget that they are only doing their job.

Mylor Yacht Harbour Marina

HARBOURS AND MARINAS

VHF

The primary working channel between vessels and marinas covered in this book is Channel 80, or alternatively, the secondary working Channel M. Harbours, for the most part, maintain a listening watch on Channel 16 and you will then move to their working channel as advised; increasingly, though, many will often respond if you call them in the first instance directly on their working channel.

CHARGES

To give an overall indication of the sort of charges you can anticipate, the price shown under OVERNIGHT CHARGE in the introduction for each port is the maximum you should have to pay for an overnight stay in a boat of 10 metres LOA on Harbour Authority facilities, either alongside or on a mooring, or in other private commercial operations such as marinas.

This includes Value Added Tax (VAT) and harbour dues, if applicable, and wherever possible was correct for the start of the 2008 season. *Most harbours and marinas increase their charges annually in line with inflation, and this should always be taken into consideration.*

In a number of West Country ports there has been a growing tendency to increase charges during the peak months of July and August on prime facilities. There also seems to be a developing trend in the number of places trying to extend the sailing season with special autumn deals – three nights paid for in high season earning a voucher for a free night in September and October!

All other charges within the main text are shown inclusive of VAT.

USEFUL GEAR

The majority of the larger harbour authorities in the West Country not only provide alongside berthing but also swinging moorings as a cheaper alternative.

A chain/rope mooring strop makes good sense!

Visitors' mooring buoys with pick-up strops will be found in the River Yealm, St Mawes, Helford River and St Mary's Harbour, Scilly, but in the majority of places the buoys just have a large shackle or metal ring through which you secure your own mooring lines. With boats of higher freeboard it is often initially difficult to secure the buoy: one of the patent boat hooks with a detachable clip and pick up line, or mooring aid which can pass and retrieve a line like the Swiftie-Matic (www.derwentmarine.net) is a useful asset to secure temporarily to enable you to set up heavier lines. Dropping a doubled line over the buoy to lasso it is another option.

However, metal and rope are always an unhealthy combination, particularly if the mooring warp is doubled up for easy release and prey to the oldest enemy at sea – CHAFE! Add a bit of swell and snatching, and it will only be a matter of time, often just hours, before you are adrift. One solution is to unshackle your anchor chain and pass it through the ring, always a bit tedious, or, alternatively, to keep a length of chain aboard specifically for this job. Plastic pipe on the mooring warp will reduce chafe but best of all though, get a special mooring strop made up with nylon mooring warp spliced onto each end of a metre or so of chain, and a decent size soft eye at either end. One end can be secured on deck, and with a bit of jiggling you can usually get the other eye through the mooring ring and retrieve it with a boat hook. The strop can then be adjusted so the chain takes all the chafe, the elasticity of the nylon will reduce the tendency for snatching and you can sleep easily again!

In a number of smaller harbours you will have to lie alongside quays with wooden piles or just bare stone and a fender board can remove a lot of topside angst! Ideally it needs to be at least 5ft long, 1ft wide and a good 1in thick, and should span at least three fenders of differing size to accommodate the curve of your hull. And on the subject of fenders, don't skimp, buy the largest you can comfortably carry – in most West Country ports at the height of the season you will probably have to raft, and even if your neighbour is ill prepared and produces a motley selection of small and inferior fenders only suitable for a dinghy, you at least will not suffer.

MOBILE PHONES AND INTERNET ACCESS

Mobile phone coverage is for the most part very good throughout the area covered by this book, but you might encounter the odd blank spot in some of the inland creeks.

Internet access has burgeoned! All West Country marinas now have WiFi, and increasingly there are independent providers for most of the main harbour anchorages and facilities. Increasingly too, pubs and hotels are providing WiFi access, often free to customers. For those who do not take their laptops afloat, and I'm one of them, public libraries offer free internet access for up to 30 minutes, or for a small charge, the growing number of internet cafés make it easy to check the email.

AND FINALLY, WHAT FLAG IS THAT?

In recent years, an expanding fervour for regional identity has taken grip, and you are more than likely to spot a few lesser known flags fluttering aloft. The white vertical cross on a black background flag of St Piran, the Cornish patron saint of tin miners, was first to gain popularity. The legality of the unofficial 'Cornish ensign' is open to debate, but certainly you'll see a few of these too, a cross of St Piran with a Union flag in the upper left canton.

Not to be outdone, BBC Radio Devon promoted a project to come up with a Devon flag, and the end result, a white vertical cross with a thin black outline on a mid-green background, has been increasingly adopted. The latest, promoted by Scilly News, is known as the Scillonian Cross, a white vertical cross, with two blue lower cantons representing the sea and two orange upper cantons representing the Scilly sunset. In the outer upper canton there are also five white stars representing the five principal islands. So now you know!

Flying the flag for Devon!

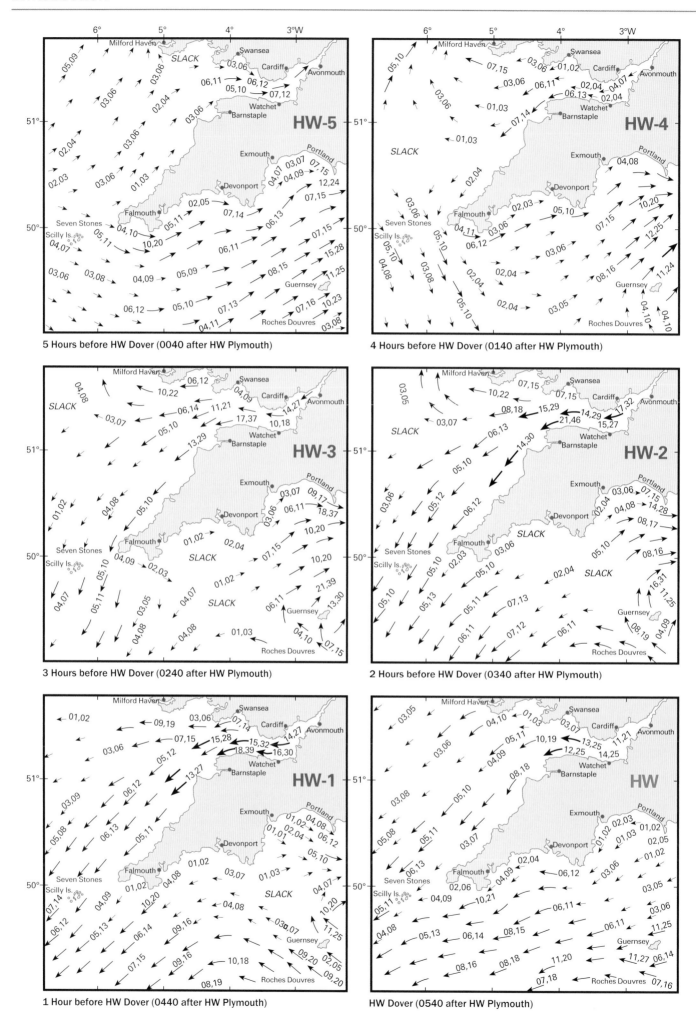

5 Hours before HW Dover (0040 after HW Plymouth)

4 Hours before HW Dover (0140 after HW Plymouth)

3 Hours before HW Dover (0240 after HW Plymouth)

2 Hours before HW Dover (0340 after HW Plymouth)

1 Hour before HW Dover (0440 after HW Plymouth)

HW Dover (0540 after HW Plymouth)

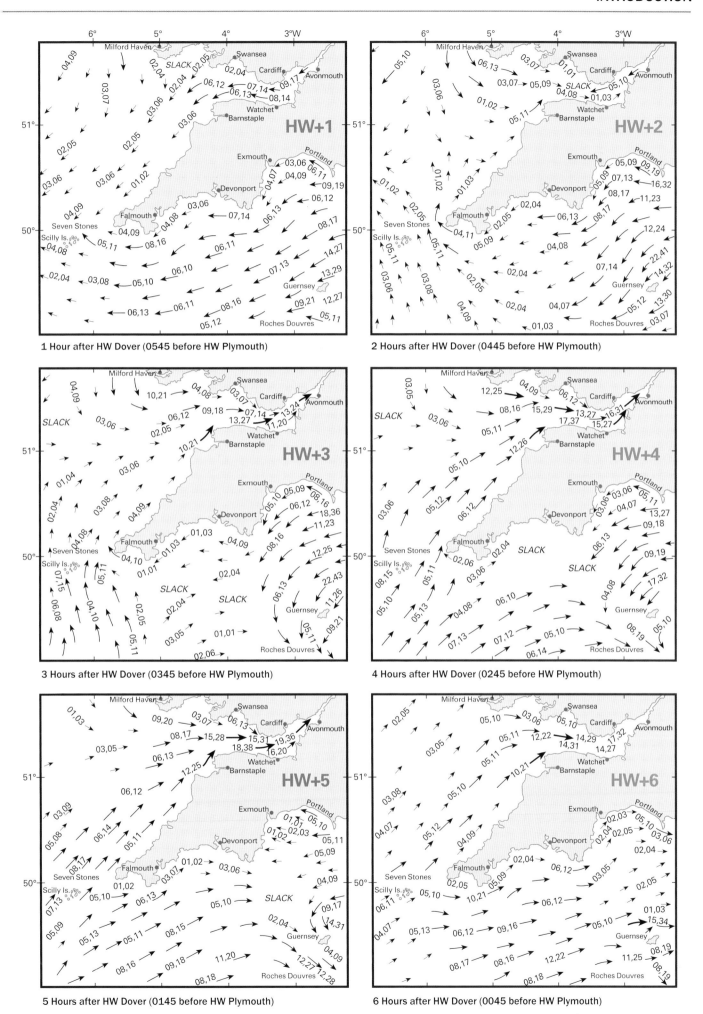

1 Hour after HW Dover (0545 before HW Plymouth)

2 Hours after HW Dover (0445 before HW Plymouth)

3 Hours after HW Dover (0345 before HW Plymouth)

4 Hours after HW Dover (0245 before HW Plymouth)

5 Hours after HW Dover (0145 before HW Plymouth)

6 Hours after HW Dover (0045 before HW Plymouth)

ABBREVIATIONS AND SYMBOLS

AB	Alongside berth	⊕	Hospital	PHM	Port-hand Mark
🔧	Boatyard	⚓	Harbourmaster	✉	Post Office
🛥	Boathoist	IDM	Isolated Danger Mark	✕	Restaurant
Ca	Cable(s)	𝒊	Information Bureau	⇄	Railway station
⚓	Chandlery	⊡	Launderette		Showers
✝	Church	Ldg	Leading	SCM	South Cardinal Mark
🔟	Diesel by cans	✦	Lifeboat	SHM	Starboard-hand Mark
	Direction of buoyage	LAT	Lowest Astronomical Tide	◣	Slip for launching, scrubbing
ECM	East Cardinal Mark	M	Nautical (Sea) mile(s)	SWM	Safe Water Mark
🧍	Fuel berth	MHWN	Mean High Water Neaps	TSS	Traffic Separation Scheme
FV(s)	Fishing vessel(s)	MHWS	Mean High Water Springs	SS	Traffic Signals
⊖	Fish Harbour/Quay	MLWN	Mean Low Water Neaps	Ⓥ Ⓥ	Visitors' berth/buoy
H+, H–	Minutes after/	MLWS	Mean Low Water Springs	WCM	West Cardinal Mark
	before each hour	NCI	National Coastwatch Institution	WPT ⊕	Waypoint
H24	Continuous	Ⓑ	Bank		
⚓	Holding tank pumpout	NCM	North Cardinal Mark		
Ⓗ	Heliport	PA	Position Approximate		

BUOY COLOURS, LIGHTS AND FREQUENCIES

R	Red		shown by number of seconds (sec or s) eg: Fl (3) R 15s. The range of the more powerful lights is given in nautical miles (M) eg: Fl (3) R 15s 25M
G	Green		
Y	Yellow		
B	Black		
W	White	L.Fl	Long flash, of not less than two seconds
RW	Red and white	Oc	Occulting light, period of light longer than darkness
YB	Yellow and black (South cardinal)		
BYB	Black, yellow, black (East cardinal)	Iso	Isophase light, equal periods of light and darkness
BY	Black and yellow (North cardinal)		
YBY	Yellow, black, yellow (West cardinal)	Q	Quick flashing light, up to 50/60 flashes per min
BR	Black and red		
FR	Fixed red light	VQ	Very quick flashing, up to 120 flashes per min
FG	Fixed green light	Mo	Light flashing a (dot/dash) morse single letter sequence, eg: Mo (S)
Fl	Flashing light, period of darkness longer than light. A number indicates a group of flashes, eg: Fl (3). Colour white unless followed by a colour, eg: Fl (3) R. Timing of whole sequence, including light and darkness,	Dir	A light, usually sectored, RWG or RG, usually giving a safe approach within the W sector. Either fixed or displaying some kind of flashing characteristic

Black Rock beacon, River Fal

Portland Bill from the south-east with tide flooding; the race and inshore passage are clearly visible

Chapter one
Portland Bill to Start Point

FAVOURABLE TIDAL STREAMS

Portland Bill
Bound west: HW Dover
Bound east: Five hours after HW Dover

Start Point
Bound west: One hour before HW Dover
Bound east: Five hours after HW Dover

PASSAGE CHARTS FOR THIS SEA AREA

AC: 2675 English Channel
              442 Lizard Point to Berry Head
              2454 Start Point to Needles
              3315 Berry Head to Bill of Portland
              1613 Eddystone to Berry Head
              1634 Berry Head to Bolt Head
              SC5601 East Devon and Dorset Coast
Imray: C5 Portland Bill to Start Point
              WCP2400.1 Exmouth to Salcombe
              ID4 Western Channel
Stanfords: 12 Needles to Start Point. CP22

SAFETY INFORMATION AND WEATHER

Solent & Portland or Brixham & Falmouth Coastguard
makes initial announcement on VHF Channel 16 at
0110, 0410, 0710, 1010, 1610, 1910, 2210, Local Time,
to confirm working channel for broadcast, normally:
Solent & Portland: Channel 84 (Grove Point, Portland),
Channel 86 (Beer Head). Brixham & Falmouth: VHF

Channel 23 (Berry Head), Channel 86 (Rame Head),
Channel 84 (East Prawle), Channel 10 (Dartmouth)

Portland Bill NCI station Tel: 01305 860178
Exmouth NCI station Tel: 01395 222492

WAYPOINTS

1	**Portland Bill offshore clearing**	
	(6M south of light)	
	50°24'.85N 02°27'.48W	
2	**Portland Race clearing**	
	(2.5M south of lighthouse)	
	50°28'.27N 02°27'.40W	
3	**Portland Bill inshore approach from west**	
	(6ca north-west of light)	
	50°31'.31N 02°28'.18W	
4	**Tor Bay northern approach**	
	(3ca east of Ore Stone)	
	50°27'.46N 03°27'.79W	
5	**Tor Bay southern approach**	
	(5ca east of Berry Head)	
	50°24'.01N 03°28'.16W	
6	**Dartmouth outer approach**	
	(4ca south-west of West Rock buoy)	
	50°19'.52N 03°32'.83W	
7	**Start Bay (1M east of Skerries buoy)**	
	50°16'.33N 03°32'.20W	
8	**Start Point**	
	(2.5M east-south-east of lighthouse)	
	50°12'.86N 03°34'.68W	

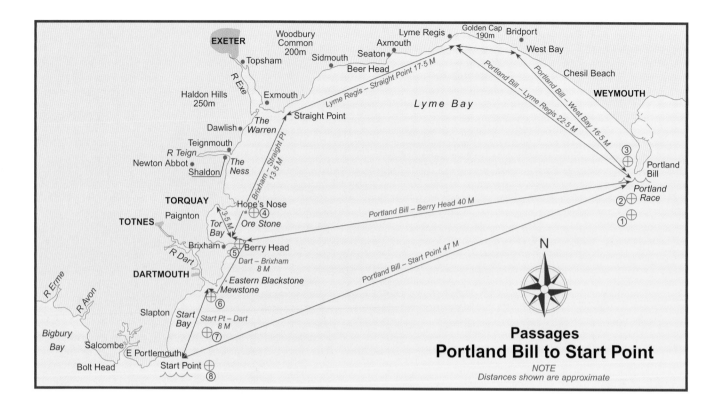

Passages
Portland Bill to Start Point
NOTE
Distances shown are approximate

'"Going West?" said the skipper of the pilot cutter. "Yes", we answered, and felt like adventurers. "And you?" He shook his head. We'd have a head wind, he reminded us, all across the bay. We knew it, but we had a good ship, too. The west wind still blew. When we were clear of the harbour we backed the jib and let the boat lie while we hoisted the dinghy on deck, and lashed it. That done, we let draw, set the foresail and mizzen, and stood away for the Shambles Light. Our voyage had begun. We were bound west, to visit a new country beyond the Bill . . .'

From Portland Bill to Berry Head it is exactly 40 miles, and 47 to the Start. It never seems less, and usually feels much further. The opening lines were written by Aubrey de Selincourt in 1948, and nothing has really changed – with the prevailing southwesterlies, the odds are still just as much in favour of being on the wind most of the way. However, you will have barely started this passage before the first major hurdle is encountered – Portland Bill and its notorious tidal race. Depending on your port of departure, the time of day and the prevailing weather conditions, there are two options for negotiating this major hazard and tidal gate: the longer but safer offshore route or the inshore passage.

PORTLAND RACE
AND HOW TO AVOID IT

The race is formed by the considerable intrusion of Portland Bill into the main English Channel tidal stream, creating large eddies on both sides of its tapering point. These run southwards for over nine hours out of every 12 at Springs and collide just to

seaward of the Bill in an area that is already much disturbed by a shallower ledge (10.4m), which extends nearly half a mile south of the Bill and over which the main tidal stream tumbles east and west.

The situation is further exacerbated by the three-mile-long Shambles Bank (least depth 3.4m) to the east-south-east, which deflects the main stream towards the tip of the Bill at rates of up to seven knots at Springs, and even more, up to 10 knots within the Race. And that is just the tide – add a bit of wind and sea and you get the general picture!

To avoid Portland Race completely you will have to pass well south of the Shambles, and a good five to six miles south of Portland Bill. In heavy weather an offing of 10 miles would be preferable and still very uncomfortable. It is easy enough to allow for this southerly offshore course if you are bound up or down Channel. Departing from the Needles (Bridge buoy), it is about 35 miles to a waypoint five miles due south of Portland Bill, a course that will also take you clear to the south of St Alban's race. However, if you break the passage with a stop in Weymouth, you will then be faced with a detour of about 15 miles to take the safe course east and south of the Shambles.

Although it seems tempting to cut through to the west of the Shambles, in anything other than a high powered vessel this is asking for big trouble, except perhaps at Neaps and in very calm weather; at any other time you will be in grave danger of being swept inexorably into the Race, or set onto the Shambles, so for me the extra miles are well worth the peace of mind.

It is seven miles from Weymouth to the East Shambles BYB east cardinal buoy (Q (3) 10s) and you will need to leave in time to get to the buoy at about HW Dover –0030, just as the tide is beginning to turn westwards. At night Portland Bill has a powerful light of a 25-mile range with interesting characteristics. Approaching from the east, its single flash gradually increases to four every 20 secs between 221° and 244°, it shows four flashes every 20 secs through the southern sector between 244° and 117°, and to the west four flashes decreasing to one every 20 secs between 117° and 144°. In addition, it also has a very useful (FR 19m 13M) sector light (271° to 291°) covering the danger area to the east-south-east over the Shambles.

The alternative is the shorter but much more demanding passage inside Portland Race, which should only be attempted in daylight, moderate weather, and avoided at the top of Springs. Although this inshore passage is often described as an area of relatively smooth water extending two to three cables from the shore, the key word here is relative, and that is relative to the far greater turmoil a short distance further to seaward!

The timing of the passage is fairly critical, but with the benefit of an engine it is easy enough to judge, although this too can be hazardous due to the many pot buoys in the inshore passage which are often submerged just below the surface by the strength of the tide. On one memorable occasion when I was berthed in Weymouth, no less than three disabled boats were towed in by the lifeboat with pot lines around their propellers in the course of two days.

Bound west, aim to be at the tip of the Bill at, ideally, HW Dover, certainly no earlier than half an hour before HW Dover and no later than two hours after HW Dover, which will normally mean a departure from Weymouth at about HW Dover –0100 (about two hours after HW Portland). You will then have a south-going stream right down the eastern side of the Bill. Aim to close the land off Grove Point, keep within 200m of the shore and as you round the tip of the Bill you should then run into the favourable north-west going stream to shoot you clear of the Race. The prominent isolated flat-topped Pulpit rock stands at the south-western extreme of the Bill and you can start to bear away to the west once this draws abeam. If you attempt the passage any later than an hour after HW Dover, you will encounter a strengthening south-going stream on the west side of the Bill that will do its very best to force you back into the Race.

Bound east, the approach to Portland Bill inshore passage is more complicated because of the problem of accurately timing your arrival after the 40 mile crossing of Lyme Bay. Ideally you should be at the tip of the Bill at HW Dover +0530, but as you approach the Bill steer towards the high northern end of Portland to counteract the south-going stream along its western side. You should then hold close down the western shore and, as you approach the old High Light and the tip of the Bill, keep about 200m off.

If you have any doubts about the timing, or if the weather is deteriorating as you cross Lyme Bay, don't take a chance. Alter course in good time to pass well south of the Bill and the Shambles, where the main east-going flood will become favourable at HW Dover +0600.

If treated with the respect it deserves, given careful planning and in suitable weather, the reality of Portland Bill is rarely as bad as the anticipation. Hundreds of small craft safely pass this way in the course of an average season, but admittedly the first time is always the most daunting. Nevertheless, the sight of Portland dropping safely astern is always accompanied by

West Bay has been much improved by the long Jurassic Pier. The visitors' pontoon is clearly visible in the outer harbour

a certain nervous relief, but for many that is soon replaced by other anxieties as the long haul across Lyme Bay, in normal visibility, is often the first opportunity to make a passage out of sight of land.

There is at first the pleasant anticipation of the new cruising ground ahead, but as the hours pass and there is still nothing to be seen, those first niggling doubts begin to set in. Is the compass really accurate? Did I allow for tidal set and leeway? Is the GPS really telling the truth? Always, an anxious eye on the weather, the slight greyness to windward, and the hint of an increase in the wind. And underlying it all, that hollow awareness that there are now no real harbours of refuge under your lee; West Bay's outer harbour provides some shelter from westerlies in the lee of the new Jurassic Pier, but there is limited depth at Low Water and potential surge. Certainly it should not be considered in winds of any strength from the south or south-east, neither should Lyme Regis, which dries completely. Both, however, can provide

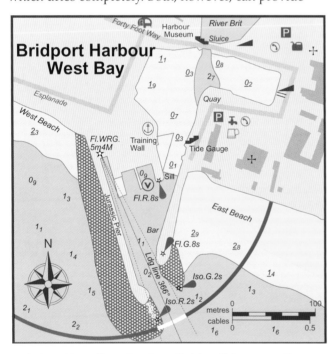

an interesting diversion in suitable offshore weather.

But then at last it is there – no longer a figment of wishful thinking, although looking not the least bit as you imagined. A featureless, thin, low line, and no sign of the two bold headlands you expected to see – Berry Head and Start Point will be indistinguishable until you are much closer.

Berry Head is distinctively square and flat topped, and the Start is an unmistakeable jagged cockscomb with a conspicuous white lighthouse and two tall radio masts close inland. It is invariably much easier to make a landfall on a strange coastline at night, ideally just before dawn, for then the lights will take away the doubts. Start Point (Fl 3 10s) has a 25-mile range and Berry Head (Fl 2 15s) has a 14-mile range. For first timers across the bay, the prospect of a night passage is

probably not very appealing and it is more likely that your approach will be a race against daylight, which is no real drawback as your probable first ports-of-call – Torquay, Brixham or the River Dart – are all well lit and easy to enter. Though tired, the excitement of landfall and arrival in the West Country should definitely carry you through.

INSHORE ACROSS LYME BAY

Given Lyme Bay's traditionally poor reputation, which to a great extent is a hangover from the days of sail when ships were regularly embayed here, most boats heading for the West Country wisely take the direct offshore route and get across as quickly as possible. However, with suitable quiet offshore weather, the longer inshore route along the coast can provide an interesting diversion, providing a closer look at the dramatic 'Jurassic Coast', renowned for its remarkable wealth of fossils. In 2001 UNESCO awarded it the status of a Natural World Heritage Site, the only one in England.

There are a couple of possible overnight or daytime stops along the way, and breaking this passage can be particularly useful when heading east to enable more accurate timing for the inshore passage at Portland Bill. Admiralty Chart 3315 covers the whole of Lyme Bay from Portland to Tor Bay, including harbour plans for both West Bay (Bridport) and Lyme Regis. Alternatively use its Small Craft Folio SC5601 (East Devon and Dorset Coast, Exmouth to Christchurch).

Running north-westwards from Portland, the spectacular low line of Chesil beach (the name derives from the Anglo-Saxon for stones) extends for nearly 15 miles as a steep and featureless shingle bank, its pebbles decreasing in size the further west you travel to such an ordered degree that local fishermen were reputed to be able to locate their position in fog or darkness by their size! There are no offlying dangers and you can follow its length just a few cables offshore if conditions permit.

Towards its western end a line of high ochre cliffs begin to rise immediately to the east of West Bay, the small tidal harbour serving Bridport, which lies just over 16 miles north-west of the Bill of Portland; there is a yellow can buoy (Fl Y 5s) marking a sewer outfall just under a mile south-south-west of the entrance.

Until recently the harbour's former 12m-wide drying entrance (approach waypoint 50°42'.23N 02°45'.86W) created dangerous seas between the two 180m long West and East piers in any sort of onshore breeze, and it could only safely be considered in settled offshore weather two hours either side of local High Water (HW Dover –0500). However, in 2005, work was finally completed on the new 240m long West Pier, now renamed 'Jurassic Pier', to the west of the existing entrance. Extending south-eastward to a position due south of the old East Pier, it forms a protective overlap, a new 43m wide entrance, and an outer harbour, improving both the accessibility and shelter, although a swell can sometimes be felt inside. A 40m long visitors' pontoon lies at the northern end of the outer harbour by the slipway on the west side of the entrance to the inner harbour. There is about 0.5m LAT in the outer harbour, the berths on the East pier are exclusively for fishing boats and the drying inner harbour, which has a sill (dries 0.1m) across its entrance, is full of local craft. Here the flood rises fast for the first hour, slackens for the next hour then continues a fast rise to High Water when there can be a stand of up to one hour.

Visitors are requested to call ahead, Tel: 01308 423222 or 078702 40636, to enable the harbourmaster, James Radcliffe, to advise on depths and allocate a berth. An intermittent VHF watch is maintained on VHF Channel 16, callsign *Bridport Radio*, working channel 11, but this cannot always be relied on. The harbour office is located at 'The Mound' on the west side of the inner harbour, and a daily weather forecast is displayed here. There is water and electricity available on both piers and also the pontoon. Although there are currently no showers or toilets for visitors, it is hoped these will be provided in the not-too-distant future.

The overnight charge for a 7m to 10m boat works out at £14, over 10m £20. If waiting for the tide, or as an alternative to entering the harbour, it is possible to anchor to the south-west of the western pier in approximately 2–3m.

A night arrival is probably not recommended for a first time visit, but there is an approach light (Dir F WRG), the white sector centred on 336°T covering the harbour entrance, with (Iso G 2s) and (Iso R 2s) on the outer end of the defensive breakwaters. There is a green light (Fl G 8s) at the outer end of the East Pier while another green (Fl G 8s) and red light (Fl R 8s) light are situated at the entrance to the inner harbour.

Thinly diguised as *Bridehaven*, West Bay achieved national prominence as the location for the 1999 BBC TV series *Harbour Lights*! There are shops, cafés and a pub, while diesel and petrol are available in cans from the local garage. However, a much wider range of facilities, including banks, can be found in Bridport, a mile inland and reached by regular buses.

Bridport was a harbour during Saxon and Medieval times when vessels could still navigate the River Brit and the proximity of much hemp and flax growing saw it develop as a major manufacturing town for rope, nets and sailcloth, an industry that continues today, albeit with synthetic material. For many years too, there was another association with small craft, for the famous 'Brit' petrol engines were manufactured here.

Because of the continual silting problems in the river, a new harbour – West Bay – was completed at the mouth of the River Brit in 1744 and, in spite of its exposed entrance, it was busy for well into the mid 1800s, both as an exporting port for the ropes of Bridport and as a shipbuilding centre. Elias Cox's yard flourished from 1779, building vessels as large as the 1,000-ton full-rigged ship *Speedy* in 1853 and the 800-ton barque *Nourmahal* in 1856 and, although the last ship was launched in 1879, repair work continued until 1885. By then the port's demise was assured, for the Great Western Railway had reached Bridport the previous year and it was proving far more cost effective to transport the town's produce by rail. Despite commercial traffic eventually ceasing during the 1960s, the port continues to provide a base for a sizeable fleet of small craft and fishing boats.

Although it is just under seven miles from Bridport to Lyme Regis, there is plenty to see as the coastline begins to take on a more dramatic aspect. The unstable coastal cliffs have been much effected by subsidence

The drying harbour at Lyme Regis is protected by the famous Cobb. There are visitors' moorings just east of the entrance

and landslip, creating many typical 'undercliff' formations, with the reddish cliffs banked above each other, undulating and rising to over 155m in places before reaching a peak at Golden Cap three miles west of Bridport which, at 190m, is the highest point on the South Coast. Its name derives from the distinctive rounded summit of yellow tinged jurassic limestone, which is particularly evident when caught in sunlight, and it tumbles away in orange cliffs towards the seaside resort of Charmouth, rising again into another spectacular stretch of jumbled coastal landslips, cliffs, gorse and bramble forming Black Ven and The Spittles, an area renowned for fossil remains. Drying rocky ledges extend to seaward from Golden Cap westwards, but as long as you keep half-a-mile offshore there are no other dangers.

Lyme Regis is an attractive stopover but the harbour dries completely. Lying just to the west of the town, the main shelter is provided by the famous Cobb, a robust and ancient sea wall immortalised in the film of John Fowles' novel *The French Lieutenant's Woman*. Built on top of a projecting reef, the Cobb dates from around 1284 and protects the artificial harbour from the prevailing southwesterly wind and sea, its outer end composed of a large rocky extension marked at its outer, eastern end by the Beacon Post – a reddish port hand beacon. The inner harbour wall, Victoria Pier, branches off the Cobb to provide additional protection to the drying harbour, while the North Wall protects it to the north-east, affording good shelter within.

There is a YB south cardinal buoy 500m east of the end of the Cobb, marking the end of the long outfall running northwards. About 100m east of the harbour entrance are four red visitors' buoys which can be used if waiting to enter the harbour or for an overnight stay. If there is any underlying swell they are liable to be rolly, and be warned – there is not much more than 1m here at Low Water Springs. Deeper draught boats can anchor further to seaward but clear of the harbour entrance where there is good holding.

Lyme Regis harbour is accessible about two hours either side of Local High Water (HW Dover –0455) and displays the same sort of tidal characteristics as West Bay. By far the best bet is to contact the friendly harbourmaster, Mike Poupard, ideally the day before (Tel: 01297 442137 or mobile 07870 240645), otherwise call Lyme Regis Harbour Radio on VHF Channel 16 – he works on Ch 14, 0800–2000 during the season – when you are about an hour away and he will endeavour to ensure there is a berth for you on arrival. His office is prominently situated in the north-west corner of the harbour opposite the large launching slip.

Normally space can be found for boats up to a maximum of about 10m LOA and deep draught boats will have to dry out on firm sand alongside the outer end of Victoria Pier, which dries between 0.3 and 1.3m

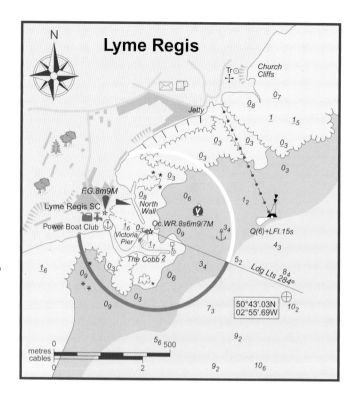

– a fender board is recommended. The overnight charge for a 10m boat alongside works out at £14, but there is a reduced rate if you remain outside on the buoys. Fresh water is available on the pier but fuel is not easy to obtain, the nearest garage being two miles away.

At night a light at the seaward end of Victoria Pier (Oc WR 8s 9M) and one on the shore (FG 9M) form a leading line of 284°T, giving a safe approach into the harbour, although a night approach is not recommended for a first time visit. A useful harbour approach waypoint 600m from Victoria Pierhead on the same leading line is 50° 43'.03N 02° 55'.69W – the south cardinal outfall buoy (Q(6) +L Fl 15s) conveniently lies 300m north of this waypoint.

Between 200 and 300 yachts a year now visit Lyme Regis, but not quite as many as during the early 19th century when as many as 600 ships a year were recorded. The need for a port developed in the 13th century to export wool from Somerset, and by 1331 it was written that the town was 'inhabited by rich and powerful merchants owning fifteen great ships and forty boats'.

But commerce finally gave way to the more genteel 19th century pursuits and it soon became the popular seaside resort it is today. Jane Austen was a regular visitor and wrote *Persuasion* while staying here, and John Fowles, who moved to Belmont House in 1968 soon after his first major literary success, lived there until his death in 2005.

The town is a short walk along the promenade from the harbour past sandy East Beach and is a very attractive place with many fine Regency and Georgian buildings. Most normal requirements can be obtained, there are plenty of pubs and restaurants, a fascinating museum in the Guildhall, and the friendly Lyme Regis Sailing Club (for contact numbers use its website: www.lrsc.org.uk) is very strategically located between the Cobb Arms pub and the Harbour Inn! When open visitors are welcome to use the club bar and showers; if the club is closed the harbourmaster can provide a key for the latter.

The shingle beach to the west of the harbour is remembered as the place where the Duke of Monmouth landed in 1685 to begin his Monmouth Rebellion with his march on London to assert his claim on the throne, an ill-fated venture that ended within weeks with his defeat and capture at Sedgemoor. He arrived in London to be executed, not crowned!

West of Lyme, the coast degenerates into another geological spectacle, the huge five mile scar of the Downlands Landslip, which became the Undercliffs National Nature Reserve in 1956. This stretch of very unstable land comprises porous chalk on top of greensand on top of clay, and is moving almost continuously, but never quite as spectacularly as in 1839 when over eight million tons – 20 acres of fields – slipped towards the sea creating a spectacular shattered landscape of deep chasms and general chaos. It attracted such great attention that Queen Victoria ordered a detour so that she could see this phenomenon from the Royal Yacht.

At the western end of Downlands, the Haven Cliff falls away to where the River Axe emerges from behind the high sheltering bank of shingle that forms the eastern end of Seaton beach. Axmouth harbour is just within the mouth of the river, a small haven with a quay and moorings which can be accessed by small shoal draught craft (max 1.2m draught) capable of taking the ground. A prominent stone pier with a starboard hand beacon at the extreme eastern end of Seaton beach deflects the river seawards through the shingle bank. There is a bar which dries to nearly 1m and access is only really feasible about half an hour either side of High Water (Dover –0440) in offshore winds and settled weather; it should not be considered in any other circumstances.

Once inside the river you turn sharply to port and follow the wall lining the starboard bank. As the river widens there are drying berths alongside the quay at the inner end of the wall, but these are mostly used by local fishing boats. Opposite are a number of drying trot moorings, max 8.5m LOA, belonging to the Axe Yacht Club, which might be able to provide an overnight berth. Due to the changing nature of the entrance, strangers are advised to contact the yacht club in advance on Tel: 01297 20742, or to anchor off and investigate by dinghy first. It is also worth knowing that the ebb at Springs can run at up to six knots within the river! However, those who attempt a visit are welcome to use the yacht club's bar and showers. Seaton, another popular seaside resort, is within easy walking distance

and all normal requirements will be found there.

In 1825 the great civil engineer Thomas Telford was engaged on a feasibility study to create a canal from Axmouth to the Bristol Channel, but like many such schemes it came to nothing. Later, the Axe's potential as a commercial port was diminished considerably with the construction in 1877 of the world's first concrete road bridge, which limits navigation just upstream of the harbour.

As you continue west of Seaton the coast trends more to the south to form Beer Roads, sheltered to the west by the last prominent chalk headland of Beer Head. The once busy fishing community of Beer still has a few of the typical East Devon full-bodied varnished clinker boats which are hauled up its steep shingle beach on wooden skids. It was also once home to Jack Rattenbury, one of Devon's most notorious smugglers who published his *Memoirs of a smuggler* in 1837 after eluding the Excisemen for nearly 50 years!

A good anchorage can be found here, well sheltered in winds through north to west if you sound in to the south of the main beach clear of the local moorings. Flanked by a stream, the attractive main street of the small town leads up from the beach. Most normal provisions are available and there is a good choice of restaurants, cafés and pubs, including the Dolphin Hotel. Chandlery and rigging is of course available from the redoubtable Jimmy Green Marine at The Meadows, Tel: 01297 20744.

It is 15 miles from Beer Head to Straight Point at the mouth of the River Exe, and from here onwards the coast is increasingly dominated by cliffs of deep red Devon sandstone topped with greenery. Just over two miles west of Beer, the long shingle beach at Branscombe attained international notoriety when the storm-damaged containership *MSC Napoli* was deliberately beached here early in 2007, resulting in a frenzy of looting as the containers began to break up and wash ashore. Thousands descended on this picturesque spot, and the iconic images of gangs hauling brand new BMW motorbikes up the beach were beamed worldwide. After months of removing the cargo, the wreck defied attempts to refloat her intact and was eventually blown into two, the bow section towed away to breakers, and a year later, the aft section still being dismantled!

Lyme Regis is ideal for boats that can take the ground

Axmouth's small haven is well hidden behind Seaton's shingle beach

THE EXE ESTUARY

Straight Point (Fl R 10s 7M) forms the eastern side of the entrance to the River Exe, a low-lying sandstone promontory with two prominent flagstaffs indicating if the rifle ranges are in use. Two yellow DZ buoys just under a mile south-east and east of the point mark the seaward limit of this range. Straight Point light has a range of seven miles, visible 246° – 071°T.

The River Exe is a broad, drying estuary, navigable for six miles inland to Topsham, but less frequented by visitors, who are often put off by the approach channel between the drying outer Pole sands and Exmouth beach. After a long period of relative stability, in the past few years this has been changing noticeably, as the Pole Sands have been shifting ever further to the south-east, reducing the depths and the width of the outer entrance channel considerably. At the same time the Pole Sands, once continuous, have split in the middle, and a new alternative channel has formed, its outer end marked by a spherical RW vertical stripe 'Exe' safe-water buoy (Fl + LFl (Morse 'A') 10s). See Exe approaches, page 33.

Dangerous in onshore winds of any strength from east through south to south-west, in favourable conditions the river is definitely worth a visit and, once in the channel, it is well-buoyed. Although lit, I would always recommend a first time approach in daylight.

The high red cliffs of Orcombe Point lead in to the beach and town of Exmouth on the eastern side of the entrance. Opposite, the Warren is a long sandy promontory which closes off the greater part of the wide mouth of the Exe from which shallow banks extend nearly a mile to seaward. To the west, the red sandstone cliffs reappear between the resort towns of Dawlish and Teignmouth, and beneath them the main London/Penzance railway line enjoys a spectacular run along the coast. Inland, the land rises to over 250m again into the Haldon Hills. There are no off-lying dangers except Dawlish Rock (2.1m), a mile east-south-east of the town, and a course half-a-mile from the shore can safely be followed if you wish to admire the weathered cliffs and sandstone pinnacles – like the fast disappearing Parson and Clerk.

Inshore, the tidal streams along this stretch of coast are generally weak and run parallel to the coast, the

Exe approach from the south-west. The high red cliffs and Sandy Bay caravan park (centre) are both conspicuous

north-north-east-going flood beginning five hours after HW Dover, and the south-south-west ebb beginning just after HW Dover, attaining a maximum of one knot at Springs. Channelled in the closer approaches to the rivers, however, rates increase considerably, attaining in excess of four knots at Springs.

THE TEIGN ESTUARY

Immediately to the west of Teignmouth, which is easily located by the prominent church tower and long pier on the seafront, there lies the narrow entrance to the River Teign, bounded on the western side by the prominent high sandstone headland of the Ness and its sectored approach light (QWRG 7M). Strangers, however, should not approach at night, for here too a sandy bar renders the entrance dangerous in onshore winds.

The river dries extensively and navigation within the river is severely restricted by a low bridge (2.9m clearance) which limits access to the upper reaches half a mile above the entrance. There are, however, a couple of convenient visitors' pontoons in the lower river off the town where you will lie afloat at all states of the tide.

A yellow sewage outfall buoy (Fl Y 5s) is situated 1.16 miles south-east of the Ness, and from here on the coast remains steep for the next four miles westwards, with no dangers except within a few boat's lengths of the shore. Topped with fields, trees and isolated houses, the red sandstone gives way to pale grey and ochre limestone off Babbacombe Bay, where there is a reasonable anchorage in westerly winds. Anstey's Cove to the west of quarry scarred Long Quarry Point is another good temporary anchorage, although care must be taken to avoid three drying rocks near the southern entrance point to the cove.

TOR BAY

In contrast to the high cliffs further to the east, Hope's Nose, the eastern boundary of Tor Bay, slopes gently down to the sea, its grassy turf and low rock ledges and cliffs home to the largest kittiwake colony in Devon.

Just under four miles away, the distinctive flat-topped line of Berry Head marks the western limit of the bay, which takes a deep, sheltered bite into the Devon coast. Well protected in westerly winds, it was a traditional anchorage for the Navy prior to the development of Plymouth, and it has always been a popular venue for yacht racing, notably the magnificent J Class during their brief heyday in the 1930s. More recently the punishing Cowes/Torquay Race has been a longstanding powerboat racing event.

To seaward, the low, flat Lead Stone and the 32m high Ore Stone, a mile offshore, are also popular with the seabirds and white with droppings. There is a deep

Tor Bay from the north-east. Hope's Nose, right, Thatcher Rock, Lead Stone and Ore Stone, with Berry Head in the distance

passage between the two islands, but do not pass too close to the south-west of the Ore Stone where the Sunker lurks awash at LAT. In calm weather, with an absence of swell, it is possible to land on the Ore Stone, anchoring just north of the island on the rocky ledge which has 3m LAT. Pick anywhere on the rocky shore and lift your inflatable on to the rock platform. I would not, however, recommend leaving your mother ship entirely unattended!

The last of the Hope's Nose islands is Thatcher Rock, a jagged pyramid rising to 41m south-west of the point. Behind it, the concave sweep of the large hotel high on the cliffs is a foretaste of what will be seen as Torquay opens beyond the next point. Just under a mile west of Thatcher Rock lies Morris Rogue, a shoal with a least depth of 0.8m LAT. Keep the Ore Stone open of Thatcher Rock and you will clear this hazard, otherwise deep water extends safely right to Torquay harbour entrance.

Although the actual harbour mouth is not easy to spot until close, Torquay is an unmistakeable proliferation of large buildings and tower blocks, with the large façade of the Imperial Hotel high on the cliffs just south of the harbour. It is easy to enter, both by day and night, and there are excellent facilities for visitors, including a large marina.

The whole of the coast backing Tor Bay is one large urban sprawl. The English Riviera is an unbroken line of busy beaches comprising Preston sands, Paignton sands, Goodrington sands and Broad sands, with promenades, resorts and holiday camps in the hinterland. Along their length yellow speed limit buoys are positioned about two cables offshore during the summer, with '5 KTS' on square topmarks, restricting the areas for swimming. Inside these controlled areas you should proceed with extreme caution.

Paignton, just under halfway across the bay, is a popular resort with a traditional pier; a quarter of a mile south of this is the sandstone bluff of

Roundham Head, and Paignton's small drying harbour is situated on its northern side. Given over completely to local moorings and busy with tripper boats, the harbour is only suitable for visitors in smaller craft able to dry out easily, which can sometimes be allocated space against the East Quay. It is always advisable to call ahead on VHF Ch 14, callsign *Paignton Harbour,* or Tel: 01803 557812 for berthing instructions.

Drying rocky ledges extend south and east of the harbour's East Quay, their outer limit marked by a BYB east cardinal mark, and the final approach is interesting in that Paignton, to my knowledge, is unique among British harbours in having an unconventional fairway where ingoing vessels must hold to the port hand side of the channel rather than the normal starboard side. This anomaly provides a safer line of approach from the north-east and is indicated by a unique seasonal red port-hand buoy flying a Code flag 'N' (chequered white and blue).

Facilities are limited, there are taps on the Quays, but no fuel. There is a restaurant, pub, café and a few shops, including a small chandlery beside the harbour.

The once-peaceful anchorage of Elberry Cove in the extreme south-western corner of the bay is now usually busy with water-skiing activity. East of it, the houses give way to the large expanse of Churston golf course, beneath it the cliffs, broken with many disused quarries, fall steeply into the sea with no dangers at their feet. Just west of the wide entrance to Brixham outer harbour is Fishcombe Cove, a quiet, secluded anchorage in westerly winds. Brixham, a busy fishing port, has a large deepwater outer harbour that is easy to access in all conditions and provides all weather shelter within its large marina. Visitors' berths are usually available.

Berry Head from the south with Tor Bay beyond

BRIXHAM TO DARTMOUTH

With the exception of rocks extending a cable to the north of Shoalstone Point, the coast between Brixham and Berry Head is steep-to. The headland, 55m high, is an impressive sight, rising steeply and heavily quarried on its northern side. A coastguard lookout with latticed radio mast stands beside the lighthouse at the eastern end. This drops almost vertically into the sea and, though not recommended, you could sail to within a boat's length of the foot of the cliffs. Off the point the tide attains 1.5 knots at Springs, the north-going flood begins five hours after HW Dover, the south-going ebb one hour before, the streams running parallel to the coast.

Half a mile south of Berry Head, off Oxley Head, which has a ruined fort and car park on its top, are the Cod rocks – two steep islets, with the largest, East Cod, 9m high. Between them lie the drying Bastard Rocks and, although it is quite safe to enter the bay to the north to admire the impressive limestone cliffs overhanging a large cave, keep well to seaward when leaving and do not attempt the inshore passage between the rocks.

Various dangers and shallows extend for about half a mile to seaward for the rest of the four mile passage along this stretch of coast, and a sensible offing should be maintained. Mostly high, rolling turfy hills, sloping to low irregular limestone cliffs, it is interspersed with several beaches and coves backed by steep valleys. Mag Rock, drying 0.3m, lies 1 cable east of Sharkham Point, and to seaward, Mudstone Ledge, safe enough, with a least depth of 5.4m does, however, kick up an uncomfortable sea at times. It is also a popular spot for crab and lobster pots, and their markers and buoys, the scourge of the whole Devon and Cornwall coastline, will be found in abundance from here on. Many do not have visible dan-buoys with flags, and are just inflatable floats, 'buffs' as they are known locally, barely awash, often semi-submerged in the tidal stream and posing a real propeller fouling hazard. A constant lookout must be kept at all times, which renders inshore passages particularly wearisome and ill advised at night under power.

A course at least half a mile from the coast will clear both Druids Mare, a group of rocks (drying 2.1m) one cable south-south-east of Crabrock Point, and Nimble Rock, a particularly insidious outcrop (0.9m LAT), which lurks nearly two cables south-south-east of Downend Point. Start Point lighthouse open of Eastern Blackstone will clear the Nimble.

Eastern Blackstone, steep and 16.5m high, is not difficult to miss, nor too, the much larger, 35m high jagged outcrop of the Mewstone beyond it to the south-west. Pass to the south of the Mewstone YB south cardinal buoy (VQ(6) + LFl 10s). Do not be tempted to cut the corner from here into Dartmouth as submerged

Dart approach from the south

rocks extend nearly three cables to the south-west of the Mewstone, marked at their outer extremity by the West Rock YB south cardinal buoy (Q (6) + LFl 15s). Inshore, high on Froward Point is the prominent Dartmouth day beacon, a tower with a wide base that is particularly valuable for locating the Dart when approaching from the south or south-west, as the narrow entrance to the river is very difficult to distinguish in the high folds of the coastline.

START BAY

The wide sweep of Start Bay extends nearly 8 miles south-west from Dartmouth to Start Point, and inshore the high cliffs undergo a dramatic transformation into Slapton Sands, a long low beach enclosing the fresh water lake of Slapton Ley, a valuable wildlife sanctuary.

During the Second World War, this area was used extensively by the American forces practising for the D-Day Normandy landings, but tragedy struck on the night of the 28 April 1944 when eight tank landing craft engaged in 'Exercise Tiger', a rehearsal for Operation Overlord, using live ammunition for full effect, were

chanced upon by German E-boats. The effect of their topedo attack was devastating, sinking two of the landing craft and badly damaging a third, resulting in the loss of 986 American soldiers, sailors and their armament. The disaster was caused by typographical errors in radio frequencies and a lack of sufficient Naval escort, and the whole episode remained top secret for over 40 years. Today, on Slapton Sands there is a memorial to the dead, its centrepiece a battered Sherman tank. This was salvaged from the bay by Ken Small, who campaigned tirelessly to establish the memorial, all recounted in his fascinating book *The Forgotten Dea*d.

Start Bay has no inshore dangers, and with an offshore breeze a fine sail in calm water can be enjoyed along its length close to the shore.

West of Torcross, the cliffs begin to rise again, with the tiny fishing village of Beesands at their foot, and its less fortunate neighbour, the ruined village of Hallsands. During the latter part of the nineteenth century nearly 700,000 tons of shingle were removed from this corner of the bay to build the new docks in Devonport. Without these vital natural defences the small fishing village met its fate on 26 January 1917 when an easterly gale and high tide destroyed the entire settlement, leaving just one ghostly ruin which remains today. In settled offshore weather, if time permits, or waiting for the tide west around the Start, this is a handy anchorage, although a trip ashore has a distinctly ghoulish fascination.

Ironically, it is further offshore that Start Bay poses problems, for it is here that you encounter the only real offshore bank in the West Country, the Skerries, which extends three miles in a northeasterly direction from a position six cables north-east of Start Point. On old charts from the early 18th century a possible derivation of the name is found, for on these the bank is called *The Scary*, which it can be at times! Although the depths over the bank are adequate for most small craft, the shallowest point being the

The Mewstone and Dart approach from the north-east. Note the daymark on the skyline to the right of the yacht

Dartmouth is particularly elusive from the south-west, although the Mewstone, far right, the daymark, right of centre, and cottages, left, are all good pointers

south-west end with a depth of 2.1m LAT, it creates dangerous breaking seas in bad weather, when it should be given a wide berth. An approach to Dartmouth from the south should not be attempted until the red Skerries can buoy at the north-east end of the bank has been passed.

Deriving its name from the Anglo-Saxon word for a tail, Start Point is one of the more distinctive West Country headlands. Five grassy hillocks topped with rocky outcrops about 60m high range along its prickly spine, topped by two BBC radio masts (264m). Built in 1836, the white buildings and lighthouse (Fl (3) 10s) perch neatly above the low cliffs at the eastern end, the fixed red sector of which covers the Skerries Bank (210° – 255°T).

In fog or poor visibility, the only audible aid to navigation is the foghorn on Start Point (60s). As ships bound down Channel for Plymouth and Fowey close the land at this point, there is a noticeable increase in traffic.

Although weak in Start Bay, tidal streams now have to be reckoned with again, becoming much stronger off Start Point. They attain up to 4 knots at Springs and extend about a mile to seaward from the lighthouse. Three miles south of the point the streams are weaker, just over two knots at Springs, the east-north-east flood beginning five hours after HW Dover, and the west-south-west ebb about one hour before HW Dover. Closer inshore the tide turns about half an hour earlier.

There is no inshore passage as such, but in fair weather less turbulence can sometimes be found closer to the point, taking care to avoid Start Rocks and the numerous pot markers. In bad weather, especially with wind against tide, the race should be taken seriously as it produces heavy overfalls, and the point should be passed at least two miles to the south. On one of my first early outings along this coast in my father's small sloop, boldly we had set off for Salcombe with a strong weather going tide. The sudden increase in the apparent wind speed, the sight of cresting seas and doubtless my anxious face prompted Dad's typically wry comment '… probably not the best day to be doing battle with the Cape Horn of the West Country'. We turned tail for the welcome sanctuary of the Dart, and ever since, for me, Start Point has always conjured up that enduring image!

Start Point and Start Rocks from the east, with Prawle Point in the distance

River Exe

Tides	HW Dover −0445
Range	Exmouth MHWS 4.6m–MHWN 3.4m, MLWN 1.7m–MLWS 0.5m
	(HW Topsham approx 20 mins after HW Exmouth). Spring ebb can attain
	five knots off Exmouth docks and runs hard in the Bight
Charts	AC: 2290, SC5601.6; Stanfords: CP 22; Imray: WCP2400.2
Waypoints	East Exe buoy 50°36'.00N 03°22'.37W – see Approaches on page 33
	Exe safe water buoy 50°35'.90N 03°23'.70W – see Approaches on page 33
Hazards	Pole Sands, Maer and Conger rocks (lit by fairway buoys). River approach dangerous in
	strong easterly and southerly weather. Strong tidal streams in entrance channel. Large
	part of river dries
Harbour speed limit	10 knots
Overnight charge	Exmouth Marina £15. Exe Harbour Authority, river moorings £8.
	Topsham Quay £6. Trout's Pontoon £17.50

As most yachts heading west make a landfall on Berry Head or Start Point, the River Exe, lying inshore of the normal track across Lyme Bay, tends to be overlooked by visitors, which is a shame as it differs greatly from its deeper, wooded companions further west.

At Low Water it is but a meandering channel amidst a wide expanse of glistening mud and clean yellow sandbanks. The entire estuary is a designated Site of Special Scientific Interest (SSSI) and internationally renowned as a haunt of waders and seabirds; in the upper reaches summer fishermen still shoot their long seine nets on the last of the ebb in pursuit of wild salmon. At full flood it metamorphoses into a broad but shallow lake over six miles long and a mile wide; an atmospheric place of optical illusion and frequently changing light, Turner was but one of the many artists to succumb to its subtle drama. If transposed to the East Coast the Exe would slot very neatly into that shifting maze of swatchways and creeks and could easily be dubbed the Blackwater of the West.

Deflected eastwards by the long beach and scrubby dunes of Dawlish Warren, the river's exit to the sea is flanked by drying sands to seaward and the extended, narrow approach channel along the Exmouth seafront has always been a bit of a deterrent to visitors although it has always been well-buoyed. For many years this was my home patch, and my father's boat was based at Topsham. Though commercially far less busy than it used to be, in contrast the leisure boating industry has expanded dramatically. If the weather permits, the Exe can provide an interesting diversion, particularly for shallower draught boats, and those able to dry out easily. It is unlikely that you will sail away disappointed with what you have found.

The Exe dries extensively, and the channel holds close to Exmouth beach on the right. Note Pole Sands in the foreground, Dawlish Warren on the left and the entrance to Exmouth Marina just right of centre

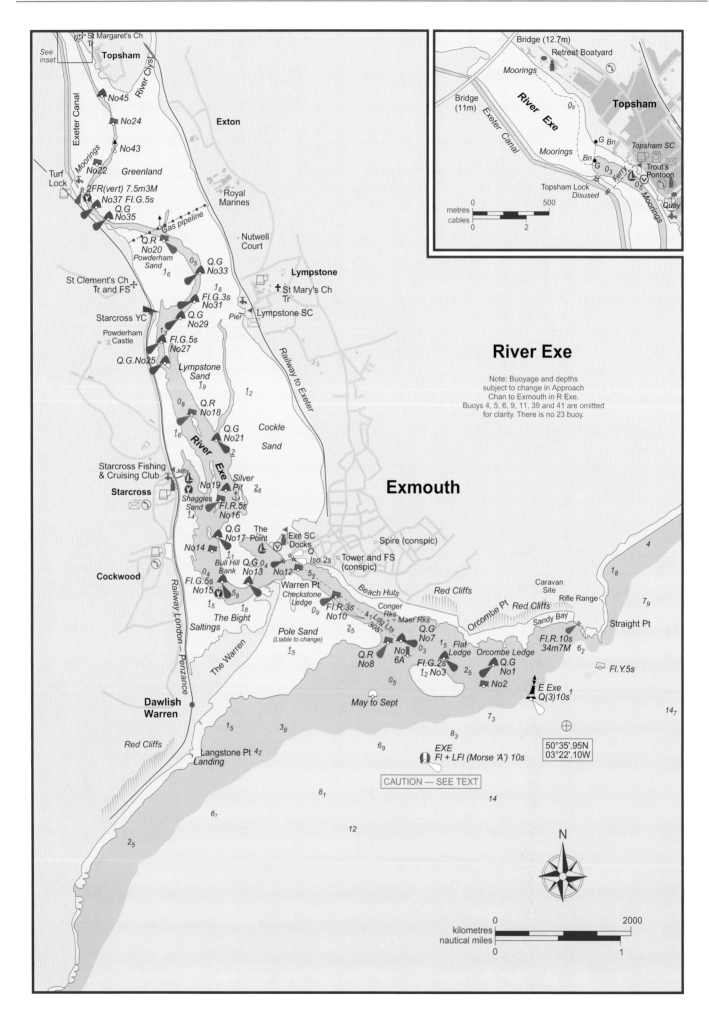

Topsham

St Margaret's Ch Tr

See inset

Exeter Canal

No45

No24

River Clyst

No43

Moorings

No22

Turf Lock

Greenland

Exton

Royal Marines

2FR(vert) 7.5m3M

No37 Fl.G.5s

Q.G
No35

Gas pipeline

Nutwell Court

Q.R
No20
Powderham Sand

0₅

1₆

Q.G
No33

Lympstone

St Mary's Ch Tr

St Clement's Ch Tr and FS

1₈

Fl.G.3s
No31

Starcross YC

Q.G
No29

Lympstone SC

Pier

Powderham Castle

1₃

Fl.G.5s
No27

Q.G.No25

Lympstone Sand
1₉

Cockle Sand

0₈

Q.R
No18

Railway to Exeter

1₆

Q.G
No21

River Exe

1₂

1₂

2

Starcross Fishing & Cruising Club

Jetty

No19

Silver Pit

2₆

Starcross

Shaggles Sand

Fl.R.5s
No16

1₄

Q.G
No17

The Point

Exe SC Docks

Spire (conspic)

Q

Iso.2s

Tower and FS (conspic)

No14

Bull Hill Bank

1₁

Q.G
No13

0₄

No12

Q

5₂

Cockwood

0₄

Fl.G.5s
No15

5₈

1₅

1₈

The Bight

Saltings

Warren Pt
Checkstone Ledge

0₉

Fl.R.3s
No10

Beach Huts

Conger Rks

Maer Rks

Red Cliffs

Caravan Site

Rifle Range

4

1₈

7₉

4 Ldg Lts
305°

Orcombe Pt

Red Cliffs

Sandy Bay

Straight Pt

2₅

Q.G
No7

Railway London – Penzance

The Warren

Pole Sand
(Liable to change)

1₅

Q.R
No8

No
6A

0₃

1₅

Flat Ledge

Orcombe Ledge

Fl.R.10s
34m7M

6₂

Fl.Y.5s

Fl.G.2s
No3

1₂

2₅

Q.G
No1

Dawlish Warren

No2

0₅

E Exe
Q(3)10s

1

14₇

Red Cliffs

Langstone Pt
Landing

4₂

1₅

3₈

May to Sept

7₃

8₃

6₉

2₅

50°35'.95N
03°22'.10W

8₁

14

6₇

EXE
Fl + LFl (Morse 'A') 10s

CAUTION — SEE TEXT

12

2₅

N

River Exe

Note: Buoyage and depths subject to change in Approach Chan to Exmouth in R Exe. Buoys 4, 5, 6, 9, 11, 39 and 41 are omitted for clarity. There is no 23 buoy.

Exmouth

Inset (Topsham)

Bridge (12.7m)

Retreat Boatyard

Moorings

Bridge (11m)

River Exe

Topsham

Exeter Canal

0₈

Moorings

G Bn

Topsham SC

Bn
G

0₃

Ferry

Trout's Pontoon

Topsham Lock
Disused

0₅

Quay

metres

0   500

cables

0   2

kilometres

0   2000

nautical miles

0   1

APPROACHES

In suitable settled offshore conditions and a flooding tide, the entrance to the Exe is relatively straightforward, but a first time visit should not be considered in onshore winds of any strength, especially from the east through south to south-west. A confused area of breaking seas soon builds up in the approaches, and the run in along the uncomfortable lee shore of Exmouth beach leaves little room for mistakes. Once the sands begin to uncover, the tide in the channel can run hard, particularly on the ebb at Springs.

Approaching from the south-west, Straight Point lies to the east of the river and, although this fairly low headland is not easy to spot, it can be located by the far more conspicuous white-diamond shape of Sandy Bay caravan park just inland. There are two flagpoles on the headland, and in its vicinity are invariably large numbers of small local angling boats. There is also a yellow sewer outfall buoy (Fl Y 5s) just under 0.5M south of the point.

Straight Point is used as a military firing range and its seaward limits are marked by two yellow DZ buoys to the south-east and east, both Fl Y 3s. From March to October firing can take place on weekdays between 0800 and 1600, and the danger area should be avoided. When firing is in progress a safety boat patrols the area, and red flags are flown from the flagstaffs on the point. No flags mean no firing, a flag on each pole indicates firing in progress and two flags on each pole means firing temporarily ceased. The range can also be contacted on VHF channel 08, callsign *Straight Point Range*.

Rising immediately to the west of Straight Point, the undulating line of high red sandstone cliffs ends at Orcombe Point where Exmouth's long sandy beach begins.

For many years the approach to the river comprised a long, narrow channel running south-east/north-west parallel to the beach and foreshore at Exmouth, flanked to seaward by the Pole Sands, an extensive area of drying shallows.

However, in the last few years there have been increasingly problematic changes to the seaward end of the channel, as the Pole Sands began to encroach ever further to the east. The depths reduced, and also the channel width, as the buoyage was moved even closer to Exmouth beach from which the rocky Paige and Flat ledges extend. By late 2007 the channel had almost disappeared, depths had reduced to 0.3m LAT and No 6 buoy was drying at Low Water Springs.

However, the news is not all bad! This dramatic shift of sand has effectively split the Pole Sands, the problem area evolving into the separate and still growing Outer Pole Sand, and a new swatchway with an average depth of 1.5m LAT forming further to the west, on a roughly north-north-west/south-south-east alignment, with the prominent spire of Exmouth's Holy Trinity Church

bearing about 330°T. This has been increasingly used by local craft, and with ongoing surveys predicting that the original channel is likely to become non-existent sometime during 2008, new buoyage was introduced in anticipation of this. The buoyage comprises a new spherical RW vertical-striped 'Exe' safe water buoy (Fl + LFl [Morse 'A'] 10s) established at the seaward end of the emerging channel at 50°35'.90N 03°23'.70W.

From here you steer to a new style No 8 port hand buoy – a red catamaran base with square cage (QR) situated at 50°36'.41N 03°24'.17W. The starboard side of the channel is indicated by a new No 6A ' preferred channel to starboard marker' – a port hand buoy with a green band and striped RGR topmark at 50°36'.30N 03°23'.83W, indicating the divide in the main (exisiting) channel and the new alternative. At this point you will rejoin the original main channel, which is well marked with even numbered red cans to port and odd numbered green conical buoys to starboard.

This kind of fluid situation is never easy for the author of a book like this! Due to the frequently changing nature of the sands and buoyage within the Exe an up-to-date copy of Admiralty Chart 2290, SC5601.6, CP22 or WCP 2400.2 is essential, but given the current uncertainties, I would also advise anyone intending to visit the Exe to check the latest Admiralty Notices to Mariners, www.hydro.gov.uk, and to contact the harbour office, Tel: 01392 274306, for an update as they are monitoring the situation constantly. I would also suggest that for boats of deeper draught an approach is only made on a rising tide no earlier than three hours after Low Water with a careful eye on the sounder. Although lit, I would definitely not recommend it at night for strangers.

Currently (2008) the East Exe BYB east cardinal buoy (Q (3) 10s) marking the entrance to the main buoyed channel lies just under a mile south-west of Straight Point. **If the channel does close completely, this, and the subsequent buoyage, to nos 6 and 7 will be removed.** It is anticipated that additional buoys will be added to the new channel as it becomes more established.

If the original channel does not close completely, it will remain buoyed. The shallowest water lies between Nos 3 and 7 buoys where there is little more than 0.3m LAT in places; No 6 buoy is aground at Low Water Springs, and you need to keep well over to starboard towards No 5, following the line of small yellow buoys that mark the outer boundary of a jet-ski area, and only swing gradually back to port towards Nos 7 and 8 buoys.

THE INNER CHANNEL BEYOND NUMBER EIGHT BUOY

From No 8 buoy, No 9 buoy takes you clear of Maer and Conger rocks and you run in with Exmouth beach and promenade, with its brightly painted beach huts, close on your starboard hand. This is followed by a long terrace of typical Edwardian seaside hotels as you close the real mouth of the river, between the Warren, the long sandy promontory ahead to port, and the pierhead at the entrance to Exmouth Marina to starboard. Do not be tempted to stray from the channel as there is little room outside of it, and the Pole Sands are steep-to and surprisingly hard if you run aground.

Leave No 10 buoy well on your port hand; this marks Checkstone Ledge, a rocky outcrop which lies to the west of the buoy, and do not be tempted to cut the corner towards the low sandy promontory of Warren Point as this is continually extending south-east, forming a large area of gravelly shallows. Note that there is no No 11 buoy, and leave No 12 buoy well to port, holding a course towards Exmouth pierhead end before turning west across the river. There is a marked pontoon just off the north-eastern end of the Warren which can be used by visitors for berthing overnight or temporarily if they are waiting for sufficient tide to get into Exmouth Marina. If you want to get ashore easily, a water taxi operates from Exmouth Dock to anywhere in the lower Exe; callsign *Exeplorer*, VHF Ch M or Mob: 07970 918418.

FUEL, FRESH WATER AND GAS

Diesel can be obtained alongside the south side of the outer entrance to Exmouth Dock during normal working hours as well as from Trout's pontoon and Retreat Boatyard, Topsham. Petrol can only be bought in cans from Starcross garage and Pretty's garage, Topsham. Water is available at Exmouth Marina, Exe Sailing Club, Turf Hotel, Trout's boatyard, Topsham SC and Retreat Boatyard. Calor and Camping Gaz are available at Garners Home

Hardware, Exmouth, Starcross garage, and Trout's boatyard, Topsham.

EXMOUTH MARINA

The tidal streams run strongly, in excess of three knots on the ebb at Springs, creating a confused tidal lop in the narrows, and a very strong run across the narrow entrance to Exmouth Marina, which is hidden almost until you draw abeam of it. Beware of the frequent passenger ferries and other boats emerging. Beware, too, if approaching on the flood as, as you turn into the entrance, there is an equally strong counter eddy that can take you by surprise.

The former Exmouth Dock is privately owned and was regularly used by coasters until 1989, since when it has undergone a major transformation into Exmouth Marina, which is surrounded by a large luxury housing development. The old dock is now full of pontoon berthing with bridges to the shore. Although originally dredged to 2m LAT, there has been noticeable silting in recent years and in places there is visibly little water here at Low Water Springs, although you will sit comfortably in soft mud. Despite the berths being private, space can usually be found for visitors if berth owners are away. Call *Exmouth Dock* on VHF channel 14 or Tel: 01395 269314 or, alternatively, berth alongside the pontoon on the starboard side of the long dock entrance and see the harbourmaster, Keith Graham, whose office is close by on the quay on the upper level of the building. The overnight charge for a 10m boat is £14, which includes the use of showers and toilets.

The bridge across the inner end of the dock entrance lifts on request during normal working hours (VHF Ch 14) and is then opened on the hour until 2300, after which it remains open until 0800.

Looking towards the Warren and Bight from Exmouth dock entrance. The waiting pontoon is up to the right of the motor boat; note the tidal stream on No 12 buoy (left)

Exmouth Marina

supermarket in the Magnolia Centre, along with the usual high street names, Boots, WH Smith, Woolworths and Superdrug, a post office and branches of all main banks with cashpoints. There's also a good smattering of local shops incorporating butchers, bakers and fishmongers.

Lively pubs, cafés and restaurants abound and include the Seafood Restaurant Tel: 269459, Franklins Tel: 263086, Sophie's Tel: 222257, several Italians – Donatos Tel: 279644, Nico's Tel: 276734 and Branzinos Tel: 279720 – Mexican at The Mexican Tel: 223388, Thai at Lemongrass Tel: 269306 and a surprisingly large choice of Indian and Chinese. There's no shortage of fastfood outlets either, with burgers, fish and chips, KFC and kebabs galore!

DAWLISH WARREN

Just a short distance across the water, the eastern end of the Warren always used to provide a peaceful contrast, but sadly the once popular anchorage is now very restricted by moorings which run parallel to the beach along the curve of the river known as the Bight, opposite No 13 buoy.

In the 1930s this end of the Warren was covered with a large number of bungalows and holiday homes, but the winter storms and shifting sands allow no such permanence. As a boy, I can remember the last few houses high on the dunes on the seaward side of the beach, and the fascination of seeing their broken remains after they had been undermined and began to collapse. The sea broke right through the Warren in the 1960s during a winter storm, although the massive repair works and new groynes on the seaward side have resulted in a steady re-growth ever since.

The western end of the Warren is a popular golf course, but is within an extensive 500 acre nature reserve and bird sanctuary protected under by-laws passed in 1983. These have been enforced with increasing vigour over the past few years, particularly with regard to access to the remoter eastern end of the Warren, which is regularly patrolled by wardens.

It used to be possible for bilge-keelers to dry out along the edge of the Bight, however, this is now judged to be a protected area for birds. Avoid it at all times as

Peter Dixon's Chandlery, Tel: 01395 273248, is conveniently close to hand on Pilot Wharf on the south side of the entrance, along with a newsagents, café, wet fish shop, the Beach Hotel, a popular pub with good food, and right on the pierhead Olivants Restaurant, Tel: 01395 227145. There are marine and electronic engineers close by; ask the harbourmaster for directions.

The pool to the north-west of the dock entrance off The Point is completely taken up with local moorings, including that of the Exmouth Lifeboat. Anchoring is not recommended due to the risk of fouling moorings and the strong run of the tide. With sufficient water, a boat capable of taking the bottom comfortably can always anchor round the back of The Point. Here, out of the main stream and clear of the local moorings, you can dry out on hard sand on Shelly Bank, at about half tide, just off the Exe Sailing Club, Tel: 01395 264607; www.exe-sailing-club.org. Its large clubhouse was built in the 1970s after its previous one on the old north side of the dock entrance was spectacularly destroyed when the quayside collapsed. Visitors are welcome to use the showers and bar when open.

EXMOUTH FACILITIES
(Local phone code 01395)
Exmouth, the oldest seaside resort in Devon, dates from the 1750s and is a typical busy holiday town in season, with its long sandy beach, amusements and traditional donkey rides. Attractive Georgian buildings rise along the elevated Beacon area and the adjoining seafront, but much of the newer town centre, about half a mile from the dock area, is fairly bland. It caters well for all the normal requirements, with a large Somerfield

your presence is not likely to be appreciated. The beach along the very eastern tip and part of the seaward end of the Warren – Warren Point – is now designated as very sensitive, being the only roosting area for birds when the tide rises over 3.2m. Wardens will clear it of people on these occasions. In other words, there's a lot less space for visitors of the human variety than there used to be!

I am fortunate, I suppose, to have been able to enjoy it long before these restrictions were imposed. Then there was nothing more than the low sweep of the beach and the dunes behind – a wilderness of lupins and marram grass. At dusk it became the silent haunt of the rabbits and birds, while just across the water the cheerful glare of the lights along Exmouth sea-front emphasised the pleasant isolation of the place. Nothing, except the rumble of the main line trains along the western shore, disturbed its peace.

In complete contrast, though, a mile or so along the beach, the village of Dawlish Warren is a sprawl of amusement arcades, gift shops and even a betting shop, catering for the large holiday chalet villages nearby. There's also a grocery, newsagent, post office and pub.

STARCROSS
(Local phone code 01626)
To avoid the encroaching edge of Bull Hill Bank do not steer directly for No 15 buoy – keep out towards the large ship mooring buoy in mid-channel. This is primarily for commercial vessels but can be used if you are not too worried about your topsides. Just to the north-west are four yellow Harbour Authority visitors' buoys (up to 12m LOA, marked ECC Visitors) at £8 per day. They do not have pick-up strops. To check availability you can try calling *Port of Exeter* or *Harbour Patrol* on VHF Ch12 during normal working hours, although a reply is not guaranteed. Your best bet is usually to call the water taxi *Exeplorer* on Ch M or Mob: 07970 918418 who will advise. Here again, given the strong tidal streams, the water taxi is also the easiest way to get ashore!

Above No 14 and No 17 buoys a channel branches away to port towards the mass of moorings off Starcross, where there is a good Londis convenience store with off-licence, a baker, newsagent, post office, chemist, three pubs serving food, including the large Courtenay Arms, and a fish and chip shop. Starcross garage can supply diesel and petrol in cans and has a convenient all-tide pontoon (about 1m Mean Low Water Springs) moored just south of the end of the pier to which you can secure while you go ashore. If you contact the garage, Tel: 890225, it is often possible to lie here overnight, or they might be able to find a spare mooring for you.

The Starcross Fishing and Cruising Club, Tel: 01626 891996; www.starcross-fcc.com, has one visitors'

mooring off the village (see website for coordinates), although more are available if members are away cruising. Visitors are welcomed to its fine clubhouse in the old Brunel Tower at the inner end of the pier on Ashes Quay. To access the village and club, use the small landing hard and underpass beneath the railway line at the inner end of the pier, clearly indicated by the large SFCC sign. Note that Starcross pier is private and should not be used for landing; the locked gates to the shore are only open when the Exmouth ferries arrive.

The main channel continues between No 16 Shaggles buoy and No 19 buoy, with the line of moorings to port marking the edge of the drying Shaggles Sand; to the east of the larger moorings on your starboard hand the whole area of Cockle Sand dries completely at Low Water. Just south of No 19 buoy and out of the fairway there is a deeper hole known locally as 'Silver Pit', which provides a very useful anchorage in just over 2m.

LYMPSTONE, AND UPRIVER TO TURF LOCK
From No 19 buoy head for No 21 buoy. The drying channel to Lympstone, a former fishing village nestling between two red cliffs on the eastern shore, branches off just above No 21 buoy and this can provide an interesting diversion, sounding in on a rising tide, for a quick dinghy ride ashore. Here, thatched cottages mingle with more elegant and substantial Georgian houses, and facilities include a good Londis store/ butchers, post office/newsagent, The Swan, Globe, and Redwing pubs and Lympstone Sailing Club, Tel: 01395 278792; www.lympstonesailingclub.org.uk. A number of local boats have drying moorings off the small boat shelter but the bottom is mud, and it will be a messy walk ashore if you stay to dry out!

Back in the main channel **there is no No 23 buoy**. Leave No 18 buoy and the moorings to port, and opposite No 25 (Powderham Perch) buoy, the extensive estate of Powderham itself lies behind the railway embankment. Through the trees and across an elegant deer park you can just glimpse Powderham Castle, which had been the seat of the Courteney family since the 14th century and is at present home of the Earl and Countess of Devon.

From the next buoy, No 27, the channel is well marked as it turns north-east past the white buildings and slipway belonging to Starcross Yacht Club, Tel: 01626 890470; www.starcrossyc.org.uk, which has the distinction of being one of the oldest in the country, formed in 1773. Today it is a very popular dinghy racing club and also has an active cruiser section. The moorings in the pool off the club mostly dry at Low Water.

Next, steer for Nutwell Court, a large buff-coloured Georgian house set among trees on the eastern shore.

Keep well to the starboard side of the channel, past No 29 buoy, and hold very close to No 31 (Lympstone Perch) buoy as the channel here is extremely narrow and shallows rapidly on the port hand side. Follow the outside curve of the channel to No 33 buoy, taking care not to cut across the shallow edge of Powderham Sand to port, before leaving the yellow can buoy on your port hand. This is one of four isolated danger buoys in the vicinity marking a gas pipeline which carries North Sea Gas and runs east-west across the river, and anchoring should not be attempted anywhere in the vicinity. Steer directly to red No 20 (Nob) buoy. From here, leave the next two conical yellow buoys on your starboard hand, as well as the beacon with a triangular topmark and yellow Gas Pipeline sign, and then leave the next yellow can to port.

As well as the original pipeline, you will also be passing over a new tunnel at this point, driven under the river in 2007 to carry an even larger gas pipeline from the National Grid to service a power station in Plymouth. Built to have the least environmental impact on the estuary, the 2.4m diameter tunnel is 1.8km long and cost over £7m!

During the summer months, as in several of the other West Country rivers, these upper reaches are frequently used by salmon fishermen who shoot long seine nets from small rowing boats, usually on the last of the ebb and first of the flood. They are likely to be encountered anywhere between here and Topsham.

The few licences granted for these fisheries are jealously guarded and passed down from father to son, but disease and pollution have seen a dramatic decline from the heady days when up to 99 prime fish were caught in a single shot of the net. Nor, too, has a monster 61 pound salmon like the one caught close to this spot in March 1924 by netsman Dick Voysey ever been seen again. This was no fisherman's tale, it was duly preserved and can still be seen in Exeter's Victoria & Albert Museum.

The large incongruous blocks of flats on the eastern shore are accommodation blocks for the Royal Marines Training Camp at Lympstone, so don't be too alarmed if you hear the sound of gunfire along the shore!

The shallow tributary of the River Clyst joins the Exe here, meandering away through the mudbanks to the distant railway bridge on the northern shore beyond which Tremlett's, famed for high speed powerboats, has premises at Odhams Wharf.

The main channel, much narrower at this point, leads back across the river to the western shore and close to the high flood embankment past the green No 35 (Ranje) and No 37 (Barrel) buoys. The building half hidden in the trees ahead, with a conspicuously isolated tall pine,

is Turf Hotel and the entrance lock to the Exeter Ship Canal is just to the left of the building.

TURF HOTEL

Standing in splendid isolation, and uniquely one of the few pubs in Britain that the general public cannot access by car, Turf Hotel can still be surprisingly busy, particularly at weekends! A favourite watering hole for local boat owners, there is also a ferry from Topsham, and the level canal tow path is very popular with walkers and cyclists.

Built to service the thirsty crews of the ships using the canal, Turf Hotel also stabled the towpath horses, and the pub landlord doubled up as lock-keeper too. One of the last, Stan May, was a master of dry Devon humour. Back in 1973 when I locked in as the proud new owner of *Temptress* to lay up in the canal, Stan appeared above the lockpit brandishing a can of paraffin and a box of matches. 'Do y'self a favour, boy,' he growled, deadpan as ever. 'Burn her now before you waste a penny more on an old wooden boat!'

Anchor south-east of the pier on the edge of the channel clear of the local moorings, where there is about 1m LAT and a soft mud bottom, or pick up the yellow Harbour Authority's visitor's mooring for £8 per night and pay at the hotel.

Landing is easy at the steps or the inside of the landing pontoon – but do not obstruct the outer end, as *Sea Dream II*, the regular Topsham to Turf ferry, berths here during the summer. This is a great place for children, with a tree house, climbing frames, stranded boats and a huge grassy lawn leading up to the attractive slate-hung Georgian building. Turf Hotel is open during normal licensing hours, has an excellent choice of imaginative bar food and DIY barbecues throughout the summer – they provide the food, you cook it!

A popular and attractive local watering hole, Turf Hotel and lock

Alternatively, summer visitors can lock into the canal and lie in the non-tidal basin at Turf where there are good pontoons with access to the shore. You must stay in the canal for a minimum of two nights, but the charge of £9.50 per day does include the cost of locking in and out, on weekdays only. Make arrangements with the harbour office, Tel: 01392 274306, ideally the day before, to check on the locking times – normally HW Exmouth. Onshore facilities are limited to toilets and a fresh water tap as well as, of course, the delights of the pub!

Turf Basin is also popular for laying-up and there is invariably an interesting assortment of boats to peruse. From here, the towpath along the canal provides a pleasant walk of just over a mile to Topsham Lock where another small passenger ferry runs across to the town.

EXETER SHIP CANAL

The canal, which stretches five miles inland to Exeter, is the oldest pound lock canal in England. It was opened in 1566 after the river passage to Exeter was blocked by a weir upon the orders of the Countess of Devon in an attempt to force vessels to use her own port at Topsham.

The original entrance lock was just opposite Topsham, but increasingly larger, deeper vessels resulted in the extension to Turf in 1827. Despite declining importance, the Port of Exeter remained active until the late 1960s for coasters carrying petrol, timber and coal, sliding incongruously high above the reed beds opposite Topsham and creating havoc with holiday traffic on the once notorious Exeter by-pass when the swing bridge opened to let them through!

Today the M5 motorway bridge sweeps across the wide Exe Valley just upstream of Topsham and, although this ended the traffic jams, the bridge's 10m clearance also finally sealed the fate of Exeter's waterborne commercial trade. Since then the canal has seen increasing amenity use for fishing and pleasure boating, and a fascinating trip to Exeter is quite feasible by dinghy, with a bit of portage to get past the second set of Double Locks where there is another pub.

Until late 1996 the Canal Basin was home to the Exeter Maritime Museum which had struggled to survive against increasing financial odds since it was created in 1968 by David Goddard. This remarkable collection of working craft from all over the world was then moved to Lowestoft where it is still in the throes of going on permanent display under the auspices of the International Sailing Craft Association (ISCA). Many of the smaller craft were transported by sea aboard a coaster which loaded its intriguing cargo alongside Topsham Quay.

TOPSHAM
(Local phone code 01392)
The final stretch of the river from Turf to Topsham is very shallow at Low Water, with less than a metre in many places, but on the flood a few groundings in the soft mud are no problem. The channel is not difficult to follow, leaving Nos 39 and 41 green buoys on your starboard hand, No 22 red can (Ting Tong) to port. As the channel curves northwards again, do not cut too close to the BYB pole as this is a Topsham Sailing Club race mark and is outside the channel. Leave the perch with a triangular topmark (traditionally known as Black Oar) well to starboard and steer directly for No 24 red can buoy, leaving it close to port. Topsham lies ahead to starboard, and the last green channel buoy, No 45, is in the approach to the main bulk of the moorings. These have a clearly defined fairway between them.

Beyond the large modern block of flats that dominates the waterfront, Topsham Quay is easily located by the

Approaching Topsham Quay. Trout's pontoon lies beyond

large brick built former warehouse, now an antiques market. Visitors can berth alongside the quay, where you will dry out in very soft mud. The Harbour Authority charges £6 a night and payment should be made to the Ferryman, Mob: 0780 120 3338, at Topsham ferry further upriver, close to the Passage House Inn and Topsham Sailing Club. Ashore, toilets, water, refuse disposal and electricity are now available on the Quay, Sails and Canvas Sailmakers (Tel: 877527) are based here and the Lighter Inn, with its large outside seating area, is a favourite with locals on balmy summer evenings!

If space is available, the alternative for berthing is alongside the private pontoons off Trout's Boatyard – call ahead on Tel: 873044 (www.troutsboatyard. co.uk). There is 1m at Mean Low Water Springs on the outside of the three hammerhead pontoons where visitors normally berth, making it best suited for bilge keels or centreboards; deeper draught boats

Trout's pontoons looking upstream. Visitors are welcome to berth on the outer ends by arrangement

TOPSHAM FACILITIES

'. . . "not so small a Town as I find it represented in some Accounts" wrote an observer in 1754. "It has not only one pretty long Street to its Kay (where there is a Custom House) and another below it to a fine Strand, the latter adorn'd with diverse handsome Houses, but several good Bye-Streets branching out several ways; and is, in short, a very pleasant, a considerable, and flourishing place, inhabited by many Persons of good Fashion and Politeness, as well as Ship-masters, Ship-builders etc etc . . . Its chief Market, Saturdays, is well supply'd not only with Shambles Meats of all sorts, but Poultry and other Fowls, Butter Cheese and Fruits, and here being Butchers and Fishermen resident, there's seldom a total Lack of Provisions of either Kind, neither of very good Bread, nor as good Beer, Cyder, Wine, Spirit, Liquors . . . It may be concluded that 'tis no despicable or mean Town."'

The same holds good 250 years on, with just a few additions to the facilities perhaps. All provisions are available, including a Co-op, which is open late and also on Sundays, Arthur's butchers and delicatessen, a bakery, a specialist cheese shop, independent wine merchant, green grocer, two newsagents and two chandlers, The Foc'sle, Tel: 874105, which is also an Admiralty Chart agent, and Ash Marine, Tel: 876654, on the Exeter road. Westaways is a good hardware shop, and the branches of Lloyds TSB and Natwest both have cashpoints. Every Saturday morning there is a busy indoor market at the Town Hall. Just a short distance out of town on the main road to Exmouth, about 15 minutes walk or a 57 bus ride, Darts Farm Village is a gourmet's delight!

Today there are no cargoes on the quay – just cars. Those who sit beneath the cheery umbrellas outside the Lighter Inn – formerly the Custom House – are a far cry from the hardened characters that frequented its once tiny and smoke-filled bar! Despite its relatively small population, Topsham has always been renowned for an abundance of hotels and pubs. At one time there were over 20 and today 10 still remain, affectionately dubbed the 'Topsham Ten' by Exeter University students for whom this challenge has become a rite of passage. Certainly a fascinating evening can be spent finding them, and don't miss the delightfully unspoiled

and those with fin keels can sometimes lie alongside Trout's wall where they will sink into the very soft mud. The inside pontoons are all taken up with permanent drying berths for local boats. The overnight charge for a 10m boat is £17.50, and a refundable £20 deposit is charged for an electronic key to the boatyard gate. A toilet block with a shower (£1 slotmeter) is situated in the boatyard, diesel and water are available alongside (petrol can be obtained Mon – Fri in cans from Pretty's garage on the main Exeter road), and Trout's also stocks Calor and Camping Gaz. The yard has a mobile crane and services include general repairs, rigging and Paul Craven Marine Engineering (Mob: 07980 651143). Some good aerial pictures of the River Exe will be found on Trout's website, which also has an excellent roving webcam covering the river at Topsham!

The only possible anchorage off Topsham town is just downstream of the quay in mid-channel, clear of the moorings on the eastern side of the fairway. There is about 1m here at LAT, but the bottom is gravel and the holding not good, particularly on the ebb when the current can run quite fast. Alternatively, Topsham Sailing Club, Tel: 877524; www.topsham-sc.org.uk, might be able to provide a mooring if members are away cruising. The Sailing Club was founded in 1885 and today its very active cruiser fleet is one of the largest in the West Country; it is also home to a fleet of over 30 Devon Yawls (the GRP derivative of the Salcombe Yawl). Visitors are welcome, and those two cruising essentials, showers and a bar, are available on Wednesday evenings and at weekends. There is a convenient fresh water tap on its slipway, and an all-tide landing pontoon with a bridge to the shore immediately off the clubhouse.

Bridge Inn which gained nationwide fame in 1998 when Her Majesty the Queen dropped in en route to Lympstone Marine Camp!

Most of the pubs and hotels serve food, and there's a good choice of restaurants, with seafood at The Galley, Tel: 876078, or The Passage House Inn, Tel: 873653. For elegant dining try La Petite Maison, Tel: 873660, while The Globe Hotel, Tel: 873471, offers traditional English cooking. A lively atmosphere can be enjoyed at Marcello's Ristorante Italiano, Tel: 879061, or Tapas/Mediterranean at Oliva, Tel: 0845 291 7992. Alternatively, try one of two Indian restaurants – Kaptans, above Drake's Wine Bar and Ale House, or Denleys Essence of India, Tel: 875675, on the main road to Exeter – the latter has live music on Wednesdays and Fridays. Close by, the Bamboo Topsham Fryer, Tel: 876463, does takeaway Chinese or fish and chips! There are several cafés and tearooms, including The Café, which provides a good breakfast and a varied lunch menu.

The large Antiques Market in the old Tuborg lager warehouse on the Quay has made the town something of a focal point for antique collectors and Joel Segal's is a good secondhand bookshop. Even more used nautical books will be found for sale in the unlikely surroundings of Paul Properties estate agent's office just across the road!

Topsham is well placed for a visit to the historic cathedral city of Exeter, just three miles away. Frequent buses or half hourly trains go right into the centre.

TOPSHAM PAST AND PRESENT

Though small, Topsham is both attractive and always surprisingly busy! It was once an important Roman and medieval port and was particularly prosperous in the mid-17th and early 18th centuries when it flourished as a shipbuilding centre. During the Napoleonic wars no less than 27 warships were built here for the Royal Navy by Davy's yards, and in 1850 John Holman opened a new yard with a plan to rejuvenate Topsham as a major port. Wooden vessels up to 600 tons were

The Strand is a real architectural delight!

built, and a dry-dock capable of handling 1,000-ton ships was opened. But within 15 years Holman died and there the dream ended, the silting river finally sealing Topsham's fate in the late 1970s, when the last of the timber and lager ships regularly used the quay.

The link with the name remains, however, for John Holman's great grand-daughter, Dorothy, established Topsham Museum in her house at 25 The Strand, and left it to the town on her death. It is manned by volunteers, and is open 1400 – 1700 on Monday, Wednesday, Saturday and Sunday.

Architecturally Topsham has many gems, particularly its heritage of Dutch Style houses along the Strand, built by local shipowners inspired by their frequent trips to Holland – interestingly many of Topsham's houses are also built of clinkers, small Dutch bricks that were used to ballast empty ships. A rabbit warren of narrow streets runs inland from the elegant Strand – humbler cottages and houses, now smartly renovated and bedecked with overflowing window boxes and hanging baskets. Once the homes of the fisherfolk and watermen, property in Exeter's satellite town is much sought after today, the EX3 postcode pushing prices through the £1M ceiling, and in the wake of this a predictable flurry of 'lifestyle' shops and smart boutiques!

The locals' favourite circular walk continues beyond the end of the Strand and along the raised foreshore footpath known as the Goatwalk, with more expansive views of the river. The leafy road at its end skirts Bowling Green Marsh, owned by the RSPB, where you will find an informative bird hide, and continues to the top of Monmouth Street, which leads back to the quay.

UPRIVER TO THE RETREAT BOATYARD

The Retreat Boatyard, Tel: 874720; www.retreatboatyard. co.uk, lies half a mile beyond Topsham, nestling just downstream of the M5 motorway bridge. The boatyard is accessible two hours either side of High Water for an average draught boat, when diesel and water are available alongside. Onshore services include a 36-ton crane, one of the best chandleries in the area, rigging, general repairs and electronics. The yard is also an appointed Yamaha, Volvo Penta and Mercruiser main dealer and service engineer.

To reach the Retreat Boatyard continue upstream through the moorings past the sailing club, leaving the old lock entrance on your port hand and the outfall beacon with green triangular topmark to starboard. Keep a few boat lengths off the shore and pick your way through the large number of moorings. Beyond them the river mostly dries at Low Water, leaving a large area of mud, gravel and reedbeds, with the narrow channel following the reed-fringed edge of the playing field on the starboard hand. The next beacon with a triangular green topmark off a dinghy park and landing jetty is also left to starboard. From here the channel holds close to the right hand shore, overlooked by a number of substantial detached houses; there is a large drying bank to port, so don't be tempted to cut the corner. It is then a straight run past Retreat House, a large white Georgian building, towards the moorings and landing pontoons off the boatyard. Do not try to anchor as the bottom is foul, but berth alongside the pontoon, rafting if necessary, as this is only used for short stay visitors. If you wish to remain longer, drying moorings are sometimes available off the yard if residents are away.

River Exe Port Guide – Area telephone code: 01392

Harbourmaster: Exeter, City Canal Basin, Tel: 274306.

Exmouth Dockmaster: The Docks, Tel: 01395 269314.

VHF: Normal working hours only, Ch 12; callsign *Port of Exeter* or *Harbour Patrol*; Exmouth Dock, Ch 14, callsign *Exmouth Dock*; Retreat Boatyard Ch M.

Emergency services: Lifeboat at Exmouth; Brixham Coastguard.

Anchorages: Below No 19 buoy; off Turf; Topsham. Various possibilities within river.

Mooring/berthing: Exmouth Marina, Tel: 01395 269314; Harbour Authority visitors' moorings in lower Exe and at Turf; drying alongside quay or Trout's pontoons at Topsham, Tel: 873044; drying moorings at Retreat Boatyard, Tel: 874720. Lock into Exeter Canal, Tel: 274306.

Dinghy landings: The Point, Exmouth; Starcross Pier; Turf; public slipways at Topsham, ladders on Quay; Topsham SC; Trout's Pontoon.

Water taxi: VHF Ch 80 or M, callsign *Exeplorer* or Mob: 07970 918418.

Marina: In Exmouth Dock.

Charges: Exmouth Marina: 10m boat per night £17.60; Harbour Authority visitors' moorings £4.50 per night; Exeter Canal (minimum two nights), berth below M5 bridge, £9.50; Exeter Canal basin £15, including locking and transit; Trout's Pontoon, Topsham, from £14 or £17.50 per night, depending on size; alongside Topsham Quay £6.

Phones: Dock entrance, Exmouth; Starcross; High Street by Church, Topsham.

Doctor: Exmouth Tel: 01395 273001; Topsham Tel: 874648.

Hospital: Exmouth Tel: 01395 279684; Exeter Tel: 411611.

Churches: Exmouth, Topsham, most denominations.

Local weather forecast: Trout's Boatyard.

Fuel: During normal working hours, diesel alongside in entrance to Exmouth Marina; at Trout's Pontoon and Retreat Boatyard, Topsham. Diesel and petrol in cans from Starcross Garage, Starcross. Petrol in cans from Pretty's Garage, Topsham.

Gas: Calor and Camping Gaz, Garners Home Hardware, Exmouth town centre. Starcross Garage, Trout's Boatyard, Topsham.

Paraffin: Westaways Hardware, Topsham.

Water: Exe Sailing Club, Exmouth; Turf Hotel; Topsham SC; Trout's Boatyard and Retreat Boatyard, Topsham; Topsham Quay.

Banks/cashpoints: Exmouth: All main banks have cashpoints. Topsham: Lloyds TSB, Natwest, both with cashpoints. All main banks in Exeter have cashpoints

Post office: Exmouth, Starcross, Lympstone, Topsham

Internet access: Public Library at Exmouth and Topsham, up to 30 mins free.

Rubbish: Bins at Exmouth, Trout's Yard Topsham and Topsham Quay.

Showers/toilets: Exe Sailing Club, Exmouth; Starcross Fishing & Cruising Club; Starcross Topsham Sailing Club; Trout's Boatyard, Topsham; Retreat Boatyard, Topsham; public toilets Exmouth Dock and Topsham Quay.

Launderette: Exmouth.

Provisions: Exmouth: All facilities. Dawlish Warren: limited shops. Starcross: Provisions/chemist. Topsham: Good selection of shops.

Chandlers: Peter Dixon's Chandlery, Exmouth Tel: 01395 273248; Exe Boat Store Marine, Camperdown Terrace, Exmouth Tel: 01395 263095; The Foc'sle, Fore Street, Topsham Tel: 874105 or 0870 260 2501 (Admiralty Chart Agents); Trout's Boatyard, Topsham Tel: 873044; Ash Marine, Topsham Tel: 876654; Retreat Boatyard, Topsham Tel: 874720; John Bridger Marine, Haven Road, Exeter (close to canal basin) Tel: 250970.

Repairs: Exe Boat Store Marine Ltd Tel: 01395 263095; Rowsell Morrison Ltd Tel: 01395 263911; Global Boat Works Tel: 01395 272100, all in Camperdown Terrace (behind marina), Exmouth. Trout's Boatyard Tel: 873044; Retreat Boatyard Tel: 874720, both in Topsham.

Marine engineers: Starcross Garage Tel: 01626 890225; Paul Craven at Trout's Boatyard Mob: 07980 651143; Retreat Boatyard Tel: 874720.

Electronic engineers: Trout's Boatyard Tel: 873044, and Retreat Boatyard Tel: 874720.

Sailmakers: Rowsell Sails Tel: 01395 263911, Camperdown Terrace, Exmouth; Sails and Canvas Tel: 877527, The Quay, Topsham.

Transport: Frequent bus and train connections from Exmouth via Lympstone and Topsham to main line at Exeter, Tel: 08457 484950. Buses and trains to Exeter from Starcross. M5 motorway at Topsham. Exeter Airport, Tel: 367433, 15 mins away, with UK, Ireland and continental connections.

Car hire: Exmouth, Rentex Tel: 01395 278294; Exeter, Hertz Tel:0870 850 7196; 1car1 Tel: 278575; National Tel: 250858; Hendy Tel: 275136.

Yacht clubs: Exe Sailing Club, 'Tornado', Estuary Road, Exmouth, Devon EX8 1EG, Tel: 01395 264607. Starcross Fishing & Cruising Club, Brunel Tower, Starcross EX8 8PR, Tel: 01626 891996. Starcross Yacht Club, Powderham Point, Starcross, Exeter, Devon, Tel: 01626 890470. Topsham Sailing Club, Hawkins Quay, Ferry Road, Topsham, Exeter, Devon EX3 0JN, Tel: 877524. Lympstone Sailing Club, The Harbour, Lympstone, Exmouth, Devon, EX8 5AJ, Tel: 01395 278792.

Eating out: Exmouth: Pubs, restaurants, cafés and fish & chips. Starcross: Pubs and fish & chips. Topsham: Good selection of pubs and restaurants, cafés, fish & chips.

Things to do: Swimming/walking at Exmouth and Dawlish Warren. Attractive cathedral city and major shopping centre of Exeter within 15 minutes of Topsham.

The Lighter Inn at Topsham (right) is a favourite among locals

Teign entrance at half-flood. Shaldon, left, Den Point, centre, and Teignmouth, right. Note the extent of the central Salty Bank

River Teign

Tides	HW Dover −0450
Range	MHWS 4.6m–MHWN 3.6m, MLWN 2.0m–MLWS 0.7m. Spring rates can attain up to five knots in entrance
Charts	AC: 26, SC5602.5; Stanfords: 12; Imray: WCP2400.3
Waypoints	Abeam south-west end Den Point 50°32'.39N 03°30'.07W
Hazards	Shifting bar, dangerous in easterly or southerly winds and swell, particularly on the ebb. Strong tidal streams in river. Large part of harbour dries. Low bridge across river half a mile from entrance
Harbour Speed limit	Six knots/minimal wash
Overnight charge	Harbour Authority pontoon or swinging mooring: £10

Just over five miles west of the Exe, and in many ways similar, the River Teign has less immediate appeal from a visitor's point of view. Not only does it have an outer bar in the approaches, but, sadly, the wide and drying upper reaches of the estuary are effectively closed to sailing boats by the 2.9m Mean High Water Springs clearance of the road bridge just above the town of Teignmouth. The Salty, a large sand and gravel bank which dries 3.3m, fills much of the central part of the harbour, space is at a premium and within the main channel and the entrance the tides run fast, between four and five knots at Springs. However, in spite of the difficult entrance, a considerable amount of commercial shipping uses the docks – there are around 800 ship movements a year, vessels in excess of 100m LOA and up to 5m draught at Springs. The harbour developed during the 19th century around the export of ball clay which continues today, and imports include animal feed, fertiliser, timber building material, stone and coal, amounting in total to about 600,000 tons per annum.

It is an interesting small port and worth a visit if time and weather permit. The Harbour Authority has two deep-water pontoon islands for visitors and can also provide swinging moorings if local boats are away.

It is not possible to anchor anywhere in the river due to the number of local moorings and in the fairway, which must be left clear.

APPROACHES

The Bar has a justifiably unpleasant reputation and in fresh winds from the south or east, especially on the ebb, it can become a treacherous area of steep breaking seas and surf. In offshore winds, however, and after half-flood, with no likelihood of southerly or easterly weather in the offing, the river is not particularly difficult to enter, and once inside, perfectly sheltered.

The approach should be made from a position east of the Ness, the prominent red sandstone headland on the south side of the entrance and, although lit, I would only recommend a first visit in daylight. A yellow buoy 1.16M south-east of the Ness, marking the end of a sewer outfall, is useful to gauge your distance off. The Harbour Authority endeavours to maintain a dredged fairway running east/west into the river mouth flanked by the East Pole Sand (dries 0.3m), on the southern side, and Spratt Sand (dries 2.7m) to the north, both of which extend nearly half a mile to seaward. It should be noted that this channel cannot be relied on, particularly after any strength of wind from the east, when it can silt up very rapidly. A seasonal red can buoy (Fl R 2s) is positioned on the north-east side of the East Pole Sand in the approach to the Bar marking the port hand side of the approach channel. Small yellow, black or orange buoys are often positioned along the south side of this channel to assist the pilots. Once past the bar, Spratt Sand is marked midway along its length

by a conical green buoy (Fl G 2s) which should be left on your starboard hand. However, due to the changing nature of the bar, you are strongly advised to call ahead before entering either by phone (Tel: 01626 773165) or VHF Channel 12 during office hours, callsign *Teignmouth Harbourmaster*.

Directly below the Ness, the white Lucette beacon (Oc R 6s) marks the southern side of the channel. It stands on a training wall just off the shore which dries 2m; behind it, right on the shore there are two prominent rectangular white marks painted on the seawall. The Lucette beacon lined up between these two marks gives a transit of approximately 265° along the dredged channel. Approaching the Lucette beacon, leave it several boat lengths to port and steer towards the beacon with a triangular topmark (Oc G 6s FG vert), which marks the end of Den Point, the low sandy spit on your starboard hand. Beyond it, Shaldon and a large group of moorings in the pool lie ahead, but the main channel turns sharply to starboard, with the moorings and waterfront of Teignmouth opening up before you. Here the tide runs strongly – do not cut the corner, but keep in midstream. The eastern edge of the Salty is marked by the Lower Salty red can buoy (Fl R 2s), which should be left to port, with a conical green starboard hand buoy (Fl G 2s) further upstream on the opposite side of the fairway.

BERTHING

The Jubilee and Trafalgar visitors' pontoons lie beyond the buoy, on your starboard hand, and are clearly marked. Both are 20m long and can accommodate up to

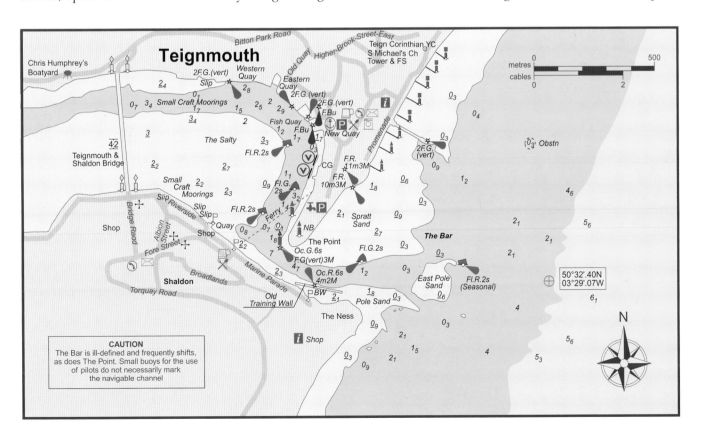

10 rafted boats depending on size, and you will remain afloat in 2.5m LAT. The overnight charge is £1 per metre. From here you will have to dinghy ashore and land on the nearby Back Beach.

The harbour office, Tel: 01626 773165; www. teignmouth-harbour.com, is situated on New Quay, a bit further upstream on the starboard hand, and is usually open during normal working hours, 0800 – 1700 weekdays, 0900 – 1200 Saturdays. On arrival contact the harbourmaster, Commander David Vaughan, or his staff, unless they have already spotted you. In season, during busy times and particularly at weekends a harbour patrol boat is usually on duty.

FUEL, FRESH WATER AND GAS

Marine diesel is available alongside the quay at Chris Humphrey's boatyard, Tel: 01626 772324, just upstream of the bridge, during normal working hours, but it is usually worth calling ahead. If your mast height prohibits access under the bridge, it is an easy dinghy trip with cans. Petrol is only available in cans from fuel pumps at Tesco Express (and taxed diesel too), which is a 15-minute walk from the harbour. Fresh water can be obtained in cans from fresh water taps at Polly Steps, the main launching slip just upstream of the docks, or in the corner of the lower car park on Den Point. Calor and Camping Gaz are available from Brigantine Chandlers in Shaldon, and depending on draught, ideally at around High Water, it is possible by arrangement to obtain water alongside from a hose on the quay.

FACILITIES

(**Local phone code 01626**)

A recorded port for nearly 1,000 years, today Teignmouth is an intriguing mixture. It is a typical beach resort with reddish sands, and was developed early in the 1800s with a traditional pier, elegant seafront, and all the usual diversions, novelty golf, a seafront theatre, children's rides and amusement arcades. In marked contrast, behind the town, the jumble of brightly painted fishermen's beach huts, slipways, alleyways and small quays along the shingly Back Beach have their own particular charm.

Salmon fishermen work the river in season, often shooting nets right across the river mouth at Low Water. The famous Morgan Giles Shipyard was located here from before the war until it closed in 1969, once employing over 150 local people designing and building fine wooden yachts – many of which are still sailing today. The Teign Corinthian Yacht Club, Tel: 01626 772734; www.tcyc.org.uk, was established in 1886, and for many years had its clubhouse on the pier. Since 1995 it has been enjoying panoramic views from its impressive clubhouse at the Eastcliff end of the seafront, and visitors are welcome when it is open – see website for times.

All the usual facilities can be found in the town, with public showers and toilets (open daily 0800 to 2200 in summer) just a short walk from Back Beach at the Den, the seafront lawns and gardens adjacent to the promenade and pier. There are also public toilets at The Point and in Brunswick Street, in the centre of town. Under local bylaws it is an offence to discharge sewerage or rubbish into the Teign estuary – it is not only popular for bathing but also an important shellfish producing area.

Rubbish can be disposed of in bins at the harbourmaster's office, New Quay, Fish Quay, Polly Steps and on The Point. There is a town centre Co-op supermarket in Lower Brook Street (0800 – 2200 Mon – Fri, 0730 – 2200 Sat, 1100 – 1700 Sun), and a new Tesco Express (0800 – 2200) which was scheduled to open in

Teign approach from the east, with the red cliffs of the Ness just left of centre

Looking towards Shaldon and the Ness. The Teign dries extensively at Low Water

Spring 2008 on the site of the former County Garage, a 15-minute walk from the harbour. You will find a number of smaller convenience stores and a launderette (open 0900 – 1900 seven days a week) in George Street as well as a post office and branches of all main banks with cashpoints. The Tourist Information Centre, Tel: 01626 215666; www.teignbridge.gov.uk, is on the Den near the pier. The Teignmouth and Shaldon museum is close to the railway station, which is about a five-minute walk from New Quay. There are frequent main line rail connections to London and the North, while regular local buses connect to all the main towns, Torquay, Exeter and Newton Abbot.

Should you have any problems with your boat, there's plenty of help on hand with Chris Humphrey boat builder, repairs and marine engineering, Tel: 772324, as well as several other marine engineers, GEMS Marine, Tel: 879879, Seaworthy Marine, Tel: 879977, and Marks Mechanical & Marine services, Mob: 07831 134813. Other useful numbers include Addicots Electrics, Tel: 774087, and Teign Diving Centre, Tel: 773965.

There's no shortage of cafés and pubs here, which include the popular Ship Inn, right by the water, The New Quay Inn, The Blue Anchor, Ye Olde Jolly Sailor and The Teign Brewery Inn. The choice of restaurants is also good: Nautilus Seafood, Tel: 776999, Trade Winds, Tel: 773181, The Owl & the Pussycat, Tel: 775321, Carlino's Bistro/Bar, Tel: 879241, Italian at The Colosseum, Tel: 870000, and two Indian restaurants, Naz, Tel: 774786, and Taj Mahal, Tel: 870223. If the tide permits, two hours either side of High Water, try an upriver foray in the dinghy to the Coombe Cellars Inn or the Passage House Inn. The channel is marked with small port and starboard hand buoys.

SHALDON

Just across the water, Shaldon is a smaller, quieter place, an unspoilt waterside village with much attractive architecture and a delightful central square surrounding a bowling green. There is less choice of facilities, but all the basics are obtainable at the Londis Waterside Village Stores (open 0800 – 1800 Mon – Sat, 0900 – 1500 Sun).

The extremely well-stocked Brigantine Chandlers, Tel: 01626 872400; www.thebrigantine.com (open 0900 – 1700 Mon – Sat, 1000 – 1400 Sun), is on the foreshore by the quay, while Mariners Weigh, Tel: 01626 873698, specialises in motor boat gear, outboard engines and repairs, and Sleeman and Hawken, Tel: 01626 778266, is a marine diesel engineer situated on Bridge Road.

For its size Shaldon has a surprisingly good choice of places to eat and drink. There's the Hunters Lodge restaurant, Tel: 873177, along with five pubs – The London Inn, Shipwright's Arms, Ferry Boat Inn, Royal Standard and The Clifford Arms – all of which serve food.

If you don't want to use your own dinghy to get across, a distinctive black and white open ferry with painted gunports runs from Teignmouth Back Beach to Shaldon, 0800 to sunset, in summer. For the energetic the coastal footpath up to the summit of the Ness and beyond provides good exercise and fine views. There is also an old smugglers' tunnel through the Ness to Ness Cove, a secluded shingly beach. The south-west's smallest zoo, the Shaldon Wildlife Trust, Tel: 872234; www.shaldonwildlifetrust.org.uk, is located just by its entrance. Specialising in the breeding and conservation of rare breeds, it is open 1000 – 1800 daily during the summer.

Torquay

Tides	HW Dover −0500
Range	MHWS 4.9m–MHWN 3.7m, MLWN 2.0m–MLWS 0.7m. Tidal streams weak in Tor Bay. Stand of 1 hour can occur at High Water
Charts	AC: 26, SC 5602.5; Stanfords: 12. CP22; Imray: C5, WCP2400.3
Waypoints	Haldon Pier Head 50°27'.43N 03°31'.74W
Hazards	Narrow harbour entrance, often busy. Approach poor in strong southeasterly winds. Inner harbour accessed via half tide sill
Harbour Speed limit	Five knots/minimal wash
Overnight charge	Harbour Authority £15 alongside pontoon. Marina £30

Centre of the self-styled English Riviera, visually Torquay is the nearest thing to Cannes or Nice you are likely to find on a West Country cruise. Once described by Tennyson as the 'loveliest sea village in England', he would see some considerable changes today from the small fishing village that he knew as a fledgling resort.

Torquay's inhabited existence has a definite pedigree. Nearby, within an easy bus ride, in the famous underground caves at Kent's Cavern you can see spectacular Stone Age remains dating from circa 35,000BC. By the 12th century Torre Abbey had been established and the small stone quay built by the Monks to serve it became known as Torre Quay. However, its real growth and prosperity came during the Napoleonic Wars, when Tor Bay was much used by the Royal Navy as an alternative to Plymouth before its breakwater

was built, being accessible and better sheltered in south and southwesterly weather. With the Fleet often anchored in Tor Bay for months at a time, the town soon found favour among Naval officers, with smart lodging houses rising beside the old thatched medieval cottages. The unusually mild climate was another obvious attraction. Large hotels quickly began to rise on the seven surrounding hills, palms and other sub-tropical plants flourished in the new parks and gardens and elegant Georgian terraces began to grow around the small harbour. As Macaulay observed, ' . . . a great watering place to which strangers are attracted by the Italian softness of the air; for in that climate the myrtle flourishes unsheltered . . . with white streets, rising terrace above terrace, and gay villas peeping from the midst of shrubberies and flower-beds.'

Town Dock
opening 2008

Torquay Harbour's continuing redevelopment includes a new 'Town Dock' in the area indicated, which was due to open in 2008

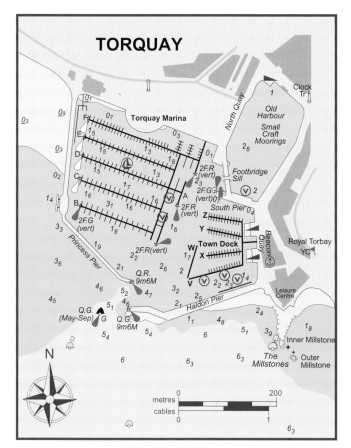

The final element in this transformation from humble hamlet into the West Country's premier seaside resort came with the arrival of the Great Western Railway in 1848, which inevitably unleashed a huge increase in holidaymakers.

At this time, though, there was still only a small drying harbour and it was customary for vessels to lie at anchor offshore. Here, in August 1868, RT McMullen had a very close shave with his 16-ton cutter *Orion* as he lay among the fleet of boats anchored in the bay for the annual regatta:

'. . . awakened at 2am by the uneasy motion of the vessel, I immediately struck a match over the barometer, and, perceiving that its state was unsatisfactory, hastily dressed myself and called up the men to make snug, as a precaution . . . we first stowed the boat, then housed topmast, and hove the bowsprit short in. Meanwhile the rain was pelting down and the wind gradually backing to the SE, throwing in a nasty sea. The mainsail in very short time became so thick and heavy with the rain, that the labour of reeving the earrings and taking reefs down was very great indeed. At 4am it blew a heavy gale SE . . . 5am there was a terrible sea, all the yachts were pitching bows under, and most of them beginning to drag home. I was glad to see three or four yachts that lay in our way slip and run for the harbour, although it was only half-tide. Having unshackled our chain at 30 fathoms and buoyed it, we set mainsail with four reefs down, reefed foresail and storm jib and slipped at 5.30am.'

Not exactly the perfect start to a day, but unlike several of the vessels that went ashore, *Orion* and her crew managed to beat out to sea without mishap.

Torquay developed early as a popular yachting centre. The Royal Torquay Yacht Club was founded in 1875 and, with the completion of the large outer harbour in 1880, the fashionable resort soon became a firm favourite in the grand era of Edwardian yachting growth, but as Frank Cowper wryly observed in the 1880s, 'I find the prices a little prohibitive, and my tastes are simpler, which may or may not be deficiencies.'

Although the outer harbour provided infinitely better shelter than the open roadstead, it still suffered from an uncomfortable heavy surge in southeasterly weather. Amazingly, the short extension to Haldon Pier that eliminated this problem was not built until over a century later when a 2,500-ton caisson was towed into position and sunk here in 1984 to protect the new marina that had begun construction a year earlier!

The opening of Torquay Marina in 1985 greatly enhanced the facilities for yachts and since then the port has become an increasingly popular stopover for visitors, with a considerable amount of harbourside regeneration in recent years and ongoing improvements to attract visitors.

APPROACHES

There are no immediate hazards in the approach to Torquay, and there is deep water to the harbour mouth, but as this is narrow it should be approached with care in strong southeasterly winds, which kick up an uncomfortable backwash. In these conditions Brixham is usually a far easier option for those seeking shelter in Tor Bay.

The entrance is only just under 50m wide and is well hidden at a distance because of the overlapping outer end of Haldon Pier. To direct vessels into the harbour mouth between May and September, a green conical buoy (QG) is situated approximately 70m west of the end of Haldon Pier – leave this to starboard and keep

The entrance to Torquay Harbour is not easy to spot at first – the green approach buoy lies on the far right

The entrance to the inner harbour boasts a very stylish footbridge! Sill closed

to starboard between the pierheads. The yellow buoy, situated to seaward and marked 5KTS, is one of the limits of the controlled inshore swimming areas around Tor Bay, within which the speed limit of five knots must not be exceeded. Take care in the final approach as the entrance is invariably busy. If closed due to navigational hazards three vertical red balls are displayed on the pierhead (three vertical red lights at night), and no vessels are allowed to enter or leave.

Entry at night is not difficult. Haldon Pier displays a green light (QG 6M) and Princess Pier a red one (QR 6M), although it is not always easy to pick them out against the blaze of lights from the town. Once inside, two green lights (2FG vert) mark the end of the South Pier and the entrance to the Inner Harbour. There are three (2FR vert) lights on the outer ends of the marina pontoons.

FUEL, FRESH WATER AND GAS

Diesel, petrol and LPG are available from the easily accessed pontoon on the outer end of South Pier (call *Riviera Fuel* on Mob: 07786 370324), which is open 0830 – 1900 Mon – Sat, 1000 – 1900 Sun, April – Sept. Fresh water taps are on the Harbour Authority visitors' pontoons and in the marina. Calor and Camping Gaz can be obtained from Torquay Chandlers, which is located in the Pavilion.

BERTHING

The outer harbour and the marina have an average depth between 1.5m and 1.9m and from May to September there is a Harbour Authority visitors' pontoon on the inner end of Haldon Pier. However, during the winter of 2007 as part of the continuing redevelopment of the harbour, a much larger complex

of purpose-built pontoons was being installed in the outer harbour, with walkways ashore, to create a 'Town Dock' accommodating an extra 150 boats, with berthing for visitors on the south side of the 'V' pontoon.

The fairway leads past the marina to the previously drying Inner (Old) Harbour. This is now accessed from 3.5 hours before and up to 3 hours after High Water over a hydraulic sill at the entrance. There is a free pontoon on the seaward side of the entrance strictly for vessels waiting for adequate tide to enter.

Adorned with sculptural 'sails' at either end, the stylish footbridge above the sill opens on request (call *Torquay Harbour* on VHF Ch 14), tide permitting, during operational hours, 0700 – 2100 May to September, 0800 – 1700 October to April. There are traffic control signals on both sides of the bridge. **Three vertical red lights = vessels shall not proceed. Two vertical green over white light = vessels may proceed, two way traffic subject to headroom; otherwise bridge will be lifted on request.** Boats passing through the entrance must keep to the central bridge span where the sill gates open, on either side of this the sill is a fixed structure between the harbour wall and the central bridge supports. It is prohibited to pass under the footbridge when the sill gate is not open. When it is open, at half tide there is usually 2.2m in the entrance. When closed, the sill maintains a depth of between 1m and 2.8m in the Old Harbour, which is mostly given over to local trot moorings, but there is another 33m long Harbour Authority visitors' pontoon on the inside of the South Pier with coded walkway access. This can be used by prior arrangement only, depending on draught, and wherever you berth the Harbour Authority's overnight charge for vessels over 7m LOA is £1.45 per metre, smaller craft are charged between £6 and £8 per night according to length. If you stay on any of the Harbour Authority visitors' pontoons for three nights you will get the fourth night free!

The Harbour Authority office is easy to spot in the smart new development on Beacon Quay where you will also find visitors' showers and toilets. There are heavy penalties for discharging marine toilets within the harbour.

Water is available on the pontoons and electric cards for shore power can be purchased from the harbour office, although you will need your own extension cable.

Anchoring is prohibited anywhere within the inner and outer harbours, but quite feasible in suitable offshore conditions either to the south-east of Haldon Pier or south-west of Princess Pier, where there is good holding in sand and mud.

Torquay Marina can usually provide berths for visitors

TORQUAY MARINA

The 500-berth Torquay Marina, Tel: 01803 200210; www.mdlmarinas.co.uk, occupies most of the western side of the outer harbour. For berthing availability and instructions call *Torquay Marina* on VHF Ch 80 or phone ahead (the office is manned 24 hours a day). Report to the marina office once secure.

The visitor charge of £3 per metre per night up to 15m, £3.50 per metre over 15m, is based on overall length – including bowsprits and davits. Although there is technically a 25% surcharge for multihulls, this is rarely imposed unless the boat is of exceptional beam or takes up more than one berth. If you take up free membership of the MDL Cruising Club and stay a week here or in any of MDL's marinas, you will get the seventh night free!

Facilities include luxury showers and toilets, fresh water, shore power, payphones, refuse and recycling, a self-service launderette and MDL WiFi. There is a large adjoining car park and excellent 24-hour security with coded locks to the marina and onshore facilities.

The extravagant Art Deco Edwardian Pavilion dates from 1812 and overlooks the marina. It was built as a 'Palace of Pleasure' to attract visitors, with music and theatre, enjoying its heyday between the wars, when the Torquay Music festival attracted top composers and conductors and performers, including Sir Henry Wood, Sir Edward Elgar, Sir Malcolm Sargent, Sir Adrian Boult and Dame Nellie Melba! Narrowly escaping demolition in the early 1970s, it is now a Grade II listed building and houses an elegant shopping mall,

with a variety of specialist and eclectic shops and galleries. It is also home to Torquay Chandlers, Tel: 0870 260 2500, open seven days a week, the Pavilion Bar and Terrace Restaurant (Tel: 211801) and Le Petit Gourmet, café/delicatessen.

FACILITIES
(Local phone code 01803)

As might be expected in a popular holiday resort, facilities in Torquay encompass most large retail outlets and branches of all major banks in the town centre. However, the only supermarkets within walking distance of the harbour are Tesco Metro in Fleet Street or Iceland in Union Square Mall, otherwise a taxi will be required to get to Sainsburys, M&S, Co-op or Somerfield. There are a number of smaller convenience shops closer to hand.

The choice of hotels, pubs and restaurants is vast, many of which are conveniently located close to the harbour on Beacon Hill, Victoria Parade, the Strand and Vaughan Parade, by North Quay. The Wetherspoons London Inn opposite the inner harbour has good value meals and WiFi access, and the Yacht, on Victoria Parade, a lively ambiance. A large pub/restaurant, with an elevated outside seating area, is situated right on Beacon Quay, where you'll also find the Below Decks Café/Bar.

Enjoy excellent seafood at No 7 Fish Bistro, Tel: 295055, Ocean Brasserie, Tel: 292359, the Hole in the Wall, Tel: 200755, Edwards' Brasserie, Tel: 290855, Café Sol, Tel: 296090, The Marina Restaurant, Tel: 292255,

Built as a 'palace of treasure', Torquay's elegant Pavilion is now a shopping mall

The Elephant bar & restaurant, Tel: 200044, or Steps Bistro, Tel: 200770. There's Italian at Prezzo, Tel: 389525, or Portobello, Tel: 296558, Indian and Chinese abound, with Thai, too, at Thai Star, Tel: 297631. For an evening out with a difference try a medieval style banquet at Camelot, Tel: 215399, or sample Moroccan at Al Beb Tapas Bar, Tel: 211755, with belly dancing at weekends!

If it's just a quick fix you need, sprint over to Fleet Street for an abundance of fast food outlets – Burger King, KFC, Pizza Express, McDonalds, Wimpy and Pizza Hut!

Although Torquay lacks the restful charm of the peaceful rivers, the contrast can make an interesting change, with plenty of nightlife for the younger members of the crew. Older hands will probably prefer the more comfortable surroundings of the Royal Torbay Yacht Club, Tel: 292006; bar Tel: 297271; www.royaltorbayyc.org.uk, and visiting members of other yacht clubs are welcome to use the showers, bar and restaurant, open daily for lunch, 1200 – 1400 with evening meals 1900 – 2230 Wednesdays and Fridays. The club's keen interest in racing goes right back to its creation in 1885 from a merger between The Royal Torquay YC and the Torbay and South Devon YC. Early regattas had their moments: in 1888 the first turning mark failed to appear and, according to the records, 'the committee launch was found to be in the charge of two boys, without orders, with no fires lit and no coal aboard!'

During 1934 and 1935 the club organised the J Class trials for the America's Cup, and hosted the 1948 Olympic sailing events. It organises the annual Torbay Royal Regatta at the end of August and is active throughout the season with local racing as well as hosting national championships and mini regattas. Since 1986 it has also organised the Triangle race to north Brittany and southern Ireland bi-annually in June. Inevitably, the harbour is particularly busy during these events!

Agatha Christie was born in Torquay in 1890 and is undoubtedly one of the town's better known former residents. This is celebrated today by the walk known as the *Agatha Christie Mile* and a permanent exhibition in Torquay Museum in Torwood Street, which leads up from the Strand. Several of the locations for her mystery stories were located in and around Torquay, including the *ABC Murders*, which features the spacious Princess Gardens adjoining the marina.

The most recent tourist attraction is the Living Coasts Centre at the seaward end of Beacon Quay, a marine conservation exhibition with a large and ingenious aviary as its centrepiece. Here seabirds from all over the world, including penguins and puffins, can be viewed at close quarters from acrylic tunnels which lead under the artificial pools and lakes or the many viewing platforms, with the coastal effects created by wave making machines and large dump buckets which drop two tons of water at a time! Included in this attraction, with splendid views over Tor Bay, is the Azure@living coasts, Tel: 202499 – a café by day, which becomes a smart *à la carte* restaurant in the evening.

A fascinating excursion well worth the effort is to the remarkable model village at Babbacombe, which will amaze adults and children alike. This, and Kent's Cavern, can be reached on buses that depart from outside Debenhams on the Strand. In contrast to the model village, Cockington, about two miles away, is the real thing – picturesque with its thatched cottages and carefully preserved vision of rural tranquility. This veritable time capsule can be reached by bus, on foot if you're in need of a good walk, or even by horse and carriage from the far western end of the Torquay seafront, where you can also enjoy the Low Water expanse of Torre Abbey Sands if you're looking for a traditional beach.

Alfresco wining and dining is all part of Torquay's lively waterfront scene

Torquay Port Guide – Area telephone code: 01803

Harbourmaster: Captain Kevin Mowat, Harbour Office, Beacon Quay, Torquay, TQ1 2BG, Tel: 292429; Fax: 299257. Office manned 0900 – 1700 Mon – Fri and weekends also, May – Sept. Email: marine.services@torbay.gov.uk; website: www.tor-bay-harbour.co.uk.

VHF: Ch 14, callsign *Torquay Harbour*, office hours.

Mail drop: Harbour office. Marina will hold mail and messages for customers. Royal Tor Bay Yacht Club will hold mail.

Emergency services: Lifeboat at Brixham. Brixham Coastguard.

Anchorages: In offshore winds, Torquay Roads, three

A stylish harbour office, too!

cables south-west or south-east of harbour entrance, clear of approaches. Anchoring prohibited within the harbour.

Mooring/berthing: Harbour Authority pontoon berthing for visitors in eastern side of outer harbour. Visitors' pontoon in inner harbour, by prior arrangement, draught restrictions apply, and access limited to 3.5 hours before High Water to 3 hours after High Water.

Marina: Torquay Marina, Torquay, TQ2 5EQ, Tel: 200210; Fax: 200225; email: torquaymarina@mdlmarinas.co.uk; website: www.mdlmarinas.co.uk. Equipped with 500 berths, including visitors. VHF Ch 80 (24 hours), callsign *Torquay Marina.*

Charges: Harbour Authority, up to 4m £6, 4m to 5.5m £7, 5.5m to 7m £8. Over 7m £1.50 per metre per day. Torquay Marina, £3 per metre per night up to 15m. £3.50 per night over 15m. Short stay of up to 4 hours, £8.50.

Phones: Beacon Quay; Torquay Marina.

Doctor: Tel: 298441 or 290000.

Dentist: Tel: 613236 or 291919.

Hospital: A&E, Torbay Hospital, Tel: 614567, 2 miles from town centre on A380.

Churches: All denominations.

Local weather forecast: Daily at harbour office and at the marina.

Fuel: Petrol, diesel and LPG alongside South Pier fuel pontoon from Riviera Fuels, Mob: 07786 370324. Open during the Summer, 0830 – 1900 Mon – Sat, 1000 – 1900 Sun.

Water: On pontoons in outer and inner harbour; Torquay Marina.

Gas: Calor and Camping Gaz available from Torquay Chandlers.

Tourist Information Centre: Adjacent to inner harbour slipway, Tel: 211211; www.englishriviera.co.uk.

Banks/cashpoints: All main banks in town have cashpoints.

Post office: Centre of town.

Internet access: MDL WiFi at marina. WiFi at London Inn.

Rubbish: Skips and waste oil disposal on Beacon Quay. Compactor, bottle and can bank in marina car park.

Showers/toilets: Harbour Authority showers and toilets, Beacon Quay; showers and toilets in marina for customers; showers available at Royal Torbay YC.

Chemical toilet disposal: At marina.

Launderette: At marina and in town.

Provisions: Everything available, with most shops open on Sundays.

Chandler: Torquay Chandlers, The Pavilion, Tel: 0870 260 2500; Riviera Boats, Beacon Quay, Tel: 294509.

Crane: Torbay Seaways & Stevedores, Tel: 296570.

Marine engineers: Able Marine, Tel: 606906. Ask at marina or harbour office, see Brixham Port Guide on page 56.

Electronic engineers: None, ask at marina or harbour office; see Brixham Port Guide on page 56.

Sailmakers: None, nearest in Dartmouth.

Transport: Regular branch line services from Torquay station (5 mins bus/taxi ride from marina) to main rail network at Newton Abbot,

No shortage of places to eat

Tel: 08457 484950. For bus information contact Traveline, Tel: 0871 200 22 33. M5 motorway (20 mins). Exeter Airport, Tel: 01392 367433 (approx 45 mins by car) has UK, Ireland and continental connections.

Car hire: Riviera Rentals Tel: 612622; 1car1 Tel: 201600; United Tel: 612622; Thrifty Tel: 294786; Practical Tel: 323323.

Bike hire: None.

Taxi: Tel: 292292; 297070; 211611; 390390; 393939.

Car parking: Beacon Quay car park; marina car park; many public car parks.

Yacht Club: Royal Torbay Yacht Club, Beacon Hill, Torquay TQ1 2BQ, Tel: 292006; email: admin@royaltorbayyc.org.uk; website: www.royaltorbayyc.org.uk.

Eating out: Wide selection from fish and chips to bistros, restaurants and ethnic food.

Things to do: Living Coasts Centre; Torre Abbey – art gallery; Kent's Cavern, underground prehistoric remains; Model Village, Babbacombe; Cockington preserved village; Paignton Zoo Environmental Park; Quaywest Waterpark at Paignton; Safe swimming from Torre Abbey sands, a 400-yd walk from marina; Torbay Royal Regatta, which takes place in August.

Inner harbour pontoon – the Living Coasts aviary is in the background

Berths in Brixham's colourful inner harbour are entirely restricted to local boats which all dry out at Low Water

Brixham

Tides	HW Dover −0505
Range	MHWS 4.9m–MHWN 3.7m, MLWN 2.0m–MLWS 0.7m
Charts	AC: 26, SC5602.5; Stanfords: 12, CP22; Imray: WCP2400.3
Waypoints	Victoria Breakwater Head 50°24'.33N 03°30'.77W
Hazards	Very busy fishing and pleasure boat harbour. Inner harbour dries
Harbour speed limit	Five knots/minimal wash
Overnight charge	Marina £30. Harbour Authority town pontoon £15. Brixham Yacht Club island pontoon £13

'Next day was the day of the trawler's race. It was still blowing extremely hard from the west but the rain had stopped. When we came on deck the smacks in the harbour already had their mainsails up, double reefed with big topsails over them. Those reefs were a good enough indication of the strength of the wind. One smack was lying right at the head of the harbour hemmed in by the dense crowd of yachts which always filled the harbour at regatta time. It was a lovely thing to watch her get under way. Just before she cast off her mooring she set a great balloon staysail, filled on the port tack, and with not an inch to spare began to forge ahead down the narrowest of lanes between the anchored craft. She was squeezed so close to the wind, and I could not but tremble to think what would happen if a puff came foul and she lost way; for there was no room to tack – indeed, there was no room to deviate a yard from her direct line. But such things do not happen to Brixham trawlers; their skippers I believe,

possess a secret magic to circumvent them. She passed within a dozen yards of *Sybil*, going fast now, her deck lined with crew – there must have been fifteen of them. Then when she was clear of the harbour, her jib was blown to ribbons. In a couple of minutes she had set another, and was away for the starting line.'

Brixham and trawlers are synonymous. In the last century the port was renowned for the powerful gaff ketches that so entranced Aubrey de Selincourt, who was writing here of a pre-war Brixham when a few of these fine vessels still regularly fished as far afield as the North Sea. Today, the large fleet of sizeable steel vessels that continue the tradition are also graphic evidence of the remarkable reversal of the port's commercial fortunes; in the late 1960s the fishing fleet was struggling to survive. The creation of the Brixham and Torbay Fishermen's Co-operative resulted in this turn around and as new, much larger vessels were introduced the fish quays grew to accommodate them.

Since then Brixham has flourished and now ranks as one of the main fishing ports in England, a success story that is impressive when compared to the recession that has dogged so many other places.

If you're here for the Spring Bank Holiday, late May/early June – during Brixham Heritage Festival – the Brixham Sailing Trawler race has been revived, and in contrast to the tanned sails you can also watch their modern counterparts racing in a haze of diesel in the Port of Brixham Trawler Race on the third Saturday in June. Brixham Regatta takes place on the third weekend in August.

Much has changed since I first began to visit Brixham over 40 years ago – there was far less commercial activity then and always

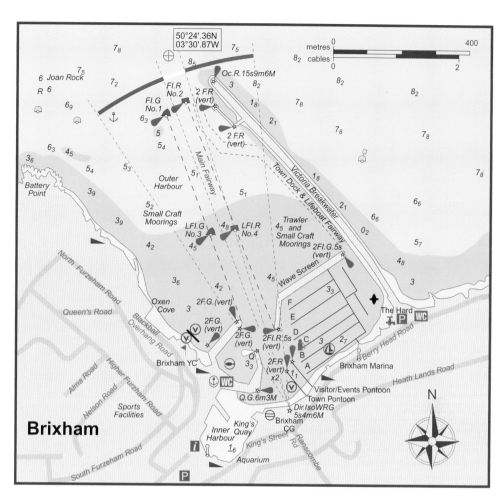

plenty of room to anchor. We frequently used to nose our way in to find space to dry out alongside the wall in the inner harbour, but nowadays this is all given over to grids and concrete hard standing for repair work. Today, first and foremost, Brixham is a busy fishing port, secondly it is an important pilotage station with large vessels regularly entering Torbay to take on or land Channel pilots, and there is also a sizeable fleet of trip and angling boats. Brixham Marina opened in 1989, and its safe and easy access has made it an increasingly popular port of call for pleasure craft.

There are huge regeneration plans for the town and harbour currently under consideration, including revitalising the town centre with a large Tesco supermarket, and the possibility of building a northern breakwater, and development of reclaimed land. Time will tell . . .

APPROACHES AND ANCHORAGE
Brixham's half-mile long Victoria breakwater has a white lighthouse at the outer end (Oc R 15s) and is easy to locate about a mile west of Berry Head. Give the breakwater end a wide berth as large beam trawlers can often emerge from behind it at speed and you should then keep to the starboard side of the 75m wide fairway, which is clearly marked by port hand (Fl R) and starboard hand (Fl G) buoys right up to the fish quays and the marina. There are two (2FR vert) lights

on the jetty on the outer, inside end of the breakwater. At night the fairway is covered by the white sector of a Dir Iso WRG 5s light located on the southern side of the harbour, which has a quick flashing light immediately above it to help identify it against the background lights of the town. The eastern end of the marina wave screen breakwater is indicated by 2 Fl G 5s vert lights, the south-western end by 2 Fl R 5s vert.

Anchoring is prohibited in the fairway, and the only feasible place to lie to your own gear is to seaward of the moorings on the west side of the harbour, which is sheltered in all but northwesterly winds, but uncomfortable in northerly or northeasterly conditions when a ground swell runs in. The bottom is foul in places and a trip line is essential.

Anchoring is also prohibited in the fairway along the inside of Victoria Breakwater, which is kept clear for the lifeboat that is berthed at the inner end.

An alternative anchorage, though less convenient for the town, is Fishcombe Cove, just west of the harbour. It is sheltered and peaceful in southerly and westerly weather, and also free. On arrival in Brixham the harbour office requests all vessels to make contact on VHF Ch 14 prior to entering the fairway.

FUEL, FRESH WATER AND GAS
Diesel is available from Brixham Marina fuel berth, which is easily accessed on the outer end of 'C' pontoon,

Brixham's outer harbour and large marina have easy all-weather access

0900 – 1800 May to September, 0900 – 1700 winter. Petrol is only available in cans from the garage; the nearest petrol alongside is in Torquay. Fresh water taps can be found in the marina, at Brixham Yacht Club and on the town pontoon. Calor and Camping Gaz are available from The Boat Shop chandlers, close to the marina.

VISITORS' BERTHING

Brixham Yacht Club, Tel: 853332; website: www.brixhamyachtclub.com, situated in the south-west corner of the outer harbour, has two 10m island pontoons immediately off the club, which can be used by visitors at a daily rate of £1.30 a metre. During the season it has a limited water taxi service, callsign *Shuttle*, VHF Ch M, otherwise it's a very short dinghy ride ashore!

However, most visitors to Brixham usually opt for the convenience of MDL's 500-berth Brixham Marina, Tel: 882929; website: www.mdlmarinas.co.uk, which fills the greater part of the south-eastern corner of the harbour and is well protected by its wave screen breakwater. Visitors' berths are usually available, often on the visitors' pontoon extending from the promenade just to the west of the main marina if it is not being used for a specific event. Please call ahead on VHF Channel 80, callsign *Brixham Marina*, or phone for berthing instructions. Once secure, walk along to the marina control office for registration. Vessels over 18m LOA must make prior berthing arrangements with the dockmaster. The overnight charge works out at £3 a metre up to 15m, £3.50 per metre over 15m. The charges on the visitors'/events pontoon are less, as there is no shore power or water, £2.10 per metre up to 15m, £2.40 over 15m.

The facilities are very good: in addition to the diesel and water, there's shore power, showers, toilets, launderette, payphones, MDL WiFi, and excellent 24-hour security, with coded access to both the pontoons and amenities block. Leaving the marina reception, turn left for the breakwater beach and you'll spot the Breakwater Bistro, Tel: 856738, which serves seafood and steaks in very artistic surroundings. Alternatively, turn right to reach The Prince William bistro/bar and carvery restaurant, Tel: 854468, and The Boat Shop chandlers. From here it's an easy 10-minute stroll along the harbourside promenade to reach the centre of town.

Facilities for visitors were further enhanced by Torbay Harbour Authority in 2000 with the creation of a large new town pontoon adjacent to the marina visitors' pontoon in the approach to the inner harbour. This was partly funded by a European Regional Development Fund and provides a base for the Brixham Heritage Fleet, which includes to date the trawlers *Pilgrim* 1895, *Vigilance* 1926 and *Regard* 1933, and the Trinity Sailing Foundation's three vessels, when they are not busy sail training, the Brixham trawlers *Leader* 1892 and *Provident* 1924 and gaff cutter *Golden Vanity* 1908.

The pontoon also provides limited berthing for visitors, with power and water available. The berths are allocated according to draught, in clearly indicated spaces, and usually you will have to raft. Depending on LOA, boats between 4m and up to 7m pay between £6 and £8 per night. Boats over 7m are charged £1.45 per metre, multihulls £2.11 per metre, and the good news is if you stay three nights the fourth is free! There is no charge for short stays of up to two hours. Shore power can be obtained with an electric card from the harbour office.

From the marina and town pontoon it is a short walk to the centre of town, past the Brixham Coastguard headquarters on King's Quay, where interested visitors are welcome, providing they are not too busy.

FACILITIES
(Local phone code 01803)
The town retains much of its original fishing village atmosphere, climbing in a colourful profusion around the steep hills overlooking the drying inner harbour,

Visitors can berth on the Town Pontoon (left)
or the adjacent marina pontoon

which is given over to local moorings, repair work and trip boat activity. A popular but unsophisticated tourist spot, Brixham has a very distinctive character and is always bustling with waterside activity, from traditional artists painting on the quay to the holidaymakers swarming over the jaunty 'replica' of Drake's *Golden Hind* in the inner harbour.

Most other facilities can be found in the pedestrianised Fore Street, the main shopping centre which follows the valley leading inland from the harbour. There's a Somerfield supermarket, open 0800 – 2000 Monday – Saturday and 0900 – 1600 on Sundays, as well as branches of all the main banks, which all have cashpoints. The Brixham Tourist Information Centre, Tel: 211211; www.englishriviera.co.uk, is located on the inner Quayside in the old Market House.

It comes as no surprise to discover that many of the local restaurants specialise in seafood! Nor too that many will be found along the inner harbour quayside, sporting inevitable nautical nomenclature. Among these are Beamers, Tel: 854777, the Poopdeck, Tel: 858681, Shores Family Restaurant, Tel: 853131, Tides, Tel: 852195 and Yardarms wine bar and restaurant, Tel: 858266. Others include Bistro 46, Tel: 858936, Saxtys, Tel: 858519, No 15, Tel: 853418, and Damar Bistro, Tel: 854469. Head further into town for Number Eleven, Tel: 857205, and Pilgrims, Tel: 853983. Remarkably in this day and age, there is no Indian or Chinese food to be found, but Café Bar Louise does fast food if you're in a hurry!

There are plenty of pubs to choose from too, all of which serve food, including the Blue Anchor, the Rising Sun, and the Sprat & Mackerel. Cafés (a Devonshire cream tea perhaps?) and seafood stalls abound on the harbourside, and no visit to Brixham is really complete without a hefty helping of fish and chips, enjoyed in the cheerful bustle of the Brixham Fish Restaurant or alfresco on the Quay.

If you continue around the inner harbour and up the steep hill past the fishmarket you will reach Brixham Yacht Club, Tel: 853332, where visitors are welcome. There are showers, a bar and the Jubilee Room restaurant for evening meals, with memorable views over the outer harbour and Tor Bay.

The club was established in 1937 and its burgee includes a crown with an orange in the hoist. This is derived from the landing of Prince William of Orange in Brixham in 1688 when, supported by a Dutch invasion force of nearly 15,000, he set out to restore the throne of England to Protestantism and was in due course crowned as William III. A statue at the head of the inner harbour commemorates the event.

Adjacent to the marina, the large slipway was built for a much later invasion, embarking troops and vehicles for the D-Day Normandy landings, and in order to provide access a number of houses on the approach road above had to be demolished; today this is the site of the Churchill gardens! Another WWII relic is the restored Emergency Coastal Defence Battery in Battery gardens, above Freshwater quarry. This scheduled monument is one of the best preserved of its kind in the UK and houses a small museum. There is also an excellent local Heritage Museum at the top end of Fore Street in the former Police Station.

If time permits and you're in need of a good walk, head for the Berry Head National Nature reserve, with splendid airy views of Tor Bay from the south-west coastal foopath. There are two Napoleonic Forts that were built to house guns protecting the Naval anchorage, WWII defences, the lighthouse, Coastguard lookout and a visitor centre with café.

And finally, there's Brixham's celebrated musical heritage too! When All Saint's parish Church was completed in 1823, its first Vicar was the Reverend Henry Francis Lyte, who dabbled between sermons in a bit of poetry and hymn writing, including the haunting *Abide with Me*, which was written in the garden of his home – today, the Berry Head Hotel. A worldwide favourite, the church bells play the tune every evening, and if you're lucky, on a balmy summer one, you might come across the Brixham Orpheus Male Voice Choir singing it in the old fishmarket on the inner quay, or perhaps the Brixham Town Band in suitably rousing form. . .

Brixham Marina is within an easy walk of the town centre

Brixham Port Guide – Area telephone Code: 01803

Harbourmaster: Captain Paul Labistour, The Harbour Office, New Fish Quay, Brixham, TQ5 8AJ, Tel: 853321/851854; Fax: 852434. Office manned 0900 – 1700 Mon – Fri; 0900 – 1600 Sat; 0900 – 1700 Sun; email: marine.services@torbay.gov.uk; website:www.tor-bay-harbour.co.uk.

VHF: Ch 16, working Ch 14, callsign *Brixham Harbour Radio* (office hours).

Mail drops: Brixham Marina; Brixham Yacht Club.

Emergency services: Brixham Lifeboat; Brixham Coastguard.

Anchorages: To seaward of moorings on west side of harbour, 4 to 5m LAT. Fishcombe Cove, situated west of harbour.

Mooring/berthing: Brixham Marina; Harbour Authority town pontoon; Brixham Yacht Club pontoon.

Dinghy landings: At Yacht Club, and public slipways/steps west and east side of outer harbour.

Marina: Brixham Marina, Berry Head Road, Brixham, Devon TQ5 9BW, Tel: 882929; Fax: 882737; email: brixham@mdlmarinas.co.uk; website: www.mdlmarinas.co.uk. Equipped with 500 berths. VHF Ch 80 (24 hours), callsign *Brixham Marina.*

Charges: Per night, Brixham Marina: £3 per metre up to 15m; £3.50 per metre over 15m; Marina visitor/events pontoon (no power or water) £2.10 per metre up to 15m; £2.40 over 15m. Short stay up to 4 hours, £6.
Harbour Authority Town Pontoon: up to 4m, £6; 4m to 5.5m £7; 5.5m to 7m £8; over 7m £1.50 per metre. Multihulls £2.11 per metre. Brixham Yacht Club pontoon: £1.30 per metre.

Phones: Brixham Marina; at yacht club; payphones by harbour office and at the head of inner harbour.

Doctor: Tel: 852731.

Dentist: Tel: 855292 or 853980.

Hospital: A&E, Torbay Hospital, Torquay, Tel: 614567.

Churches: All denominations.

Local weather forecast: At marina and harbour office.

Fuel: Diesel from fuel berth, Brixham Marina (0900 – 1800 in summer, 0900 – 1700 in winter). Petrol in cans from garage or alongside in Torquay.

Water: Brixham Marina; town pontoon; tap at yacht club.

Gas: The Boat Shop chandlery, by marina, Calor and Gaz.

Ice: Ask at marina dockmaster's office.

Tourist Information Centre: On Old Fish Quay, Tel: 211211.

Banks/cashpoints: Branches of all main banks, all with cashpoints.

There is no shortage of pubs in Brixham!

Post office: Fore Street, centre of town.

Internet access: WiFi at Brixham Marina.

Rubbish: Marina has skips and can/bottle bank.

Showers/toilets: In marina and yacht club. Public toilets on New Pier and Fishcombe car park.

Chemical toilet disposal: In marina's facilities block.

Launderette: At marina and also in Bolton Street, centre of town.

Provisions: Everything available. Somerfield supermarket open 0800 – 2000 Mon – Sat, 0900 – 1600 Sunday.

Chandlers: The Boat Shop, Tel: 882055; Bayside Marine, Tel: 856771, Higher Furzeham Road, on top of hill above yacht club.

Repairs: Drying grid in inner harbour by arrangement with harbour office.

Marine engineers: Hubbard Engineering, Tel: 853327;

Oxley Marine Engineering, Tel: 855903; Marine Engineering Looe, Tel: 844777; CF Bowles, Tel: 853670; Brixham Marine Services, Tel: 854224; or ask at marina.

Electronic engineers: Speeder, Tel: 883833; Chris Rutherford Marine Electrics, Tel: 850960; Geoff Ogborne Marine Electrics, Mob: 07976 179924; Selex Communications, Tel: 851993; JK Max Navigation, Tel: 690625; or ask at marina.

Sailmakers: Nearest is in Dartmouth.

Transport: Buses to Paignton station to connect with branch line to main line at Newton Abbot, Tel: 08457 484950. Frequent ferries to Torquay.

Car hire: Ask at marina.

Car parking: At marina multi-storey or car park in centre of town.

Yacht club: Brixham Yacht Club, Overgang Road, Brixham TQ5 8AR, Tel: 853332.

Eating out: Wide selection from fish and chips to restaurants and bistros.

Things to do: Brixham Museum, including Coastguard Museum in centre of town; aquarium; walks to Berry Head Country Park.

Brixham Yacht Club's pontoons are another option for visitors

River Dart

Tides	HW Dover −0510. Standard Port
Range	MHWS 5.5m–MHWN 4.4m, MLWN 2.2m–MLWS 0.8m. Can attain over three knots in entrance at Springs
Charts	AC: 2253, 1634, SC5602; Stanfords: CP 22, L15; Imray: WCP2400 1 & 4
Waypoints	Castle Ledge Buoy 50°19'.99N 03°33'.11W
Hazards	Mewstone and rocks to south-west of Mewstone (lit), Western Blackstone (unlit). Castle Ledge, Homestone, Checkstone (all lit). Approaches rough in strong southerly weather/ebb tide. Fluky winds in entrance. Ferries between Kingswear and Dartmouth. Chain ferry just downstream of Dart Marina, both have right of way. Large part of upper reaches dry
Harbour Speed limit	Six knots/minimal wash. Dead slow in Home Reach to Totnes
Overnight charge	Harbour Authority £26.50 alongside Town Jetty, £17.50 alongside yacht club pontoon or embankment, £13 on mooring or pontoon island (50% surcharge for multihulls). At anchor £6.50. Darthaven Marina £29.50. Dart Marina £47.10. Noss Marina £31.25. Baltic Wharf, Totnes £12.33. South Hams DC quay, Totnes £16

'A shipman was ther, woning fer by weste: For aught I woot, he was of Dertemouthe . . .'

Steeped in a seafaring tradition stretching back way beyond Chaucer's time, when the Shipman's goodly barge *Maudelayne* plied her trade from 'Gootland to the Cape of Finistere, and every cryke in Britayne and in Spayne', the deep, natural harbour of the River Dart is a must on any cruising itinerary. Often the first port of call after the long haul across Lyme Bay, its steep wooded shores and peaceful upper reaches provide a classic introduction to the area. Epitomising the essential character of West Country cruising, it provides a tantalising foretaste of the further delights to come.

APPROACHES
Approaching the Dart from Berry Head and the east, it is not difficult to find the entrance to the river as the jagged triangular Mewstone, white with seabird droppings and gulls a-wheeling, soon appears to seaward of the eastern side of the entrance, standing well clear of the land to provide a distinctive seamark. From further offshore though, to the south and the south-west, this island is lost against the shore and the entrance is completely hidden in the folds of the 170m high cliffs. It would still be a notoriously elusive haven if our predecessors had not bothered, in 1864, to build a 25m high column with a wide base high above Inner Froward Point to the east of the entrance, a fine daymark that is easy to spot.

On the west side of the entrance, the row of white coastguard cottages about 100m above Blackstone Point is very conspicuous against the green hillside. However, once located, there are few other problems. Although the entrance is relatively narrow, it is

The Dart's deep but narrow entrance is memorably flanked by two castles

Overlooked by the Royal Naval College, the Dart has plenty of options for visitors, including Darthaven Marina off Kingswear in the foreground. Alternatives include Dart Marina Yacht Harbour in the far centre or Noss Marina, just visible on the top right

if a ship is anticipated during the night these buoys are lit (Fl Y).

Though straightforward at night, the whole approach should ideally be timed for daylight, as the imposing scenery, St Petrox Church and the two castles guarding the narrow entrance are a sight not to be missed!

Kingswear Castle is privately owned, but Dartmouth Castle, to the west, dates from 1481, and at one time a 750ft chain resting on six barges was stretched from here to the opposite shore to protect the port from raiders. It is now administered by English Heritage and open daily 1000 – 1700 during the summer (until 1800, July/Aug) for a small charge. Walk out from the town or, easier still, take the small ferry from the Embankment to enjoy fine views of the entrance from the castle, where there is also a café. From here you can continue the walk through the woods and along the cliffs to Compass Cove, a shingly beach which is safe for bathing.

In daylight a closer approach can be made from the south-west, keeping near to the red can Homestone buoy (QR) marking a rocky ledge (least depth just under 1m LAT) to the north-west. A course can then be laid along the shore, keeping clear of the two Western Blackstone Rocks off Blackstone Point and the red

extremely deep with the few hazards close to the shore.

Take care, though, in strong southeasterly to southwesterly winds and an ebb tide, which can run out at over three knots at Springs after heavy rain or strong northerly winds. Confused seas will be found in the immediate approaches, and the high surrounding shore tends to create rapid and baffling shifts of wind, a factor that should be considered if entering under sail alone. Once inside, the shelter is excellent.

From the east, give the Eastern Blackstone and the Mewstone a wide berth as there are a number of drying rocks extending to the west, clearly marked by two YB south cardinal buoys, Mew Stone (VQ(6)+ LFl 10s), just to the south-east of the Mewstone, and West Rock (Q(6) +LFl 15s), just to the south-west of West Rock. From here hold your course for the conical green Castle Ledge buoy (Fl G 5s), which should be left on your starboard hand. This buoy lies on the seaward limit of the harbour (an imaginary line joining Combe Point and Inner Froward Point) and from here on the six knot speed limit is strictly enforced throughout the river as far as the weir at Totnes.

Approaching at night, keep both Start Point (Fl (3) 10s) and Berry Head (Fl (2) 15s) visible until Castle Ledge buoy is located. This will bring you into the sectored light on the Kingswear shore (Iso RWG 3s) which covers the entrance to seaward, an area known as the Range, the red sector just clearing hazards to the west and the green sector hazards to the east. Keeping in the central white sector you have a safe and easy run in, leaving the red can Checkstone buoy (Fl (2) R 5s) on your port hand. Passing through the narrows, wait until the white sector of the inner light low down by Bayards Cove (Fl RWG 2s) is open before turning north-west into the harbour, keeping in midstream and taking care to avoid the large, normally unlit, mooring buoys in the centre of the channel just beyond Kingswear, although

Royal Dart Yacht Club looking across to Bayards Cove. Note the lower ferry on the right

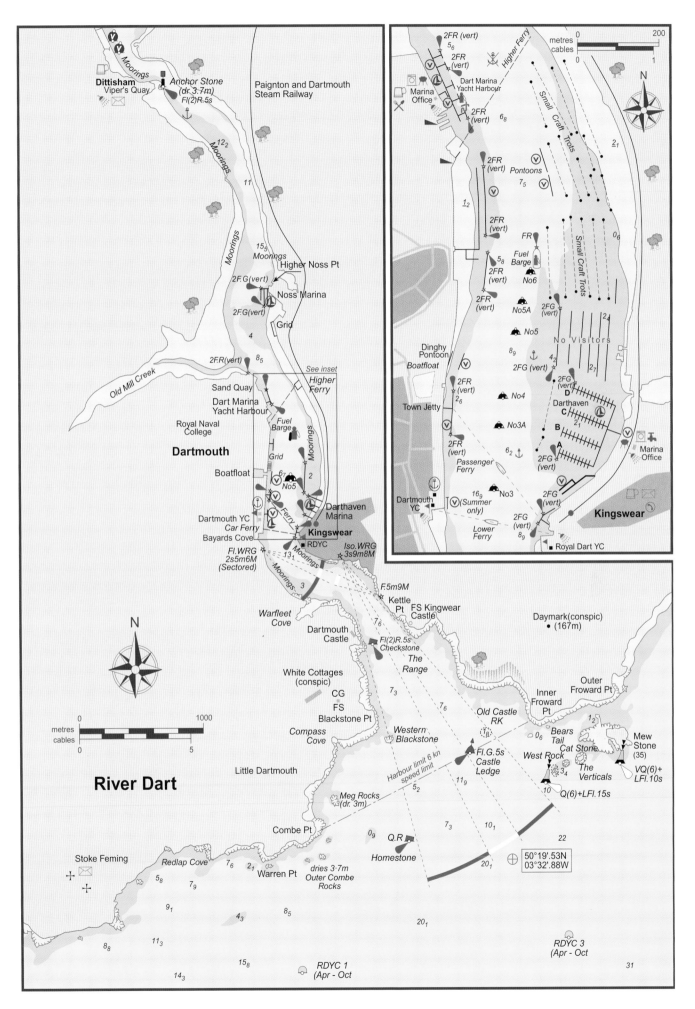

Dittisham
Viper's Quay
Moorings
Anchor Stone
(dr 3.7m)
Fl(2)R.5s
Paignton and Dartmouth
Steam Railway

Moorings
12₂
11
Moorings

15₅
Moorings
Higher Noss Pt
2F.G (vert)
Noss Marina
2F.G(vert)
Grid
4

Old Mill Creek
2F.R(vert)
8₅
See inset
Higher Ferry
Sand Quay
Dart Marina
Yacht Harbour
Royal Naval
College
Fuel
Barge

Dartmouth
Grid
Moorings
67₉
2
Boatfloat
No5
Darthaven
Marina
Dartmouth YC
Car Ferry
Bayards Cove
Ferry
Kingswear
RDYC
13₁
Moorings
Fl.WRG
2s5m6M
(Sectored)
Iso.WRG
3s9m8M
3

Marina Office
Dart Marina
Yacht Harbour
2FR (vert)
5₆
2FR
(vert)
Higher Ferry
metres
cables
0   200
0   1
2FR
(vert)
6₈
N

2FR
(vert)
Pontoons
7₅
1₂

Small Craft Trots

2₁

0₆
2FR
(vert)
FR
Fuel
Barge
No6
5₈
2FR
(vert)
2FR
(vert)
No5A
2FG
(vert)
No5
Small Craft Trots
2₄

Dinghy
Pontoon
Boatfloat
No Visitors
8₉
4₂
2₇
2FR
(vert)
2₆
2FG (vert)
No4
2FG
(vert)
D
Darthaven
C
B
2₁
A
Town Jetty
No3A
2FR
(vert)
6₂
2FG
(vert)
Marina
Office
Passenger
Ferry
Dartmouth
YC
16₉
No3
(Summer
only)
2FG
(vert)
Kingswear
Lower
Ferry
2FG
(vert)
8₉
Royal Dart YC

F.5m9M
Kettle
Pt
FS Kingwear
Castle
Warfleet
Cove
Dartmouth
Castle
7₆
Fl(2)R.5s
Checkstone
The
Range
Daymark(conspic)
• (167m)

White Cottages
(conspic)
CG
FS
Blackstone Pt
7₃
7₆
Old Castle
RK
1₈
Outer
Froward Pt
Inner
Froward
Pt
0₆
Bears
Tail
Cat Stone
1₂
Mew
Stone
(35)
Compass
Cove
Western
Blackstone
Fl.G.5s
Castle
Ledge
West Rock
3₄
The
Verticals
VQ(6)+
LFl.10s
Little Dartmouth
Harbour limit 6 kn
speed limit
11₉
5₂
10₁
10
Q(6)+LFl.15s

N
metres
cables
0   1000
0   5

River Dart

Meg Rocks
(dr. 3m)
7₃
Combe Pt
0₉
Q.R
Homestone
Stoke Feming
Redlap Cove
7₆
2₁
5₈
7₉
Warren Pt
dries 3·7m
Outer Combe
Rocks
8₅
22
20₁
50°19'.53N
03°32'.88W
9₁
4₃
8₅
20₁
8₈
11₃
15₈
RDYC 1
(Apr - Oct)
31
RDYC 3
(Apr - Oct)
14₃

Ever popular, Dartmouth Town Jetty is the most convenient walk ashore berth for visitors

FUEL, FRESH WATER AND GAS

Diesel and petrol are easily obtainable (0800 to 1800 daily in summer) from the large blue fuel barge moored in the centre of the harbour just upstream of the Resnova Floating Inn. Call *Fuel Barge* on VHF Ch 6 or Tel: 07801 798861. Once alongside, be aware that although there are a number of pumps, this is definitely not self-service and await your turn!

Fresh water is available from the following places: on the North & South Embankment, the town jetty, at all marinas and the Royal Dart YC. Fresh water taps can also be found at Dittisham, on the dinghy landing pontoon at Stoke Gabriel, the Maltsters Arms Tuckenhay and the Steam Packet Inn, Totnes. Calor and Camping Gaz are only obtainable at Darthaven Marina.

ANCHORAGE, BERTHING AND MOORINGS

At first glance the harbour is one large mass of moorings and, though crowded in the season, you will always be able to find a berth somewhere in the Dart – even during the very popular Port of Dartmouth Royal Regatta which runs for three days at the end of August. If anything, you are spoilt for choice, but one thing is certain, wherever you go, it will cost you something, for the whole river as far as Totnes is administered by the Dart Harbour and Navigation Authority (DHNA) and dues are payable throughout the river at a rate of £0.65 per metre per day, which makes anchoring the cheapest but probably the least convenient option. The harbour office is on the South Embankment, with its entrance in Oxford Street, and a particularly nice touch is the daily and five-day weather forecast which they hand out in a free booklet form.

The anchorage is on the Kingswear side of the river between the line of large midstream mooring buoys and Darthaven Marina and the private pontoon moorings. Do not let go too close to the midstream buoys as their ground chains extend for quite a distance. The holding is good, but the ebb can run at up to two knots at Springs, and it is a good dinghy ride across to Dartmouth. If the anchorage is crowded, wind against tide can also produce quite a few unpredictable antics, and a sudden glut of neighbours in embarrassingly close proximity. The other disadvantage with anchoring is that the Harbour Authority does not allow boats to be left unattended at anchor except for short periods

Checkstone buoy just south of Dartmouth Castle and St Petrox Church, which is perched on the western shore. Once past the castle, keep to starboard and follow the eastern shore and the line of moorings below the Royal Dart Yacht Club, a gabled red brick building with a veranda, flagstaff and prominent dinghy pontoon. Immediately beyond the yacht club, frequent passenger and car ferries ply between Kingswear and Dartmouth. They have priority at all times, care should be taken to keep well clear particularly under sail, and always pass astern.

Don't be taken aback if you hear a loud whistle and the sudden puffing of a steam train. Close by on the Kingswear shore the railway station is now the terminus for the Paignton and Dartmouth Steam Railway, Tel: 01803 555872; www.paignton-steamrailway.co.uk, a popular tourist attraction which is just guaranteed to send boys of all ages into nostalgic euphoria!

Stretching before you, the large and virtually landlocked harbour is an impressive sight. Dartmouth and Kingswear overlook it from their respective steep hillsides in a colourful profusion of pastels, intermingled with the odd splash of black and white half-timber, and upriver, the imposing facade of the Britannia Royal Naval College, designed by Sir Aston Webb, which has dominated the view since 1905 when it replaced the old wooden walled ships *HMS Britannia* and *Hindustan*. Dartmouth has been the Royal Navy's primary officer training establishment since 1863, a proud association with the town which has, in its time, seen several Kings of England and the current heir to the throne among the cadets. From Easter to October there are guided tours of the College, tickets can be purchased from the Dartmouth Tourist Information Centre, where you will have to produce some form of ID, preferably with photo.

(for shopping or meals ashore) and vessels must not be left unmanned during the turn of the tide. Local fishing vessels work in and out of the adjacent moorings and an anchor light is essential.

The DHNA is a totally independent and self-financing body which maintains all the facilities in the river, including lights, buoyage and waste disposal and recycling. Visitors' berths are clearly marked with blue flags and information signs with a blue background; all other information signs have a yellow background. Visitors' dinghy berths are marked by blue flags with a black St Andrew's cross. Further upriver, visitors' moorings are all blue and clearly marked with a black 'V'.

The daily rates (not inclusive of harbour dues) vary according to location: a berth on the lower South Embankment walk ashore pontoons off the Dartmouth Yacht Club (maximum 9.5m LOA) works out at £1.10 per metre – very convenient for the town. There are also walk ashore berths alongside the inner, downstream end of the Town Jetty, charged according to size in clearly designated spaces: up to 9m £15, 9.1m to 12m £20, 12.1m to 15m £25, 15.1m to 18m £30. Electricity is available at extra cost. Between 1700 and 0845 (after the passenger boats close down) visitors can also use the outside berths for an overnight charge of £1.10 per metre. In all cases owners of multihulls will be charged 50% more. There is no charge for short stays of up to a maximum of two hours on all the pontoons except the Town Jetty, thereafter you will pay a half-day charge of half the full daily rate for vessels using the port between 0600 and 1800.

The DHNA has a number of cheaper berthing options for visitors, a pontoon island just north of the Town Jetty, another at the northern end of the Embankment for boats up to 8m LOA and 1.25m draught, and a long deepwater pontoon island outside the residents trot moorings above Kingswear for larger vessels, which can raft two deep if necessary. Charges on both these pontoons are £0.65 per metre plus dues, 50% extra for multihulls. It is worth noting that chargeable length for vessels under 12m will be rounded up to the nearest half metre; over 12m it will be rounded up to the nearest metre. Unattended vessels will be charged double after 14 days.

During the summer, 0800 to 2300, the Harbour Authority runs a convenient water taxi service that can be hailed on VHF Ch 69 callsign *Yacht Taxi* (Tel: 07970 346571). The Resnova Floating Inn also runs water taxis that can be called on VHF Ch 08, callsign *Puffin Water Taxi* (Tel: 07787 504007). Fares start from £1.50 per person, one way.

If you decide to go ashore under your own steam, contrary to its name, The Boatfloat, an enclosed dinghy harbour entered under a bridge just upstream of Town Jetty is not, however, the place to leave your dinghy as

it dries completely! By far the most convenient spot is the landing pontoon alongside the embankment just a bit further upstream at Double Steps. The upper end is used by the water taxis and Dittisham Ferry, dinghies can be left for up to six hours in the clearly marked area at the lower end. In addition, just below the higher ferry, dinghies may be left on the outer end of the long, low tide pontoon off the embankment.

Up river at Dittisham and beyond (see Dittisham and the Upper Reaches) there are visitors' swinging moorings, where you will also pay £0.65 per metre plus dues. Berths and moorings are normally allocated by the river officers who are out on the water during the season from 0800 until dusk daily during the summer; VHF Ch 11 callsign *DART NAV*. Volunteer staff also patrol outside of these hours for safety purposes, but do not collect fees or dues. If you arrive after hours take whatever seems to be the most convenient option. During the height of the season you will invariably have to raft up.

Temporary berthing is also possible alongside the North and South Embankment in available space when the tide permits, which is handy for a quick shopping expedition. The North Embankment upstream of the ferry pontoon dries on most tides, while the South Embankment below the pontoon dries at Springs. Daily Quay dues are applicable for anything more than a short stay at £1.10 per metre, multihulls 50% extra. Note, too, that a very good scrubbing grid is situated on the Embankment which can be booked through the DHNA. Both water and electricity are available here.

Showers will be found to the rear (car park side) of the public conveniences on the North Embankment. Both the Dartmouth Yacht Club, Tel: 01803 832305; www.dartmouthyc.org.uk, and the Royal Dart Yacht Club, Tel: 01803 752496; steward Tel: 752272; www.royaldart.co.uk, extend a friendly welcome to all visitors, with excellent showers and comfortable bars where meals and bar snacks are served at lunchtime and in the evening. The Royal Dart YC has a convenient dinghy pontoon with a handy fresh water tap.

On the South Embankment the Dartmouth Yacht Club is just a few steps away from the lower walk ashore pontoon for boats up to 9.5m LOA

Finally, there are the three private berthing options – Darthaven Marina off Kingswear, Dart Marina Yacht Harbour just above the higher ferry and Noss Marina further upstream on the eastern side of the river.

DARTHAVEN MARINA

On the southern side of its 270-berth marina, Darthaven Marina, Tel: 01803 752545; www.darthaven.co.uk, has a clearly marked visitors' pontoon which can accommodate up to 25 rafted boats. Adjacent to this, the inner pontoon has DHNA short stay berths (up to two hours) which are clearly indicated along with a visitors' dinghy berthing area. This and the visitors' pontoon are both linked to the shore by the same bridge. Space for visitors within the rest of the marina is limited but it can often accommodate you if berthholders are away. Advance booking is not possible so call *Darthaven Marina* on VHF Ch 80 or phone ahead. Alternatively, on arrival, berth temporarily in any available space and check in at the berthing office. Latecomers will find vacant overnight berth numbers chalked up on the notice board by the office, and if your berth is not shown as vacant, move to one that is. Visitor charges are £2.35 per metre per night plus harbour dues of £0.60 metre.

Facilities, including showers, toilets, launderette and a large chandler, are all located in the shoreside administration and amenity building on the other side of the railway line, and onshore services include a 35-ton boat hoist and shipwright. During the summer their electronics engineer operates a seven day service, Tel: 07767 250787, and their marine engineers a seven-day 24-hour emergency call out service in season, Tel: 07973 280584. The marina is also a Volvo Marine Centre with full breakdown facilities.

DART MARINA YACHT HARBOUR

Opened in 1961, Dart Marina was the very first marina to be built in the West Country, and during 1997 it underwent a complete rebuild to a very high standard.

Dart Marina Yacht Harbour

Darthaven Marina's visitors' pontoon off Kingswear is clearly marked and of easy access

As a result it gained the prestigious Five Gold Anchors award from the Yacht Harbour Association. With the completion of the adjacent colourful quayside housing development of luxury designer houses and apartments, all the 110 berths have since been taken up by annual berthholders, and Dart Marina has now restyled itself as the Dart Marina Yacht Harbour. Although there are no longer any designated visitors' berths, if berthholders are away there is always a possibility the marina can accommodate you. Call *Dart Marina* ahead of time for berthing availability on VHF Ch 80 or Tel: 01803 83716. The marina office is open 0800 – 2000 during the season, 0800 – 1700 in winter. The fully serviced pontoon berths each have water, electricity, phone, fax and television terminals, and are accessed via a PIN code security gate. Onshore facilities include luxurious showers and toilets and the ultimate cruising luxury – baths – in the quayside amenity building. All this does come at a price, the visitor charge during the season is £4.11 per metre per night plus harbour dues, which easily makes this the most expensive stopover in the West Country.

The smart Dart Marina Hotel and Health Spa, situated adjacent to the marina, is open to non-residents along with the stylish Wildfire Bistro, Tel: 837180, with an outside terrace dining area, and the sophisticated River Restaurant, Tel: 832580. Close by, with a terrace overlooking the upper ferry slipway and the river, The Floating Bridge Pub provides more traditional fare, including excellent fish and chips!

NOSS MARINA

Further upstream on the opposite shore, surrounded by high woods, Noss Marina, Tel: 01803 835620; www.nossmarina.co.uk, has 180 pontoon berths and

Noss Marina is located on a peaceful wooded reach just upstream of Dartmouth

45 trot moorings and is a quieter option for berthing, particularly if you are not planning an evening out in town! The overnight visitor charge on the pontoons is £2.52 per metre per night, trot mooring £1.58, both plus harbour dues; shore power is available at extra charge, and onshore facilities include toilets and showers, laundry, payphone, WiFi. The marina office can also arrange for provisions to be delivered. Noss Marina monitors VHF Ch 80 from 0730 to 1800 daily, callsign *Noss Marina*.

The site surrounding Noss Marina was previously Philip & Sons shipyard; established in 1858 it finally closed in 1999. Builders of many larger commercial vessels and lightships, it was also the birthplace of several famous yachts, notably Claud Worth's lovely *Tern IV* and Chay Blyth's original *British Steel*.

Yet more change is now in the pipeline! Major £100m development plans for the site were announced by the new owners of Noss Marina in 2007, including an enlarged 300-berth luxury marina, Five Star hotel and conference centre, a Marine Academy and around 70 houses costing upwards of £1m each. At the time of writing the full planning application was in the process of being submitted so, as they say, watch this space. . .

FACILITIES
(Local phone code 01803)
Facilities in Dartmouth are excellent. Just a short walk from the Embankment, in Mayors Avenue, there is a large Marks & Spencer 'Simply Food' supermarket (open daily 0800 – 2100, 1000 – 1600 on Sunday). Sadly one of my old Dartmouth favourites, Cundells delicatessen, is no more, replaced somewhat appropriately by an outlet of the Fat Face fashion chain! However, the Smith Street Delicatessen, Real Food Deli, Duke Street, Deli-Licious, Lower Street, and The French Bread Shop in the Market provide ample choice for some guzzling! The well stocked Dartmouth Vintners is in the Butterwalk and sells ice to go with the G&T!

An open-air market takes place in the Market Square on Tuesdays and Fridays, and the Dartmouth Launderette (open seven days, 0800 – 2000) is just opposite in Market Street. Lloyds TSB, HSBC and Natwest all have cashpoints (there is no branch of Barclays Bank). Shipmates Chandlers, Tel: 839292, is conveniently right in the centre of town, open seven days a week, and here you will also find a Somerfield supermarket, open 0800 – 2000 Mon – Sat, 1000 – 1600, Sundays. In addition there's a Spar supermarket in Victoria Road, open 0700 – 2200, where the post office is located, too.

The Tourist Information Centre, Tel: 834224; www.discoverdartmouth.com, is situated in the corner of the large central car park. Opposite this, in Flavel Place, the Flavel Centre houses a cinema, café and public library with free internet access. WiFi coverage is available in the main harbour between higher and lower Ferries – visit www.blackspotbroadband.co.uk.

All repair facilities are on hand, from rigging to electronic engineers, divers to marine gas engineers, yacht valeting to sailmakers!

Restaurants abound and include television chef John Burton-Race's one Michelin star New Angel, Tel: 839425, on the South Embankment, Taylors Restaurant, Tel: 832748, for good seafood and Nu at the Castle Hotel, Tel: 833033, both overlooking the Boat Float, as well as Jan and Freddie's Brasserie, Tel: 832491. Among the bistros, including the Anzac Street Bistro, Tel: 835515, RB's Restaurant, Tel: 832882, The Embankment Bistro, Tel: 833540, Brown's tapas restaurant and bar, Tel: 832572, and '24', Tel: 833804. Alternatively, try Kendricks, Tel: 832328, for a Californian menu, La Casa Di Tudor, Tel: 839278, for Italian, Taj Mahal, Tel: 835050, or The Spice Bazaar, Tel: 832224, for an Indian meal, Tzangs for Chinese, Tel: 832025, or Khrua, Tel: 835069, for Thai!

There are plenty of pubs too, with excellent food. The Cherub Inn, Tel: 832571, dates from 1380 and has a comfortable upstairs restaurant and good bar meals, while the Dolphin, Tel: 833835, offers an impressive seafood menu. For beer, a pizza or a succulent Dartmouth crab sandwich perhaps, the Dartmouth Arms, Tel: 832903, remains the favourite with locals. Among the numerous cafés, one definitely stands out – the bohemian Café Alf Resco is an absolute must for breakfast or lunch!

The Resnova Floating Inn, a converted Dutch barge moored in the centre of the river, is open from 1000 until late and visiting yachts can berth alongside to use the facilities, which include morning coffee, lunch, an all-day bar and evening meals. Showers and overnight B&B accommodation are also available and there is a water taxi service to the shore. Resnova monitors VHF Ch 08, Tel: 07770 628967, if you want to go alongside.

Overlooked by the Royal Castle Hotel, the Boatfloat is Dartmouth's central feature

DARTMOUTH, PAST AND PRESENT

Ashore, Dartmouth has plenty to offer. Now a busy and popular holiday town, its growth as a major seaport like Plymouth or Falmouth was always restricted by the hilly hinterland which made transport to and from the port exceedingly difficult. Even in the 19th century it proved impossible to bring the Great Western Railway right into the town and they had to make do with it running down the opposite shore to Kingswear. But the advantages of Dartmouth as a secure deepwater anchorage and safe haven have always been utilised and it has enjoyed a rich maritime history. As early as 1147, 164 ships assembled here to begin the second crusade and 31 ships departed from here to assist with the seige of Calais in 1346.

In 1550 John Davis, the Elizabethan explorer, was born at Sandridge in the upper reaches of the Dart, and it was from Dartmouth that he set out on his three unsuccesssful voyages in search of the fabled north west passage. His contemporary, Sir Humphrey Gilbert, half brother of Raleigh, lived at Greenway, opposite Dittisham and, although his expedition to find the north-west passage was also unsuccessful, he did take possession of Newfoundland, the first English colony in north America, in 1583. Not that he was able to reap the benefits. Homeward bound, his ship the *Squirrel* was overwhelmed by heavy seas off the Azores and all hands were lost.

In more recent times Dartmouth has celebrated other notable arrivals and departures. In 1923 George Muhlhauser ended his three year circumnavigation in the 36 ton, 40 year old yawl *Amaryllis*. It was a very significant milestone in the history of English cruising, for this was the first time a lightly crewed British yacht had achieved such a feat, although at the time it passed virtually unsung.

'We struck a fine day', he wrote to a friend, 'and Dartmouth, as we came in from the sea looked lovely'.

Having encountered much bureaucracy and, far worse, much interest from the press in Australia, Muhlhauser was secretly dreading the arrival and was greatly relieved when the Customs Officer cleared them with the minimum of fuss. 'Here', he continued, 'not a soul has taken the slightest notice. It is delightful. I smile when I think of the ruses I planned to avoid reporters. Not a reporter has shown up. I am immensely relieved. This is a real homecoming to dear old casual England.'

Tragically, within weeks of his return Muhlhauser was dead, his life shortened by the physical extremes of the voyage. He left *Amaryllis* to the Royal Naval College where she remained in use for cadet sail training until 1951 when she was towed to sea and scuttled on the 12 June.

In 1949 the intrepid brothers, Stanley and Colin Smith, arrived in Dartmouth in their diminutive home built 20 foot sloop, *Nova Espero*, after a 44-day voyage from Dartmouth, Nova Scotia. In 1951, rerigged as a yawl, she set sail again from Dartmouth crewed by Stanley Smith and a friend Charles Violet on another even more arduous east – west voyage across the Atlantic, making a landfall on Nova Scotia after 33 days and then proceeding on to New York to promote samples of British goods they had carried across from the Festival of Britain. In 1977, Dame Naomi James chose Dartmouth to begin and end her solo circumnavigation in the Gallant 53 *Express Crusader*.

Commercially, much of Dartmouth's wealth was founded around the export of cloth in the middle ages. The magnificent Butterwalk, a half-timbered row of former merchants' houses with their upper storeys perched on granite columns, dates from 1640 – its size and fine carvings are an indication of its former importance. The fascinating Dartmouth Borough Museum is now part of this fine building, and a foray into the steep winding back streets will reveal several other splendid examples of 17th century architecture. The attractive cobbled quayside of Bayard's Cove, just beyond the lower ferry, became familiar to many during the 1970s when the BBC used it as one of the locations for its *Onedin Line* series. More recently the Dartmouth waterfront and other south Devon locations such as Burgh Island have featured in the BBC's *Down to Earth* drama series.

A grumpy EE Middleton passed this way in 1869, early on in his *Cruise of the Kate*, an epic single-handed circumnavigation of Britain in a 21ft yawl. Weatherbound in a southwesterly gale, true to his gentlemanly form, he slept on board and 'went to the Castle Hotel for meals'. He could still do that today in surroundings that have probably not changed a lot! A good meal can be enjoyed at the Royal Castle Hotel, Tel: 833033, either in the smart Nu Restaurant, Tel: 833033, with river views, the lively Harbour bar, a popular haunt of the Britannia Cadets which often has live music, or the quieter Galleon bar, where themed evenings and a weekly curry night are a regular feature.

If you're feeling like a quiet walk, take the higher ferry across to the Kingswear side of the river and, as you begin to climb up the road, look out for the marked footpath on the right which will take you up the steep-wooded hillside to an elevated and easier path that eventually leads you through the woods to Kingswear, with some fine glimpses of the river along the way. From Kingswear, catch the lower ferry back to Dartmouth to complete this pleasant circuit. This is part of the much longer Dart Valley Trail, a circular route from Dartmouth to Dittisham (where you can cross by ferry to Greenway), and then back to Kingswear. The Dartmouth Tourist Information Centre can provide full details.

KINGSWEAR AND FURTHER UPSTREAM

Kingswear is a much smaller, quieter place than Dartmouth. Kingswear Village Store has a good selection of provisions, including off-licence and a cash machine. There's a newsagent, post office and, as well as the Royal Dart Yacht Club, three more good watering holes, the Ship Inn, the Steam Packet and the Royal Dart Hotel, all of which serve food. Alternatively, try Zanne's Bistro, Tel: 752294. Situated upriver, it provides good seafood and stunning views. Darthaven Chandlers, Tel: 752733, open seven days a week 0830 – 1800 (1700 winter) is one of the largest in the south-west. Chris Hoyle Marine outboard motor specialist and engineers are based in Lower Contour Road, Tel: 752221.

The steam trains, Tel: 555872, run regularly to Paignton and back – a great way to keep the kids occupied for an afternoon. The bridge over the railway from Darthaven emerges at The Banjo, where buses to Brixham depart regularly.

'I grudged the delay at Dartmouth', continued Middleton, 'but was recompensed in some measure by the natural beauty of the place, which gains its greatest charm, to my way of thinking, from the entrance to the harbour. I pulled some little distance up the river in the dinghy, but the scenery appeared much tamer, not nearly so beautiful as at the mouth.'

Sadly, the poor chap did not pull quite far enough! The name 'Dart' is derived from the Old English word for oak, of which there is plenty upstream where the real delights of the Dart emerge as the navigable river winds 10 wooded miles inland to Totnes. Until 1996 coasters of up to 1,000 tons and 4m draught regularly discharged timber just below the town, but this traffic has now ceased completely and the only commercial craft using the upper Dart are the many large trip boats. The channel is well-buoyed and well worth exploring on a rising tide if time permits, and a number of secluded and peaceful anchorages can be found in the upper reaches.

The first section of the river as far as Dittisham is quite straightforward, wide and deep with over 5m throughout the channel at LAT. The only real hazard is the upper car ferry, a sizeable vessel that runs across the river on wires and berths just downstream of the Dart Marina. Always pass astern and give it a wide berth, as the wires close to it are near the water surface.

Beyond Dart Marina Yacht Harbour, to port, the jetties and moorings all belong to the Britannia Royal Naval College, and a wary eye should be kept out for the numerous small naval craft running around with midshipmen under training.

The wide mouth of Old Mill Creek dries completely, and at low tide the remains on the northern mud, marked by two cardinal beacons, are those of one of the last Irish three-masted trading schooners, *Invermore*, abandoned after an abortive attempt to sail her to Australia.

From here on, beyond Noss Marina, the shores are steep and wooded, the trees brushing the high tide mark along a wide reach lined with local moorings. It narrows considerably at the Anchor Stone, a 3.7m drying rock with a beacon and square red topmark (Fl (2) R 5s). This should be given a good berth and left well to port.

Here, according to local tradition, Sir Walter Raleigh reputedly smoked the first pipe of tobacco in England after being banned from trying it in his half-brother's house at Greenway! The tight passage between the rock and the western shore is definitely not recommended – this can be a spectacularly embarrassing spot to be stranded!

Anchoring is not allowed off Dittisham because of the extensive moorings and the anchorage just downstream of the Anchor Stone is the nearest, if not the most convenient for the village. Sound in just to the edge of Parsons Mud, upstream of the local moorings. The tide can run quite hard here and it can be uncomfortable with a fresh breeze against it; the mud drops away steeply and, as I have found out myself, it is not unknown for boats to drag into the deeper water.

The pontoon islands upstream of Kingswear are always a quieter berthing option for visitors

A brave row against the ebb, an outboard puts the Ferry Boat Inn within more tenable reach! However, if you are merely looking for a peaceful anchorage in sylvan surroundings and wish to go nowhere else you have found it – at least, once the trip boats wind up for the day.

DITTISHAM

There are a number of clearly marked pale blue DHNA visitors' moorings available just downstream, directly off, and upstream of Dittisham and during the season you will invariably have to raft. Landing is easy at all states of the tide on the large short stay dinghy pontoon where berths are clearly indicated – do not obstruct or leave your dinghy on the very outer end as this is used by the passenger ferry to Greenway Quay, which also operates as a water taxi (call *Greenway Ferry* on VHF Ch 10), and also the Dartmouth to Dittisham ferry during the season.

Water is available from a public tap on the foreshore at the front of the Ferry Boat Inn, Tel: 722368. Ever popular, and inevitably crowded in season, there's a good selection of bar food and drink in undeniably convivial surroundings. On the opposite side of the road, overlooking the river, The Anchorstone Café, Tel: 722365, is a lovely spot for breakfast, lunch and early evening dinner.

From here Dittisham, pronounced locally as 'Ditsam', straggles up the steep hill, a mixture of pretty thatched stone and cob cottages leading to the village centre, which has a small but surprisingly well stocked grocery store/post office, payphone and another pub, The Red Lion, with fresh local salmon one of its specialities during the season. When the tide permits, walk along the foreshore from the Ferry Boat or along the lane that branches right just up the hill above the pub, to reach a grassy playing field known as the Ham, where you'll find a rubbish/recycling facility and a free shower in the public convenience block!

There are fine views upriver from higher Dittisham.

With plenty of visitors' moorings, Dittisham is always popular and landing is easy on the dinghy pontoon off the Ferry Boat Inn

Widening into a shallower tidal lake thick with moorings, the water stretches for a mile towards the distant buildings of the boatyards in Galmpton Creek, where the steep wooded shores fall away into gently rolling fields.

THE UPPER REACHES

Above the moorings, the large area of Flat Owers Bank dries at Low Water and the main channel keeps close to the wooded south shore, swinging round across the entrance to Galmpton Creek where the Dartside Quay and Dolphin Shipyard are both situated at the head of the drying creek.

Dartside Quay is a major repair facility owned by MDL, Tel: 01803 845445; www.dartsidequay.co.uk, with 53-ton and 16-ton hoists and a six-ton mobile crane. On site services include repairs in wood, GRP and steel, chandlery, engineering, rigging, electronics and sailmaker. There is a vast area of hard standing. Normally the yard is accessible two hours either side of High Water.

A number of moorings lie along the deep water, but care should be taken to avoid the Eel Rock (dries 1.5m), on the eastern edge of the channel south of the gabled boathouse on Waddeton Point. With sufficient water, there is a short cut to the west of Flat Owers Bank and from Greenway Quay steer straight for Waddeton boathouse, a course of about 020°T, until abeam of the port hand Flat Owers buoy, before altering slowly towards the second boathouse, Sandridge, and steering about 310°T. There are a few shallow patches, but with a couple of hours of flood you should get across.

From Sandridge boathouse, the channel deepens again and swings back close to Higher Gurrow Point. Steer for the port hand beacon ahead at the entrance to Dittisham Mill Creek, keeping close to Blackness Point, and then working back across the river to the delightfully named Pighole Point on the eastern shore. In the right conditions and providing you are clear of the main channel, it is possible to anchor just west of Higher Gurrow Point or just west of Blackness Point.

This wide reach of the river is known locally as the 'Lake of the Dart', as it is impossible to see a way out from the centre at High Water. It is not, however, a deep lake, for Middle Back, a large drying bank, extends right up its centre. Keep close to the line of moorings along the eastern shore and just south of the beacon with a green triangular topmark (Q Fl G) marking the entrance to the drying Stoke Gabriel creek. Here you will find the last three pale blue DHNA visitors' moorings, which can be used by vessels up to 9m LOA. A channel marked by two R/W port hand beacons with square red topmarks leads to a dinghy pontoon and a small quay where it is possible to land, but beware, do NOT proceed any further than the quay – there is a tidal dam right across the creek, submerged at high tide.

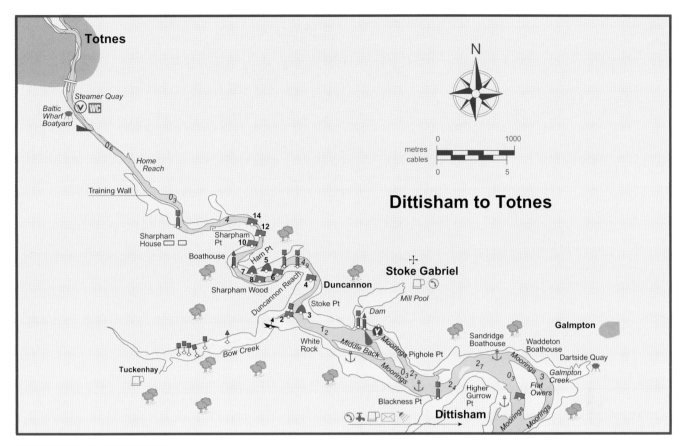

STOKE GABRIEL

A picturesque Devon village, with three pubs, a hotel, limited provisions and a fresh water tap on the dinghy pontoon, its claim to fame is the massive yew tree in the church yard, reputedly the oldest in England. A fleet of salmon seine boats lies here in the creek and during the season (16 March – 16 August) the netsmen can be encountered anywhere in these upper reaches and should be given a wide berth if fishing.

BOW CREEK

Beyond Stoke Gabriel creek the channel holds close to the east side of the river as far as Mill Point, then swings about 45° to port towards White Rock, which is prominent on the western foreshore, then north again at the mouth of Bow Creek, passing between No 2 Bow Creek, port hand buoy and No 3 Langham Wood, starboard hand buoy. It then turns sharply to the east and narrows towards the tiny hamlet of Duncannon.

Bow Creek is accessible for shallower draught boats and the quay at Tuckenhay can be accessed almost three hours either side of High Water. For deeper draught boats, a convenient anchorage is just under the northern shore by Langham Wood Point. From here it's just over a mile in the dinghy up to the pub, and for the most part the tortuous channel is marked. You will be venturing as deep as you are likely to get by boat into the depths of rural Devon. The shoreline is of overhanging trees and rough pasture right to the water's edge where cattle graze and silently watch as you slip past through the brown, soupy water.

Passing to the north of No 2 Bow Creek buoy the channel follows the north shore then crosses to the south bank, taking care to avoid the old wreck, then holds mostly to the south bank, past the derelict barn on the north shore, from where you will be able to see Tuckenhay. You will then steer for the first green post with triangular topmark, which must be left on your starboard hand, then leave the next five red posts to port, which mark the channel very accurately as it swings back across the creek, close to the north bank. After the last red post, keep the blue mooring buoys about 4m to starboard, and once past them aim directly for the pontoon by the quay.

Tuckenhay is still a forgotten, sleepy place and today it seems amazing that in 1806 it was the ambition of Mr Abraham Tucker to develop it as a major port. That grand plan never came to much, although local trade kept the quay busy until 1939 when the last large vessel, the 240 ton coaster *Reedness,* made her final visit.

However, Mr Tucker's gas house did put the village on the wider map as one of the first places in England to receive gas lighting, even before London! For many years the nearby paper mill produced paper for banknotes, and from the mid 1800s cider and malt were both produced here. When I first visited the creek, the ancient cider factory on the crumbling quayside was derelict, but developers of a different kind to Abraham Tucker have since moved in and converted the fine stone buildings into luxury homes. In the early 1990s the Maltsters Arms was owned by the ebullient television gastronome Keith Floyd, during which time, in his typically flamboyant style, he changed the name to Floyd's Inn (sometimes). Perhaps that should have read (briefly)!

The pub welcomes visiting boats, dinghies can berth on the pontoon and larger boats alongside the quay. It is possible to stay for up to a maximum of two nights, drying out alongside in soft mud, but you are advised to phone ahead to check availability, Tel: 01803 732350. There is no overnight charge (apart from harbour dues), water and shore power are available; the latter costing £5 a visit. As well as local ales, The Maltsters Arms restaurant specialises in fresh local produce, including salmon – reservations definitely advised – and during the summer its quayside barbecue is very popular, even more so when it coincides with the live music events. Basic provisions, milk/bread, are available from the pub; www.tuckenhay.com contains regularly updated navigational and tidal access information for the creek.

A pleasant half-mile walk along the tree-lined lane leading towards the head of the creek will bring you to another friendly pub/restaurant, the Waterman's Arms, Tel: 732214.

TOTNES

Beyond Duncannon the river remains narrow and generally shallow on the inside of the bends. A large number of sizeable pleasure boats run regularly between Totnes and Dartmouth as the tide permits, and in these restricted waters passing can be tricky at times. They are plying their trade and you are there for fun, so pull in and let them pass, a courtesy they will greatly appreciate.

Leave No 4 Duncannon buoy to port and keep close to the rocky east shore, leaving the two red beacons to port to enter Ham Reach, where the shores are again steep and wooded. Keep red can buoys Nos 6 and 8 to port and Nos 5 and 7 conical buoys to starboard, after which remain close to the west shore under Sharpham Woods, leaving the starboard hand beacon well to starboard as this is inshore of the edge of the bank.

Sharpham House, an impressive Georgian mansion standing high above the trees, was reputedly built with 365 panes of glass in its windows and has many other calendar inspired features, and is set in the 500-acre Sharpham Estate, which includes an 11-acre vineyard (Tel: 732203; www.sharpham.com).

The vines saddle the hillside above the river in orderly ranks and produce around 30,000 bottles of white wines from its Madeleine Augevine grape, which has, to date, won the Best English Wine award five times. The vineyard also vinifies a red from Cabernet Sauvignon and Merlot grapes produced at the nearby Beenleigh Estate. The vinyard is open to visitors daily throughout the season, 1000 – 1700 and a variety of tours, all including wine tasting sessions, are available at differing charges.

The Sharpham Creamery is another success story, producing a luscious Brie style cheese from the estate herd of Jersey cows. Both the wine and cheese can be bought from the farm shop. The restored Sharpham Quay is actually around the next big bend, and it is possible to berth here for about two hours either side of High Water to stroll up to the shop.

Steer back to the eastern shore beyond Ham Point, leaving the next three can buoys Nos 10, 12 and 14 to port, and into Fleet Mill Reach, avoiding the saltings to port as the channel lies closer to the starboard bank past the remains of the old paddle steamer *Kingswear Castle* on the shore. Then edge back to the western side, past Sharpham Quay, and onwards to the next port hand beacon before swinging back starboard, holding a course close to the rocky outcrop on your starboard hand. A final swing back to port brings you into Home Reach, where the buildings and distant tower of Totnes church will be in sight beyond the flat marshy fields and saltings.

The deeper water lies along the centre of the river for the next 200m, then veers closer to the stone training wall to port, built by French prisoners during the Napoleonic war. From here head back to the starboard bank past the open fields and riverside footpath known as the Range, until you reach Baltic Wharf, the 400m long former timber quay on the west side of the river that is now the home of the Baltic Wharf Boatyard. It has an extensive area of hardstanding and undercover storage, can undertake all repairs and has a 16-ton hoist, a 10-ton crane and a large slipway. A chandler is also located on site. This quay can be used by visitors for overnight berthing by prior arrangement (Tel: 01803 867922) – here you will begin to dry out a couple of hours after High Water in reasonably soft mud and

The sylvan upper reaches – Sharpham House and vineyard emerge from the trees

it will cost £12.33 for a 10m boat. There are showers, toilets, water and electricity and very good 24-hour security in the boatyard.

Part of this long quayside is where Pete Goss and his Goss Challenge team built the massive but ill-fated *Team Phillips* catamaran. It was launched in March 2000 to worldwide media interest and named in London by the Queen. A catalogue of disasters dogged their attempt to enter *The Race* – the non-stop around the world challenge – culminating in December 2000 with abandonment in mid-Atlantic during sea trials due to steering failure during a severe storm.

There is space for up to five bilge keel or shoal draught boats to berth and dry out alongside the wooden public quay on the opposite side of the river, by the prominent blue office buildings, where South Hams Council charges £1 per metre per night (plus dues).

Upstream, at Mill Tail, the river divides around Vire Island. The Steamer Quay to starboard is private and in constant use by pleasure boats, and beyond it the channel leading to the bridge is full of local moorings. The Totnes Boating Association has its clubhouse on the Steamer Quay and visitors are welcome when it is open at weekends.

The port hand branch leads to the old Town Quay, which is private and berthing is not allowed. The only other berths available for visitors are by the Steam Packet Inn, Tel: 863880, where there is about 20m of quayside by the pub garden with nearly 3m Mean High Water Springs, and a clean, hard bottom to dry out on. Adjacent to the pub's children's play area is a further 25m of quay with a muddier bottom.

On arrival, check with the pub that you are in a suitable spot. The Steam Packet has a restaurant as well as bar meals, and even provides breakfasts! No charge is made as long as you use its facilities. A slot metered electricity supply by the quay, a washing machine and dryer, as well as bathroom facilities and fresh water are all available, but are charged for separately.

Totnes is a very attractive and unspoiled medieval town, rising up a steep main street to a hilltop surmounted by the remains of the Norman motte and bailey castle. For those interested in little known facts, it apparently has more listed buildings relative to its population than any other town in Britain! There's also an Elizabethan museum, a 900-year old Guildhall and a Museum of Period costume – visit the Tourist Information Centre for full details. Interestingly, it has been the home to a number of famous writers over the years, including Mary Wesley, Desmond Bagley and Sean O'Casey.

Totnes has a bustling shopping centre, with all normal facilities available, including pubs, restaurants, bistros, banks, art galleries and it is renowned for secondhand bookshops. There is a lively open-air market on Fridays and Saturdays, an Antiques Fair on Fridays and a large Somerfield (open 0800 until 2000, Mon – Wed, 2100 Thurs – Sat and 1100 – 1700 on Sundays) and Morrisons (0800 – 2000 Mon – Thurs, 2100 Fri/Sat, 1000-1600 Sundays). Fuel is only available in cans from the local garage. The mainline railway station is on the outskirts of town, with frequent connections to London and the North. Should you have need to leave your boat in the Dart for a while, there are buses from Dartmouth direct to the station, or much more fun, catch one of the Riverlink ferries if the tide permits!

Be warned, though, that if you're here on a Tuesday during the summer, when the Charity and Craft market takes place, your shopkeeper is quite likely to appear in a ruff and pantaloons, for traditionally the locals like to dress up in Elizabethan attire for this event!

River Dart Port Guide – Area telephone code: 01803

Harbourmaster: Captain David White, Dart Harbour & Navigation Authority, 6 Oxford Street, Dartmouth TQ6 9AL, Tel: 832337; Fax: 833631. 0900 – 1700 Mon – Fri, 1000 – 1600 Sat & Sun. Email: info@dartharbour.org; website: www.dartharbour.org.

VHF: Ch 11, callsign *DART NAV*, office hours.

Mail drop: Harbour Office, Marinas, Royal Dart YC.

Emergency services: Lifeboat at Brixham. Brixham Coastguard.

Anchorages: Between large ship buoys and moorings on Kingswear side of river.

Below Anchor Stone. Various possibilities upriver – call *DART NAV*. Vessels must not be left unattended at anchor for any length of time.

Moorings/berthing: Harbour Authority visitors' pontoons on Dartmouth waterfront, upstream of Kingswear and visitors' moorings off Dittisham and Stoke Gabriel. Check availability with river officers. Berthing alongside the barge *Resnova Floating Inn*.

Dinghy landings: At pontoons. Steps on embankment and Low Tide pontoon, all indicated by blue flags with black St Andrew's Cross.

Water taxi: VHF Ch 69, *Yacht Taxi* (Tel: 07970 346571) 0800 – 2300 daily during summer; VHF Ch 08 *Puffin Water Taxi* (Tel: 07770 628967); Dittisham, VHF Ch 10, *Greenway Ferry*.

Marinas: Darthaven Marina, Kingswear, Tel: 752545; www.darthaven.co.uk, 270 berths, including visitors' berths. VHF Ch 80, callsign *Darthaven Marina*.

Dart Marina Yacht Harbour, Sandquay, Dartmouth, Tel: 837161; www.dartmarina. com, 110 berths, visitor berthing only when space available. VHF Ch 80, callsign *Dart Marina*.

Noss Marina, Tel: 839087; www.nossmarina.co.uk, 180 berths including visitors' berths. VHF Ch 80 callsign *Noss Marina*.

Charges: Harbour dues £0.65 per metre per day payable throughout river to Totnes plus visitors' charges: Town Jetty between £15 and £30 depending on LOA; £1.10 per metre per night on Yacht Club walk ashore pontoon or alongside Embankment; £0.65 per metre per night on pontoon island or visitor mooring. Dart Marina £4.11 per metre per night plus harbour dues. Darthaven Marina £2.35 per metre per

River Dart Port Guide (Cont) – Area telephone code: 01803

night plus harbour dues. Noss Marina on pontoon £2.52 per metre per night plus harbour dues.dues. Noss Marina fore & aft moorings £1.58 per metre plus harbour dues. Baltic Wharf 10m boat drying alongside £12.33.

Phones: By Boatfloat, opposite the Butterwalk. At marinas, yacht clubs, harbour office.

Doctor: Tel: 832212.

Dentist: Tel: 835418.

Hospital: Dartmouth, Tel: 832255 – minor injuries only. Nearest A&E, Torbay Hospital, Tel: 614567, 2 miles from centre of Torquay on A380.

Churches: All denominations.

Local weather forecast: At harbour office and marinas.

Fuel: Diesel and petrol from fuel barge, Tel: 07801 798861, or VHF Ch 06 callsign *Fuel Barge*. Open daily 0800 – 1800 in Summer; 0900 – 1600 Mon/Wed/Fri, 0800 – 1200 Sat in winter.

Gas: Calor and Gaz, Darthaven Marina.

Water: Taps on embankment, at all marinas. Tap at Dittisham, in front of Ferry Boat Inn. Public tap on pontoon at Stoke Gabriel. Maltsters Arms, Tuckenhay. At Steam Packet Inn, Totnes, charged by quantity.

Tourist Information Centre: Adjoining Newcomen Engine House in car park behind Embankment, Tel: 834224.

Banks/cashpoints: HSBC, Lloyds TSB and Natwest have cashpoints. No Barclays.

Post office: In Spar supermarket, Victoria Road. Kingswear by ferry slipway.

Internet access: WiFi in lower harbour: www. blackspotbroadband.co.uk. Free (first 30 mins) public internet access, Dartmouth Library.

Rubbish: Dispose in bins marked Y*acht Waste* on DHNA facilities and at marinas. Floating skip off Dartmouth and Dittisham. Harbour Authority will dispose of pyrotechnics and other toxic waste, including batteries by arrangement – a charge will normally be made for this service.

Showers/toilets: Available at Royal Dart YC, Dartmouth YC, Dart Marina, Darthaven Marina and Noss-on-Dart Marina, Resnova Floating Inn. Free showers in public toilets on Dartmouth Embankment and the 'Ham' Dittisham.

Launderette: Dartmouth Launderette, Market Street. Launderettes at all marinas.

Provisions: Everything available. Marks & Spencer supermarket in Mayors Avenue open 0800 – 2100 weekdays, 1000 – 1600 Sunday, Somerfield supermarket in centre of town, 0800 – 2000, 1000 – 1600 Sunday. Spar supermarket, Victoria Street, 0700 – 2200.

Chandlers: Shipmates, Newcomen Road, Tel: 839292; Dartmouth Boating Centre, clothing, Tel: 832093; Darthaven Chandlery, Kingswear, Tel: 752733; Baltic Wharf Chandlery, Tel: 867362. The Harbour Bookshop, Fairfax Place, Dartmouth has a wide range of nautical books, Tel: 832448.

Repairs: Darthaven Marina, Kingswear, Tel: 752545; Creekside Boatyard, Old Mill Creek, Tel: 832649; Dartside Quay, Galmpton, Churston, Tel: 845445; Dolphin Shipyard, Galmpton, Churston, Tel: 01803 842424; Baltic Wharf Boatyard, Totnes, Tel: 01803 867922.

Marine engineers: Darthaven Services, Tel: 752242 or Mob: 07973 280584, 24-hour, seven-day emergency call out; Riverside Marine Engineering, Tel: 835166; Tonto Marine Services, Tel: 844399; Marine Wise, Tel: 868757 or Mob: 07768 437996; Stevenson Marine, Tel: 814011 or Mob: 07855 255217; Chris Hoyle Marine, outboards, Tel: 752221; Marine Engineering Looe, Tel: 844777.

Electronic engineers: AK Marine Electronics, Tel: 833300; Darthaven Services, Tel: 752242 or Mob: 07767 250787, operates seven days a week in season; Yacht Electrical Services, Tel: 01626 870167 or Mob: 07734 053874.

Gas engineer: Andrew McGuinness, Tel: 782988.

Sailmakers: Dart Sails & Covers, Tel: 839196.

Riggers: Barry Hollis Rigging, Tel: 833094 or Mob: 07977 451197; Atlantic Spars, Tel: 843322; Harris Rigging, Tel: 840160 or Mob: 07970 712877; Bay Rigging, Tel: 846333 or Mob: 07816 925666.

Divers: Millennium Marine, Tel: 856060.

Taxi: Dartmouth, Tel 833778; Kingswear, Tel: 752626; Totnes, Tel: 864745, 863017, 865575.

Car hire: None. Nearest at Paignton Railway station, United, Tel: 520494, or SIXT, Tel: 0870 1567 567; Totnes United, Tel: 864651.

Bus/train connections: No 111 or 112 Stagecoach bus, hourly connection to Totnes, Tel: 664500, or Traveline, Tel: 0871 200 22 23. Main line railway station at Totnes, Tel: 08457 484950. Also regular River Link ferries, Tel: 834488, to Totnes Steamer Quay in season when tide permits, but a good 10 minutes walk to station – best to book taxi in Totnes, see telephone numbers above. Paignton and Dartmouth Steam Railway, Kingswear, Tel: 555872, connections from Paignton to main rail line at Newton Abbot.

Car parking: Off Mayors Avenue behind Embankment, short stay only. Long stay park & ride car park is situated on outskirts of town with bus to Embankment/ town centre.

Yacht clubs: Royal Dart Yacht Club, Kingswear TQ6 OAB, Tel: Office 752496, Steward 752272; email: office@royaldart.co.uk; website: www.royaldart.co.uk. Dartmouth Yacht Club, South Embankment, Dartmouth TQ6 9BB, Tel: 832305, email: post@dartmouthyc. org.uk, website: www. dartmouthyc.org.uk.

Eating out: Very good selection of restaurants, bistros, pubs and cafés.

Things to do: Dartmouth Borough Museum, Butterwalk; Newcomen Engine House, Mayors Avenue; Dartmouth Castle/ St Petrox Church; open-air market, Friday and Tuesday; steam railway; guided tours of Royal Naval College; good walks on both sides of harbour entrance and river.

Regatta/special events: The Port of Dartmouth Royal Regatta, three days at end of August; South Western Area Old Gaffers Race around end of July; Dartmouth Music Festival, May.

THE place for breakfast!

A fair wind and tide! Start Point from the south

Chapter two
Start Point to Rame Head

FAVOURABLE TIDAL STREAMS
Start Point
Bound west: One hour before HW Dover
Bound east: Five hours after HW Dover
Rame Head
Bound west: Two hours before HW Dover
Bound east: Four hours after HW Dover

PASSAGE CHARTS FOR THIS SEA AREA
AC: 1613 Eddystone Rocks to Berry Head
            1634 Berry Head to Bolt Head
            SC5602
Imray: C6 Salcombe to Lizard Point
            WCP 2400.8 Start Point to Fowey
            ID4 Western Channel
Stanfords: 2 English Channel western section. Chart
            Pack 22 The South Devon Coast

SAFETY INFORMATION AND WEATHER
Brixham & Falmouth Coastguard makes initial
announcement on VHF Channel 16 at 0110, 0410, 0710,
1010, 1610, 1910, 2210 Local Time, to confirm working
channel for broadcast, normally: VHF Channel 23
(Berry Head), Channel 86 (Rame Head), Channel 84
(East Prawle).

Prawle Point NCI station Tel: 01548 511259
Rame Head NCI station Tel: 01752 823706

WAYPOINTS
1   **Start Point (2.5M east-south-east of lighthouse)**
        50°12'.86N 03°34'.68W
2   **Prawle Point (1M south of headland)**
        50°11'.14N 03°43'.26W
3   **Salcombe approach**
        (1M south-south-east of Mewstone)
        50°11'.57N 03°46'.68W
4   **Bolt Tail (1.5M south of headland)**
        50°13'.04N 03°52'.21W
5   **Hillsea Point**
        (1.2M south-south-west of Hilsea Point)
        50°16'.59N 04°02'.25W
6   **Yealm approach**
        (6ca south-west of Yealm Head)
        50°17'.90N 04°05'.30W
7   **Great Mewstone (0.5M south of**
        southern tip of Great Mewstone)
        50°17'.86N 04°06'.46W
8   **Rame Head (5ca south of headland)**
        50°18'.10N 04°13'.42W
9   **Eddystone (1M north of lighthouse)**
        50°11'.89N 04°15'.95W

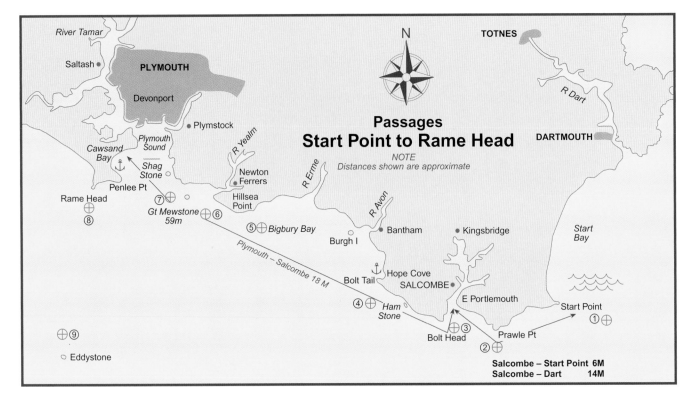

With some romanticism, Frank Carr summed it up very well. . .'West of the Start one begins to have the feeling that one is at last getting to deep seas and blue water; and although the mouth of the Channel is no more from Ushant to Scilly than thirty-nine leagues, it is quite wide enough and deep enough for small craft to be able to be caught out pretty badly . . .'

After the gentle, protected sweep of Start Bay, the rock fringed coast beyond Start Point can often feel exposed and almost inhospitable which, in poor weather, it most certainly is. Here, Devon projects its southernmost point far into the English Channel, prey to the weather and the full strength of the tidal streams. This combined assault on the coastline is clearly reflected as you move further west to the high cliffs between Bolt Head and Bolt Tail.

START POINT TO SALCOMBE

In the prevailing southwesterlies, a long ground swell and much larger seas will be encountered once clear of Start Point. Carrying a fair tide westwards, the odds are certainly in favour of the wind being against it, and this can worsen wind and sea conditions.

Salcombe, six miles west of Start Point, is the most likely destination for cruising boats from Dartmouth. It is a particularly unspoiled estuary with excellent facilities for yachts, but does, however, have a bar which is extremely dangerous in strong southerly weather and certain combinations of ground swell and ebb tide. With a least depth of 1m LAT (1.3m on leading line), it is always best to arrive after half flood.

Plymouth, the next real port of refuge, is accessible in all weather and lies almost 25 miles west of Start Point. These factors should be considered before setting out from the Dart or making a landfall on the South Devon coast.

However, in fair weather, Salcombe presents no problem. Ideally, leave Dartmouth towards local Low Water which will bring you to the Start with the main ebb running westwards. By the time you reach Salcombe the local inshore flood should ensure ample water over the bar.

Assuming that you pass over a mile to seaward of the Start to avoid the race, your course will take you well clear of any inshore dangers such as the isolated Blackstone and Cherrick rocks, and the Sleaden rocks,

Prawle Point from the south-east, with Bolt Head misty in the distance and Salcombe just coming into view

which extend about 400m south of Peartree Point. In calm weather, it is possible to pass much closer inshore, where the tidal streams turn approximately half an hour earlier, but attain considerably greater strength – up to four knots at Springs. For this reason the fisherman's passage inside the Blackstone is definitely not recommended!

Beyond Start Point the coast is lined by low cliffs, ledges and small rocky bays backed with steep, higher land, a mixture of fields and heathland, with extensive gorse and ferns and just a few isolated houses. There are no dangers more than three cables offshore, but the large numbers of pot buoys can turn the passage into a veritable slalom at times and a sharp lookout is essential. Note that frequently you will only spot them at the last minute as they are often dragged under by the tide.

Prawle Point, three miles west, is not particularly spectacular. There is a conspicuous terrace of old coastguard cottages immediately east of the Point which features a prominent NCI lookout on its flat, grassy top, with cliffs falling away to a rocky outcrop forming a natural arch when viewed from the west. As you pass the point, the few rusting remains at the foot of the cliffs are of the Greek-registered *Demetrios*, wrecked here in December 1992 while on tow to the breakers. Just to the north, Elender Cove is an attractive daytime anchorage in offshore winds, popular with local boats. Beneath the jagged rocky outcrops on Gammon Head there's a clean expanse of low tide sand and the inlet is just indented enough to get you out of the tidal stream. This runs at up to two knots at Springs around Prawle Point, kicking up another small race which can be uncomfortable at times; ideally keep a good half mile offshore.

In contrast to Prawle, Bolt Head is a dramatic sight as it emerges in the distance, over 100m high, and steep-to with distinctive jagged rocky ridges and pinnacles. Salcombe lies at the head of the bay formed between Prawle Point and Bolt Head, and a course should be held towards the western side before turning north towards the entrance, which is not easy to spot from a

Elender Cove is a popular and attractive daytime anchorage

distance. At night, Start Point light is obscured north of a line extending from the Start through Prawle Point; keep the light open across the bay until the leading light into Salcombe is located before turning north.

BOLT HEAD TO BOLT TAIL

Off Bolt Head are two isolated rocks, the Mewstone (19m) and the Little Mewstone (5m), close to the shore. Overfalls extend to seaward in their vicinity and this can often be an uncomfortable corner. For the next four miles the high, dramatic cliffs between Bolt Head and Bolt Tail have a particularly rugged and rather grim appearance – an uncompromising lee shore – which should ideally be given a good offing to avoid the dangers and the severe squalls that the high cliffs can generate: a phenomenon described with suitable drama by Hilaire Belloc in his *Cruise of the Nona*.

'As for the spill off Bolt Head, it fell after a clear midnight. . . and it was more than a spill; for it blew for the best part of an hour then ceased. But like its brother off Beachy, it was peculiar to the high land, for it came due northerly whereas the main wind had east in it. I was watching the morning star burning like a sacred furnace on the edges of the black hills when

Viewed here from the south-west, the jagged profile of Bolt Head is dramatic from every angle

Bolt Tail with Bigbury Bay opening beyond

Satan sent that wind and tried to drown three men. But we reefed in time – there were three of us, one for the helm and two to reef; and when dawn broke, and the blessed colours of the east renewed the day, strange! – one end of the boom had three reefs down, and the other only two!'

The main hazards are the Gregory Rocks (least depth just under 2m) half a mile south-east of the Ham Stone, which is an isolated rocky islet (11m) off Soar Mill Cove, where a grassy valley runs down to the only major break in the line of the high cliffs. The Ham Stone is infamous for sinking one of the last great Finnish grain barques, *Herzogin Cecilie*, when she went ashore in thick fog on 25 April 1936. After seven weeks, the vessel was refloated and beached in Starehole Bay, at the entrance to Salcombe, as her rotting and fermenting cargo was unwelcome in the harbour. It proved to be her final resting place, for soon afterwards a summer gale from the south-east broke her back, and her remains can still be seen dimly today.

The *Herzogin Cecilie* was wrecked without loss of life; but in contrast the disaster of *HMS Ramillies* in 1760 was catastrophic. A 74-gun ship of the line, set to the east before a severe southwesterly, she mistook Bolt Tail for Rame Head and realised her mistake too late when steep cliffs rather than the entrance to Plymouth appeared through the murk. Unable to claw off the lee shore, she anchored, but eventually drove ashore. Only 26 survived from her complement of 734. Few ships have held out long once ashore on this particular stretch of coast; it has an uncomfortable feel about it and I, for one, invariably feel a certain relief once it is safely astern.

The cliffs remain steep right to Bolt Tail, and west of Soar Mill Cove there is a group of three tall radio masts (50m), and then two radio towers (25m) on the grassy plateau along the clifftop. The final hazard just east of Bolt Tail is Greystone Ledge (1.8m), extending a quarter of a mile to seawards. At Bolt Tail, a precipitous cliff with an isolated rock at its foot, the coast falls suddenly back into Bigbury Bay. The cliffs are steep-to and, if followed 200m offshore, the small village and harbour

of Hope Cove will appear tucked snugly behind Bolt Tail where it is possible, in offshore winds and settled weather, to anchor in the centre of the bay.

BIGBURY BAY

From Bolt Tail the Devon coastline bears away to the north-west, and the seven mile indentation of Bigbury Bay is usually passed by most cruising boats, as it lies inside the direct course for the Yealm or Plymouth. Although normally a lee shore, in easterly or northerly weather it can be further explored by visiting the seldom frequented rivers of the Avon and Erme.

About a third of the way across the Bay, off the holiday resort of Bigbury-on-Sea, is the distinctive hump of Burgh Island, which lies just to the west of the hidden entrance to the drying River Avon, bounded on the east by the beach and sand dunes, along with a line of low rock-strewn cliffs below the golf course at Thurlestone Links. Further east, isolated Thurlestone rock (10m) is a conspicuous feature, rather like a large boat aground on the beach. Only accessible near High Water in favourable conditions to boats of shallow draught, the Avon is a particularly beautiful small river where those able to dry out will find good shelter once inside. There is a temporary anchorage to the east of Burgh Island if waiting for the tide.

The River Erme, three miles to the north-west,

Tucked just inside Bolt Tail, Hope Cove is only a feasible anchorage in easterly winds

Approaching Plymouth and the Yealm, with Hillsea Point on the right and the Mewstone beyond

although attractive, is very open and only really feasible as a daytime anchorage. Wells Rock and several other shoal patches extend a mile south of Erme Head, the eastern side of the river mouth.

Within Bigbury Bay the tidal streams are considerably weaker, attaining a maximum of one knot at Springs on the flood, which rotates in an easterly direction, beginning HW Dover +0415. The weaker ebb runs to the west-north-west, beginning HW Dover –0200.

Closing the western shore, Hillsea Point, rounded and grassy with low cliffs, has an old coastguard lookout and flagstaff just to the east. Hillsea Rocks and shallow patches lie up to a mile offshore. Do not close the land if bound for the Yealm, but hold a course away from the the shore towards the Great Mewstone, an unmistakeably large pyramid-shaped island, until the marks into Wembury Bay can be located, leading into the well-hidden delights of the River Yealm. One of the classic West Country havens, this is popular and inevitably crowded in season.

RIVER YEALM AND APPROACHES TO PLYMOUTH

Dominating Wembury Bay, the Great Mewstone (59m) is an impressive lump of rock, with sparse sea turf and ferns on the steep slopes that are now just the haunt of the sea birds that give it its name. At one time it was inhabited and the ruin on the eastern side, a single storey circular stone building with an unusual conical roof, was possibly built with the remains of a small medieval chapel that is recorded as being sited there. The last known inhabitants of the Mewstone were Sam Wakeham and his wife in the 1820s. It was their rent-free domicile in return for protecting the island's rabbits during the off-season for the Calmady family. Now owned by the Ministry of Defence, the island is a wildlife conservation area and closed to the public.

Shoals extend nearly a mile south-west and east from the Mewstone, and the passage between it and

the mainland is rock strewn. Beyond it, the huge bay enclosing the naval and commercial port of Plymouth opens to the north. With the exception of the Shagstone, an isolated rock on the eastern shore marked with an unlit beacon, there are no hazards for small craft, and deep water is carried right into Plymouth Sound. The large outer harbour is enclosed by a central breakwater, with entrances to its east and west.

Tidal streams in the approaches to Plymouth are complicated by a clockwise rotation – at the eastern entrance the main flood commences half an hour after HW Dover, the ebb at HW Dover –0530. Streams in the entrances attain just over a knot at Springs but they can be considerably greater in the Narrows within the harbour.

The approach to Plymouth is easy at night. It is well lit, with plenty of water, and the only real problem is likely to be distinguishing the navigation lights from the huge mass of the city lights. Care should be taken to keep a careful watch on other shipping, as the harbour and approaches are invariably busy.

Penlee Point on the western side of Plymouth Sound is a wooded and rocky headland with white buildings low down on the point. Shoals extend two cables to the south-east, and are marked by the Draystone red can (Fl (2) R 5s).

A mile and a half to the west, Rame Head, the western extremity of Plymouth Sound, is a distinctive cone shape, its grassy slopes climbing to the conspicuous ruins of a chapel on the summit where there is also an NCI Lookout. The shore is steep-to and can be approached to within two cables, although rocks extend from the western side, and in conditions of wind against tide overfalls will be encountered for about half a mile south of the headland.

In good visibility, eight miles south of Rame Head, the thin pencil of the Eddystone lighthouse rises

The Eddystone lighthouse, a lonely but vital navigational aid

Heading west from Plymouth, Rame Head has a pleasing conical appearance

incongruously from the sea. A lurking nightmare for ships running into Plymouth, a light on this curious isolated reef was first established in 1698 by an aggrieved shipowner, Henry Winstanley, who had lost two vessels. His distinctly Heath Robinson structure, somewhat akin to a Chinese pagoda, survived a mere five years before it was washed away, taking by chance the luckless Winstanley and some workmen with it. In 1709 John Rudyerd erected a wooden lighthouse with considerably more success, but this was destroyed by fire, not water, after 47 years.

Four years later, John Smeaton's elegant granite column began a vigil that was to last for 120 years, his design setting the pattern for many others, and were it not for the rocks crumbling beneath it, it would probably still stand there today. Instead, when the present lighthouse designed by Sir J N Douglass replaced it in 1882, Smeaton's dismantled tower was re-erected on Plymouth Hoe and is open to visitors.

Just awash at High Water Springs, the rocks extend in a radius of about three cables around the lighthouse, which is a grey tower with a helicopter pad. The major light in this section of coast, it has a 17 mile range (F1(2) 10s 17M & Iso R 10s 8M)), the red sector (110.5° – 130.5°T) covers the paradoxically named Hand Deeps – in reality a shoal with least depths of 7m – three miles north-west of the Eddystone. Hand Deeps, which breaks heavily in bad weather, and the Eddystone are both very popular with sea anglers and in fine weather there are invariably a number of boats in the vicinity.

This passage area is not easy in fog. There are few aids and, although most of the dangers lie inshore of the 10m line, particular care should be taken to avoid being set into Bigbury Bay, the hazards approaching Yealm Head and the Great Mewstone and surrounding rocks. It is generally the best policy to maintain a good offing. The only sound signals are at Start Point (Horn 60s), the Eddystone (Horn 30s) and Plymouth West Breakwater end (Horn 15s). As an alternative to feeling your way into Plymouth, where the shipping movements continue in spite of fog, the anchorage in Cawsand Bay on the western side of the approaches is of easy access and well worth consideration in suitable weather.

Attractive and well-sheltered from the west, Cawsand Bay is a popular anchorage in the western approach to Plymouth

Salcombe in high summer! The main visitors' moorings can be seen along the channel, centre, with Batson Creek beyond

Salcombe

Tides	HW Dover –0523
Range	MHWS 5.3m–MHWN 4.1m, MLWN 2.1m–MLWS 0.7m. Spring ebb attains up to three knots off town
Charts	AC: 28 and SC5602.10; Stanfords: CP 22, L14; Imray: WCP2400.5
Waypoint	Wolf Rock Buoy 50°13'.53N 03°46'.58W
Hazards	Bar dangerous in strong southerly weather and ebb tide. Bass Rock (lit), Wolf Rock (lit) Blackstone (lit) and Poundstone (unlit). Very crowded in season and cruising yachts are not permitted to sail within harbour during July and August. Large part of upper reaches dry
Harbour Speed limit	Eight knots/minimal wash
Overnight charge	Harbour Authority mooring or visitors' pontoon island £18. At anchor £9

'Sunset and evening star, And one clear call for me!
And may there be no moaning of the bar,
When I put out to sea . . .'

So begins Tennyson's famous *Crossing of the Bar* inspired by the sound of the breaking sea upon Salcombe Bar during a stay in the harbour as a guest aboard Lord Brassey's yacht *Sunbeam* in 1889. Even then this was a popular if somewhat exclusive haunt of the wealthy, who were attracted by the romantic beauty and the mild, almost Mediterranean, climate.

That has changed little, and today Salcombe is one of the most popular cruising stopovers in the West Country, attracting over 6,000 visiting boats a year. Tucked away from the main tourist track through Devon, the small town has managed to resist most attempts to over-develop the area, relying totally on its natural attractions. There's definitely an exclusive feel to the place, there are several smart hotels, and the limited amount of accommodation ashore and lack of amusement arcades or similar diversions has kept the masses away. Apart from the small fleet of 15 or so fishing boats, mostly crabbers, and the Kingsbridge ferry, there is no commercial traffic within the river and it is totally committed to pleasure boating in all its forms.

As harbours go, Salcombe is super-efficient, managing the ever increasing numbers of visitors with a polite but necessary authority. At times such as during the regatta weeks at the beginning of August – a tradition dating back to 1857 – the numbers have to be seen to be believed.

During the busiest months of July and August for

Always popular, the unspoiled Salcombe estuary stretches inland to distant Kingsbridge, top left.
Limebury Point and Sunny Cove are on the right, while the powerboat, centre, is just crossing the Bar

safety reasons cruising yachts are not permitted to sail within the harbour and power boats will always find the speed limit of eight knots strictly enforced.

The estuary is a classic ria (a valley drowned as water levels rose after the ice ages) and is something of an anomaly as there is no Salcombe River flowing into it, merely a number of small streams that emerge from the eight large creeks that stretch inland into the attractive and rolling hinterland of Devon's South Hams.

This large area of inland saltwater is an important natural habitat and was made a Site of Special Scientific Interest (SSSI) in 1987. Navigable for four miles to Kingsbridge, a large area of the upper reaches dries, but within the lower half of the estuary there is plenty of deep water, some memorable scenery and a number of superb clean sandy beaches.

Salcombe never developed as a major port, partly because of its remote position right at the southernmost tip of Devon, but also because of the shallow bar at the entrance. This becomes very dangerous with strong onshore winds or swell and an ebbing tide, when an approach should never be attempted.

APPROACHES

The wide bay to seaward of Salcombe's entrance is known as the Range and the approach from the east is memorable, the dramatic profile of Bolt Head forming a succession of jagged pinnacles and gullies rising 100m to a flat grassy top. Keep a good half mile off the shore to avoid the Chapple Rocks, least depth 2.7m, and close the steep western shore to within a cable of the Eelstone, before turning northwards. However, be ready for very strong gusts and fluky winds beneath the cliffs. From the west, the Mewstone (19m) and

Little Mewstone (5m) are large prominent rocks several cables to the south of Bolt Head. They can be passed within a cable and the harbour will then begin to open.

The Bar (least depth 0.7m) extends in a southwesterly direction from the rounded fern-covered Limebury Point, footed with low sloping cliffs on the eastern shore. A leading line (000°T, least depth 1.3m) is formed by the beacon on the Poundstone (a red and white-striped pole with red topmark) and another beacon elevated behind it on Sandhill Point (white with a horizontally striped red and white diamond topmark). The latter displays a directional flashing light (RWG 2s) and its white sector (357° – 002°T) indicates the leading line. It is perhaps easier to enter at night, as in daytime the beacons are not easy to spot.

From a distance Sandhill Point appears as an evenly rounded hill, its wooded slopes dotted with detached houses. Prominent in the centre is a large red brick house with two white dormer windows in the roof and gables at each end – the beacons lie exactly below the left hand gable.

The depths are actually better just west of the leading line, with over 2m close to the rocky shore. Normally, in offshore winds, preferably after half flood with minimal ground swell, Salcombe Bar will present no problems, but if you have any misgivings, and particularly if you can see any breaking seas, call *Salcombe Harbour* on VHF Ch 14 or Tel: 01548 843791 for advice before you attempt to enter.

Once over the Bar, the red can Bass Rock buoy (QR) marks this 0.8m drying rock off Splat Point; steer up to leave the conical green Wolf Rock buoy (QG) close on your starboard hand. Wolf Rock dries 0.1m and only shows on the lowest of tides, but beyond it the

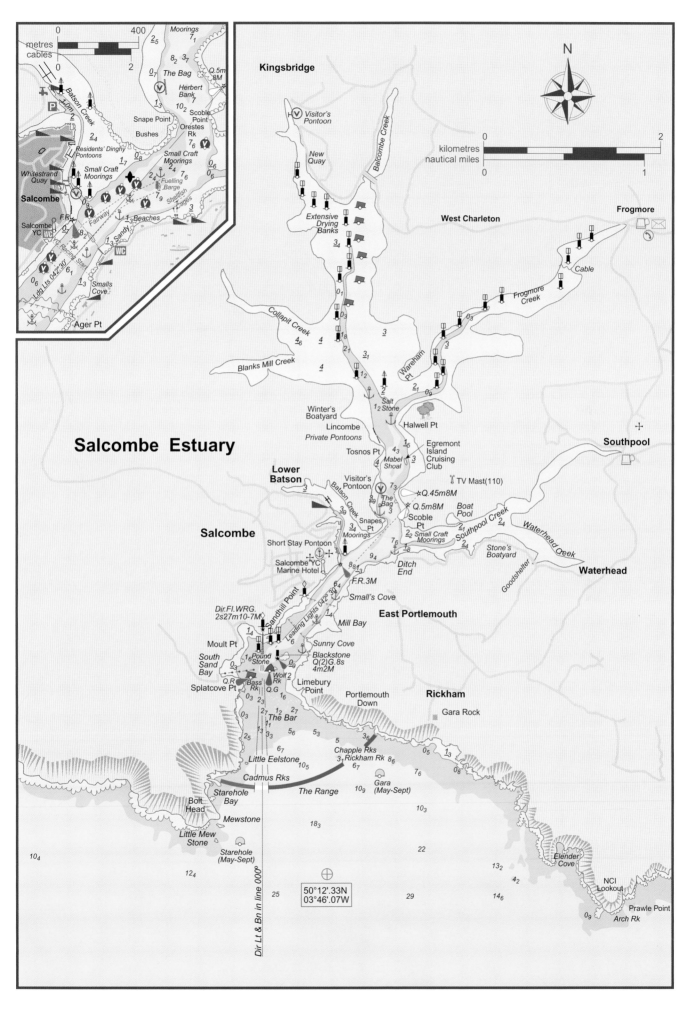

Kingsbridge

Salcombe Estuary

Salcombe

West Charleton

Frogmore

Southpool

Waterhead

East Portlemouth

Rickham

Bolt Head

Prawle Point

50°12'.33N
03°46'.07W

Salcombe Bar: the gabled house and leading marks, 000°T

Blackstone, which dries 5m, is nearly always visible. The extensive rocky shoal around its base is marked by a green and white beacon on its western extremity (Q (2) G 8s), and the channel lies between this and the line of red and white beacons on the western shore off the remains of Fort Charles. At night, a pair of quick flashing (Q) leading lights, situated just west of Scoble Point, give a transit of 042°T that will take you up the centre of the harbour in clear water (least depth 5m) right to the town.

ANCHORAGES AND MOORINGS

In settled weather you will find a pleasant and popular daytime anchorage with a little under 2m at Low Water just north-east of the Blackstone off the sandy beach at Sunny Cove.

Because of underwater cables, anchoring is prohibited anywhere off the next inlet at Mill Bay.

The adjacent sandy cove on the starboard shore, Smalls Cove, is also a popular spot, along with Fisherman's Cove just upstream of the East Portlemouth ferry landing slip. Sound in to the edge of the beach where there is about 2m at Low Water. Both have clean

sand with safe swimming and, although Fisherman's Cove does not have a lot of sand left at High Water, there's a convenient retreat nearby – the award winning Venus Café – for a sandwich, baguette or pasty!

On the opposite side of the channel, the first of the yellow visitors' moorings lie off the prominent Marine Hotel, with two more moorings for larger craft on the east side of the fairway. All the visitors' moorings are clearly marked with a 'V', are numbered and have the maximum permitted LOA indicated on them. They do not have pick-up buoys so you will need a line ready to pass through the large ring. In season it is likely that one of the harbour patrols will meet you in the vicinity and allocate a berth if you have not already contacted them on VHF Ch 14. Due to the popularity of Salcombe, during the height of the season you will invariably have to raft up. The bulk of the visitors' swinging moorings are just a bit further upstream off the town and the Harbour Authority also has a large deep-water visitors' pontoon island just under half a mile beyond the town in the area known as 'The Bag'. The overnight charge for a visitors' swinging mooring or berthing on the pontoon is £1.80 per metre. This includes two free shower tokens per boat that can be used at Salcombe Yacht Club!

If you pay for a week's moorings in advance you will be charged at 5.5 times as opposed to 7 times the daily rate. Craft attending rallies, club cruises and other such events are offered a discount of 20%, with the sum collected en bloc by the organisers.

In addition to this the Harbour Authority is actively trying to encourage visitors outside the main summer season with various incentives. If you stay three or more nights during July or August and pay on arrival you will get a free night in September or October. If you stay for three or more nights and pay on arrival any time outside of July and August you will get an extra free night.

Finally, except in July and August, stormbound

In fair weather the anchorage off Sunny Cove definitely lives up to its name!

The Normandy short stay visitors' pontoon

vessels may, at the discretion of the harbourmaster, be offered a concession of a 50% reduction in mooring charges after the first three days, up to a maximum of seven days, after which full charges will be levied.

Just upstream of the Marine Hotel, Salcombe Yacht Club, Tel: 01548 842872; www.salcombyc.org.uk, enjoys a commanding view of the estuary from Cliff House on the hillside, a large red brick building with a prominent tower, veranda and terrace. The club was founded in 1894 and a warm welcome is extended to visiting yachts and their crews, with showers, bar and meals all available. Its starting line and dinghy landing with running mooring are on the waterfront below the club and beyond the first visitors' moorings on the west side of the harbour, the line of smaller yellow buoys running parallel to the shore marks a fairway that must be used when races are starting as the centre of the river gets very congested.

The Ferry Inn, beside the ferry steps, has a beer garden and bars overlooking the harbour and is a popular spot for the pundits to gather and watch everyone else's mistakes from behind the safety of a pint!

Beyond the ferry, Batson Creek bears away to port, much of it drying but there is a clearly marked channel (G/W and R/W poles with topmarks) dredged to 1m. A floating waste recycling facility is moored on the north side of the channel entrance. The channel leads to the Normandy short stay visitors' pontoon (least depth 1m), which is linked to the shore by a bridge onto Whitestrand Quay where the harbour office is located. A weather forecast and outlook are posted here daily. Vessels over 12.2m (40ft) and 2m draught should first check access with the harbour patrol.

This convenient daytime facility is for stays of up to half-an-hour only, for shopping or topping up water and must not be used overnight between 1900 and 0700. Tenders from visiting boats can be left on the inside of this pontoon providing they are marked with the parent craft's name. Beyond Whitestrand, the dredged channel continues along the creek to

an all-tide small craft launching slip at Batson.

The main fairway, which must be kept clear, runs up the centre of the harbour. Most of the visitors' moorings, predominantly yellow again but with some orange buoys for smaller craft, are clearly marked along both sides. Anchoring is not possible on the Salcombe side of the channel because of the large number of local moorings. By far the best spot is opposite, off East Portlemouth's sandy beach, well upstream of the ferry towards Ditch End. The overnight charge for anchoring here or anywhere else in the estuary is £0.90 per metre. Let go along the edge of the bank, which drops off steeply, and don't skimp on the cable as the tide can run fast and many a relaxed drink at the Ferry Inn has terminated prematurely with the sight of one's boat dragging resolutely to seaward!

A lone Salcombe yawl ghosts through the visitors' moorings – you will invariably have to raft in high season

The Harbour Authority runs a convenient water taxi service which can be summoned on VHF Ch 12, callsign *Salcombe Harbour Taxi* or by phoning the harbour office, Tel: 01548 843791. During the peak season, 7 July – 26 August, it operates (weather permitting) from 0800 to 2300, in May, June and early September 0800 – 2200; the harbour staff will advise at other times. Charges, one-way, are £1.50 per person off the town, from 'The Bag' you'll pay £2. Discounted tickets are also available, for example a book of 20 tickets at £1.50 will cost just £20.

FUEL, FRESH WATER AND GAS

During the season (end of June to mid-September), diesel and petrol are easily obtained from the fuel barge (open daily 0830 – 1700) moored off the entrance to Southpool Creek, opposite the town; VHF Ch 06, callsign *Fuel Barge*, Tel: 07801 798862. Fresh water can be obtained alongside from the taps and hoses on the Normandy short stay visitors' pontoon. Calor and Camping Gaz refills are obtainable from The Salcombe Boatstore chandlery (open seven days a week), and Salcombe DIY Centre, both in Island Street.

FACILITIES
(Local phone code 01548)

Nowadays, the invasion is annual, and although not quite as swamped with visitors as some of the West Country's main holiday resorts, it is probably a good guess that in Salcombe's case 90 per cent of the people walking the narrow streets in mid-summer are doing something with some kind of boat. Once renowned for the number of dories, today it's the RIB that seems to rule. The town is compact and most likely has more designer label shops for its size than anywhere else in the West Country: Weird Fish, Quba, Musto, Jack Wills, T&G, White Stuff, Fat Face, Crew and Moshulu no less! The rest of the main shopping street, Fore Street, provides for most other requirements. Here Cranch's Pantry has a good selection of groceries, fruit and vegetables, there's an excellent fishmonger, fresh bread at the Upper Crust Bakery and Coleman's Butchers can provide ice as well as the obvious! Other shops include Bowers Wines off-licence, a newsagent, chemist, a number of smart gift shops and galleries and Salcombe Deli or Casse-Crout Bakery/Deli for some sheer indulgence! To keep on top of the spending there's a Lloyd's TSB bank with cashpoint and, although the HSBC branch is only open 0930 – 1530 Mondays and Thursdays, it has a convenient cashpoint facility in the Whitestrand car park adjoining the public phone box. The post office will be found inside Shipwrights of Salcombe – confusing at first for those who have known Salcombe for a while for this was until recently The Shipwrights Arms pub. Alas, no more, it's a 'lifestyle' and gift shop now!

There are, however, still four pubs remaining – The Ferry Inn, King's Arms, The Victoria and the Fortescue – all of which do good bar food. Most of the restaurants are along Fore Street, or just off it, including Dusters Bistro, Tel: 842634, a regular venue for live jazz on Sundays, and Catch 55, Tel: 842646, which serves seafood. The ever popular Galley, Tel: 842828, and Restaurant 42, Tel: 843408, both have great views of the harbour, while Boatswain's, Tel: 842189, is tucked cosily away in Russell Court. Captain Flint's, Tel: 842357, does a good pizza and is a great favourite with children. At the far end of town, in Island Street, at the new Hannaford landing building overlooking Shadycombe Creek, you'll find The Oyster Shack, Tel: 843596, serving oysters from the River Avon and other local seafood, and Jack Sprats, Tel: 844747, a popular family restaurant. There are also several coffee shops and cafés as well as good fish and chips.

Do not miss the fascinating Maritime Museum, located beneath the Tourist Information Centre, Tel: 843927; www.salcombeinformation.co.uk, in Market Street, and the excellent Lifeboat House Museum on the waterfront.

WiFi is available both off the town and in The Bag; for more information contact the harbour office. There's also public internet access at the local library (varying

As good as it gets! Another popular anchorage is off East Portlemouth's fine sandy beach

opening times and closed Tuesdays) in Cliff House, next to the Yacht Club, at The Coffee Shop in Fore Street or at Blue Water Surf Café, which is situated round the back of the town in Island Street.

Finally, no visit is complete without a taste of delectable Salcombe Dairy ice cream. Such is its pedigree, it's even sold at Sadlers Wells!

SALCOMBE, PAST AND PRESENT

Salcombe was not always the smart, respectable town that it is today. In 1607 the harbour was a much busier place and the justices reported that the town was 'full of dissolute seafaring men, who murdered each other and buried the corpses in the sands at night'.

The forlorn remains of Fort Charles at the harbour mouth date from the mid-1600s. The last garrison in England to hold out for Charles I, it endured six rather uncomfortable months while the Roundheads bombarded it from the Portlemouth shore.

As a commercial port, its heyday was in the mid-1880s when a large number of schooners were built to engage in the salt cod trade with Newfoundland and Labrador, many launched from the famous yard of William Date in Kingsbridge. After buying the fish, these small British vessels crossed the Atlantic to sell their cargoes in Spain, Portugal and the Mediterranean and through this a new trade developed bringing citrus and soft fruit to England. Speed was of the essence for this financially precarious activity, and it produced a small but extremely fast type of schooner that was able to set large amounts of sail. They were typical of the ports of South Devon and of Salcombe in particular.

By the beginning of this century the port had lapsed into total decline and it was then that its new popularity as a select holiday resort was established. However, apart from the bombardment of Fort Charles, undoubtedly the most dramatic event to engulf the town was the arrival in 1943 of 137 officers and 1,793 men of the US Naval Construction Battalion in preparation for the D-Day landings. The old Salcombe Hotel and many other properties were requisitioned, several rows of old cottages were bulldozed to make a loading ramp which has since become Whitestrand, and the large concrete slipway was built in Mill Bay. An impressive fleet of landing craft was assembled in the estuary and practice landings carried out on nearby Slapton Ley. On 4 June 1944, 66 vessels sailed from Salcombe. For the small town its invasion had ended, and in Europe, it was about to begin.

From a family point of view, the attraction of Salcombe today has to be the number of splendid beaches. Apart from those already mentioned, South Sands, at the entrance, is one of the safest and can be reached by a regular ferry. Refreshment, including excellent cream teas, can be found at the South Sands Hotel. Close by, North Sands is smaller and here you'll

also find the Winking Prawn Waterfront brasserie, Tel: 842326.

From South Sands a signposted walk up through the woods brings you to the Overbecks Museum of natural history and curiosities and Sharpitor Gardens, boasting many exotic plants normally only grown under glass – such as banana, fig and lemon trees. From here press on to the spectacular viewpoint at Sharpitor and then on to Bolt Head.

If the tide is very, very low, you might just glimpse the ghostly outline of the ill-fated barque, *Herzogin Cecilie*, in her last resting place far below in Starehole Bay. This is all National Trust land and if you're feeling particularly energetic the fine elevated coastal path will take you all the way to Bolt Tail.

'For beauty and romantic walks', wrote Cowper 'especially along Sharpitor to Bolt Head, I think it beats every other place on the South Coast.'

As well as the beaches on the opposite side of the estuary, which are all easily reached by dinghy or the ferry, there are also good walks eastwards along the coast towards Start Point. A particularly pleasant round trip can be enjoyed by following the coastal footpath from Mill Bay out past Limebury Point and towards Prawle Point before turning inland to Gara Rock and following the quiet lanes back to East Portlemouth. Here there is a church (and telephone) as well as some lovely views of Salcombe and the upper harbour from its lofty heights. You can then descend back to the harbour via the steep and shady steps of Ferry Hill.

The harbour's large area of sheltered, clean water provides excellent sailing for dinghy sailors, not least the fleet of pretty Salcombe yawls. The clinker construction, broad transom and short bowsprit are the key to their ancestry, for they evolved from the traditional local fishing vessels of the early part of the 19th century. Three-quarter decked or open, between 14ft and 18ft overall, they were also used by local licensed watermen for hiring out to picnic parties and racing once a year during the local regatta.

The birth of the racing yawl is generally attributed to Jim Stone, a young local shipwright who built himself a 14ft yawl purely for racing in 1917. Unable to afford the paint, he finished her off with creosote, decided to call her *Blackbird*, and appropriately this dark horse won every race!

The design was further refined by Morgan Giles in 1937, when the overall length was standardised at 16ft with a heavy iron bulb keel and centreboard. They are still constructed locally, and open meetings often attract well over 50 boats for some very close racing.

Excellent sailing is also one of the main reasons that the famous Island Cruising Club has been based here since 1954, its members enjoying a varied fleet of vessels (www.icc-salcombe.co.uk). It has been a widely recognised RYA Training Centre for decades where thousands of children and adults have acquired their sailing skills!

The club's name was derived from the Island, the area to the south of Shadycombe Creek where its original clubhouse (sold in 2000) backed onto the pleasantly salty backwater at the rear of the town. Today the clubship is the former Mersey ferry *Egremont*, moored further upriver in The Bag. Visitors are welcome to use the showers (for a small donation) and bar. You can also book breakfast, lunch or dinner on Tel: 01548 531176 or 531775 out of office hours.

All manner of nautical activity still lurks in Island Street – boatyards, engineers and various other boating businesses, including two chandlers, The Salcombe Boatstore (open seven days a week) and Blue Water Marine, the latter holding a good stock of stuff for powerboats, oils and engine accessories.

Even if you're not in need of anything, a pleasant hour can be spent nosing around the colourful old boatsheds, heavy with the tang of fresh sawdust and old hemp. You may chance on a new yawl being built, or an old clinker launch under repair. If time further permits, it's a pleasant walk onwards around Shadycombe Creek to the sleepy backwater of Batson, with its picturesque hamlet at the head of the creek.

THE UPPER REACHES

However, nowhere is absolutely perfect. There are two things that can detract from a visit to Salcombe – the sheer number of boats at the height of the season and the swell in a southerly blow. In spite of the apparently landlocked nature of the harbour, this will be experienced as far up as Scoble Point, rendering the anchorage and moorings surprisingly rough and uncomfortable, particularly on the ebb.

The solution to both these problems is to seek out one of the quieter, more sheltered spots further up the estuary. Southpool Creek dries almost to its mouth, but boats able to take the ground might find a spot just upstream of the moorings, grounding at Low Water. Ideally this is best explored by dinghy, slipping away from the bustle of Salcombe between the steep-wooded shores and following the rising tide as it creeps along the muddy shores. At Gullet Point the creek divides, the starboard arm becoming Waterhead Creek where you will find the small, forgotten hamlet of Goodshelter; Southpool Creek is very shallow beyond Gullet but the quiet village of Southpool can be reached a couple of hours either side of High Water. There are no facilities except a phone, although if you time it right a pint at the Millbrook Inn awaits.

Opposite the entrance to Southpool Creek Middle Ground is a bank (least depth 1.5m) extending south and east from Snapes Point – deep water lies on the Scoble side of the channel. The ebb funnels through this gap at up to two knots at Springs.

Looking upstream to Snapes Point and The Bag – the fuel barge is on the bottom left

Opening before you is the traditional upper anchorage of The Bag, although now most of it is given over to permanent moorings. Shoal draught boats might just squeeze into the handy corner and tuck themselves in just north of wooded Snapes Point, close to the edge of the drying mud, where you will be sheltered from most weather. Alternatively, for the more convivial, there is a large visitors' pontoon island a little distance upstream, providing a secure and sheltered berth. You will find recycling bins here, but no other services.

The oldest objection to The Bag used to be the long row to town. The outboard dealt with the worst of that, although in a fresh southerly breeze it can still be a long, wet ride in an inflatable! By far the most convenient solution is the Salcombe Harbour taxi service, call VHF Channel 12, and the round trip fare will be £4 per person.

Mabel Shoal (1.2m LAT) lies inconveniently right in the middle of The Bag, and care should also be taken to avoid the rocks extending from Tosnos Point at the northern end of this stretch. The best course to avoid both hazards is to follow the line of moorings along the eastern shore past the wooded outcrop of Halwell Point, where an anchorage can be found close to the shore.

Just upstream of Tosnos, the remains on the foreshore are those of the 108ft yacht *Iverna* built by Fay in 1890 – she was winner of the Big Class in 1890-92. When I first visited The Bag in the 1960s, this and several other elegant large vessels were still afloat as houseboats along this reach.

Nestling in the small inlet at Lincombe you will see the buildings and slipways of Winter's Boatyard, which is approached by a narrow winding channel marked by small buoys. Ahead, the Saltstone Beacon, a striped pole with green triangular topmark, marks a large rock drying to 4.9m. This was once used by 17th century Non-Conformists for illegal religious meetings, as it belonged to none of the local parishes and was out of legal jurisdiction.

Between it and Halwell Point lies the entrance to Frogmore Creek. This, too, dries extensively, but a very peaceful anchorage can be found just inside the mouth, with 2m at Low Water, or you can anchor just west of the Saltstone in the same sort of depth. The latter berth is more likely to be affected by passing traffic, such as ferries, but with a bit of luck, you will find welcome solitude as evening descends.

After supper, dinghy over for a leg stretch on the lonely, pebbly, foreshore of Wareham Point, then drift back as dusk descends over the silent wooded shore, the ebb rippling quietly out of the creek and the peace broken only by the sudden startled cries of the birds settling for the night. With luck the morning will dawn warm and calm, the distant wooded shores indistinct in a gentle but rising mist as the early sun tries to burn through – it does sometimes happen!

If the tide permits, it's time for another trip in the dinghy, following the twisting creek further inland between the rolling fields and grazing cattle to the village of Frogmore. The channel is well marked along its port side by red and white striped poles with square topmarks, and shoal draught boats can get right up to Frogmore on a rising tide, although the final half mile is very shallow. Here a grocery, post office and the Globe Inn cater for most immediate needs.

After the grandeur of the entrance, above Frogmore Creek the character of the estuary changes completely, becoming wide and flat and meandering gently into peaceful South Hams – the name derives from the old English word *hamme*, meaning a sheltered place – and for an average draught boat it is a pleasant run up to Kingsbridge on a rising tide. There is a limited amount of drying berthing if you are interested in staying overnight, but it is always advisable to check availability with the harbour office first. The visitors' mooring charges at Kingsbridge are the same as Salcombe!

The large visitors' pontoon in The Bag is a more peaceful alternative to a mooring off the town

KINGSBRIDGE APPROACHES

Leave the Saltstone well to starboard, and off the wide entrance to Collapit and Blanks Mill Creeks pass the striped red and white poles with red topmarks, which clearly mark the western side of the channel, to port.

On the western bank, at the north side of Collapit Creek, is a conspicuous house with a mooring off it.

Here the channel divides, the line of numbered red can buoys marking a subsidiary channel that leads away to the distant group of moorings by the bridge across Balcombe Creek. These buoys should all be left well on the starboard hand and, following the poles, the main channel takes you north towards High House Point, where the outskirts of Kingsbridge, a rather unsightly development of modern houses sprawling across a low rounded hill, can be seen. Beneath this point the channel turns sharply back to the western shore, there are a number of local moorings along its edges, and upstream Kingsbridge begins to appear.

The bank on the eastern shore is large and shallow, so do not cut the corner. In contrast to the development opposite, trees and fields run down close to the channel on the western shore, which swings northwards again past a private pontoon with numerous local boats alongside. Just upstream is New Quay, formerly the site of Date's shipyard, and the boatyard and private pontoons all belong to the Kingsbridge ferry.

BERTHING

No public berthing is allowed anywhere along the length of this quay, but keep close and continue past the new buildings at its northern end before turning across the entrance of the inlet where there are a number of local boats moored on your port hand.

The channel now heads towards the slipway and quay on the western shore, which marks the beginning of the tree-lined basin enclosing the head of the creek. The visitors' pontoon, with a bridge to the shore, will be found on the starboard hand; shoal draught boats should berth on the outside at the downstream end, whereas visitors with deeper draughts should use the berths which are clearly marked alongside the wall opposite. These berths are suitable for vessels of up to 11m, dry completely to soft mud and are only safely accessible two hours either side of High Water.

FACILITIES

Kingsbridge, an unspoilt country town with many fine Georgian buildings, forms the junction of four busy roads through South Devon. Although long dead as a seaport, it is an important shopping centre and bustles with activity, with a street market on Tuesdays and Thursdays, and a farmers market on the Quay the first Saturday of the month. All normal requirements except fuel can be found. Pubs, restaurants and cafés abound, and after the distinctly nautical atmosphere of Salcombe a taste of the country makes a pleasant contrast before returning downstream to the sea and yet another *Crossing of the Bar*:

'For though from out our bourne of Time and Place,
  The flood may bear me far,
  I hope to see my Pilot face to face,
  When I have crost the bar.'

Salcombe Port Guide – Area telephone code: 01548

Harbourmaster: Ian Gibson, Harbour Office, Whitestrand, Salcombe TQ8 8BU, Tel: 843791; Fax: 842033. Open 0900 – 1300, 1400 – 1645 daily during season, otherwise Mon – Fri only. Email: salcombe.harbour@southhams.gov.uk; website: www.salcombeharbour.co.uk

VHF: Ch 14, callsign *Salcombe Harbour*, office hours. Harbour patrols, callsign *Salcombe Harbour* all monitor Ch 14 and 12 and operate 0600 – 2200 during season.

Mail drop: c/o Harbour Office or Salcombe Yacht Club.

Emergency services: Lifeboat at Salcombe; Brixham Coastguard; Prawle Point NCI Lookout, Tel: 511259.

Anchorages: Sunny Cove, Smalls Cove, East Portlemouth beach, entrance to Frogmore Creek, west of Saltstone and shoal draught/drying anchorages in many other parts of estuary. Anchoring prohibited in area off Mill Bay.

Moorings: Numbered, marked with a 'V' and details of maximum size, 21 visitors' swinging moorings off Salcombe for up to 15m, larger moorings available up to 17m, and three for up to 100 tons TM. Normandy short stay daytime visitors' pontoon off town for up to half-an-hour only, no berthing between 1900 and 0700. Large deep water visitors' pontoon island in The Bag. Drying visitors' pontoon and berthing alongside wall at Kingsbridge.

Dinghy landings: Inside Normandy pontoon. Salcombe Yacht Club steps. Ferry steps, East Portlemouth beach.

Water taxi: Harbour launches double up as taxi service. Call *Salcombe Harbour Taxi* on VHF Ch 12, 0800 – 2345 during season, shorter hours at other times. Charges, one-way, from £1.50 to £3 per person depending on location, landing/departing Whitestrand pontoon. Regular ferries from Salcombe to East Portlemouth, South Sands and Kingsbridge when tide permits.

Marinas: None.

Charges: Overnight charge on pontoons or moorings £1.80 per metre per night. At anchor £0.90 per metre per night. Special rates for stays over a week.

Phones: Whitestrand Quay.

Doctor: Health Centre, Tel: 842284.

Dentist: Tel: 844844.

Hospital: South Hams Hospital, Casualty, Kingsbridge, Tel: 852349.

Churches: C of E and RC.

Local weather forecast: Outside harbour office.

Fuel: Diesel and petrol alongside fuel barge, end June to mid-Sept only, 0830 – 1700 daily. Monitors VHF Ch 06, callsign *Fuel barge* or Tel: 07801 798862.

Water: Hoses on Normandy short stay visitors' pontoon.

Gas: Calor and Camping Gaz from Salcombe Boatstore, Tel: 843708, and Salcombe DIY Centre, Tel: 843623, both in Island Street.

Tourist Information Centre: Town Hall, Salcombe, Tel: 843927; www.salcombeinformation.co.uk. The Quay, Kingsbridge, Tel: 853195.

Banks: Lloyds TSB with cashpoint. HSBC (open 0930 – 1530 Mon, Thurs) has cashpoint in Whitestrand car park. All main banks in Kingsbridge, but cashpoints only at Lloyds and HSBC.

Post office: Fore Street, Salcombe; Kingsbridge.

Internet access: WiFi in lower harbour and The Bag, contact harbour office. Coffee Shop, Fore Street, Blue Water Café, Island Street, Public Library, Cliff House (opening times vary daily).

Rubbish: Floating recycling facility in entrance to Batson Creek and visitors' pontoon, The Bag.

Showers/toilets: Salcombe Yacht Club. Public toilets at Whitestrand and Shadycombe car park.

Launderette: Fore Street, Salcombe (seven days), also in Kingsbridge.

Provisions: All normal requirements in Salcombe. All requirements at Kingsbridge.

Chandlers: Salcombe Boatstore, Tel: 843708; Blue Water Marine, Tel: 843383, both in Island Street.

Repairs: Yeoward & Dowie, Island Street, Tel: 844261; Winters Marine, Lincombe Boatyard, slipping to 30 tons, Tel: 843580. Drying out alongside by arrangement with harbourmaster.

Marine engineers: Sailing, Island Street, Tel: 842094; Winters Marine, Lincombe Boat Yard, Tel: 843580; SMS, Lincombe, Tel: 843655, VHF Ch 13 0830 – 1700; 24 hour breakdown service Tel 01548 843053; Reddish Marine, Tel: 844094; Wills Bros, The Embankment, Kingsbridge, Tel: 852424.

Electronic engineers: Andrew Jedynak, Tel: 843321; Richard Lewis, Tel: 843223.

Sailmakers: J Alsop, The Sail Loft, Croft Road, Tel: 843702; J McKillop, The Sail Loft, Ebrington Street, Kingsbridge, Tel: 852343; Westaway Sails, Ivybridge, Tel: 01752 892560, local pick up from Salcombe Boat Store.

Riggers: Salcombe Boatstore, Tel: 843708; Harris Rigging, Tel: 01803 840160.

Liferaft/inflatable repairs/servicing: Danby Maritime Safety, Tel: 842777.

Transport: Regular local buses, Tel: 853081, and ferries on tide to Kingsbridge, with Western National bus connections, Tel: 01752 402060, to main line trains at Plymouth (1 hour) or Totnes (40 mins): Tel: 08457 484950 or Traveline 0870 6082608.

Taxis: Clark Cars, Tel: 842914/Mob: 07976 551532, or Moonraker, Tel: 560231.

Car hire: Alpha, Kingsbridge, Tel: 856323.

Car parking: Large car park at Shadycombe, Salcombe. Large car park on Quay at Kingsbridge.

Yacht club: Salcombe Yacht Club, Cliff Road, Salcombe TQ8 8JQ, Tel: 842872.

Eating out: Varied choice of restaurants/bistros, pubs, cafés and fish and chips.

Things to do: Salcombe Maritime Museum; Lifeboat Museum; Sharpitor Gardens and Overbecks Museum; spectacular walks on both sides of estuary entrance; good swimming from many sandy and protected beaches within the harbour.

Regattas/special events: Salcombe Festival early June; Salcombe Town Regatta and Salcombe Yacht Club Regatta during first two weeks in August; harbour is also popular for dinghy championships throughout the season.

Salcombe shopping – not a supermarket in sight!

Bigbury Bay

Tides	River Avon/River Erme: HW Dover −0525
Charts	AC: 1613, SC5602.4; Stanfords: 13; Imray: C6, WCP2400.8
Hazards	**River Avon:** Tidal entrance with bar, dangerous in onshore wind. Strong currents within entrance. River mostly dries. Murray's Rocks in approach (unlit)
	River Erme: Wells Rock to south-east, Edward's Rock, East and West Mary's Rocks in entrance (all unlit). Drying tidal river, dangerous in onshore winds

The seven mile stretch of Bigbury Bay can often be a bit of a plod in prevailing southwesterly winds and boats heading across it will usually remain a good two to three miles offshore en route for Plymouth or the Yealm. However, in calm, settled weather, there are several places within it which make an interesting detour from the normal track.

Hope Cove is a small fishing village tucked away on the north side of Bolt Tail, which can sometimes provide a temporary anchorage in easterly winds. There are no off-lying dangers; sound into the centre of the cove between the small pier and the south shore, but beware the Basses Rock closer inshore which dries 1.3m.

THE RIVER AVON

The River Avon is, however, the real gem of Bigbury Bay, and for owners of shallow draught boats capable of drying out it can be a delightful spot for an overnight stop, providing there is no inkling of a change of weather to the south or west. Although perfectly sheltered within, in an onshore breeze and any ground swell, the river entrance is inaccessible. Once inside, if the weather does turn, you might not be able to get out for some time . . .

To find it, initially steer directly for the flattened pyramid of Burgh Island (pronounced Burrr), then hold more to the east and approach midway between the island and Longstone Point. The extensive sand dunes and beach of the Ham extend west from Longstone Point, concealing the tortuous entrance to the Avon and, apart from a very narrow channel, the whole of the approach dries at Low Water. Ideally it is best to enter an hour before High Water (HW Dover −0525) as the current runs strongly in the entrance, up to 4 knots at Springs.

I would personally recommend an earlier arrival when the drying Murray's Rocks, which extend nearly 2.5 cables to the south-east of the island, will still be visible. However, beware the outermost, Blind Mare, which has just over 1m over it at Mean Low Water Springs. A useful beacon used to mark Murray's Rocks but now only the base remains, a stumpy post that is just awash at High Water. I am informed by the harbourmaster that the topmark is unlikely to be replaced and that the post probably will not survive much longer either!

Sounding in with due care, a good anchorage in firm sand will be found just north-east of Murray's Rocks

Hope Cove is a pleasant daytime anchorage in offshore winds. Hillsea Point is just visible on the distant side of Bigbury Bay

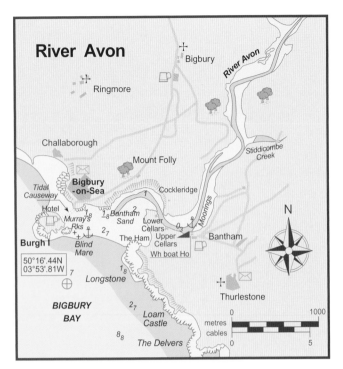

River Avon

Avon approach: Burgh Island Hotel is conspicuous on the left, with Mount Folly rising on the right and the entrance to the river in the centre

in about 2m. From here it is wisest to reconnoitre the channel by dinghy if you plan to enter the Avon, as it has become increasingly silted in recent years.

Alternatively it's a handy daytime anchorage just for a visit to Burgh Island, which is tidal, linked by drying sands to the mainland and the trippery resort of Bigbury-on-Sea. At high tide, a remarkable 'sea tractor' with seats on an elevated platform maintains the link with the shore. In contrast to the mainland resort,

privately-owned Burgh Island sports an elegant Art Deco hotel, where Agatha Christie wrote several of her books. Today, it has become a popular location for films of similar style and period. On the foreshore, by the landing place, there is also a small pub, the atmospheric 14th century Pilchard Inn.

Returning to the Avon – the entrance to the river is backed by a high cliff, Mount Folly, and the deepest water over the bar is found on a transit of the two conspicuous houses just east of the group of trees on the clifftop. Keep close to the beach on the western side, following the steep shoreline, until the white mark painted on the rock is abeam, before turning to starboard towards Lower Cellars Point, which is covered in turf and ferns and above which protrudes the top of a solitary pine tree. Do not rely on spotting

Burgh Island and approach to the Avon at half flood. Note Murray's Rocks extending to the south-east of the island

Looking upstream to Bantham, where much of the Avon dries

the white mark though, it has been known to disappear in land slips as the cliff is quite unstable! Here the river narrows considerably, with a shingly bank along the northern shore. Steer close to the point, where the current can run up to five knots through the narrows on the ebb if the river is in flood.

Once through the gap, you have entered a real hideaway. The river widens, with the landing beach and houses ahead, and immediately to starboard there is a sheltered pool off the quaint thatched boathouse and grassy quay, tucked beneath the dense foliage of the steep protective cliff. At first sight, with 2m at Low Water, this would seem to be the ideal anchorage, but holding is poor and the current runs strongly. Instead, follow the southern shore upstream towards the white building with a long thatch on the foreshore and anchor anywhere clear of the local small boat moorings, which now amount to no less than 85 during the season, and you will have to navigate carefully if the tide is flooding hard.

You will ground and probably dry out at Low Water, and there is a token charge of around £2 a night for anchoring which should be paid to the harbourmaster, Mr Marsh Dawes (Tel: 01548 561196; 0900 – 1600 Mon – Fri), who will usually be found in or near the large thatched building on the foreshore. In spite of its medieval appearance, this was actually built in 1937 to celebrate the accession of King George VI, and is nothing more than an enormous boathouse with two fine figureheads at each end. There is a further surprise within, for you will probably find some of the lovely traditional varnished clinker Bantham dinghies, many of which were built and maintained by Hugh Cater, who sadly died in 2007. The tradition is, however, being continued by Marsh Dawes, who has taken over their care and repair.

After the busier anchorages that you have probably visited so far, this delightful place is a rare find, even mobile phone coverage has yet to intrude and is practically non-existent on the river. Disappearing beyond cornfields sloping down to wooded shores, the river winds upstream between drying sandy banks

and reedy saltings for another four miles to the village of Aveton (pronounced Orton) Gifford. It is a sleepy, almost forgotten waterway, but 50 years ago barges regularly worked their way inland with cargoes of lime, stone and coal for the South Hams farms, and the tiny quays at Bantham reeked of the pilchard catches as they were landed and cured. On a rising tide, it is well worth further exploration in the dinghy, with the enticing prospect of a pint and a snack at the Fisherman's Rest pub at Aveton, perhaps?

Bantham itself is little more than a hamlet, a row of well cared-for cob and stone cottages, with deep overhanging thatches and tiny windows. The village is privately owned by the Evans Estates, which accounts for the admirable lack of development. Both Bantham and Aveton Gifford once had a post office and village stores and it is a sign of the times that these have now closed. However, the beach shop does stock an increasing amount of basic provisions as well as all-day breakfasts and other treats on their terrace, which has splendid views of the bay and Burgh Island. The mainstay of Bantham, though, is inevitably the very popular Sloop Inn which does excellent bar food.

THE RIVER ERME

Nearly three miles further north-west, the other 'forgotten' river of Bigbury Bay, the Erme, though very attractive and completely unspoiled, is only really feasible as a daytime anchorage in favourable conditions, and is not suitable for an overnight stop. Lacking a sheltering natural breakwater like the Ham, the river mouth is wide open to the south-west and dries completely beyond the entrance. As it is privately owned by the Flete Estate and designated as a wild life sanctuary, permission is needed to enter the inner reaches. However, in settled weather and an offshore breeze, a pleasant daytime anchorage can be found in the mouth off the fine sandy beaches at Mothecombe and Wonwell.

Although there are no offshore hazards, care must be taken in the approach to the Erme. There are several dangerous unmarked rocks, in particular Wells Rock (least depth 1.2m) just over half a mile

The approach to the River Erme: Landmarks include Owen Hill, centre, the isolated row of cottages, right, and Fernycombe Point, far right

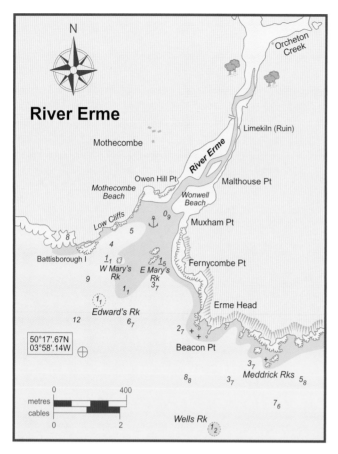

River Erme

Mothecombe

Orcheton Creek

Limekiln (Ruin)

River Erme

Owen Hill Pt

Malthouse Pt

Mothecombe Beach

Wonwell Beach

Low Cliffs

Muxham Pt

Battisborough I

W Mary's Rk

E Mary's Rk

Fernycombe Pt

Edward's Rk

Erme Head

Beacon Pt

Meddrick Rks

Wells Rk

50°17'.67N
03°58'.14W

metres
cables

0   400

0   2

south of Erme Head, the eastern flank of the river mouth. Within the entrance there are three more rocks, West and East Mary's Rocks (dry 1.1m and 1.5m respectively) and further to seaward, three cables south of the low grassy Battisborough Island on the northern shore, Edward's Rock (least depth 1.1m). Shallow water extends south-west from the Mary's Rocks, and the deeper channel runs parallel to the sloping slab-like cliffs of the northern shore.

Keep to the west of all the hazards and steer for the southern end of Owen Hill, the prominent isolated cliff topped with a group of conspicuous pines. Mothecombe beach lies just to the west and, by sounding in towards it, a good sandy anchorage will be found inside the Mary's Rocks in about 3m, two cables due south of Owen Hill.

The River Erme is probably unique in that there are absolutely no facilities within a mile; the clean sandy beaches and clear water are perfect for swimming and, if time permits, a dinghy trip should certainly be made some of the way upstream, following the tide up the twisting channel between the sandy banks and steep-wooded shores, past the old lime kiln to the dark and silent Salmon Pool. There are few places on the South Coast that remain quite so unspoilt.

The Erme from the south-east. Fernycombe Point is in the foreground, with East Mary's Rock covered and Mothecombe beach on the far side of the river next to Owen Hill

The entrance to the River Yealm. Note the sand bar shallows on the left side of the river, with Cellar Bay to the right. The visitors' pontoons and Yealm Steps landing pontoon are visible where the creeks separate

River Yealm

Tides	HW Dover –0520
Range	MHWS 5.4m–MHWN 4.3m, MLWN 2.1m–MLWS 0.7m
	Attains up to three knots in entrance at Spring ebb
Charts	AC: 30 and SC5602.8; Stanfords: CP23; Imray: C14, WCP2400.6
Waypoint	Outer sand bar buoy 50°18'.59N 04°04'.12W
Hazards	West and East Ebb Rocks, Mouthstone Ledge from east; Outer and Inner Slimer Rocks from west (all unlit). Bar across northern side of entrance (buoyed and lit). Under 2m within entrance at Springs. Not recommended in strong southerly or southwesterly wind and swell. Newton Arm and large area of upper reaches dry
Harbour speed limit	Six knots/minimal wash
Overnight charge	Harbour Authority mooring or pontoon island: £14.50

Undoubtedly one of the classic havens of the entire South Coast, the small and beautiful River Yealm probably owes much of its unspoilt character to the fact that for many years the narrow and twisting entrance was a strong deterrent to visitors by sea, making it very difficult to enter under sail alone. With no beaches or attractions for holidaymakers other than the natural beauty of its wooded shores, it was still very undeveloped well into the 1930s, and it is only since the war that the small cottages have become highly desirable as holiday and retirement homes. Ironically, as reliable auxiliaries overcame the problem of the entrance, they inevitably created another, for the river is now so popular in the height of summer that it is often a very tight squeeze to find a berth.

The harbour is leased from the Crown Estate Commissioners and administered by the River Yealm Harbour Authority, a statutory non-profit-making organisation. In 1989 the Harbour Authority decided that, depending on the space available, the number of visiting boats would have to be restricted at the busiest times of the year, usually during spells of settled weather and particularly on summer Bank Holidays. In general terms this usually means about 90 boats, but obviously the size and type of vessels has a significant bearing on the total. It is therefore sensible to aim to arrive early if possible to avoid disappointment.

Don't be put off though. As long as you are not averse to rafting up, or are determined to have a secluded mooring all to yourself, the Yealm is undoubtedly

The inner reach, with *Temptress* lying on the large visitor mooring, left

another essential on any West Country cruise. Ideally, visit it early or late in the season when it is altogether a different place.

APPROACHES

In spite of the bar, the approach is not as difficult as it might at first seem, although the entrance to the river is totally hidden behind Misery Point. Care must be taken rounding Yealm Head from the east to avoid the Eastern and Western Ebb Rocks, which are just awash LAT three cables south-west of Garra Point. Normally they can be seen by the seas breaking, but are particularly insidious in calm weather. Keep a good half-mile off the shore and do not turn north into Wembury Bay until the church tower at Wembury is bearing 010°T.

Approaching from the west, the sloping pyramid of the Great Mewstone provides a fine landmark to locate the river, but keep clear of the Mewstone Ledge (least depth 2m), which extends a cable south-westward, and the Outer and Inner Slimers (drying 1.5m and 0.3m respectively) two cables east of the island. Continue eastwards until you are on the same 010°T bearing on Wembury Church and these will safely be avoided.

The bottom of Wembury Bay is uneven and rises quickly to around 6m LAT. This can produce very rough seas in strong winds from the south and west, when no approach to the river should be attempted – the safe and easy entrance to Plymouth is close by.

Holding 010°T, the first indication of the river mouth is usually other boats in the vicinity and, if the wind is off the land, vessels anchored in Cellar Bay. As Mouthstone Point draws abeam, the leading marks will be seen above and to the left of Cellar Beach – two white triangular beacons with a black line down the centre, giving a transit of 088.5°T to clear rocky Mouthstone Ledge which stretches west for one cable from the point.

This leading line does not clear the sand bar which dries 0.6m LAT and extends from Season Point. Its southern end is clearly marked by the red can Bar buoy (Fl R 5s), which should be left on your port hand. This is the only light in the river, so entry at night without local knowledge, except in ideal conditions and with a good moon, is not recommended, particularly on a first visit!

A green beacon with triangular topmark on a white backboard, perched almost opposite, marks the southern side of the 40m wide channel, and between the two there is a least depth of almost 3m LAT.

Once past the beacon, continue into Cellar Bay, where you will leave the second red can buoy (unlit), marking the eastern extremity of the bar, well to port before heading onto 047°T towards the square white leading mark with red vertical stripe, high in the gorse on the opposite cliff. If the weather is fair you can anchor off Cellar Beach where there is no charge; usually, though, it is crowded during the day.

Across this section of the river, on the lowest tides there will be no more than 1.2m of water until the sharp turn to starboard around Misery Point is completed and you are into the first inner reach. If in any doubt about the depth, do not attempt the entrance until a good hour after Low Water.

Yealm outer approach: the red Bar buoys are to port, the green beacon to starboard and the leading marks to the left of Cellar Bay

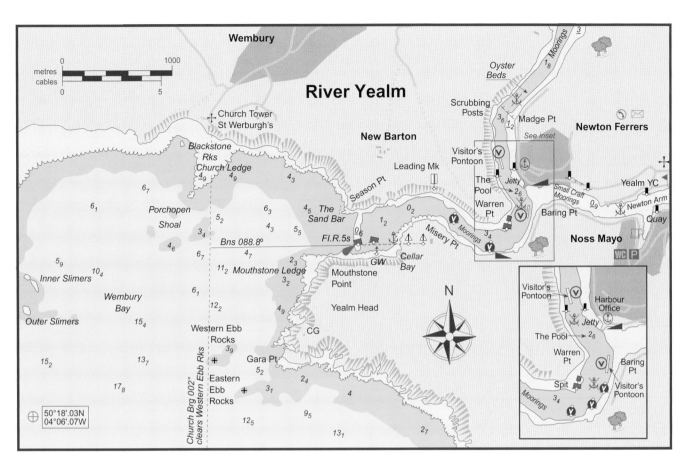

MOORINGS

Once inside Misery Point you enter a different world as the sea vanishes astern. The channel deepens to well over 2.5m and runs between steep-wooded banks, with little indication that there is any kind of settlement, other than the sudden proliferation of moorings. Due to the lack of swinging room, anchoring is not permitted anywhere in the river beyond Misery Point.

The first visitors' mooring, a red buoy with a heavy duty anti-chafe pick-up strop, is just east of Misery Point at the outer end of the local moorings. This is for larger craft (up to 18m/25 tons max). Continuing inwards down the fairway between the moorings, the red can Spit buoy is not always easy to spot until you're almost upon it. This marks the drying sandy spit extending south from Warren Point and, in spite of the buoy, this is a regular spot for unintentional grounding as there seems to be a compulsion for many to cut inside this port hand mark!

Opposite the Spit buoy, on the south side of the channel, are two 25 ton moorings which can accommodate up to three visitors at a time, red buoys marked 'visitor' again with heavy duty pick-up strops. A short distance further upstream on the starboard hand, the 150ft long visitors' pontoon can take up to about 26 rafted boats, with a maximum of three abreast on the deep water channel side. The overnight charge for using any of the harbour mooring facilities is £1.45 per metre.

Yealm visitors' moorings, right, and Spit buoy, left

You are now in the Pool, a fine landlocked natural haven surrounded by high hills, wooded right to the water's edge. However, though well protected from any seas, the inner river can be surprisingly dramatic in a bad blow, as the wind eddying round the high shores creates williwaws and very strong gusts. On several occasions in this seemingly perfect shelter, I have seen and experienced myself small craft laid over almost on their beam ends and great columns of spume and spray whipped off the water!

The river divides at the Pool, which is overlooked by the prominent Yealm Hotel. Newton Arm leads off to the east, while the Yealm itself continues northwards beyond Warren Point. Here another visitors' pontoon along the western, Wembury shore is situated, with the

A glorious mooring! Yealm Pool looking downstream from Yealm Steps

capacity to raft up to about 20 boats. In addition to the Harbour Authority facilities, there is also an unwritten understanding in the Yealm – where space is at such a premium – that visitors can pick up any vacant mooring providing there is no tender or note attached to it. However, if you do so, you should not leave your boat unattended without the prior approval of the harbour staff.

The harbourmaster and his staff are invariably out on the water first thing in the morning and after 1600 in the afternoon to assist with settling people in. If you pick up a vacant mooring during the day, nip ashore to the smart new harbour office, Tel: 01752 872533, at Yealm Steps by the main landing pontoon. You can land and leave your dinghy here, but do not obstruct the outer end of the pontoon where there is a fresh water hose, as this all-tide berth (least depth 2m) is kept clear for temporary stays of up to half an hour to take on water. There is also a holding tank pump-out facility on the pontoon – contact the harbour office if you wish to use it.

Alternatively, you can hail Bill Gregor's Water Taxi on VHF Ch 08 (Tel: 01752 880079), which operates daily from 1000 to 1600 subject to demand, and evenings only by prior arrangement.

The harbour office, an intriguing and sympathetically designed building perched on legs on the foreshore (Tel: 01752 872533), is normally manned from 0900 – 1200 daily during the season. There is no VHF watch, so if you wish to contact the harbourmaster at any other time you will either have to spot him on

the water, leave a message on the answerphone or post a note through his letterbox. Here you'll also find visitors' showers (£1 slotmeter) and toilets, a holding tank pump-out facility, local weather and tidal information and rubbish disposal – use the green bags provided and place it in the bins by the steps.

Due to the surrounding hills you might have problems with mobile phone access, there used to be a payphone at Yealm Steps but the nearest is now in the village by the post office. Should you have need to get to Plymouth, to catch a train perhaps, there is a convenient weekday bus service that leaves by the Yealm Hotel.

The Newton Arm dries almost completely, but two hours either side of High Water, the villages of Newton Ferrers, half a mile upstream on the northern shore, and the delightfully named Noss Mayo, opposite, can be reached by boats of average draught. At the head of the creek, another quarter of a mile or so, is a public quay at Bridgend and boats drawing up to 2m can get to it a couple of hours either side of High Water Springs. Here you will find berths alongside for scrubbing or repairs, with power and water available.

This and the other drying berths at Pope's Quay, Noss Mayo, can all be used on arrangement with the harbourmaster.

Bilge-keelers can dry out comfortably on the foreshore off Newton or Noss on reasonably hard ground. The centre of the creek should be kept clear, and take care to avoid the 'Voss', a tidal causeway which links the two villages at Low Water, as well as the clearly marked underwater power cables between Newton Ferrers and the eastern side of Noss Creek.

FUEL, FRESH WATER AND GAS

There is no diesel or petrol available in Newton Ferrers or Noss Mayo. The nearest fuel alongside is in Plymouth. Fresh water can be obtained from the hosepipe on the outer end of the Yealm Steps Pontoon. No Calor or Camping Gaz is available.

FACILITIES

From the Pool, Newton Ferrers is easily reached by dinghy if the tide permits or by a 10-minute walk along the pleasant footpath overlooking the steep sided creek. This bears off to the right of the road just a short distance up the hill from Yealm Steps. Alternatively, there are two landing places, Wide Slip and Parish/Kilpatrick Steps, opposite the visitors' pontoon on the south side of the entrance to Newton Arm. A delightful footpath leads through the National Trust woodlands to Noss Mayo.

Newton was presented to Henri de Ferrieres by William the Conquerer as a reward for his assistance in the Norman invasion, which explains the strange name – Noss derives from the Old English for promontory. Both villages have been very well preserved, although in recent years there has been an inevitable spread of modern bungalows and houses around them. Looking out over the creek, the older cottages are immaculately kept, the crisp whitewash emphasising doorways overhung with wisteria and roses. Their well-tended gardens are ablaze with flowers, and neat stone walls and lawns drop away to the water's edge.

Though small, Newton Ferrers has a post office/newsagent/general store, butcher, chemist and at the top of Newton Hill, a Co-op/off-licence and grocery (0800 – 2000 Mon – Sat, 0900 – 1900 Sun) with a cash machine. There are no shops or a post office in Noss Mayo, but there's a choice of three worthy pubs which also do good food – The Swan and The Ship at Noss, and The Dolphin on the foreshore at Newton Ferrers.

Close by, the fourth option is the Yealm Yacht Club, Tel: 01752 872291 or bar 0560 1125871; www.yealmyachtclub.co.uk, which is open every evening during the season (1800 – 2300), and lunchtimes Sat (1200 – 1500) and Sun (1200 – 1700). The club was founded in 1933, and visitors are very welcome to use its bar and showers (£1 slotmeter). Hot and cold bar meals are available as well as evening meals in the club's bistro restaurant. Call 01752 872232 to make a reservation. The Club also has WiFi and internet access available for a small fee.

The Yealm remains a quiet, relaxing sort of place. The walks in the surrounding woods and beside the river are lovely, reflecting the origins of the river's name which is Celtic for 'kind'. The Wembury shoreline and the larger part of the upper reaches are Sites of Specific Scientific Interest (SSSI) and the tidal reaches have been designated as a Special Area of Conservation (SAC). Much of the surrounding coastline and hinterland is owned by the National Trust.

The walk over Warren Point out to Season Point, which overlooks the river mouth, is particularly fine, with good blackberrying in late summer. It is a memorable spot to watch the sunset over Wembury Bay and the Mewstone. Alternatively, land at Parish Steps, turn right and follow the lower path past Ferry Cottage, through Passage Wood and then onto the coastal path which will take you out past Cellars Bay to Mouthstone and Gara Points. Enjoy the fine views of the mouth of the river, before continuing to the National Trust car park. From here it is possible to return along the road via Hannaford to Noss Mayo and back to Parish Steps along the creek. In all, it is a 7km circuit of about two hours.

THE UPPER REACHES

Beyond the Pool, the upper reaches are well worth a trip on the tide and in a small boat they are navigable for another two miles, although anchoring is prohibited throughout. Between Madge Point and the moorings further upstream at Thorn Pool the open area of water is reserved for recreational use, while along the shores there are extensive oyster beds marked by withies and small yellow and black marker buoys. The deepest water lies in the centre of the river and depths vary, with as little as 0.3m LAT in places.

Beyond the oyster beds, upstream of the marked underwater power cable, the river is all privately owned by the Kitley Estate. **Here, too, anchoring and also landing anywhere on the foreshore are totally prohibited**, as the owner is attempting to maintain it as a nature reserve. At Steer Point the river divides, Cofflete arm to port and the larger Yealmpton arm to starboard. Both are muddy and dry at Low Water, but these wooded and peaceful backwaters, rich in bird life, can be explored by dinghy on a rising tide.

Always popular, you will have to raft on the lower visitors' pontoon in Yealm Pool

River Yealm Port Guide – Area telephone code: 01752

Harbourmaster: Mr Robin Page, The Harbour Office, Yealm Road, Newton Ferrers PL8 1BN, Tel: 872533. Open 0900 – 1200 daily in season. Harbour staff afloat in launch early morning and evenings. Email: ryha@eclipse.co.uk; no website.

VHF: No radio watch.

Mail drop: c/o Harbour Office.

Emergency services: Lifeboat at Plymouth. Brixham Coastguard.

Anchorages: Cellar Bay in offshore winds.

Mooring/berthing: Harbour Authority has several swinging moorings to accommodate visitors from 18m – 7m LOA. Two visitors' pontoons. Local moorings available to visitors if unoccupied. Scrubbing/repair berths available alongside by arrangement with the harbourmaster.

Dinghy landings: By harbour office at Yealm Steps all-tide pontoon. Parish Steps, opposite visitors' pontoon. High water landing at Newton Ferrers slip, Noss Creek, Yealm Yacht Club, Bridgend Quay.

Newton Ferrers looking towards Noss Mayo. The picturesque upper reaches of the Yealm dry completely

Water taxi: Yealm Water Taxi, VHF Ch 8; Tel: 880079, from 1000 – 1600 during season, evenings by arrangement only.

Marina: None.

Charges: £1.45 per metre per night. Cheaper rates for longer periods and boats can be left by arrangement with the harbourmaster.

Phones: Outside post office, Newton Ferrers, and by Swan Inn, Noss Mayo.

Doctor: Health Centre Yealmpton, Tel: 880567. Out of hours emergency, Tel: 880392.

Hospital: Derriford, Plymouth, 10 miles, 24 hours casualty, Tel: 777111.

Churches: Newton Ferrers; Noss Mayo, both C of E.

Local weather forecast: At harbour office.

Fuel: None, nearest in Plymouth.

Gas: None, nearest in Plymouth.

Water: Hose at outer end of Yealm Steps pontoon at all states of tide. Maximum 20 minute stay.

Tourist Information Centre: None.

Banks/cashpoint: Co-op has cash machine.

Post office: Newton Ferrers.

Internet access: WiFi and internet access available through Yealm Yacht Club for small fee.

Rubbish: Bins by harbour office, Yealm Steps.

Showers/toilets: At harbour office, Yealm Steps; Yealm Yacht Club. Both have £1 slotmeter.

Launderette: None, but limited local facility at Briar Hill Farm campsite – ask at harbour office for directions.

Provisions: All basics available in Newton Ferrers, including meat, groceries, off-licence and chemist.

Chandler: None.

Repairs/marine engineer/ electronic engineers/ sailmakers: Enquire at harbour office.

Transport: Six buses a day, Tel: 222666, weekdays, to Plymouth (time table available at harbour office). Main line train connections at Plymouth, Tel: 08457 484950. Airport at Plymouth, Tel: 204090.

Taxis: Coombe Cabs, Tel: 872052; Bridge Cabs, Tel: 696969.

Car hire: None, but most national networks in Plymouth.

Car parking: Very restricted.

Yacht Club: Yealm Yacht Club, Riverside Road East, Newton Ferrers, Plymouth, Tel: 872291; www.yealmyachtclub.co.uk.

Eating out: Meals at pubs in Noss Mayo and Newton Ferrers. Evening meals at Yealm Yacht Club bistro

Things to do: Many good local walks; swimming at Cellar Beach; tennis court in Noss Mayo.

Fresh water tanks can be topped up on the outer end of Yealm Steps pontoon (left) at all states of the tide

Plymouth

Tides	HW Dover –0540. Standard Port
Range	MHWS 5.5m–MHWN 4.4m, MLWN 2.2m–MLWS 0.8m. Ebb streams can attain in excess of three knots in Narrows, and five knots in upper reaches of Tamar.
Charts	AC: 30, 1967, 1900, 1901, 1902, 871, SC5602.8&9; Stanfords: L13; Imray: C14, WCP 2400.13
Waypoints	Knap buoy 50°19'.56N 04°10'.02W. East Tinker Buoy 50°19'.20N 04°08'.30W
Hazards	Shagstone (unlit). Much commercial and Naval shipping. Strong tidal streams in places. Much of upper reaches dry
Harbour Speed limit	10 knots north of breakwater. Eight knots in Cattewater, five knots in approach to Sutton Harbour and QAB marina. Dead slow/no wash in all marinas
Overnight charges	Marinas: **Mayflower** £27.50; **QAB** £30; **Sutton** £30; **Yacht Haven** £28; **RWYC** mooring £12.50; **RPCYC** mooring £10; **Weir Quay** mooring £10

'Plymouth is a Naval and commercial port and has one of the finest natural harbours in the country. It is not frequently used by yachts. . .' When my predecessor, D J Pooley, was writing the original *West Country Rivers* in 1957, this paradox held true, and remained so for many years afterwards. Perfect for fleets of warships, the sheer physical scale of Plymouth had little to offer smaller craft, and apart from a few rather dirty commercial basins, there was never a really convenient place for visitors to lie. Most of the better anchorages are a long way from the town and are exposed in bad weather.

How things have changed! Today, there are four large marinas which have excellent facilities for visitors and a number of smaller marina and berthing options. Although still primarily a naval port with considerable commercial traffic, including regular ferries to Brittany and Spain and a busy fishing fleet, Plymouth has become internationally renowned as a premier yachting centre and the venue for a number of major events. These include the Single and Double Handed Transatlantic races as well as the Round Britain, and the city has been the finishing point for the often gruelling Fastnet race for over 70 years. It has also established itself as a popular location for club rallies and championship racing events, including powerboats.

Plymouth's expansive seafront, looking west from the Yacht Haven Marina and Mountbatten. Sutton Harbour and marinas are on the right, The Hoe, centre. The River Tamar is in the distance wending its way inland

OUTER APPROACHES

There are few natural hazards in the approaches to this vast harbour, which is bounded on the east by the Great Mewstone and Rame Head to the west. However, one danger to be aware of is the off-lying Shagstone on the eastern shore, which has an unlit beacon and is linked to the land by a partially submerged reef. Otherwise, the hazards are entirely man-made, with shipping and much naval activity the main considerations.

The port is under the jurisdiction of the Queen's Harbourmaster. All movements are controlled by the Longroom – the port's nerve centre – which is located in a tower just west of the entrance to Millbay Docks – VHF Ch 16 and 14, callsign *Longroom Port Control*.

Warships have the absolute right of way and if you are in any doubt about that the escorting MOD Police, in their RIBS and launches, will be onto you in a trice and you will be far from popular! It is not permitted to pass within 50m of berthed warships and 100m of berthed submarines. All warships and particularly submarines should not be approached within 200m when under way and you must cross astern by at least 800m. Under Schedule 2 Rule 2 of the Dockyard port of Plymouth Order 1999, '*all navigable waters north of 50° 20'.00N (in effect, the breakwater) shall be deemed a narrow channel. Vessels of less than 20 metres in length, sailing vessels and vessels engaged in fishing shall not impede larger vessels manoeuvring within the port.*'

In practice there is absolutely no reason why small craft should get embroiled with big ship movements in Plymouth, as for the most part there is no need to follow any of the deeper buoyed channels, there is plenty enough water and depth outside of them. Keep well clear and let common sense and good seamanship prevail, and keep aware of impending shipping movements by monitoring VHF Channel 14 while underway.

The Great Mewstone from the west

Plymouth eastern approach, with the Shagstone, centre

The vast open roadstead of Plymouth Sound was transformed as a fleet anchorage by the completion of Sir John Rennie's central breakwater in 1841. Just under a mile long, Plymouth Breakwater consumed four million tons of materials and took 29 years to build. The large round fort in the centre is its most conspicuous feature in daytime when the breakwater ends are not immediately easy to spot from well offshore. There is, however, a wide, safe passage around either end.

Plymouth's western breakwater light

FROM THE EAST: After passing the Great Mewstone, the Shagstone, a rock marked with an unlit white beacon, can be passed reasonably close, keeping you well east of the deep water channel, which is bounded on its western side by the Tinker shoal, least depth 3.5m.

This is marked on its eastern extremity by the East Tinker BYB east cardinal buoy (Q (3) 10s) and to the west by the West Tinker YBY west cardinal buoy (VQ (9) 10s). Although normally not a problem, seas break heavily on this shoal in southerly weather, when the western entrance is far better. Whidbey Light (Oc (2) WRG 10s 5M) on the eastern shore is the first of several complex sectored approach lights for the eastern deep water channel. The next, Staddon Point, east of the breakwater end, has a light beacon (Oc WRG 10s 8M) with R/W horizontal bands around its daymark base.

The eastern breakwater end is marked by a conical daymark surmounted by a beacon with round ball topmark and a sectored light (L Fl WR 10s 9m 8/6M) showing: Red 001° – 018°, White 018° – 190°, Red 190° – 353°, White 353° – 001°.

The East Tinker buoy lies in the narrow white sector and you soon pass into the red. Large ships will then come onto the leading lights situated on and to seaward of the Hoe, the upper Oc G 1.3s, the lower sector Q WRG, with the white sector covering the leading line of 349°T.

Once past the breakwater end, a YBY beacon with west cardinal topmark (Q (9) 15s) marks the eastern side of the deep water channel; closer inshore 2FG vert lights mark the outer end of Fort Bovisand pier. Several large Admiralty moorings are laid inside the breakwater, all of which are lit (Fl Y, 15s to 2s).

FROM THE WEST: Once past Rame Head keep to seaward of the Draystone red can south-east of Penlee Point (Fl (2) R 5s) and then steer straight for the lighthouse on the western end of the breakwater (Fl WR 10s 19m 12/9M, Iso 4s 12m 10M over sector 031° – 039°).

Plymouth Sound and approaches

CAWSAND ANCHORAGE

Cawsand Bay lies on your port hand providing an excellent anchorage in southwesterly and westerly weather, off the pleasant twin villages of Cawsand and Kingsand. This is a handy overnight stop on passage along the coast to avoid the detour into Plymouth and has the additional advantage of being free!

Anchor anywhere clear of the local moorings in about 2.5m with good holding, keeping well into the head of the bay to avoid the degaussing range limits as shown on the Admiralty chart. This extends well along the north-eastern side of Penlee Point and anchoring is

prohibited. At weekends Cawsand is a popular spot for local boats and is often very crowded.

Ashore the facilities are surprisingly good. A good selection of provisions, including fresh vegetable, frozen meat and off-licence will be found in Kingsand's Premier Store which is, amazingly, open every day 0630 – 2100! The Shop in the Square in Cawsand is mostly limited to takeaway food, including good pasties and baguettes. Shipshape in Kingsand has a small amount of chandlery and also houses the local post office, while Morans delicassen/café sells freshly baked bread and speciality cheeses. A public telephone

Colourful Kingsand, a very popular anchorage and handy on a coastal passage to avoid the detour into Plymouth

is situated up the road to the left of the prominent Kingsand clock tower.

There is definitely no shortage of eating and drinking places though, with four pubs – the Cross Keys, Halfway House, Rising Sun and Devonport – as well as the Cawsand Bay Hotel, which is open to non-residents!

Summer ferries operate to and from the Barbican, which is within easy walking distance of Plymouth City centre. If you follow the delightful coastal footpath through the Mount Edgcumbe Country park, Cremyll ferry to Plymouth is just over three miles away – about an hour's walk. It is advisable to leave someone on board, if such an expedition is planned, in case the wind hooks round to the east when you should get out fast and into the shelter of Plymouth before Cawsand becomes untenable.

PLYMOUTH SOUND

Approaching Plymouth from the breakwater, the most distinctive features are Drake's Island to the west, the large square hotel building in the centre, and to the east the high ground of Staddon Heights, topped with radio masts.

Two prominent forts sit on either side of the Sound just inside the breakwater, Picklecombe on the western shore, now luxury flats, and Bovisand, opposite, which is the British Sub-Aqua Club diving training centre. Two of 'Palmerston's Follies', they were built in the 19th century as part of a defensive chain of forts along the south coast in anticipation of a French invasion that never materialised. Two very noisy annual events now take place in the Sound, the British Power Boat Grand Prix in July and the National Fireworks Competition, a truly amazing display of pyrotechnics in August!

FUEL, FRESH WATER AND GAS

Diesel and petrol are available alongside at Queen Anne's Battery Marina (0830 – 1830) and Mayflower Marina (24hrs, but only accessible four hours either side of High Water depending on draught). Diesel only from Plymouth Yacht Haven (24hrs) and Sutton Marina (0830 – 1830 summer). See the Port Guide on page 118 for other sources further upriver. Fresh water can be obtained at all the marinas, as can Calor and Gaz (24hrs at Mayflower; from chandlery at Plymouth Yacht Haven).

ANCHORAGES AND BERTHING

Decide early where you intend to berth, as Mayflower Marina is to the west of the town centre; Sutton Harbour Marina, Queen Anne's Battery Marina and Plymouth Yacht Haven are to the east. The other alternatives depend very much on the prevailing weather conditions – either anchoring or picking up a mooring, although here the choice is very limited.

The anchorages in the Sound are all free, but suffer from the disadvantage that they are remote from the centre of Plymouth. The southern end of Jennycliff Bay, protected by Staddon Heights, provides good shelter in easterly weather, although you will often be subjected to strong and squally downdraughts. Sound in to about 2m at Low Water, well clear of the conical green buoy (Fl G 6s) marking the wreck of the MV Fylrix, which dries LAT. The inshore area to the north of the buoy, across Batten Bay, is a water-skiing area.

Both Drake's Island and Barn Pool afford shelter in westerly or southwesterly conditions and can be approached either by following the main deepwater channel round to the east of Drake's Island, or west of it by using the short cut across 'The Bridge', providing you have sufficient rise of tide.

THE BRIDGE, BARN POOL AND APPROACH TO MAYFLOWER MARINA

The water is shoal and littered with the dangerous remains of concrete wartime defences on both sides of the narrow passage through The Bridge. However, between them there is 1.7m LAT, and the channel is clearly marked by four lighted beacons: the outermost No 1 green, with a green conical topmark (QG), which should be left on your starboard hand, No 2 a red port hand beacon with red can topmark (QR), No 3 green with green conical topmark (Fl (3) G 10s) and the innermost, No 4 red with red can topmark (Fl (4) R 10s). Nos 1 and 4 have tide gauges, graduated in metres, indicating the height of tide above Chart Datum.

At Springs, the stream can run through here at three knots, so use the passage with caution, ideally no earlier than an hour or so after Low Water, and do not wander from the channel. Unless you have a good following wind, proceed under power.

Once through, Barn Pool lies to port, under the wooded Mount Edgcumbe shore. Deep water carries close to the pebbly beach, so sound in and anchor in about 3 – 4m. A trip line is recommended as there are many underwater obstructions and the southern end of the bay is foul, supposedly with the remains of an old sunken barge. Although eddies extend into the pool at times, you will lie here comfortably out of the main tidal stream.

This is a delightfully peaceful spot surrounded by the magnificent woods and grasslands of the 800-acre Mount Edgcumbe Country Park, which is free and open to the public daily. In this former deer park, Sir Richard Edgcumbe built Mount Edgcumbe House between 1547 and 1553. It survived a direct hit by bombs in 1941 and this fine red stone Tudor mansion was extensively restored between 1958 and 1964. It is open during the summer (1100 – 1700 Wed – Sun, entry charge), and a café in the old orangery normally operates during the summer. There is also a fine coastal footpath through

Overlooked by tranquil parkland, Barn Pool is another popular spot

the park which eventually takes you to Cawsand.

You can either stroll through the park or along the foreshore (except HW± 2hrs) to Cremyll for a pint at the Edgcumbe Arms, which also serves good food. Close by you will find Mashfords Cremyll Shipyard, a family business for many years, run by the six Mashford brothers from the 1930s until 2004 when it came into the current ownership. Both Chichester and Rose fitted out here for their circumnavigations, as well as Ann Davison in 1952 prior to her transatlantic crossing in *Felicity Ann*, a Mashford built 4-tonner. Described in her book *My ship is so small*, the epic voyage to New York in this 23 foot sloop took 254 days and established her as the first woman to sail the Atlantic single-handed.

Today Mashfords specialises in traditional and modern repair and restoration, and can slip vessels up to 325 tons on the largest of its six slipways. A regular passenger ferry runs from Cremyll to Stonehouse from where there are buses right into the centre of Plymouth.

The only other feasible anchorage lies north-east of Drake's Island, east of the pier, well clear of the local moorings and the underwater obstruction (least depth 0.9m), 400m due north of the pier. Reasonable shelter will be found in winds between south and west, but the proximity to the busy main channel can make it rolly at times. Once known as St Nicholas's Island, this is traditionally where Francis Drake lay with his battered *Golden Hind* on the return from his circumnavigation in 1580, cautiously waiting for news of the political climate that might greet him, before sailing on to be knighted at Deptford by Queen Elizabeth I.

Drake's Island is now privately owned and has been used in the past for a variety of purposes including adventure training, but is now uninhabited apart from a caretaker. Landing is not permitted.

Approaching the Bridge, a useful shortcut when the tide permits

MAYFLOWER MARINA

The Mayflower Marina, Tel: 01752 556633; www.mayflowermarina.co.uk, was the first in the south-west to be awarded the prestigious Five Gold Anchors by the Yacht Harbours Association in 1986, and still retains Four Gold Anchor status today. If tidal conditions are not suitable for The Bridge, you will have to pass to the east of Drake's Island and approach along the deep and well-lit Drake's Channel, leaving the conical green West Vanguard (Fl G 3s) buoy to starboard before heading on through the narrows between Cremyll and the orange and white beacon on Devil's Point (QG).

From here the modern buildings of Ocean Court and the forest of masts in the marina are unmistakeable – either call Mayflower Marina on VHF Ch 80, phone ahead for a berth allocation, or tie up in the reception berth on the outer pontoon and report to the office. This is clearly marked between the striped flags.

At night the marina has an approach light (Dir QWRG) and the south-eastern end of the outer pontoons is marked by 2 FR vert lights.

Much of the Mayflower's success is due to its ownership by a consortium of its berth holders. It has a particularly relaxed, quiet and friendly atmosphere and is a popular stop for long distance cruisers, giving it a genuinely international flavour. It is also a favoured venue for club rallies and cruises in company. Although its position away from the main centre of Plymouth would seem to be a disadvantage, it is in fact quite self-contained and the facilities are excellent. The Performance Yachting Chandlery & Store, Tel: 01752 565023, has been expanding fast under new ownership and stocks, among other things, locally sourced frozen meat – venison, beef, pork, bacon and sausages! As well as general groceries, it also has an off-licence and sells newspapers and magazines, fresh sandwiches, hot

Approaching the Mayflower Marina, Ocean Court is unmistakeable. Devil's Point is on the right

pies and pasties daily, and a wide range of chandlery. Moreover, it provides internet access. The shop is open 0800 – 1800 Mon – Sat (1730 Oct to Feb), 0900 – 1600 Sundays. The Brasserie café/bar and restaurant, Tel: 500008, is right on site, there are excellent self-contained showers, toilets and a good self service launderette.

Diesel, petrol, Calor and Gaz are available (seven days/24 hours) from the fuel berth, which is located on the eastern, inner side of the marina. For boats of average draught this is normally accessible four hours either side of High Water. To reach it, continue past the outer ends of the main pontoons and then bear round to port, where the fuel berth will be seen ahead next to the travelift dock. Leave the YBY west cardinal beacon (unlit), marking the outer end of the Cremyll ferry slipway, on your starboard hand.

Other facilities include electricity, latest weather information, WiFi broadband access at all berths (log on to www.mymarina.co.uk and click 'My Square Mile' on the homepage), marine and electronic engineers, riggers, a 1.5-ton crane and 33-ton travelhoist. The excellent 24-hour security makes it an ideal place to leave a boat for longer periods of time, and the marina tariff has a built-in discount rate for stays of over a week.

There are 396 deep water berths for up to 25m LOA and 4m draught, with about 30 for visitors, although even at the height of the season they always manage to fit you in somehow. Larger craft can usually be accommodated by arrangement if they call ahead. The overnight charge is £2 .75 per metre, including electricity, while a multihull surcharge of LOA x 1.5 will only be made where the vessel takes up two berths. A short stay of up to four hours will cost £3.50 an hour. There are competitive rates for stays of over a week and over a month. Mayflower Marina is also a member of TransEurope Marinas, a group of independent UK and European marina operators offering reciprocal berthing arrangements for their berth holders, who are entitled to a 50 per cent discount for the first five nights.

For a pleasant short evening stroll, leave the marina

Mayflower Marina is of easy access at the mouth of the River Tamar. Cremyll lies opposite, with Barn Pool to the upper left

Mayflower Marina enjoys a peaceful setting with fine views and sunsets to the west

entrance and turn left along the footpath opposite, which leads to Mutton Cove and into the public gardens bordering Mount Wise. Here, on the restored site of the 17th century Redoubt, there is a spectacular 40m high landmark feature – a futuristic stainless steel mast and viewing platform – created in 1999 as part of the Mount Wise Park regeneration. This striking structure is loosely derived from the historical use of the Redoubt as a signalling station during the early 1800s. It was the westernmost end of the chain of shutter telegraph stations that once linked Devonport and other naval bases, like Sheerness and Portsmouth, directly with London.

This form of visual communication comprised six pivoted rectangular boards that could be read at a great distance, the message being relayed onwards along a chain of 28 telegraph stations. The Admiralty in London could receive a reply from Plymouth within 20 minutes! After the shutter telegraph was discontinued in 1814, a mechanical semaphore mast was erected here to communicate with ships in the Hamoaze, and the two uppermost features of the new mast hark back to these semaphore arms.

Right opposite the marina, there is another piece of very prominent Naval heritage, the impressive Georgian buildings of the Royal William Victualling Yard. Designed by Sir John Rennie, this was completed in 1835 and, named after William IV, it provided all the essentials to keep the hungry fleet in food and drink. The brewhouse could produce 30,000 gallons of beer a day, the mill had the capacity to grind over 120,000 kilos of flour a week, and the slaughterhouse could deal with up to 80 head of cattle simultaneously. A large cooperage made barrels for salt beef, beer, spirits, water,

ships' biscuits and also gunpowder, all of which were ferried out to the Royal Naval ships in the Hamoaze and Dockyard in barges from the all-tide basin in the centre of the Yard. It closed in 1992, and after several ambitious plans, the Scheduled Ancient Monument began its new lease of life by undergoing a conversion into luxury apartments and offices, with ongoing developments including cafés, restaurants and shops. The yard is open to the general public and well worth a look: the architecture, a mixture of Portland stone and granite, is fabulous, and quite evidently, no expense has been spared. You can sit amongst all this splendour enjoying refreshment at Caffe Latte! The walk from the marina is not very inspiring so the best plan is to dinghy over to Freemans Wharf, just north of the Yard, and land at steps there.

APPROACHES TO QUEEN ANNE'S BATTERY MARINA, SUTTON HARBOUR MARINA, AND PLYMOUTH YACHT HAVEN

As you approach from seaward and pass to the east of Drake's Island, Plymouth Hoe lies ahead. It runs east-west and on its high grassy slope the old Eddystone lighthouse, banded horizontally red and white, and the tall obelisk of the war memorial, are both prominent. At its eastern end the conspicuous fortress of the Royal Citadel and below it the Royal Plymouth Corinthian Yacht Club (RPCYC), Tel: 01752 664327; www.rpcyc.com, overlooks the entrance to the Cattewater and Sutton Harbour.

The RPCYC extends a warm welcome to visitors

Queen Anne's Battery Marina, bottom right, lies in the approach to Sutton Harbour Marina, which is accessed by a 24 hour lock, centre. The impressive Citadel fortress and the Barbican are on the left

and has two daytime moorings off the clubhouse for temporary use (although they can be very rolly) and two visitors' moorings in the Cattewater available at £10 a night. The impressive clubhouse has spectacular views of Plymouth Sound and is open daily 0900 – 1500, 1800 – 2300 (closed all day Monday and Sunday evenings). The club monitors VHF Ch M (37) and is equipped with showers as well as a bar/restaurant with lunch menu that is available daily except on Mondays. Its elegant restaurant is open 1930 – 2230 Weds – Sat evenings, with a Sunday carvery lunch 1230 – 1430.

Directly opposite, Mount Batten is a promontory with an isolated hill and old artillery tower which dates from the 1600s. Formerly the RAF's area maritime base, it is now home to the Mount Batten Centre, a major regional dinghy sailing and watersports centre. This is run by an amalgamation of all the watersports organisations in Plymouth following the allocation of £4 million of lottery sports funding and European finance at the end of 1997. It was opened by Prince Philip in 1999.

The surrounding area, which had been closed to the public since it was requisitioned in 1916, has since been landscaped with walks, viewpoints, picnic spots, a refurbished breakwater and the Mount Batten Bar and Shaw's Restaurant. If more clues as to who lived here are needed, look at the street names hereabouts – Shaw Way and Lawrence Road – for this is where TE Lawrence arrived in 1929 to spend four years seeking anonimity as Aircraftsman Shaw after his First World War activities in Arabia.

Mount Batten was originally a seaplane base and became home to two squadrons of flying boats during the 1920s, for which the large hangers were built. From 1952 onwards it was an air-sea rescue training centre, finally closing in 1992. The west hanger is now the base for two boat building companies, while the east hanger is part of the Plymouth Yacht Haven complex. Access is by a regular water taxi service from the Barbican.

The long Mount Batten breakwater extends towards a large dolphin on the Mallard Shoal (least depth 3.5m) and a somewhat confusing cluster of buoys marking the deep water channel. The dolphin has a triangular white topmark surmounted by a sectored light (QRWG) and is the lowest of the two leading marks for the main deep water channel. The upper, a beacon with white triangular topmark and Oc G light, is on the eastern side of the Hoe, giving a transit of 349°T. In practice there is no need for small craft to follow this line – instead pass between the South Mallard YB south cardinal buoy (VQ(6) + Fl 10s) and the end of Mount Batten breakwater (2FG vert) into the Cobbler Channel.

Ahead, Queen Anne's Battery Marina (known locally as QAB) has a breakwater fronted by vertical piling, with a red and white horizontally-striped beacon and red spherical topmark with (FR) light on the southern side. This is the front mark of a leading line (048.5°) for the Cobbler Channel approach, with the rear light (Oc R 8s) situated in the small clock tower on top of the marina building/RWYC clubhouse. The breakwater also has an Oc G 8s light on the south-western corner, and a Fl (2) G 5s light on the inner breakwater end on its southern side. Both QAB and Sutton Harbour are approached past Fisher's Nose, a granite quay on the western shore with *Speed Limit 8 knots to the east* painted on it and a Fl (3) R light at night. You must proceed under power in Sutton Channel (to the north of Fisher's Nose). This is always a busy corner as most of the large trip boats operate from here, besides which it is also the entrance to two marinas and the fishing harbour.

The River Plym continues eastwards, its mouth known as the Cattewater, which is commercial and administered separately by the Cattewater Harbour Commissioners. Due to the local congestion, anchoring is prohibited here. Plymouth Yacht Haven soon comes into view on your starboard hand, extending from Mount Batten across Clovelly Bay, the southern shore of the Cattewater. Beyond it, the houses and foreshore of Turnchapel are just under a mile upstream. Vessels proceeding to and from the marina pass through the approaches to Cattedown Wharves, so maintain a vigilant lookout and keep well clear of the deepwater channel and larger vessels at all times. A mile further on, the road bridge at Laira has a 5m clearance, which effectively closes the river to all but small craft.

QUEEN ANNE'S BATTERY MARINA

To enter, keep to the starboard side of the channel and follow the marina breakwater, watching out for and giving way to boats emerging, as they have priority.

Opened in 1986 and taking its name from the former use of the site as a gun emplacement built during the Napoleonic War, Queen Anne's Battery Marina, Tel: 01752 71142; www.mdlmarinas.co.uk, is run by Marina Developments Ltd. Call *QAB* on VHF Ch 80 or phone ahead to request a berth – around 40 are normally available for visitors alongside the continuous pontoon on the inside of the breakwater, although at the height of the season you will probably have to raft up. The finger piers are all reserved for the 235 permanent berth holders, but may be allocated to visitors if berth holders are away. The overnight charge is £3 per metre for craft up to 15m and £3.50 per metre for those over 15m. A short stay will cost £10.

Water and electricity are available on the pontoons, all of which are accessed through coded security gates. MDL WiFi internet access is also provided. Diesel and petrol are available from the fuel station (0830 – 1830) on the outer pontoon, adjacent to the marina entrance. Ashore you will find showers with coded access and toilets, as well as a launderette. Situated by the marina office in the main building overlooking the marina are a small provisions shop, which also sells ice, the ever popular Chandlers Bar and Bistro, Tel: 257772,

and The Sea Chest, Tel: 222012, an excellent new and secondhand maritime bookshop and Admiralty Chart agent. Also on site, beyond the large car park you'll find Sound Bites Café, ideal for a hearty breakfast or lunch, Yacht Parts Plymouth chandlers, Tel: 252489, Dinghy & Rib Warehouse, Tel: 222265, and Waypoint 1 Marine Electronics, Tel: 661913. Other marine-orientated businesses encompass a broad spectrum from liferaft repairs to stainless steel fabrication, diving air to sailmakers and riggers. There is a large slipway adjacent to the marina with a 25-ton travelhoist for haul out, scrubbing and repairs.

The Royal Western Yacht Club of England (RWYC), Tel: 01752 660077; www.rwyc.org, founded in 1827, is the fifth oldest yacht club in England. In early 1989 it moved to its smart premises on the first floor of the marina building after 25 years at the western end of the Hoe in the building that is now the Waterfront Restaurant. RWYC has four visitors' moorings in the Cattewater available on application (£12.50 a night), and visitors are welcome to use the club (open 0900 – 2300), as well as its showers, bar and popular restaurant .

QAB is a major venue for international yachting events, most of which are organised by the RWYC, such as the Round Britain and Ireland Race, Fastnet finish and, of course, the OSTAR Singlehanded Transatlantic race, which has taken place regularly since 1960 when Lt Col 'Blondie' Haslar's idea came to fruition. Just five yachts set out and it was won by Francis Chichester in *Gypsy Moth III*. The numbers have grown to in excess of 50 starters over the years and the next will take place in 2009.

During these big race events, space at QAB is inevitably at a premium and it is unlikely that you will find a berth without a prior booking.

The main nautical centre of Plymouth, the Barbican, and access to the rest of the city lie just across the water

Visitors to Queen Anne's Battery Marina usually berth on the pontoon along the inside of the breakwater

and can be reached easily on foot. Turn left at the main marina entrance and follow the road, then footpath past the National Marine Aquarium, which overlooks the marina. This large and fascinating complex demonstrates the circulation of water from a stream on Dartmoor to coastal reefs, deep oceans and coral reef, and includes a large shark tank. It is a favourite tourist attraction, so during the height of the season you will probably have to queue to get in! The swing bridge across the entrance lock into Sutton Harbour takes you right into the Barbican.

Barbican Leisure Park in Coxside is also within easy reach, providing a variety of diversions including a multiplex cinema, superbowl ten pin bowling, a health club and a variety of bars, restaurants and clubs.

SUTTON HARBOUR MARINA

Sutton Harbour, for years the base of the Plymouth fishing fleet and sea-angling boats, became home to the first marina to be built in Plymouth in 1973 when Sutton Harbour Marina, Tel: 01752 204702; www. suttonharbourmarina.com, was established. In those days the harbour, which is privately owned by the Sutton Harbour Company, was tidal and, although dredged, much of the periphery dried. However, that all changed dramatically in 1993 when the 44m long x 12m wide lock was opened as part of the Barbican flood prevention scheme, which now maintains an approximate depth of 3.5m above Chart Datum within Sutton Harbour. This large area of enclosed water has had a considerable impact on the surrounding regeneration of the area, with the building of new apartments, bars and cafés with alfresco seating on the quaysides, and a major expansion of the marina, which is now the largest in Plymouth with 467 berths.

Entry and exit through the lock are available 24 hours daily and are free of charge. Towards High Water the gates remain open to allow free flow, although the footbridge still has to be opened to accommodate craft with masts. Otherwise, the lock and footbridge are opened on request by the Harbour Control Office, which overlooks the lock on the eastern side (VHF Ch 12,

Sutton Harbour lock opens on request day and night and has convenient pontoons for transit berthing

Sutton Lock). If without VHF, stand by in the immediate vicinity, noting the traffic light signals displayed from the lock entrance: three vert red = STOP; three vert green = GO; three flashing red = serious hazard, WAIT.

Transit is made easy with floating pontoons for temporary berthing inside the lock. At night, the lock is floodlit and the entrance is indicated by reflective chevrons, R/W to port, G/W to starboard.

Sutton Harbour Marina, the centrepiece for an area of major regeneration

Once inside Sutton Harbour, the old fishmarket and Barbican quays lie on your port hand, along with West Pier Marina, which is mostly given over to local berth holders. The large new fishmarket is to starboard and Sutton Marina is dead ahead, with the visitors' arrival berth clearly marked on the outer end, adjacent to the fuel pontoon. At night the eastern end of the outer pontoon displays a red light (QR). Guys Quay Marina, again mostly for local berth holders, is in the inlet to the left of the main Sutton Harbour Marina. Subject to availability, Sutton Harbour Marina can accommodate between 25 and 30 visitors (maximum 21m LOA). It is always best to contact them in advance, especially during the season; a 24-hour VHF watch is maintained on VHF Ch 16 and 12, callsign Sutton Harbour Marina, or telephone ahead. The marina office is located right at the end of Sutton Pier, overlooking the fuel pontoon.

On-site facilities include very luxurious showers, toilets, launderette and 24-hour security. Marine & Leisure chandlery, Tel: 268826, is located on Sutton Pier beside the marina, with shops and the facilities of the Barbican just a short walk around the quayside, including the Sutton Marina Club, bar and restaurant just opposite the marina entrance. Water is available on the pontoons, and the diesel fuel berth is open daily (0830 – 1830 in summer, daylight hours in winter). Calor and Gaz are available. The overnight charge includes electricity and is based on £3 per metre LOA bands, a boat between 10m and 10.9m for instance will cost £30 per night, 11m to 11.9m, £33, et al, with reduced rates for longer stays. Short stays (max four hours), irrespective of size, are £10.

Close by on the eastern side, Harbour Marine's comprehensive boatyard has a 25-ton slipway hoist, a crane and full repair facilities. Here, you will also find the Shipwrights Arms and the China House Restaurant which, in spite of its name, is not a Chinese restaurant!

PLYMOUTH YACHT HAVEN

The 450-berth Plymouth Yacht Haven, Tel: 01752 404231; www.yachthavens.com, which opened in April 1998, lies in Clovelly Bay immediately to the east of Mount Batten and is easily approached through the entrance to the Cattewater. Call *Plymouth Yacht Haven* on VHF Ch 80 for berthing instructions or Tel: 01752 404231. Visitors normally lie on pontoons P6, P7 and P8, the section of the outer marina breakwater immediately adjacent to the shore, the first you will see as you approach, and clearly marked by signs. Here berths of up to 20m are available and larger vessels can be accommodated by arrangement. Overnight visitors' charges are £2.80 per metre inclusive of electricity, with reduced rates for longer stays.

Facilities include showers and toilets with coded access, a laundry (tokens from reception), telephones, an internet café in the marina reception, as well as WiFi: visit www.myoceanwave.com. There is excellent 24-hour security, Mob: 07721 498422, which also monitors VHF Channels 80 and 37, and coded access gates to the marina.

In the nearby eastern hanger Mount Batten Boathouse, Tel: 482666, is open seven days a week and has a large selection of chandlery and electronics. It also provides a marine engineering and electronics service and supplies Calor and Gaz. Diesel is available (24 hours) from the fuel berth, which is equipped with a holding tank pump-out facility.

The hefty 65-ton travel hoist is the largest in the area and there is a significant amount of laying up space and undercover storage. Other services include Hemisphere Riggers, Tel: 07790 225511, Yacht Rigging Services, Tel: 0800 9158609, and Slik Cut Sailmakers, Tel: 401904. Boat repairs, stainless fabrication, heating/air-conditioning and upholstery specialists are all located in the eastern hanger. The Bridgend Boat Company and Western Marine Power occupy the western hanger.

Plymouth is easily accessed using the regular Yellow Boat water taxi service, Tel: 07930 838614, to the Barbican from the Mount Batten landing stage. Weather permitting, the taxi leaves Mountbatten on the hour and half hour, and leaves the Barbican at a quarter to and a quarter past the hour. During the season it runs 0745 – 2300 Mon – Thurs (2315 Fri), 0845 – 2315 Sat and 0845 – 2230 Sun.

The nearest supermarket is at the broadway shopping centre, Plymstock, about 10 mins on No 7 bus from the marina entrance, departing every 20 mins. Alternatively, there is a mini-market/post office in

Mount Batten protects the entrance to the Cattewater and the approach to the large Plymouth Yacht Haven complex in Clovelly Bay. The convenient water taxi to the Barbican uses the jetty closest to the long breakwater

Still within easy reach of the city, Plymouth Yacht Haven provides a quieter alternative for visitors

Hooe, which is only a 10-minute walk away.

Right by the Mount Batten Boathouse, Café Crew has a limited stock of provisions and is a handy spot for breakfast and lunch, and if you walk around the back of the hangers you'll find Val's Galley Café and takeaway. The marina is due to open its own onsite bar/restaurant, The Bridge, in 2008. The nearby Hotel Mount Batten has a bar, restaurant and carvery, Tel: 405500, while the foreshore walkway from the marina followed by a footpath take you within a few minutes to Turnchapel village where the traditional Boringdon Arms and Clovelly Bay Inn both serve good value pub meals.

THE BARBICAN
(Local phone code 01752)
The bustling and historic area of the Barbican is the tourist centre of Plymouth and is where the Pilgrim Fathers embarked aboard the *Mayflower* and sailed for the New World in 1620, although there is an ongoing debate as to whether this was indeed their last port of call (see Newlyn on page 190)! This proud naval city was blitzed more heavily than anywhere else in Britain during the last war and, with large areas being completely destroyed, only the Barbican remains as an example of what this medieval city was like before 1941. It is a maze of intricate narrow streets, with fine examples of Tudor buildings, many of which are now shops – including a handy grocery mini-mart/off-licence.

The cosmopolitan mix of bistros and restaurants ranges from seafood at Piermasters, Tel: 229345, Joined up Whiting, Tel: 665325, or Barbican Seafood and Pasta Bar, Tel: 671299, and steaks and fish at Platters, Tel: 227262, to Italian at Zucca Brasserie, Tel: 224225, Greek cuisine and fish at the Village Restaurant, Tel: 667688, Japanese at Yukisan, Tel:254240, and Indian at the Jaipur Palace, Tel: 668711. Cafés and bars

with alfresco seating, such as Bacaro, Rakuda, Cider Press, Smokey Joes and The Blues Bar, have sprung up all around the quayside. Pubs include The Dolphin, Maritime Inn and Three Crowns, all of which are very lively at the weekend. No visit to the Barbican is quite complete without a massive bacon sandwich and steaming mug of tea from Captain Jaspers right on the quayside!

Along with the café culture, the interesting and attractive area surrounding Sutton Pool has definitely come alive with a dramatic proliferation of art galleries and antique shops. There are several museums, including the Elizabethan House in New Street, and nearby the 16th century Merchant's House in St Andrew's Street, which houses the Museum of Plymouth History (weekdays 1000 – 1300, 1415 – 1730, 1700 on Saturdays).

Plymouth fishmarket was the focal point of the old quayside until 1995 when the business was transferred to the new buildings on the opposite side of Sutton Harbour. Since then the old fishmarket has been stylishly transformed into an intriguing tourist attraction – the Barbican Glass Works – where the public can watch skilled Dartington glassmakers producing the goods, and hopefully buy them too!

In Southside Street, the former Dominican Priory where the Pilgrim Fathers reputedly spent their last night in England is now part of the premises of the famous Plymouth Gin Distillery. Established in 1793, it is famed as the basis for Royal Naval officers' pink gins. Guided tours are available Mon – Sat throughout the season, and a Beefeater restaurant/pub, Tel: 224305, is located within the distillery.

THE CITY OF PLYMOUTH
Plymouth has a population of over 250,000 and the city centre is 10 minutes' easy walk from the Barbican. The post-war redevelopment of the main shopping area surrounding Royal Parade is mostly redbrick and architecturally unimaginative, with wide boulevards and large shopping precincts; somehow one feels a great opportunity was lost in the rebuilding. There has been a new wave of recent activity though, with the opening of the Drake's Circus undercover shopping centre, in the heart of the town. In this extravagant temple to retail therapy, you'll inevitably find most of the mainstream fashion retailers, but there is also a Boots and M&S. The older Armada Centre on the far side of the town centre has a large Sainsbury's supermarket or, alternatively, there's a Tesco Metro in New George Street. Both are a taxi ride from the marinas, but useful if you're planning a major provisioning expedition.

Yet more pubs and restaurants abound – everything from Burger King to expensive brasseries! But if you're weatherbound with a restless family there are plenty of shoreside diversions – two multi-screen cinemas, the famous Theatre Royal, Plymouth Pavilions (swimming and ice skating) and ten pin bowling, as well as the City Museum and Art Gallery. It is also a convenient place to leave the boat for a day or two if you wish to hire a car and explore south Devon – Dartmoor is within easy reach. The main line railway station is to the north of the city centre, while the Bretonside bus and coach station, situated between the Barbican and the city centre, is nearer.

However, in contrast to the mid-20th century centre, the seafront is a grand spectacle. It is a short walk from the Barbican – follow Madeira Road up past the Citadel, and the elevated promenade winds beneath the grassy slopes of the Hoe, overlooking the rocky foreshore and cliffs below, which are dotted with bathing platforms, pathways and the large, restored Art Deco Tinside Lido open-air swimming pool.

If you're feeling particularly energetic, seek out the full Plymouth Waterfront Walk, which was created in 1999 to celebrate Plymouth's history and its waterfront. It runs from Admiral's Hard, Stonehouse, opposite the Mayflower Marina, all the way to Mount Batten and Jennycliff. Points of interest along the way are highlighted with features and plaques, and full details and a map can be obtained from the Plymouth Tourist Information Centre in the Barbican, Tel: 01752 306330; www.visitplymouth.co.uk.

Climbing higher onto the open space of the Hoe, the views across the Sound from this natural grandstand are magnificent, and even more so if you pay to climb the extra 72 feet to the top of Smeaton's former Eddystone lighthouse, which is open daily in season from 1000 – 1600, adults £2, children £1 (free if under 5). It was built in 1759, dismantled in 1882, and rebuilt on the Hoe in 1884, and its continuing longevity was assured in 2000 when £400,000 was donated from the Heritage Lottery Fund towards its restoration.

Sir Francis Drake's remarkable display of sang-froid – contentedly playing on as the vast Spanish Armada sailed unchallenged into the Channel – means that the Hoe, bowls and Drake will forever remain synonymous. Far more a seaman than a bowls player, Drake knew only too well that his ungainly ships could not leave the Sound against the head wind until the ebb began . .

THE HAMOAZE AND BEYOND

One of the real advantages of Plymouth if the weather turns against you is the great potential for exploring further inland along the Rivers Tamar and Lynher. Heading west past the Hoe, Millbay Docks is commercial and of no interest to visitors. It is the

The powerhouse of Plymouth's heritage, Devonport's Royal Naval Dockyards dominate the lower Tamar

terminal for the RoRo ferries to Roscoff and Santander, and care should be taken when these large vessels are entering and leaving.

On the starboard side of the docks' entrance, the cluster of masts belongs to boats moored in Plymouth's fifth marina, Millbay Marina Village, owned by MDL. This is private and has no facilities for visitors, except for berth holders at other MDL-owned marinas, but only by prior arrangement (phone ahead on Tel: 226785). Plymouth lifeboat is based within this marina.

Beyond the Narrows and the Mayflower Marina you enter the wide Hamoaze, its curious name derived from the thick mud that once oozed out of Ham Creek, long since buried beneath the extensive Royal Naval Dockyards that line the eastern Devonport shore. Established by King William III in 1691, these are now privately run by Devonport Management Ltd (DML), which is better known in the sailing world for the fleet of 16 identical 67ft racing yachts that were built here (1990 – 1992) for Chay Blyth's around-the-world British Steel Challenge. More recently 12 new 72-footers were launched for the 2001 BT Global Challenge, and the company has become increasingly involved in building and developing lifeboats for the RNLI, which incorporate the Severn and latterly the Tamar class. Specialist vessels, including smaller warships and superyachts, are other areas of its expertise.

This is always a fascinating stretch of water, particularly for younger crew members, as there are invariably a variety of warships and submarines berthed along the quays. For the skipper, however, it is a more demanding exercise as it is usually busy and a careful eye should be kept on other ship movements. **Remember, too, that civilian craft are not permitted to pass within 50 metres of military vessels or Crown Property or enter the dockyard basins**.

The large figurehead of King William III at the southern end of the dockyards is known locally as King Billy. Behind him, the sizable covered slipway is the oldest in any of the former Royal dockyards and, as you pass upstream, the first group of three huge sheds is the undercover frigate repair facility, while the next complex with the big crane is where Britain's nuclear submarines are refitted.

Large chain ferries link Devonport with Torpoint on the Cornish shore and, until 1962 when the Tamar road bridge was opened at Saltash, a mile further upstream, these and the Saltash chain ferry were the only road links across the river. The ferries have right of way and display flashing orange lights at their forward end to indicate the direction in which they are moving. Give them a good berth.

In contrast the western shore is much less developed, and beyond Mashfords Shipyard the shallow drying inlet of Millbrook Lake stretches away to the west for over a mile to the village of Millbrook, making an interesting diversion for shallower draught boats on the flood, ideally three hours after Low Water.

Initially the channel heads directly for the buildings and slipways at Southdown Marina, on the northern side of the creek where there are moorings and pontoon berths that dry out in soft mud at Low Water. Visitors' berths are £17.50 per day, but it is usually best to phone ahead to check availability, Tel: 01752 823084; www.southdownmarina.com. This is a peaceful sort of backwater, shore facilities include toilets, showers, telephone, washing machine and tumble drier, diesel and fresh water. The marina is run by the Huggins Bros Marina Group, a local private business, which also owns Torpoint Yacht Harbour and the boatyard at Carbeile Wharf, both just a short distance further up the Tamar.

Southdown Marina's location has a fascinating history – the old quays first date from 1650 when a gunpowder factory was established here, while during the early 1700s the King's Brewhouse was also constructed on this site to provide ale for the Navy (it was used in preference to water as it tended to keep better!) In its heyday over 20,000 gallons a week were produced and shipped across the water to the fleet at Devonport! A pleasant walk from Southdown will lead you to the village of Millbrook, one mile away.

Continuing afloat beyond Southdown, steer south-east towards the prominent house beneath the woods on the southern shore, which has the road running in front of it. As you pass this, bear west again, leaving both the black post with yellow 'X' topmark and the line of boats on green mooring buoys on your starboard hand, at which point you will see a long pontoon on your starboard bow extending from Foss Quay. This was once the site of a large brickworks and is now the home of the Multihull Centre Services Boatyard, Tel: 01752 82390; www.multihullcentre.co.uk, run by Pip and Debbie Patterson, names well-known in the multihull world. If there is space on the pontoon, berth here and make contact with the office, otherwise berth alongside the quay. In both places you will dry at Low Water.

Visitors are welcome to stay for up to two nights free of charge, after which they will have to pay £9 a night up to 30ft, £10 up to 40ft, £11 over 40ft. Commensurate weekly rates are £40, £50 and £60.

The yard can provide showers and toilets, chandlery, repairs, diesel in cans, water and rigging, as well as a crane. It also has a pick up box for Westaway Sails for repair and valeting.

It's an easy walk to Millbrook, which takes its name from the tide mill that once operated here. There's a a good Spar store/post office with a cash machine, a Co-op with 24 hour cashpoint, an organic wholefood grocer/greengrocer, newsagent, chemist, fish and chip café, and three pubs with memorable names – The Devon & Cornwall Inn, The Mark of Friendship and the Heart in Hand, all of which serve food! The village hall is home to a computer centre where you can access the internet.

Transport services comprise two local taxi firms and a good bus link to Plymouth via Torpoint and Cremyll, should you need to get there!

Continuing northwards beyond the entrance to Southdown Lake there is little of interest along the western shore – the wide but mostly drying expanse of St John's Lake stretches away towards the modern buildings of *HMS Raleigh*, the Royal Navy recruit training establishment. St Johns Lake is now an SSSI, but at one time it was used by Royal Navy ships, moored in the entrance to the creek, for random firing practice: you did not have to scrape much off the surface of the mud to uncover cast iron cannon balls, lead musket balls and bullets!

Torpoint Yacht Harbour nestles within the massive walls of an old Ballast Pound

The second Huggins Bros Marina, Torpoint Yacht Harbour, Tel: 01752 813658; www.torpointyachtharbour. co.uk, is on the western shore just south of the Torpoint ferries and is located inside the old Ballast Pound, built in 1783 to shelter and load the barges once used to carry rock ballast out to ships that were sailing light of cargo. This impressive square compound has walls 20ft thick, is dredged to 2m inside, and has 80 pontoon berths with full tidal access. The drying berths alongside the shoreside quay wall are accessible about three hours either side of High Water. A few pontoon berths can usually be allocated to visitors, but it is best to phone ahead for availability. A boat up to 35ft will cost £25 per night. Swinging moorings are also sometimes available off the Yacht harbour at £15 per night. Water, electricity, showers, toilets and WiFi are all provided.

Carbeile Wharf, The Huggins Bros Marina group's boatyard, is located in a drying inlet on the northern side of St John's Lake, just behind Torpoint, and is accessed from the buoyed channel leading to *HMS Raleigh* (see map on its website www.hugginsmarine.com). Facilities include a boat hoist, cranes, marine engineer, repairs and onshore storage.

Torpoint's name derives from Tar Point – originally a careening beach where vessels could be caulked and tarred. Today most normal provisions can be obtained in the town centre, just a few minutes walk away from the yacht harbour, and the Torpoint Mosquito Sailing Club, Tel: 812508; www.tmsc.org.uk, is situated right next door. Established in 1891, it derives its curious name from the Mosquito class of boats that evolved from local gaff-rigged workboats into the club's first racing fleet in the 1890s. Sporting innovative lifting keels and rudders, and furling headsails, these 16 and 18-footers with a sail area of 350sq ft were quite a handful but keenly raced! The club's best known member in recent years is Pete Goss, and visitors are always welcome to its friendly bar and good value restaurant.

THE LYNHER/ ST GERMAN'S RIVER

The Lynher or St German's River is the first opportunity to get away from the bustle of the Hamoaze. Its wide mouth opens to port, upstream of the dockyards, beyond the large warship moorings. The river dries extensively, but is navigable on the tide for four miles to the private quay at St German's where it is possible for bilge-keelers to dry out or larger boats to lie alongside by arrangement.

There are a few buoys in the lower part of the river; leave red cans to port and conical green buoys to starboard when navigating upriver. The channel enters along the northern side, past Wearde Quay, where there are local moorings and the first port hand buoy 'Lynher Entrance'(Q R). This and a second red buoy clear Beggars Island, a gravelly shoal awash at High Water Springs on the southern side of the entrance. Just east of Sand Acre Point and the first green buoy, you will find a possible anchorage, but the proximity of the main line railway tends to disturb the peace.

The channel next trends south to avoid the spit extending from the northern shore, marked by another green buoy, and you pass a number of moorings belonging to the RN School of Seamanship at Jupiter Point, a wooded promontory with a jetty and pontoons.

The next red buoy is close to the northern shore, off Antony Passage, and it is possible to anchor off the mouth of Forder Lake. West of Forder Lake, as far as the next creek, Wivelscombe Lake, an underwater power

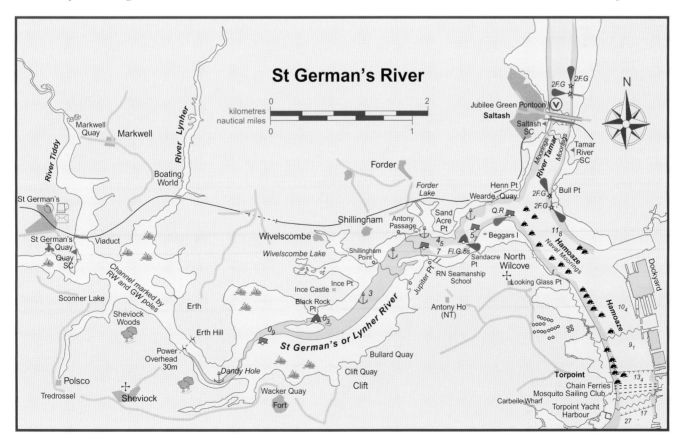

St German's Quay

between Warren Point and the bend, there is a fine and isolated anchorage in Dandy Hole, a fortuitous pool with about 3m. Overlooked by high woods, this is as peaceful a spot as you are likely to find, well sheltered and totally away from it all.

From Dandy Hole to St German's the river dries completely and is easiest to scout by dinghy. The wooded shores open out again and the twisting channel is marked by red posts to port, green to starboard, swinging from the eastern shore above Erth Hill to the western shore off Sconner Lake, then north to a striped middle ground pole where the Rivers Lynher and Tiddy part company. The latter heads west towards St German's Quay, sitting dwarfed beneath the impressive arches of the long railway viaduct across the river.

The channel of the Lynher continues north, marked by occasional white posts, before passing under another railway viaduct (21m clearance) beyond which Boating World, Tel: 851679, is situated. Here you will find a large number of second hand craft, along with a sailmaker, café, chandler, marine engineer, 10-ton hoist and 35-ton crane. Normally this is accessible for boats of moderate draught from half flood onwards.

At St German's there are a number of drying moorings off this private quay, and other local boats in berths alongside on the soft mud. Downstream of the old warehouse buildings where the Quay Sailing Club is based, no berthing is allowed, but upstream, space can sometimes be found for an overnight stay alongside by arrangement with the club. A noticeboard displays a phone number to contact when the club is closed

cable and gas pipeline cross the river and anchoring is therefore not permitted.

Ince Point, on the western side of Wivelscombe Lake, is surmounted by Ince Castle, and south of it there is another anchorage in about 3m. At high tide this is a broad expanse of water, surrounded by lush fields and gently rolling hills, peaceful and unspoiled, with very little evidence of human intrusion. However, from here depths reduce considerably, with generally less than 1m, and drying banks are extensive on both shores. The various salty creeks are ideal for dinghy exploration.

The best is yet to come! Explore further on the flood, but with a wary eye on the sounder, and keep close to the next green buoy off Black Rock Point, where the channel narrows considerably. At the next red can the shores ahead close in, becoming steep and wooded along Warren Point, the river disappearing as it turns tightly behind the rounded slope of Erth Hill. Here,

An early morning run ashore – Dandy Hole at its very best!

– normally it is open on Wednesday evenings and at weekends. Services include a small dinghy landing pontoon alongside the quay and a water tap by the club.

This is a peaceful corner with just a few cottages and the old grassy quayside – disturbed only by the rumble of the trains overhead. The village is about a mile away where there are basic provisions, a post office and the Elliot Arms pub. If you walk up the road from the quay you will pass a telephone box en route or, alternatively, follow the pleasant footpath upstream beneath the viaduct, which will eventually bring you along old Quay Lane to the village, where there is a doctor's surgery. Occasional trains run to Plymouth from St German's station.

THE RIVER TAMAR

The Tamar, however, is altogether a far bigger proposition for it is 12 miles to Calstock, and ideally a whole flood tide is needed. In the narrow upper reaches the streams run strongly, particularly on the ebb, and attain in excess of five knots when the river is in spate. In these circumstances, due to the current and the amount of floating debris, trees and branches, such a trip is not recommended.

Today, the river is a tranquil place, a quiet rural waterway that belies its former importance as one of the busiest industrial areas in the West Country. Extensive granite quarries and rich tin, copper, silver and arsenic mines in the upper reaches were all serviced from the sea, with large sailing schooners, ketches and barges plying far inland. Apart from a few overgrown and derelict quays, it is now difficult to imagine such a hive of maritime activity, but fortunately the heritage

Saltash Sailing Club's trots and short stay pontoon

has not been totally lost. At Cothele, far upstream, there is a restored Tamar barge and a museum, while Morwellham, almost at the head of navigation, is a former Victorian port that has been restored as a tourist attraction. The upper reaches have now been designated as a World Heritage Site.

Above the entrance to the Lynher, the channel runs broad and deep past Saltash on the western shore towards the twin road and rail bridges. The latter, yet another of Isambard Kingdom Brunel's remarkable achievements, took seven years to build and was opened in 1859 to carry the Great Western Railway from London into Cornwall.

There are many local trot moorings off Saltash, and the enthusiastic and welcoming members of the Saltash Sailing Club, Tel: 01752 845988; www.saltashsailingclub.co.uk, have their clubhouse on the first prominent quay, at the southern end of which you will find their short stay pontoon. There is ample water alongside it

Jubilee Green visitors' pontoon, Saltash

on all but Springs, when you should approach it with care. Berth here temporarily and seek out the club administrator if you wish to stay longer – he will usually be able to sort out a club mooring if one is available.

The club is open most lunch times and evenings and visitors are very welcome to use its bar, limited restaurant facilities and showers. There are three pubs in the immediate vicinity of the waterfront, an area known as Waterside, where the large slipway remains as the only tangible evidence of the old Saltash Chain Ferry that ran across the river until the Tamar road bridge was opened in 1962.

A short but steep climb up the hill will bring you to the main shopping area, which can provide most normal provisioning requirements, including a Somerfield and Co-op supermarket as well as a Natwest, HSBC and Barclays banks with cashpoints.

On the opposite side of the river, just downstream of the bridges at Saltash Passage, St Budeaux, the Tamar River Sailing Club, Tel: 362741; www.tamarriversailingclub.co.uk, has its premises on the waterfront, with a landing pontoon and moorings off it.

Upstream, moorings continue beyond the bridges along the western shore where there is a convenient landing pontoon off Saltash's Jubilee Green. The inner fingers are private berthing belonging to Saltash Sailing Club, but the outer end of the pontoon is available to visitors, max 10m LOA, for stays of up to 12 hours, free of charge – very handy if you want to nip into Saltash to do some shopping!

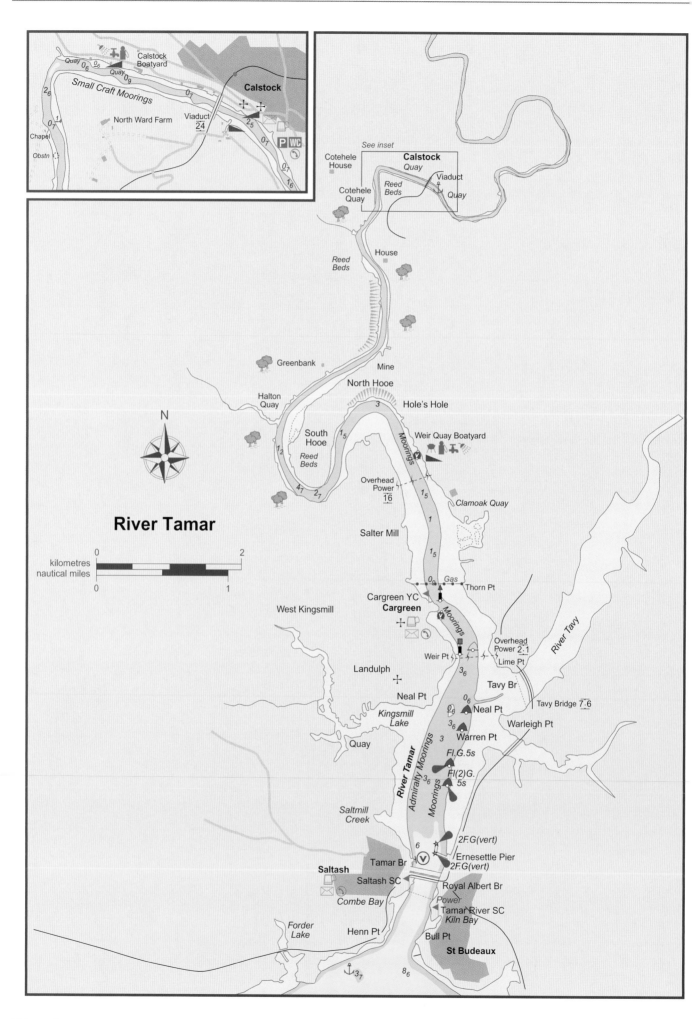

River Tamar

kilometres
nautical miles

The higher Tamar, with Cargreen in the foreground and Weir Quay Boatyard in the far distance

On the eastern side of the river Ernesettle Pier is an MOD munitions depot, while two long trots of Admiralty barge moorings run upstream on either side of the main channel.

A line of four green conical buoys marks the eastern bank, and the northernmost lies off the entrance to the River Tavy. Sadly this attractive tributary has long been denied to sailing boats by the railway bridge across its mouth, with only a 7.6m clearance. The river dries almost completely at Low Water, but power boats or dinghies can explore it on the tide as far as Bere Ferrers, which boasts a pub and limited provisions.

Between the last green buoy and Neal Point, on the western shore, is a drying bank. Keep close to the starboard side of the channel before steering north to Weir Point, a wooded promontory where a large overhead power line crosses the river. Almost directly beneath it, the channel is marked by a post with square red topmark to port and a yellow conical buoy, marking the outer edge of a water-ski area, to starboard. The latter sometimes dries at Low Water Springs, so hold close to the port-hand mark.

The small village of Cargreen lies ahead, with three parallel trots of local moorings running north-south, indicating the deeper water. You should steer for the centre trot to avoid a shallow patch which lies just downstream of the end of the western trot.

CARGREEN AND WEIR QUAY

Before WWI Cargreen was still a major crossing point of the Tamar, but the growth of motor traffic resulted in the enlargement of the Torpoint ferries and the decline of Cargreen. Today it is another peaceful village, not much more than a single street running down to the quay. There is a post office (open mornings only) and a general store that closes on Friday afternoons.

Anchor clear of the local moorings where there is about 2m, or pick up one of the visitors' moorings belonging to the Crooked Spaniards Inn, Tel: 842830, which is prominent on the foreshore, and see the landlord when you go ashore for a drink or one of their good value meals.

Cargreen Yacht Club, a little further upstream, made history in 1995 when it was the first in the West Country to be allocated lottery funds to build its fine new clubhouse – over £40,000 was given to the project. Visitors are welcome to use the bar and showers when it is open, usually on Friday evenings or weekends. A contact number is displayed on the door – somebody will normally be able to turn out and help if you have a problem, and you can often be found a mooring if members are away. A tap is located by the clubhouse and you can land at the club slip, which is particularly convenient for avoiding the extensive mud at low tide.

Beyond the moorings the channel is marked on the starboard side by a green beacon with triangular topmark, and it is a straight run northwards to Weir Quay Boatyard, Tel: 01822 840474; www.weir-quay.com, where 120 moorings lie along both sides of the deeper water. The moorings are operated at capacity,

In a tranquil setting, visitors are always welcome to Weir Quay Boatyard

but visitors are always made very welcome at a flat rate of £10 a night. Make phone contact with the office or pick up the white 'visitor' mooring or the first empty mooring nearest to the slipway and await directions.

It is a peaceful spot for a stopover and is ideal for walking and exploring this Area of Outstanding Natural Beauty. Information on walks and local attractions is available from the yard's office and visitors are welcome to use the facilities, incorporating shore power on the berthing pontoon, toilets, showers, waste disposal, diesel in cans and gas. A chandlery is also available and its small provisions store provides most cruising essentials.

The yard has been in the ownership of Mike and Lisa Hooton since 1999, and facilities include a 12-ton crane, 20-ton boat transporter, with full time staff for repairs and engineering. Fine joinery is a speciality and Weir Quay takes a special interest in traditional and classic boats.

Continuing upstream, apart from a few deeper pools, there is less than 1.5m. The river narrows considerably and winds almost back on itself. The channel is not marked, but generally the deepest water lies along the outside of the bends.

Keep close to the wooded shore beyond Holes Hole, where there is an old quay and several hulks, following the low cliffs right round the outside of this bend as the bank extending from the south shore is very shallow, with a few moorings lying along its edge. From here onwards, between March and September, salmon netsmen will be encountered and care should be taken to pass slowly, keeping a lookout for their nets extending from the banks. As the expansive reed beds come abeam to starboard, head across to the southern shore, again holding close to the steep woods.

Large trip boats run regular day cruises from Plymouth to Calstock and, if encountered in these upper reaches, there is not a great deal of water to spare. Their skippers appreciate it greatly if you can pull over to let them pass.

The channel continues to follow the western bank where Pentillie Castle is now mostly obscured by trees, and past Halton Quay with a curious building rather like a railway signal box that is, in fact, one of the smallest chapels in England. Bear across the the eastern shore past extensive reedbeds, and upstream is a house with two gables just visible in the trees. Steer towards this with an eye on the sounder, then follow the deeper water as it first swings back to the western bank, then midstream as Cothele Quay appears.

COTHELE QUAY

With sufficient water it is possible to berth very temporarily (there is only 1.2m here at High Water) alongside the quay, which has been preserved by the National Trust as part of the Cothele estate, although you are better off picking up the mooring in the river.

The quay is home to the restored Tamar barge *Shamrock*. A 57ft ketch, she was built in 1899 and, co-owned by the National Maritime Museum, is the only surviving example of the barges that were once an essential element in the life of the waterway. During the summer she is occasionally sailed by enthusiasts. There is a small museum on the quay devoted to the maritime history of the river, and about 10 minutes' walk from the quay, Cothele House, a splendid Tudor mansion and gardens, is open daily 1100 – 1800 April – October.

CALSTOCK

Beyond the moorings off Cothele Quay, the prominent building of the former Danescombe Hotel, now a private house with an elegant veranda, sits high on the hillside above the final sharp bend into the Calstock reach. As the reed beds open to starboard, the fine viaduct will come into view beyond them.

A line of moorings lies in the centre of the channel off the Calstock Boatyard on the port hand bank; some of these are kept available for visitors drawing up to 1m, but it is best to enquire in advance by calling Tel: 01822 835968 or Mob: 07969 515238. Deeper draught boats should book ahead for a mooring. A charge of £10 a night includes the use of the showers and toilets ashore. Diesel is available alongside the quay.

Anchoring is not recommended immediately above or below the viaduct because of the moorings, poor holding and the narrowness of the channel used by the pleasure boats, although it is possible a bit further upstream just beyond the last private mooring where the sounder will reveal a convenient pool.

In 1998 the Calstock Development Trust was created to rejuvenate the river frontage, since when a new landing slipway and jetty for the ferry operators have been built, but the proposed pontoon for visiting yachts has not yet materialised. The ferry operators have no objection

Calstock is as far as most intrepid explorers of the upper Tamar will probably get!

to visitors using the jetty to drop off crew as long as the ferry is not impeded and boats are not left unmanned.

Calstock was once the busiest port in the upper Tamar, but looking at it today it all seems almost inconceivable. The quays where ships lay two or three abreast have mostly crumbled into disrepair, and the attractive cluster of cottages and small Georgian and Victorian houses, mainly dating from the 1850s, clinging to the steep roads up the hillside, betray little evidence of their busy past.

On the opposite shore, now lost in the reeds and sedge, the famous shipyard of James Goss was building large wooden vessels as late as 1909. The ketch *Garlandstone* was the last of these, and today she is preserved as part of the former copper port of Morwellham just over two miles upstream, which has been restored by the Morwhellam Trust as a monument to the industrial past of the Tamar. Open daily during the season as a tourist attraction, it is even possible to take a train ride deep into one of the old copper mines. Beyond Calstock the river becomes much narrower, very shallow and tortuous, and is best explored only by dinghy or small shallow draught boats. Alternatively, take the ferry from Calstock, which runs if weather and tide permit.

If you need any further proof of all this industrial heritage, or just an excuse for a pint, go and take a look at the old photographs in the Tamar Inn where you can also enjoy a good bar meal. Other facilities include a newsagent and general food store, a post office, two restaurants and another pub/restaurant, the Boot Inn, petrol at the garage and a branch of Lloyds TSB bank (open 1000 – 1230 on Mondays). There are also trains to Plymouth.

Plymouth Port Guide – Area telephone code: 01752

Harbourmaster: Commander ID Hugo RN, Queen's Harbourmaster, HM Naval Base, Plymouth, Tel: 553740. Deputy QHM, Longroom, Tel: 663225. Cattewater Harbourmaster, Captain Tim Charlesworth, 2 The Barbican, Plymouth PL1 2LR, Tel: 665934. Sutton Harbourmaster, Mr Peter Bromley, North Quay House, Sutton Harbour, Plymouth, Tel: 204186, Mobile: 07860 863150.

VHF: HM Naval Base Ch 16, working 14, callsign *Longroom Port Control* (24 hours). Cattewater Harbour Office VHF Ch 12, 14 and 80, (0900 – 1700 Mon – Fri). Sutton Harbour *Sutton Harbour Radio* VHF Ch 16 and 12 (24 hours). See 'marinas' below.

Emergency services: Lifeboat. Brixham Coastguard.

Anchorages: Cawsand Bay; off Jennycliff; Barn Pool; Drake's Island; St German's and Tamar Rivers.

Moorings: RWYC, RPCYC; Weir Quay Boatyard, Tel: 01822 840474, email: info@weir-quay.com; website: www.weir-quay.com; Calstock Boatyard, Tel: 01822 835968.

Dinghy landings: RPCYC; Mayflower SC.

Water taxis: Mayflower Steps to Mount Batten.

Mail drop: Marinas; RWYC and RPCYC.

Marinas: Mayflower Marina, Ocean Quay, Richmond Walk,

Synonymous with Drake and Plymouth, the splendid Hoe and Smeaton's old Eddystone lighthouse overlook the Sound

Plymouth, PL1 4LS, Tel: 556633; Fax: 606896; email: info@mayflowermarina.co.uk; website: www.mayflower marina.co.uk. Equipped with 396 berths, 30+ visitors, callsign *Mayflower Marina* VHF Ch 80 (24 hours).

Queen Anne's Battery Marina, Plymouth PL4 0LP, Tel: 671142; Fax: 266297; email: qab@mdlmarinas.co.uk; website: www.mdlmarinas. co.uk. A total of 240 berths including visitors, callsign *QAB* VHF Ch 80 (24 hours).

Sutton Harbour Marina, Sutton Harbour, Plymouth, PL4 0ES, Tel: 204702;

Fax: 204693; email: marina@sutton-harbour. co.uk; website: www. suttonharbourmarina.com. Out of 467 berths, 30 are for visitors. Callsign *Sutton Harbour Marina*, VHF Ch 12. Accessed through free lock (access 24hrs), callsign *Sutton Lock* VHF Ch 16 and 12 (24hrs).

Plymouth Yacht Haven, Shaw Way, Mount Batten, Plymouth PL9 9XH, Tel: 404231; Fax: 484177; email: plymouth@yachthavens.com; website: www.yachthavens. com. There are 450 berths inc visitors, callsign *Plymouth*

Yacht Haven VHF Ch 80 (24 hours).

Charges: Mayflower Marina £2.75 per metre per night (inc electricity). Queen Anne's Battery Marina up to 15m £3 per metre per night, over 15m £3.50 per metre per night. Sutton Harbour Marina £3 per metre per night (inc electricity). Plymouth Yacht Haven £2.80 per metre per night (inc electricity). Moorings per night: RWYC £12.50. RPCYC £10. Weir Quay £10.

Note that there is no charge for anchoring anywhere within the Plymouth area.

Plymouth Port Guide (Cont) – Area telephone code: 01752

Phones: At all marinas and yacht clubs. Cawsand, Cremyll, Southdown, Millbrook, St German's, Torpoint, Saltash, Cargreen, Calstock.

Doctor/dentist: Ask at the marinas.

Hospital: Derriford, Tel: 777111.

Churches: All denominations.

Local weather forecast: At all marinas.

Fuel: Mayflower Marina, diesel, petrol 24 hours depending on tide height, Queen Anne's Battery Marina, diesel and petrol, 0830 – 1830. Sutton Harbour Marina, diesel 0830 – 1830. Plymouth Yacht Haven, diesel 24 hours. Weir Quay and Calstock Boatyard, diesel only.

Paraffin: At QAB and Mayflower marinas.

Gas: Calor/Gaz at all marinas, 24 hours at Mayflower Marina.

Water: At all marinas. In cans, Cawsand; Multihull Centre, Millbrook; St German's Quay; Cargreen; Weir Quay; Calstock.

Tourist Information Centre: Barbican, opposite old Fishmarket.

Banks/cashpoints: All main banks in Plymouth city centre, all with cashpoints.

Post offices: Barbican; Plymouth City centre; Cawsand; Millbrook; St German's; Cargreen; Calstock.

Internet access: WiFi at all major marinas and Torpoint Yacht Harbour. Internet café, Plymouth Yacht Haven. Performance Yachting Chandlery & Store, Mayflower Marina.

Rubbish: Disposal and recycling facilities at all marinas.

Showers/toilets: At all marinas; RWYC; RPCYC.

Launderettes: At all marinas.

Provisions: Everything obtainable. Many shops also open on Sundays.

Chandlers: Performance Yachting Chandlery & Store, Mayflower Marina, Tel: 565023; Yacht Parts Plymouth, Tel: 252489, and The Sea Chest, nautical bookshop/Admiralty Chart Agent, Tel: 222012, both at Queen Anne's Battery; Marine & Leisure, Sutton Jetty, Tel: 268826; Marine Bazaar, Tel: 201023; Mount Batten Boathouse, Tel: 482666; on Sutton Road (near China House restaurant); Plymouth Yacht Haven; Saltash Boat & Mooring Services, Saltash, Tel: 845482.

Repairs: Mashford Shipyard, Cremyll, Tel: 822232; M&G Marine Services, Mayflower Marina, Tel: 563345, Mob: 07831 460340; West Country Yachts, Tel: 606999; Harbour Marine, Sutton Harbour, Tel: 204690; Bridgend Boat Co Ltd, Mount Batten, Tel: 404082; Western Marine Power, Mount Batten, Tel: 408804; Booth & Wilkinson, Mount Batten, Tel: 408488; Blagdons Boatyard, Richmond Walk, Tel: 561830; Multihull Centre, Millbrook, Tel: 823900.

Marine engineers: Harbour Marine, Sutton Harbour, Tel: 204691; Marine Engineering Looe, QAB, Tel: 226143; Pro Marine, QAB, Tel: 267984; M&G Marine, Mayflower Marina, Tel: 563345; West Country Yachts, Tel: 606999; Western Marine Power, Mount Batten, Tel: 408804. Ask at marinas or boatyards.

Electronic engineers: Marine Systems, Tel: 07979 804681; Waypoint 1, Tel: 661913; Mount Batten Boathouse, Tel: 482666; Ultra Marine Systems, Tel: 07989 941020, or ask at marinas.

Gas engineer: Gas Plus, Tel: 519235; Mob: 07966 583503.

Sailmakers: Ullman Sails, Tel: 550040; Ocean Canvas UK, Tel: 609500; Slik Cut, Tel: 401904; Inshore Sails & Covers, Tel: 229661; Westaway Sails, Ivybridge, Tel: 892560). Ask at marinas.

Riggers: Yacht Rigging Services, Freephone 0800 9158609; Allspars, Tel: 266766; Hemisphere Rigging Services, Tel: 07790 225511.

Transport: Main line trains to London and the north, Tel: 08457 484950. Buses, Western National, Tel: 402060. Good road connections to M5. Plymouth airport, flights to London/Scotland/Eire, Tel: 204090. Ferries to Roscoff and Santander, Tel: 08705 360360.

Car hire: Hertz, Tel: 207207; Avis, Tel: 221550; Acorn, Tel: 253600, or ask at marinas.

Taxi: Tel: 606060; 222222; 202020; 0800 175175 or 0800 123444.

Car parking: All marinas have customer parking.

Yacht clubs: Royal Western Yacht Club of England, Queen Anne's Battery, Plymouth, PL4 0TW, Tel: 660077; email: admin@rwyc.org; website: www.rwyc.org.

Royal Plymouth Corinthian Yacht Club, Madeira Road, The Hoe, Plymouth PL1 2NY, Tel: 664327; email: club@rpcyc.com; website: www.rpcyc.com.

Mayflower Sailing Club, Phoenix Wharf, Plymouth, Tel: 662526; email: mayflowersc@hotmail.com; website: www.mayflowersc.org.uk.

Torpoint Mosquito Sailing Club, Marine Drive, Torpoint, PL11 2EH, Tel: 812508; email: website@tmsc.org.uk; website: www.tmsc.org.uk.

Saltash Sailing Club, Tamar Street Saltash, PL12 4EL, Tel: 845988; email: enquiries@saltashsailng club.co.uk; website: www.saltashsailingclub.co.uk.

Tamar River Sailing Club, 833 Wolseley Road, St Budeaux, Tel: 362741; website: www.tamarriversailingclub.co.uk.

Eating out: Vast choice from Indian to Greek, Spanish to Chinese, brasseries to bistros, pub food to pizza, fish and chips to burgers!

Things to do: Elizabethan House; Plymouth Museum in old merchant's house; Royal Citadel; Barbican; Barbican Glass Works; National Marine Aquarium; Smeaton's Tower; Plymouth Dome and Pavilions, audio/visual history of Plymouth; swimming and ice skating; The Hoe; Plymouth Waterfront Walk; Drake Circus; large indoor shopping centre, two multi-screen cinemas, theatre.

Regattas/special events: Port of Plymouth Regatta and Plymouth Classic Boat Rally take place at end of July. Venue for many special events, including dinghy championships, and start/finish of major offshore races, including Fastnet, Transatlantics and Round Britain. There's a National Fireworks Competition, August, and British Power Boat Grand Prix, July.

Café culture abounds in the revamped Barbican

Reaching down to Plymouth,
Rame Head from the south-west

Chapter three
Rame Head to The Manacles

FAVOURABLE TIDAL STREAMS
Rame Head
Bound west: two hours before HW Dover
Bound east: four hours after HW Dover
Dodman Point
Bound west: three hours before HW Dover
Bound east: three hours after HW Dover

Passage charts for this sea area:
AC: 1267 Falmouth to Plymouth.
        148 Dodman Point to Looe Bay
        (including harbour plan of Polperro).
        777 Land's End to Falmouth.
        3l Harbours on the south coast of Cornwall
        (Fowey, Charlestown, Par).
        147 Plans on the south coast of Cornwall
        (Helford River, Looe, Mevagissey). SC5602
Imray: C6 Salcombe to Lizard Point.
        WCP 2400.8, 2400.9
Stanfords: 2 English Channel western section. Chart
        pack 23, Lizard Point to Rame Head

SAFETY INFORMATION AND WEATHER
Brixham & Falmouth Coastguard makes initial
announcement on VHF Channel 16 at 0110, 0410, 0710,
1010, 1610, 1910, 2210 Local Time, to confirm working
channel for broadcast, normally: VHF Channel 23
(Lizard), Channel 86 (Rame Head), Channel 10 (Fowey),
Channel 84 (River Fal).

Rame Head NCI station Tel: 01752 823706
Polruan NCI station Tel: 01726 870291
Charlestown NCI station Tel: 01726 817068
Portscatho NCI station Tel: 01872 580180

WAYPOINTS

1	**Rame Head (5ca south of headland)**	
	50°18'.10N 04°13'.42W	
2	**Looe Island (6ca south of the Ranneys buoy)**	
	50°19'.21N 04°26'.38W	
3	**Udder Rock buoy (1ca south of buoy)**	
	50°18'.81N 04°33'.85W	
4	**Fowey approach**	
	(3½ca due south of Punch Cross)	
	50°19'.27N 04°38'.40W	
5	**Gwineas Rock (1M south-east of buoy)**	
	50°13'.83N 04°44'.17W	
6	**Dodman Point**	
	(2M south-south-east of monument)	
	50°11'.14N 04°47'.34W	
7	**Gull Rock/The Whelps**	
	(0.5M south-east of the most southern rock)	
	50°11'.11N 04°53'.91W	
8	**Falmouth approach**	
	(0.5M south-south-east of St Anthony Head)	
	50°07'.96N 05°00'.55W	
9	**Manacles (1M east of buoy)**	
	50°02'.80N 05°00'.35W	

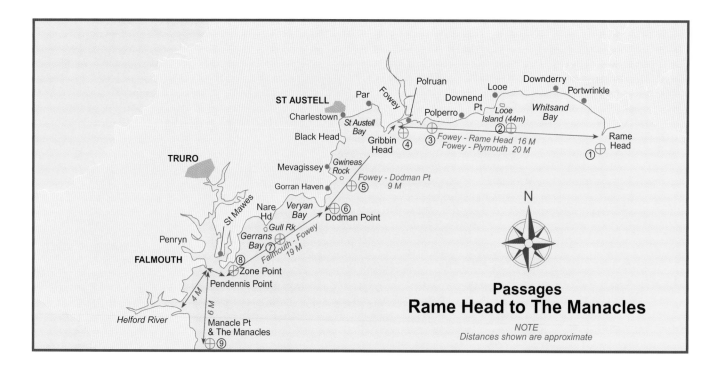

Passages
Rame Head to The Manacles

NOTE
Distances shown are approximate

West of Plymouth and the Yealm, Fowey is the next probable destination on a coast-hopping cruise and, over 20 miles away, it is one of the longest legs. Although no great distance in itself, yet again the odds are very much in favour of winds forward of the beam and once past Rame Head the tidal streams are weak inshore and of no great assistance. Three miles south of Looe the streams rotate in a clockwise direction, attaining a maximum at Springs of about one knot, east by north at HW Dover –0520, but no more than a knot west by south at HW Dover +0035. Somehow, this passage always seems to take longer than anticipated.

The Dodman is 23 miles distant from Rame Head and, given reasonable visibility, its long, flat topped headland and distinctively rounded end will be visible on the horizon. Whitesand Bay falls back immediately to the north-west of Rame Head – a succession of sandy beaches and rocky outcrops backed by a continuous line of steep and broken grassy cliffs between 30m and 76m high. Here, the Leander class frigate *HMS Scylla* (F71), the last of her kind to be built at Devonport in 1973, was scuttled spectacularly in March 2004 to form an artificial reef for divers. Now known as Scylla Reef, it lies 1.4M north-west of Rame Head, has a least depth of 8m LAT and is marked by a red can buoy (QR).

The direct course to Fowey keeps you a good couple of miles offshore, which is no great disadvantage as this is one of the less inspiring stretches of coast. Rocks extend a cable immediately to the west of Rame Head, and north-west of the point is a dangerous wreck awash at Low Water Springs and marked by a red can. Following the sweep of the bay inshore, there are rifle ranges by the old fort at Tregantle, where a

number of flagstaffs along the cliffs warn you to keep well clear if the red flags are flying. The last serious wreck in Whitsand Bay was the Maltese registered *Kodima*, which lost power in a southwesterly gale in February 2001 and ran ashore beneath Tregantle, with spectacular results as her cargo, thousands of tonnes of prime timber, began to wash ashore onto the beaches. As ever the locals were quick off the mark, a scene that was even more spectacularly repeated with *MSC Napoli's* stranding off Branscombe in 2007. Huge quantities were salvaged and hauled away up the cliffs, and local boats laden with the treasure could be seen offloading in all the nearby ports. The Receiver of Wreck was soon clamping down on the activity but to this day many garden sheds and house extensions still bear witness to the bonanza. The *Kodima* was refloated without suffering too much damage thanks to her ice-strengthened hull.

Sounding like a perfect setting for an Enid Blyton children's adventure, Portwrinkle, almost two miles west of Tregantle, is a very tiny boat harbour, which dries completely and is fringed by extensive rocky ledges. A few houses are situated nearby, while the village of Crafthole can be seen on the skyline. From here onwards, the coast continues in a long, high sweep with further extensive rocky ledges and hazards stretching up to two cables offshore, including the Longstone, a prominent rock 18m high. At Downderry, which straggles along the cliffs, precipitous paths lead down to a beach, and to the south there are the Sherberterry Rocks, a large area of shallows extending just over two miles offshore, with least depths of 4.9m. These can produce an area of rough water, particularly in onshore winds when this whole stretch of coast should be avoided and a good offing maintained.

Looe from the south-east, with Looe Island, left

LOOE AND POLPERRO

Looe Island is 44m high and pleasantly rounded. Almost linked to the mainland at Low Water, it lies close to the shore and is a perfect natural daymark for the drying fishing port of Looe just to the east. Looe is mostly commercial with very limited facilities for visiting boats, and is dangerous to approach in fresh or strong southerly or southeasterly winds and ebb tide, as it has a long and very narrow entrance. In offshore winds, however, there is a good anchorage just off the harbour.

Rounding Looe Island, the Ranneys is a group of drying rocks extending three cables south-east from the island, south of which shallower patches stretch for nearly a mile with least depths ranging between 9m and 11m – note that in fresh wind against tide this can create some unpleasant overfalls. The YB south cardinal buoy (Q(6)+LFl 15s), which lies 1M south-south-east of the Ranneys, provides a useful distance mark – keep to seaward of this and you will avoid any problems. A 586m high television mast can be seen 10 miles due north of Looe Island, displaying a number of fixed red lights at night.

Beyond Looe the coast becomes more interesting again. There is a measured mile (1,852.9m to be precise!) just west of the island, the transits formed by two white beacons with a vertical black stripe at each end, running as far as the approach to Talland Bay. This attractive sandy beach backed by trees and fields is popular with holidaymakers and stretches to the 100m high Downend Point, which has a large granite war memorial near the summit. Downend Shoals, a mile due south, have a least depth of 2.6m and should be passed well to seaward if there is any sea running.

If bound for Polperro, the small fishing village and harbour just over mile to the west, it is best not to turn inshore until the white beacon on Spy Glass Point (Iso WR 6s 7M), just east of the harbour, is bearing north. Approaching from the west, a prominent television mast will be seen high on the cliffs just before the village opens. Like Looe, Polperro is a place less frequented by yachts and space within the harbour is taken up by local boats so, weather permitting, you will either use one of the six visitors' moorings in the close approach to the harbour, or anchor just south of them. In bad weather a storm gate closes off the harbour completely.

From Polperro to Fowey, in good weather, the coast is very attractive with impressive cliffs up to 91m in height, occasionally broken by steep green and grassy coombes and gullies running down to small coves. The water is deep to within two cables of the shore and there are no hazards, except Udder Rock (dries 0.6m) two miles west of Polperro and half a mile offshore, which is marked by a YB south

Polperro lies hidden in a narrow cleft in the cliffs

Udder Rock buoy looking west to Gribbin Head

cardinal buoy (VQ(6) +LFl 10s). A white beacon on the cliffs along with a white mark on a rock on the shore also provide a transit (020°T) for this hazard, while a prominent white mark on the western side of Lantic Bay, just open of steep Pencarrow Head (135m high), gives a cross bearing of 283°T. At night, if you are in the red sector of Fowey light, you will pass Udder Rock to the south, although it is safer still to keep further to seaward in the white sector.

Generally, if making the passage from Plymouth to Fowey at night, the dominant feature is the Eddystone to the south-east (Fl (2) 10s 17M), but you will be on the 13M limit of its fixed red sector (112° – 129°T). Rame Head is unlit, but a buoy 1M south-south-east of Looe Island is lit (Q(6)+LFl 15s), as is Looe harbour entrance (Oc WR 3s 15/12M). Also look out for a light just east of Polperro Harbour (Iso WR 3s 7M) and the Udder Rock buoy (VQ(6) +LFl 10s), two miles west of Polperro, and Fowey harbour (L Fl WR 5s, W 11M, R 9M).

FOWEY

In daylight, although completely hidden from the east, the entrance to Fowey harbour is not difficult to find thanks to the huge red and white horizontally striped daymark and a square pillar 104m high built by Trinity House in 1832 on Gribbin Head – a long promontory to the south-west of the river mouth.

A mile east of the entrance and immediately west of Pencarrow Head is Lantic Bay, backed by National Trust land, and its tidal beach is a beautiful stretch of clean sand with a good anchorage off it in northerly winds.

Gribbin Head and Cannis Rock at Low Tide

Beyond it is a conspicuous white house high on the cliffs, and a ruined tower. The Polruan NCI lookout (Tel: 01726 870291), in the Old Pilots' lookout building, is also located here. As the headland draws abeam, Punch's Cross, a white cross on a large rock, will come into view to starboard, with houses along the cliff above. The river mouth and town of Fowey will now start to appear, surrounded by high ground on either side.

Deep and free from hazards, Fowey can be approached in any weather, although strong southerly winds and ebb tide will produce very rough conditions and breaking seas in the entrance. As well as being a popular yacht harbour, this is also a busy commercial port, exporting large quantities of china clay. Be ready for surprise encounters with sizeable ships in the entrance, which is only a cable wide at its narrowest point. These vessels have priority, so keep well clear!

ST AUSTELL BAY
TO DODMAN POINT

The passage from Fowey to Falmouth is another 20 miles, and the tide is once again a definite factor to consider when rounding the Dodman. The Lizard and Start Point both instantly evoke an image of overfalls and races, but somehow the Dodman seems to elude such an association, which is strange as there can often be quite an unpleasant amount of disturbance in its vicinity. Close to the point streams run at nearly two knots at Springs and, with wind against tide, the uneven depths and shoals of the Bellows and Field can produce a small, but very unpleasant race extending a good mile offshore. If a westerly wind of any strength is prevailing, ideally try to round the point at slack water just before the main ebb begins to the south-west (about three hours before HW Dover), which means leaving Fowey two hours after local HW (Dover –0600).

The whole promontory of the Dodman provides a considerable lee in westerly weather, and it should be remembered that a fresher wind and larger seas are likely to be encountered once past the point, particularly in a southwesterly when it can be a long 10-mile beat to windward along an exposed stretch of coast that provides no shelter until you reach Falmouth.

The only hazards between Fowey and the Dodman are both well marked. The first is Cannis Rock (dries

Approaching from the south past the Cannis Rock buoy, Fowey is easy to spot

4.3m) marked by the Cannis Rock YB south cardinal buoy (Q6+LFl 15s) positioned a mile south-east of Gribbin Head in the western red sector of Fowey lighthouse. The second is the Gwineas Rocks, the largest of which dries to 8m. They are just over two miles north-east of Dodman Point, with Gwineas BYB east cardinal buoy (Q (3)10s) guarding them two cables to the south-east.

St Austell Bay opens to the north-west when clear of Gribbin Head, and the coast running away towards the Dodman, nine miles south-west of Fowey, provides a good sheltered area of water in westerly winds.

This is an attractive miniature cruising ground in its own right. The land rises beyond it, where you will see the distant sprawl of houses around St Austell. The once spectacular and jagged skyline of the surrounding 'Cornish Alps' – the huge white spoil heaps from the extensive china clay workings – have now been re-profiled and planted with greenery and from offshore no longer appear as an enticing range of snow covered mountains when they catch the sun!

The once busy china clay port of Par fell victim to cheaper foreign imports, and was due to close at the end of 2007. The clay drying plants were to remain operating at a lesser scale, continuing to provide a distinctive landmark on the northern shore of the bay – four large chimneys that are even more conspicuous when belching white smoke. Par has always been closed to pleasure craft so it will be intriguing to see what happens to it once the commercial traffic has ceased. Another marina perhaps?

Further west an additional former clay port, Charlestown, shows what can be done as this is now privately owned by the Square Sail Shipyard Ltd. Home to many classic and traditional craft, it is well worth a visit if time and weather permit. An NCI lookout is located here (Tel: 01726 817068).

Your course will take you well away from the land, closing it east of the Gwineas Buoy, but the town and white lighthouse of Mevagissey are easy to spot on the

western shore, a V-shaped gap in the cliffs, surmounted by houses on both sides. Gorran Haven, a drying small boat harbour, lies due west of Gwineas rocks. As always, particularly near the rocks, keep a good lookout for pot buoys.

This course will also lead you close to the Dodman Point Gunnery Range, which was established here after the closure of Portland Naval Base in 1996. There are three yellow spherical target buoys lying approximately 3.7M south-south-east of Dodman Point, the most southerly 'A' at 50°08'.53N 04°46'.37W (Fl Y 10s), 'B' at 50°10'.03N 04°45'.00W (Fl Y 5s), and 'C' at 50°10'.40N 04°47'.51W (Fl Y 2s). Naval vessels usually fire on these from a position approximately seven miles to the north-east of the buoys, somewhere between 2.5M and 9M south-south-east of Gribbin Head. Firing takes place in daylight only, roughly once or twice a week throughout the year, except during August and for two weeks over Christmas. During exercises, which normally last for a maximum of two hours using flash/bang/smoke charges but no high explosives, a helicopter is stationed within

Mevagissey from the east

Gwineas buoy and Dodman Point from the east

1M of the target buoys and a range safety boat (23m LOA black hull/yellow superstructure) is normally on station and can be contacted on VHF Ch 16 & 10. The firing ship can be called on VHF Ch 16, 74 or 10, and it will also promulgate its intentions on VHF Ch 74 immediately prior to firing and at regular intervals throughout the exercise. Normally, the firing itself lasts little more than 15 minutes at a time.

No firing will take place if a vessel is within the safety trace area, which extends south-west and beyond the target buoys. There is no exclusion zone and vessels have a right of transit through the range area, but their co-operation is requested. Ideally try to transit the area on a north-west/south-east heading and remain two miles clear of the target buoys, and it is prudent to contact either the firing ship or the range safety vessel to discuss your intentions. Details of firings – Gunfacts – are broadcast after the shipping forecasts by Brixham and Falmouth Coastguard at 0710 and 1910 Local Time on VHF Channels 10 (Fowey), 23 (Lizard), 84 (Falmouth), 86 (Rame Head). Information is also displayed at Fowey Harbour Office and can also be obtained direct from Flag Officer, Sea Training Operations Room (FOST OPS) 24 hours a day either on VHF Channel 74 or Tel: 01752 557550.

Close to, the Dodman is an impressive 111m high rounded bluff. It is flat topped with steep cliffs along its eastern side, but with a more sloping western side comprising a lovely stretch of National Trust property covered in gorse, ferns and grass. High on the south-western tip is a large white cross erected in 1896 by a local vicar.

On a fine calm day it is quite feasible to pass within a cable of the foot of the cliffs, as the water is deep and unimpeded, but in any sort of sea or weather stand well out – up to two miles in fresh conditions. A once notorious headland for shipwrecks, particularly in fog, it is amazing that no light or fog signal was ever established here, particularly as both St Anthony light (Iso WR 15s 16/14M, Red Sector 004° – 022°) and the Lizard light (Fl 3s 25M) are obscured from the Dodman. Apart from the lights of villages ashore, there are no aids to navigation at night until St Anthony

light appears on a northwesterly bearing, although sometimes its loom will be seen sooner. There is also a noticeable set into the bays between the Dodman and Falmouth. In poor visibility or at night give this coast a wide berth.

DODMAN POINT TO FALMOUTH

Once past the Dodman, Veryan Bay opens to the north. It is an attractive but uncompromising cliff-lined stretch of coast, broken at intervals by small sandy coves. Nare Head, the western extremity of Veryan Bay, is five miles distant and looks similar to the Dodman, but has the distinctive triangle of Gull Rock, an island 38m high, a mile to the east. Although Veryan Bay is almost free from offshore dangers – with no rocks more than two cables from the shore – there is one notable exception. Lath Rock (least depth 2.1m) is almost midway across the bay, although fortunately just inside the direct line from the Dodman to Gull Rock.

Gull Rock is a jagged pyramid, with sparse grass around its whitened summit, clear evidence of the many seabirds that nest there and give it its name. In fair weather it is possible to pass between the rock and the steep 80m high cliffs at Nare Head, but the Whelps, a reef with a number of drying rocks, mostly 4.6m, extends a mile to the south-west of Gull Rock.

Gerrans Bay, much of which is surrounded by National Trust land, is of a similar aspect to Veryan, although the cliffs along its western side become less precipitous. Probably the best of all the anchorages along this section of coast is off Porthscatho, a little fishing village now popular with holidaymakers, which offers shelter from the west. There is a small pier on its southern side, affording protection to the drying foreshore, with a reasonable anchorage just to the north-east. Basic provisions, a post office and several pubs ashore make this a popular day sail from Falmouth. There is an NCI Lookout at Portscatho, Tel: 01872 580180.

Gerrans Bay has witnessed many shipwrecks in its time, with vessels mistaking it for the entrance to Falmouth, but one of the most spectacular was the capsize of pop star Simon Le Bon's maxi, *Drum*, after

Looking west from the Dodman – Nare Head and Gull Rock, centre

St Anthony light emerges to reveal the entrance to the Fal. Pendennis Head is on the left

she lost her keel in gale force conditions during the 1985 Fastnet, leaving her stunned crew stranded on the upturned hull, with thankfully no loss of life.

The Bizzies (least depth 4.2m) lie almost on the line from Gull Rock to Porthmellin Head and should be avoided in fresh winds and ground swell, which can create quite an area of overfalls around them.

Beyond Gerrans Bay, the rounded profile of Zone Point continues to hide the elusive St Anthony light (Iso WR 15s 16/14M, Red Sector 004° – 022°) and a certain nagging doubt can tend to creep in at this stage of the passage. There used to be a conspicuous row of coastguard cottages high on Zone Point, but these have since been demolished by the National Trust. It is surprising that no daymark was ever established here as the entrance is not easy to locate from the east until, at last, the white lighthouse lantern peeps into view from behind the headland. Just over a mile south of the light, a rocky shoal called Old Wall (least depth 7m) rises steeply from the sea bed and can produce an area of rough water in strong southerly winds. In fine weather it is a popular fishing area and easy to spot by the number of angling boats in its vicinity.

The entrance to the River Fal is a mile wide and safe to enter in any condition. It is flanked on the east by St Anthony Head and Pendennis Point to the west, with the only hazard being Black Rock, right in the middle, marked by a conspicuous isolated danger beacon (Fl (2) 10s) which can be passed either side. In strong southerly winds, with an ebb tide out of the estuary, rough seas will be encountered in the approach and entrance. The ebb, up to two knots at Springs if fresh water is running down the river, begins at HW Dover –0605.

HELFORD RIVER AND THE MANACLES

It is just over five miles from St Anthony Head to Manacle Point, away to the south-west, and between them Falmouth Bay is a fine natural roadstead, well sheltered from the north to south-west, but open to the east and south. It is much used by large vessels as an anchorage, and increasingly for offshore bunkering.

From Pendennis Point, neatly crowned with its castle, the hotels and beaches of the Falmouth seafront form a broad sweep to the west, and the large cream-coloured Falmouth Hotel at the eastern end is particularly prominent. Depths reduce gradually towards the shore, which is fringed with rocky ledges, but there are no dangers further than a cable from it, except large numbers of poorly marked pot buoys. In offshore winds it is possible to anchor off Swanpool Beach, just north of the prominent and wooded Pennance Point. Maenporth is another popular cove a mile to the south and, during the summer, a large inflatable racing mark is usually anchored to seaward.

From Falmouth, the entrance to the Helford River is not easy to distinguish; the various headlands of similar shape blending together. Low cliffs run between Maenporth and Rosemullion Head, which is flat topped, rounded and covered in gorse and thick bushes. Between it and Mawnan Shear there are steep grassy cliffs with a dense clump of woods and a conspicuous white house at its eastern edge.

The Gedges rocks (drying 1.4m) lie three cables east-south-east and are marked to seaward by the conical green August Rock buoy (summer months only). This is the only real hazard in the approach to the Helford River and, once past the buoy, the entrance opens clearly. It is exposed to the east, when the shallowing water produces particularly steep short seas and, being unlit, should not be attempted at night without local knowledge.

Gillan Creek is an opening in the southern approach to the Helford due south of the Gedges. This attractive, but mostly drying inlet lies between Dennis Head, which is grassy and 43m high, and Nare Point, a much lower promontory with an old square coastguard lookout on the end. Beware Car Croc, a rock just awash at Low Water in the entrance of Gillan Creek, marked with a BYB east cardinal buoy which should be left to starboard when entering. There are also rocky ledges extending a cable to seaward of Nare Point.

Proceeding south from Falmouth or the Helford, the extensive rocky nightmare of the Manacles involves a detour to the east. This part of the bay is much used for search and rescue exercises from RNAS Culdrose, and if you see Admiralty vessels and helicopters in the vicinity, keep well clear. Manacle Point is a rather untidy looking headland, badly scarred by extensive old quarry workings. Just to the north, by the small cove of Porthoustock, are the unsightly remains of the huge stone loading chutes on either side of the bay. Jagged pinnacles of rock extend from the point, which continue to form the reefs offshore, marked by the Manacle BYB east cardinal buoy (Q (3) 10s) a mile to the east. These tend to appear further out to sea than you anticipate, particularly when approaching from the south.

The Manacles are undoubtedly one of the most treacherous hazards along the Cornish coast. Lying right in the approach to a busy port, it was inevitable that this area of half-tide rocks and strong currents should claim so many ships over the years. Their sinister name actually derives from the Cornish *maen eglos*, meaning Church stones, for the spire of St Keverne Church is prominent inland.

Close to the Manacles the tidal streams run at up to two knots at Springs. If bound round the Lizard, aim to leave Falmouth or the Helford about three hours after

Calm at the Manacle buoy! Black Head can be spotted in the distance, with Coverack on the right

local High Water to gain the best advantage. There is an inshore passage through the Manacles regularly used by local fishing boats, but do not be tempted to follow them as it is very narrow in places with unpredictable eddies and currents exceeding three knots. Do not be too amazed if you see a sizeable coaster seeming to emerge from among the rocks. Incredibly, they regularly load stone at Dean Quarry alongside the cliffs just south of the Manacles. At night, if approaching from the south, the Manacles lie within the red sector of St Anthony light, 004° – 022°T.

Before radar, a very large percentage of the wrecks along this section of coast occurred in calms and fog rather than extremes of weather. It is still difficult in poor visibility, as a number of the headlands and bays have a similar appearance and audible aids are few and far between. There are just eight in total: Eddystone Light (Horn(1) 30s), Nailzee Point (Siren (2) 30s if fishing fleet at sea), Udder Rock buoy (Bell), Cannis Rock buoy (Bell) – note there is no other fog signal at Fowey – Mevagissey (Dia 30s), Gwineas buoy (Bell), St Anthony Head (Horn (1) 30s), Manacles Buoy (Bell).

Remember that there is generally a northerly set into the bays and, although the 10m sounding line provides a good indication of relative position clearing most of the hazards close to the shore, such as the Dodman, this is for the most part little more than two cables off. If in doubt, err to seawards and do not follow local fishing boats, particularly close to the Manacles – there is no telling where they might be going!

There is little to indicate the Helford from the east, except for the distant cluster of moorings within the river

Looe dries completely and the long narrow entrance is protected by the aptly named Banjo Pier!
There is a good anchorage off the beach in settled offshore weather

Looe and Polperro

Tides	Looe: HW Dover −0540; Polperro HW Dover −0555
Range	MHWS 5.4m−MHWN 4.2m, MLWN 2.0m−MLWS 0.6m. Strong streams within Looe harbour at Springs
Charts	AC: 147 (Looe), 148 (Polperro); Stanfords: CP23; Imray: C6
Waypoint	**Looe:** Banjo Pier Head 50°21'.06N 04°27'.07W
	Polperro: West Pier Head 50°19'.87N 04°30'.96W
Hazards	**Looe:** Looe Island and the Ranneys rocks to south (lit). Busy fishing port, keep clear of local boats
	Polperro: The Raney and Polca Rock in approaches (both unlit). Polperro harbour mouth closed in bad weather. Beware pot and net buoys in approaches. Both harbours dry to entrance and are dangerous to approach in onshore wind and sea
Harbour Speed limit	**Looe:** Five knots
Overnight charge	**Looe:** Harbour Authority alongside: £15
	Polperro: Harbour Authority mooring: £15

Midway between Plymouth and Fowey lie the small harbours of Looe and Polperro. Both are working fishing ports with restricted space and they dry almost completely at Low Water. Boats unable to take the ground comfortably or lie alongside can anchor off or, in the case of Polperro, use the moorings just outside the harbour. Neither harbour should be approached in onshore winds of any strength as they have narrow entrances.

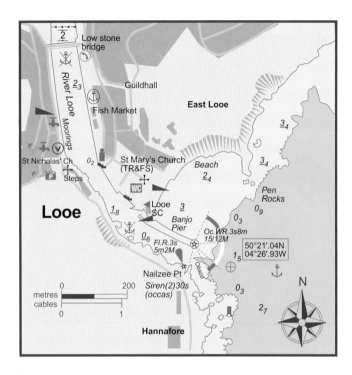

Looe
APPROACHES

From offshore, the entrance is easily located, lying to the east of the large rounded lump of Looe Island (44m) half a mile offshore. It is also known locally as St George's Island and, if approaching from the west, it is essential to keep a good half mile to the south to avoid the Ranneys, hazardous rocks drying to 4.5m. The tidal streams can at times be quite strong here and to seaward of the rocks a brisk area of overfalls will be created in certain combinations of wind and tide, extending nearly a mile to the south where a YB south cardinal buoy (Q(6)+LFl 15s) provides a useful clearing mark.

Benedictine monks were among the early settlers on St George's Island, with the remains of their chapel close to the summit dating back to 1139. Privately owned for centuries, for nearly 40 years it was home to two remarkable sisters, Evelyn and Babs Atkins, who bought it in 1965. Abandoning a civilised existence in suburban Epsom, their dramatic lifestyle change is well described in the books *We Bought an Island* and *Tales from our Cornish Island* written by Miss Evelyn who died in 1996. Miss Babs continued to live there until her death in 2004, when she gifted the island to the Cornwall Wild Life Trust, to be used as a marine nature reserve and for conservation purposes.
The island is open to visitors between Easter and September, with a ferry (Tel: 07814 139223) running from East Looe, weather permitting. Times vary according to the tide and a small charge will be incurred as well as a landing fee. Further details can be found on www.cornwallwildlifetrust.org.uk where you can also order copies of both of Evelyn's books and download an information leaflet about St George's Island and

other Cornwall Wildlife Trust nature reserves.
Do not attempt the passage between the Looe Island and the mainland, which is rock strewn and shallow. Ideally, approach Looe from the south-east, leaving the island a good two to three cables to port as you close the land, and head directly for the end of the Banjo Pier – its shape gives it the name – which forms the eastern side of the harbour mouth. On the western side of the approach, Midmain is an isolated rock south-west of the entrance identified by a lighted beacon with east cardinal top-mark (Q(3)10s), and on the rocks to the north are two red beacons closer to the harbour. On the western side of the harbour entrance the distinctive white-painted rock off Nailzee Point (Fl R 3s 2M) was for many years also emblazoned with the word *Looe*, removing any shadow of doubt – hopefully one day it will be reinstated!

The entrance is long and little more than 50m wide at its narrowest point, drying right to the mouth at Springs, and is accessible after half flood for boats of average draught. It is flanked by high cliffs along the western side, with rocky ledges at their foot. If you are early on the tide, anchor off east of the Banjo pier head in about 2–3m. At night a riding light is essential because of fishing boat movements.

Enter under power, keeping close to the Banjo Pier. The tide runs strongly, up to five knots on the ebb at Springs, and careful allowance should be made for this when manoeuvring. Beware, too, of the numerous self drive motor boats (always an unpredictable hazard), the fishing boats entering and leaving and the small passenger ferry at the southern end of the harbour.

The pier head is lit (sectored Oc WR 3s W15M R12) – the white sector (267° – 313°) covering the safe approach – and entry at night is much easier than it used to be as the entire harbour is lined with festoon lights from just inside the entrance to the bridge, which remain on all night during the season.

BERTHING
The only berth available for visitors is clearly marked *Visitor's Berth* on the small white shower building adjacent to it at the southern end of the West Looe Quay, just upstream of the ferry steps. The quay is faced with wooden piles and a fender board will be very handy; you will ground here about four hours after High Water, drying out on a firm sand and gravel bottom. The charge per night is £15, which includes free showers with special rates for a longer stay.

The quays on the east side of the harbour are reserved for the fishing fleet and, further upstream, the harbour office (open 0900 – 1700) is in the fishmarket. You should report to the harbourmaster, Mr Jeff Penhaligon, on arrival.

An occasional VHF watch is maintained – call *Looe Harbour* on VHF Channel 14 or Tel: 01503 262839; Mobile 07875 165812. Below the bridge, a number

The only visitors' berth in Looe is by the white building on the quayside, just ahead of the rafted motor boats

of local boats lie on trot moorings, all of which dry, and anchoring is prohibited throughout the harbour because of the moorings, underwater pipes and power cables.

FUEL, FRESH WATER AND GAS
Tide permitting, marine diesel can be obtained alongside at Looe Fuels on Buller Quay, East Looe, Tel: 01503 264375, but the fuel berth is not always manned as the local fishing boats are able to access the pumps with their own keys. If no one is around, and there is no reply on the phone, the harbourmaster can usually put you in touch with the proprietor. Petrol is only available in cans from the local garage. There are fresh water taps on both East and West quays. Calor and Camping Gaz are available from Marine Co chandlers, also on Buller Quay.

LOOE FACILITIES
(Local phone code 01503)
Looe is a picturesquely situated little town, which clings to the steep hills overlooking the river. During the season it pays the inevitable price and is absolutely inundated with visitors, the crowds thronging through narrow streets that were never designed for such an influx. In East Looe gift shops abound, whereas West Looe retains more of the original feel of this old fishing community, with thick-walled pastel painted cottages clustered around a network of narrow alleyways and cobbled yards.

Shore facilities are good, with plenty of shops, including a Spar in West Looe, close to the visitors' berth (0730 – 2200 Mon – Sat, 0800 – 2200 Sun), and a Somerfield supermarket in East Looe (0800 – 2200 Mon – Sat, 1000 – 1800 Sun), as well as Co-op and

Spar convenience stores. There is a launderette in both East and West Looe and a convenient shower/toilet in the small Visitors' Berth building – the key is available from the ferryman.

In East Looe you will find branches of Lloyds TSB, HSBC and Barclays, all with cashpoints, while post offices are located in both West and East Looe. Looe Chandlery, Tel: 264355, can be found at the Millpool Boatyard upstream of the bridge. The chandlery Marine Co Ltd, Tel: 265444, Marine Engineering Looe, Tel: 263009, and Marconi Marine Electronics, Tel: 265548, are based on the East Quay. Should you need medical attention, visit Looe Health Centre, Tel: 263196.

Clearly reflecting the number of hungry mouths that flock into the town, eating places abound and encompass everything from the cheap and cheerful to the more up-market. Try Tom Sawyers, Tel: 262782, in West Looe. Alternatively, there's a wide choice in East Looe, including plenty of good seafood at Trawlers, Tel: 263593, the Grapevine, Tel: 263913, or Mawgans, Tel: 265331, traditional fare at the Old Sail Loft, Tel: 262131, and the Bywater, Tel: 262314, or Mexican at Pepe's, Tel: 262057, Italian at Papa Ninos, Tel: 264231, Chinese at the Peking Gardens, Tel: 264500, Indian at Moonlight, Tel: 265372, and Greek at Pepper's Taverna, Tel: 263585. Add to this plenty of cafés and nearly 10 pubs, all of which do food and include the perennial Ship Inn, the Fisherman's Arms and the Jolly Sailor, and if you're still famished there's always fish and chips or a takeaway from the Pizza Palace.

Looe Sailing Club, in Buller Street, East Looe, Tel: 262559; www.looesailingclub.co.uk, welcomes visitors to its licensed bar, with showers also available.

The South East Cornwall Discovery Centre is in West Looe, just upstream of the old tide mill, while East Looe has a Living from the Sea exhibition in the Guildhall museum where the Tourist Information Centre, Tel: 262072, is also located. The scenic Looe Valley railway line connects with the main line at Liskeard. If the tide permits, try a dinghy excursion upstream of the bridge to explore the peaceful backwaters of the East and West Looe Rivers.

Alternatively you might feel inclined to join the masses on East Looe's sandy beach where there is good safe swimming, or on West Looe's quieter but rockier Hannafore beach.

Like many other Cornish fishing ports, Looe has had its ups and downs, suffering very lean times after the collapse of the pilchard industry in the 1930s and the mackerel fishery in the 1970s. Since then the fleet of medium-sized boats has been expanding, mostly potting, long-lining, trawling and scalloping. The holiday industry has in many ways helped to sustain the commercial fishermen through some of the harder times, as this has long been a popular sea angling port and is home of the Shark Fishing Club of Great Britain.

A surprising number of Porbeagle and Blue sharks are caught in the warm waters off Cornwall during the summer although, nowhere in the league of Jaws, they are definitely not man-eaters and are rarely found close to the shore.

At the turn of the century a fleet of over 50 large luggers still worked from Looe. These decked boats were up to 50ft long with transom sterns distinguishing them from the double-ended luggers of the West Cornish ports. Pilchards, small fish similar to herring, were traditionally caught in long seine nets during the summer months by open boats working from coves and beaches, but as the shoals moved further offshore, the larger boats were built and long drift nets began to replace the seine. In recent years there has been a big revival of interest in luggers, many have been restored and the Looe Lugger Regatta has become a bi-annual event, the next planned for June 2009.

Of all the Looe luggers, the best known and certainly the most travelled has to be the *Lily*, built by Ferris in 1896. Her fishing days were over sometime in the 1930s when a young, enthusiastic couple spotted her in nearby Polperro:

'Anne stood by the helm. "I think", she said, "we've found our ship".

We scrambled aboard and went below. The fishwell took up the whole of the middle of the ship. We pulled up the floorboards and looked into the bilge. There were firebars, cannonballs, cogwheels and shingle. She was dry as a bone but smelt to heaven of fish and tar. In the fo'c'sle was a bogie stove eaten with rust, and a single locker on the starboard side. Aft was a single-cylinder Kelvin. Anne's face was flushed with excitement. "If she only costs us twenty-five pounds, we can afford to have her converted into just what we want. It'll be like buying a new boat."

I hadn't the heart to tell her that a surveyor might find she was rotten.'

She turned out to be very sound indeed, and thus a humble Looe lugger was restored to become Peter and Anne Pye's famous gaff cutter *Moonraker of Fowey*. While her sister ships were towed to a final, rotting resting place up the Looe River, for it was considered unlucky to break them up, *Moonie* suffered no such ignominy. Ranging far and wide, her voyages from the Baltic to Tahiti and Alaska to Brazil were delightfully described by the Pyes in the classic *Red Mains'l, The Sea is for Sailing* and *A Sail in a Forest*.

Their exploits won them the prestigious Royal Cruising Club Challenge three times and three years before his untimely death in 1966 Peter Pye was elected Commodore of the RCC.

Polperro

There are no such bargains to be found in Polperro today, and the people who throng there are not searching for boats to buy, merely postcards, cream teas and souvenirs. It is not, however, a particularly recent phenomenon, as a guide book written in the 1920s reveals '. . . a human bees' nest stowed away in a cranny of rocks. Its industries are four: the catching of fish, the painting of pictures, handicrafts and – latterly – the entertainment of visitors, for it is probably the most charmingly unexpected village in all England. . .'

The pressure of visitors in recent years has resulted in the welcome banning of all cars from Polperro during the day, with a large car park on the outskirts. The 10-minute walk down the hill comes as a considerable shock to many of today's car-bound explorers unused to such inconvenience and exertion; with great relief, I suspect, they soon spot the horse drawn bus!

APPROACH AND MOORINGS

This undeniably attractive harbour is set in a narrow cleft among the cliffs just under three miles west of Looe Island, and five miles east of Fowey. It is not, at first, the easiest place to find and no attempt should be made to approach it in any southerly wind and seas, particularly from south-east. Not only are the approaches dangerous in these conditions, it is quite likely that the protective steel gate across the entrance will be closed.

Once past Looe Island when approaching from the east, a pair of transit beacons will be seen on the mainland marking the beginning of a measured mile; the second set of beacons identifying its western end lie at Downend Point just east of Talland Bay.

From south of the point, a V-shaped cleft in the high cliffs will begin to open and houses of Polperro will come into view. Steer to within two cables of the inlet and Peak Rock, a pyramid-shaped spur topped with jagged boulders, will be seen on the western side. Spy House Point, where the harbour light (Iso WR 6s) is located, is on the eastern side. The main hazard is The Polca, a rock (least depth 1.2m) about 200m south-west of the point, while the Raney, two rocks drying 0.8m, will usually be spotted awash just off Peak Rock. Proceed with caution and pass between these and the hidden Polca, before turning into the inlet and heading for the end of the East Pier. Alternatively, to pass east and north of The Polca, keep the outer ends of the West and East Piers just touching, giving a leading line of 310°T. There are up to six red visitors' moorings in the outer approach where there is about 1.8m LAT – depths begin to reduce quickly once you have passed them and the inner harbour dries as far as the outer pier at Springs, but can normally be entered after half flood. If the tide is low or you do not wish to dry out inside the harbour, moor fore and aft (north-west/south-east) between the moorings to avoid swinging into the fairway to the harbour. Alternatively, anchor to seaward clear of them in 3m – 4m LAT showing a riding light.

BERTHING

Within the harbour, the East Quay wall immediately inside the entrance must be kept clear at all times, as this is the fuel berth for the local fishing boats, a mixture of trawlers and pot boats, which also use most of the alongside berths on the West Pier, East Quay and the inner Fish Quay. The rest of the harbour has many drying fore and aft small boat moorings and berthing for visitors is therefore very limited. There is, however, usually space for up to two boats (maximum 10m LOA) to dry out alongside the wooden pile quay just beyond the *Museum of Smuggling and Fishing* on the East Quay where, conveniently, a large wooden ladder has been installed. At half tide there is usually about 1.5m here, but it is a berth best suited to bilge keelers or those with fin keel boats who are used to drying out!

The overnight charge works out at around £15 for a 10m boat, a bit less for smaller craft. The harbourmaster, Chris Curtis, who is also a full-time fisherman, or his assistant, will appear at some point to collect your dues. Their office, Tel: 01503 272809, is in the small fish market on the western side of the harbour, and they can usually be contacted on VHF Ch 10 – callsign *Polperro Harbourmaster* – should the need arise. The local trip boats work on Ch 15, and if you are not able to raise the harbourmaster they might be able to offer advice if needed. They do their best to make you welcome, and as the fishing continues to decline, Polperro, in keeping with many other West Country ports, has realised that pleasure craft might ultimately be their only route to survival and plans are still afoot to try and build a new inner pier to accommodate up to six visitors along with showers – that is, if the funding can be found, but this has so far proved elusive.

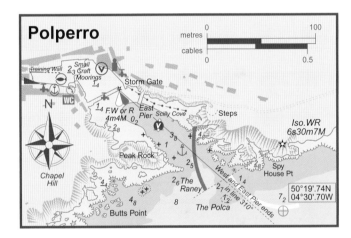

FUEL, FRESH WATER AND GAS

Diesel is only available in small quantities from the fishermen if you're really stuck, so it is best to fuel up in Fowey or Plymouth. The nearest petrol can be obtained in cans from a garage about a mile away. There are fresh water taps on both East and West Quays. No Calor or Camping Gaz.

Polperro approach from the south: Spy House Point is to the right, with the East and West pier ends coming into transit to clear Polca Rock. The yachts are on the visitors' buoys

Polperro's small drying harbour is in a spectacular setting at the foot of a steep-sided valley.
Note Peak Rock, with the Raney extending underwater, centre

POLPERRO FACILITIES
(Local phone code 01503)

In spite of its popularity the village has fortunately not been over developed. It is carefully administered by the entirely voluntary Polperro Harbour Trustees, with the declared intention of maintaining its unique character.

The tiny narrow streets and houses overhanging the harbour and the diminutive River Pol have probably outwardly altered little since 1762, when the Methodist preacher John Wesley was forced to change his lodgings because the room beneath him was 'filled with pilchards and conger eels, the perfume being too potent . . .'

Prior to the advent of the tourist industry, fishing and smuggling were the main activities, the rabbit warren of alleyways ideal for evading the Excise men. Special boats were built for the trade, and one, the *Unity*, was reputed to have made 500 successful trips, crossing to France in just over eight hours with a fair wind. Today this colourful past is well documented in the Polperro Museum of Smuggling and Fishing in the old pilchard factory on the east side of the harbour.

It is still an intriguing place to explore, particularly in the evening when the coaches and day trippers have gone on their way.

Considering the size of the village, the facilities are surprisingly good, with a grocer, butcher, baker, greengrocer, newsagents and a post office with cash machine. There's a doctor's surgery here, Tel: 272768, and you'll also find a chemist up the hill in the area known as the Coombes.

Restaurants include Neville's, Tel: 272459, for good seafood, Couch's Great House Restaurant, Tel: 272554, Nelson's, Tel: 272366, and the House on the Props, Tel: 272310. In the Coombes you'll find the Cottage Restaurant, Tel: 272217, the Kitchen, Tel: 272780, the Polmary Restaurant, Tel: 272828, and the Mermaid Hotel, Tel: 272502, which is open to non-residents. Bar meals are available at the pubs, which all have suitably nautical names: The Blue Peter, The Ship and The Three Pilchards!

In November 1824 three houses, the inner and outer piers, and 50 boats were destroyed in the worst southeasterly storm ever experienced, but on a balmy summer evening Polperro is a very different place. The cheerful red, green and yellow of the boats and the subtle backdrop of white, pink and slate-hung cottages shimmer on the water at the height of the tide, while lingering holidaymakers bask on the warm, weathered stone of the harbour wall, eking out the very last of the sun's fading glow as the valley sinks into shadow.

The harbour can also be a surprisingly musical place at times, when the Polperro Fisherman's Choir performs on the quayside and especially during the Polperro Proms, the highlight of the summer season (usually the third weekend in August), when a temporary scaffolding stage is constructed in the middle of the harbour creating a spectacular setting for jazz on the Friday night, rock and pop on Saturday and the event's climax on Sunday night, a 50-piece classical orchestra!

Fowey

Tides	HW Dover −0555
Range	MHWS 5.4m–MHWN 4.3m, MLWN 2.0m–MLWS 0.6m
Charts	AC: 31 and 148, SC 5602.7; Stanfords: CP 23; Imray: WCP 2400.7
Waypoint	Cannis Rock buoy 50°18'.38N 04°39'.95W
Hazards	Udder Rock 3M to east (lit), Punch's Cross (unlit). Cannis Rock (lit). Busy commercial port, beware shipping in narrow entrance. Upper reaches dry
Harbour Speed limit	Six knots/no wash
Overnight charge	Harbour Authority mooring or pontoon £13.50. Mixtow pontoon £15.50

'Fowey is the harbour of harbours, the last port town left without any admixture of modern evil. It ought to be a kingdom all of its own. In Fowey all is courtesy and good reason for the chance sailing man . . . and I have never sailed into Fowey or out of Fowey without good luck attending me.'

Hilaire Belloc obviously rather liked Fowey, but he was not alone among literary men and women to succumb to the romantic charm of this delightful town and deep narrow river. Daphne du Maurier lived here for many years, Sir Arthur Quiller-Couch – Q – immortalised it in his famous sagas as *Troy Town*, and his friend, Kenneth Grahame, also used it in *The Wind in the Willows*.

APPROACHES

The entrance, although only a cable wide at its narrowest, is deep and easy except in strong onshore winds over an ebb tide. The only possible problems, day or night, are likely to be a large ship emerging and fluky winds.

Keep to the middle of the channel, leaving the white cross on Punch's Cross Rock and the triangular white beacon on Lamp Rock to starboard, and high St Catherine's Point, with its small fortress, and the narrow inlet of Readymoney Cove to port.

At night, Fowey lighthouse (L Fl WR 5s) has red sectors covering the coast to the east and west. Make your approach in the white sector until the inner

'Fowey is the harbour of harbours...' and its approach is straightforward and deep. St Catherine's Point is to the left, Polruan to the right, with the visitors' moorings and Pont Pill pontoons beyond

lighthouse on Whitehouse Point, midway up the western shore, provides a sectored light (Iso RWG 3s), the white sector of which leads straight in.

Once past St Catherine's Point (Fl R 2.5s) and Lamp Rock (Fl G 5s), the only other navigation lights are the fixed red lights at the end of the Polruan ferry landing and on Fowey Town Quay, and fixed green lights on Polruan Quay. If departing at night, St Catherine's Point (Fl R 2.5s), visible 150° – 295°, and Lamp Rock (Fl G 5s), visible 010° – 205°, usefully indicate the dangers on either hand.

THE HARBOUR

Beyond Polruan fort, the river widens and the moorings, followed by the village of Polruan, will come into view along the eastern side of the harbour. Fowey stretches out along the western side in neat terraces climbing ever higher up the steep hillside overlooking the harbour. Whitehouse Quay is a small pier on the Fowey shore where a small passenger ferry runs across to Polruan, along with a seasonal ferry to Mevagissey. A little further upstream, the low black and white twin gabled building with a veranda, awning and large flagstaff is the Royal Fowey Yacht Club.

There is an average of 7m at Low Water Springs dredged right through the centre of the harbour, and plenty of water to within half a cable of the shore as far as Town Quay. This is easily located by the tower of St Fimbarrus Church and the prominent King of Prussia Hotel behind it and, except for the slipway, it dries at Low Water. It is used by local fishing and trip boats and also the water taxi.

Albert Quay, a short distance beyond, has a sizeable short stay visitors' pontoon which is dredged and accessible at any state of the tide, although further inshore it dries at Low Water. You may berth alongside this pontoon free of charge for up to two hours – handy for shopping, landing crew or taking on fresh water. Small tenders can be left for up to 12 hours on the inside. Be warned though – boats abusing this excellent facility, by using it for an overnight stop for instance, will be charged five times the normal mooring rate in the harbour!

There may be large ships moored fore and aft in the centre of the river, waiting to berth at the china clay wharves upriver, and although this narrow waterway seems on first appearance an improbable place for much commercial activity, you are now in the 15th largest exporting port in the United Kingdom, shipping one million tons of china clay a year. It sounds like a lot and it is, but sadly this trade has been steadily declining due to cheaper foreign sources, notably Brazil, and will soon be dropping to 800,000 tons and around 350 ships a year – a far cry from the heady days of 1989 when it peaked at 848 vessels and exported 1.89 million tons!

Most ships average between 7,000 and 8,000 tonnes, but the largest to date, the *Clary* and *Julie* were nearly 17,800 tons and 540ft in length, loading 14,750 tonnes for Canada.

It is fascinating to watch the apparent ease with which these vessels are manoeuvred to their berths, in particular the technique of 'drudging' them stern first up the river. This technique involves towing from aft with the anchor dragging on a short scope to hold the bows in position. Another spectacle during the summer months is the increasing number of cruise liners which are now making Fowey a regular port of call, the largest to date the 248m, 48,000 ton *Crystal Harmony*, and visitors in 2007 included *Boudicca* and *The World*.

Considering that well over 7,000 yachts also visit the port annually, the commendable Harbour Authority

Cruise ships, china clay and visiting pleasure craft are the lifeblood of Fowey. The yachts are all lying on the well marked visitors' moorings off Pont Pill

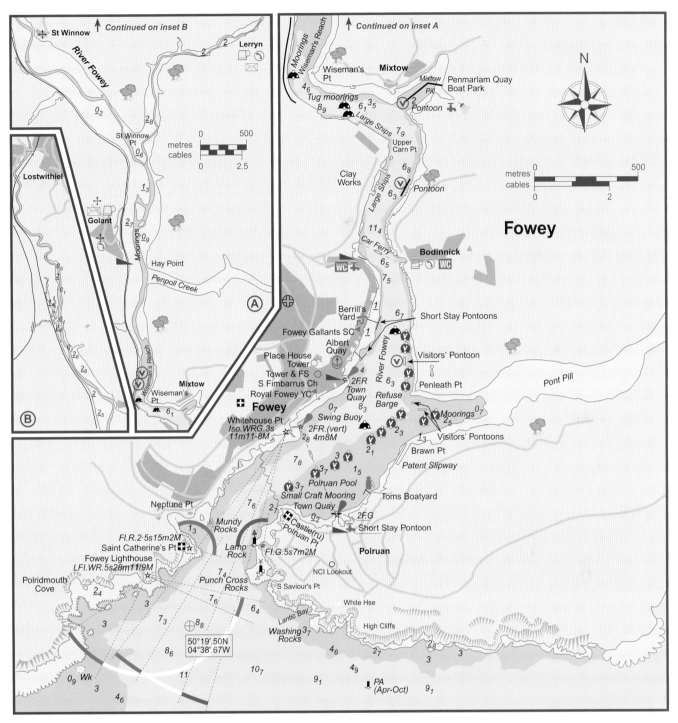

manages to achieve a remarkable balance between intensive commercial activity and a large number of pleasure craft. Facilities have been improved considerably in recent years and the main area for visitors to head for is the Swinging Ground just opposite the Royal Fowey YC.

During the season the doughty harbour launch, *Zebedee*, the harbourmaster's dory, *Dougal*, and patrol boats *Florence* and *Brian* (any similarity to the *Magic Roundabout* is not purely coincidental!) are on the water seven days a week from 0800 until dark, and in the afternoon they keep a lookout to assist new arrivals and allocate moorings. Such is the popularity of Fowey during the height of the season that you will invariably have to raft up.

Although the harbour office, Tel: 01726 832471, and launches monitor VHF Ch 16, they should be called on their working channel – Ch 12, callsign either *Fowey Harbour Radio* or *Fowey Harbour Patrol*. Note that the landlocked nature of the harbour tends to make reception poor from outside and you will probably not make contact until you are in the entrance, when you will have been spotted anyway. Because of this, the harbour office provides and maintains a direct land line VHF link to Brixham Coastguard.

BERTHING, MOORINGS AND ANCHORING

On the Polruan side of the harbour adjacent to the fairway there are several large yellow mooring buoys for larger vessels or for several smaller vessels

The Albert Quay short stay pontoon is always busy

There are three visitors' pontoons off Pont Pill, opposite the town

rafting up together if the weather is suitable. More swinging moorings for visitors lie further upstream, as you approach the entrance to Pont Pill, the creek that branches away to the north-east. These are either yellow or white buoys, all of which are clearly marked *FHC Visitor* and numbered. Three 36m long visitors' pontoons lie just within the mouth of Pont Pill (dredged 2m for some distance). Fore and aft moorings are also available in Pont Pill – handy if you want a bit of peace away from the main stream and ideal for leaving a boat if stuck for time or weather bound.

The floating rubbish and recycling skip close by should be used in preference to taking it ashore, and the Harbour Authority runs a unique daily rubbish collection service free of charge during the peak season in its dory, *Dillon*. Free rubbish bags are also available.

Just upstream of Pont Pill along the eastern side of the river, there are more swinging visitors' moorings as well as another 36m pontoon for visitors up to 16m LOA.

Opposite, on the western side of the river, a short distance beyond Albert Quay pontoon, is another short stay pontoon (max two hours) off Berrill's Yard, which belongs to the Harbour Commissioners, and also a pontoon that is the home of Fowey lifeboat. Here you will find a rubbish skip, a marine toilet pump-out facility and oily waste disposal.

Further upriver there are several other berthing options for visitors, see under 'Upper Reaches' on page 139.

Anchoring is not allowed anywhere in the fairway, near underwater cables or close to landing places. You may anchor off the entrance to Pont Pill to the east of the swinging ground, but only with the harbourmaster's permission, and this sometimes entails having to move when larger vessels are being manoeuvred.

As there is no difference in price between anchoring and using one of the Harbour Authority facilities, most visitors opt for the latter. There are seven charge bands on the visitors' buoys or pontoons (except Mixtow) – a boat between 7m and 11m works out at £13.50 per night, but there are reductions for longer stays. If you

pay in advance to stay for three days it would cost £32.50 for a boat in this charge band, or £73 for a week, except in July and August. However, if you pay for three nights in advance during these months you will be given a voucher for a free night in September or October, or two free nights if you pay for a week!

There are six charge bands for Mixtow pontoon, which is limited to a maximum size of 25m. Here a 7m to 11m boat costs £15.50 per night, with similar reductions for longer stays if you pay in advance, and vouchers during July and August.

FUEL, FRESH WATER AND GAS

Given the number of craft using Fowey annually, it comes as a surprise to many to find that fuel is not as easily obtained as might be anticipated. Diesel is available from the pontoon off C Toms & Son boatyard in Polruan during the summer, 0815 – 1615 weekdays, 1000 – 1200 weekends, call VHF Ch 10 or Tel: 01726 870232. The only source of petrol is the Four Turnings Garage, a mostly uphill walk of nearly a mile from the waterfront.

Fresh water taps and hoses will be found on the short stay pontoons at Albert Quay and Berrills Yard, and also on Mixtow Pontoon. There is no fresh water on the Polruan short stay pontoon. Calor gas and Camping Gaz refills can be obtained from Upper Deck Marine Chandlers on Albert Quay.

FACILITIES
(Local phone code 01726)
Landing is easy at the Albert Quay pontoon or Berrill's Pontoon where dinghies can be left on the inside. You can also use the landing at the Royal Fowey Yacht Club, Tel: 01726 832245, but pull dinghies clear of the steps and remember that the foreshore here dries at Low Water.

The club was founded in 1905 and members of other clubs are welcome to use its facilities, including good showers (£1 slotmeter) and comfortable bar. Here, among the various burgees that adorn the walls, is one that, for me, a dyed in the wool romantic, always induces a certain nostalgic twinge – it belonged to *Moonraker of Fowey* and was presented to the club by Anne Pye. Eagle-eyed visitors might also spot the club ensign: it is one of just a handful of clubs that have been granted a warrant to fly a defaced Red.

The club serves good value lunches, teas and dinners as well as breakfast from 0800 – 1030 during the season. Racing takes place every Wednesday evening and Sunday afternoon and visitors are welcome to join in.

The Fowey Gallants Sailing Club, Tel: 01726 832335, just upstream from Albert Quay, was founded in 1950. It has a relaxed and a pleasant family atmosphere and also extends a warm welcome to visiting yacht crews. Facilities include showers (£1), toilets and a bar that serves good food at weekends.

The alternative to your own dinghy is the popular water taxi service which runs from Town Quay. This can be hailed on VHF Ch 06, callsign *Fowey Water Taxi* (Mobile 07774 906730). It operates seven days a week in season from about 0800 until the pubs close. Charges per person are: lower harbour £2 single/£3.50 return, Mixtow £2.50 single/£4.50 return, Wisemans pool £4 single/£7 return. Children under 12 pay less. It does away with the problem of worrying about the dinghy and the sheltered cuddy is particularly enticing when it is pouring with rain and blowing.

The town is essentially just one main shopping street, very narrow in places, with houses rising up from it – still very much as Sea Rat described it in *The Wind in the Willows*: '. . . the little, grey sea town I know so well, that clings along one steep side of the harbour. There, through dark doorways you look down flights of stone steps, overhung by great pink tufts of valerian and ending in a patch of sparkling blue water. The little boats that lie tethered to the rings and stanchions of the old seawall are as gaily painted as those I clambered in and out of in my own childhood; the salmon leap on the flood tide, schools of mackerel flash and play past

the quay-sides and foreshores and by the windows the great vessels glide, night and day, up to their moorings or forth to the sea. There, sooner or later the ships of all seafaring nations arrive; and there, at its destined hour the ship of my choice will let go its anchor . . .'

It is not quite as grey today, as most of the buildings are brightly painted and very well preserved. It is also far busier than when Kenneth Grahame was writing, with cars and people competing to squeeze through the narrow bottleneck of the main street. Nevertheless, it is still a delightful place and spared the over-commercialism of so many other Cornish harbours – perhaps a reflection on the fact that such a large proportion of its visitors come in by sea.

Belloc's eulogy continues, '. . . whatever you may need in gear is to be had at once' – which is certainly true except perhaps on Sundays, with everything that a cruising crew might require including Kittows, an excellent butcher renowned for its sausages; Fowey Fish, which can also provide ice; Tiffins Delicatessen and Bakery; Fowey Mini Market (foodstore and off-licence, open 0800 – 2000 daily, 0900 – 2000 Sundays); a post office; newsagents; Bookends for secondhand nautical books; three banks which only open in the morning, although HSBC and Barclays do both have cashpoints whereas Lloyds TSB does not. There is also a cash machine in the post office. Upper Deck Marine and Outriggers chandlers are both by Albert Quay, and Mitchell Sails is a short walk away along North Street. WiFi internet access is available – visit www.myoceanwave. The only facility still noticeably lacking is a launderette, although laundry can be arranged through the Caravan Park if you are berthed at Penmarlam.

For its size, Fowey offers a wide choice of eating places. To get the day off to a good start, try the Lifebuoy Café's renowned all day breakfast or the hearty alternative at the nearby Royal Fowey Yacht Club. There's a wide choice of restaurants including Zutchis at the Toll Bar, Tel: 833001, and Food for Thought, Tel: 832221, which provides elegant dining right on the Town Quay, while the Waterfront, also situated on the quay, is a cheaper alternative, with good value family meals. The elegant Old Quay House Hotel, Tel: 833302, has a delightful waterside ambience or try the Commodore, Tel: 833594, for Italian. Sams, Tel: 832273, is a lively bistro with an excellent lunchtime menu; The Other Place, Tel: 833636, is the venue for superb seafood and Taipan, Tel: 833899, is the omnipresent Chinese!

Such is its popularity, at the height of the season you will always have to raft in Fowey

Several local hotels, like the Fowey and the Marina, with its award winning Nathan Outlaw restaurant (reservations essential, Tel: 833315), are open to non-residents for meals, while the pubs – Safe Harbour, Ship Inn, King of Prussia, Galleon, Lugger Inn and Globe Posting House – all have a good selection of bar meals. If you want a pleasant stroll before you eat, head towards the Bodinnick Ferry car park where Chuffers, Tel: 833832, resplendent in Great Western livery, harks back to the days when this was the site of Fowey's railway station. Just across the ferry at Bodinnick, you'll also find the old Ferry Inn, another pleasant pub that does lunch and evening meals.

POLRUAN

Polruan clings to an even steeper hillside than Fowey and can provide all the basics. It is an attractive, far quieter little village where visitors' cars are prohibited in season – they must be parked at the top of the hill.

During the summer there is a convenient short stay, all-tide landing pontoon provided by FHC and the Polruan Town Trust off the end of Polruan Quay, but be careful going alongside at Low Water as there is limited depth.

The village has a well-stocked mini-market/off licence/newsagent (0700 – 1700 Mon – Fri, 0730 – 1700 Sat; 0730 – 1230 Sun), a post office that can be found in the Winklepicker gift shop on the Quay, and a couple of good pubs – the Russell and the Lugger Inn (where there is a cash machine) – as well as Crumpets Teashop.

C Toms & Son boatyard is on the site of the former Slade boatyard, which built a number of well-known West Country schooners and was the inspiration for Coombes boatyard in Daphne du Maurier's *The Loving Spirit*. The yard is still very much involved with traditional boatbuilding, and a peep into its large shed often reveals a big wooden or steel fishing boat under construction. Its slipway, one of the largest in the

There is a convenient short stay and dinghy landing pontoon off quieter Polruan but check the depth towards Low Water

area, can take vessels of up to 28m and 160 tons, and there is also a 30-ton crane.

The Harbour Authority has a large slipway and its own repair yard at Brazen Island further along the Polruan shore, which is used to maintain its tugs, dredger and barges. Private vessels up to 450 tons and 30ft beam can be hauled out by arrangement. It is also possible for smaller craft to dry out alongside the wall here for scrubbing/repairs, with the harbourmaster's permission, at no extra charge.

TROYS AND GALLANTS

Fowey Classics, a gathering for traditional craft, takes place during the first week in August, culminating in a feeder race to Falmouth Classics. Fowey Regatta Week, the major sailing event of the year, is during the third week in August, when the harbour is packed to absolute capacity. Feeder races from Plymouth and Falmouth include a large contingent of their gaff-rigged working boats, and racing takes place every day both outside and inside the harbour, including the very close competition among the local one design class, the *Troys. Jocelyn*, the first of these colourful 18ft three-quarter decked, tall rig bermudian sloops, which sport a distinctive 4ft bowsprit, was created in the winter of 1928/29 by local boatbuilder Archie Watty. She was an instant hit, by the following season six more had been built and Sir Arthur Quiller-Couch allowed the name *Troy* to be adopted for what had become a new class. To date 26 have been built, of which 23 survive today, including four built since 2004. Early boat owners favoured girls' names, but later turned to gemstones – *Opal, Jade* and the very latest, *Moonstone*.

The other local class is the Fowey River, solid 15ft clinker family dinghies based on the 1945 'Knockabout' design by RF Freeman. The first of nearly 50 was built in 1950 by Hunkins Boatyard and, although many have been lost over the years, a fleet of around 16 usually turns out during Fowey Week, their brightly coloured gunter rig making them instantly recognisable!

The spectacular finale of the week is the Harbour Race for the Falmouth Working Boats. However, if you are seeking peace and quiet, be warned – this is one week to avoid Fowey altogether!

Historically, Fowey has a wild and romantic past, which started when the port began to develop in the 12th century after the previous harbour at Lostwithiel, six miles inland, began to silt up. By 1346 it was able to supply 47 ships and nearly 800 men for the siege of Calais, more than any other port in England, and it seemed to give the Fowey men a particular taste for adventure. Little more than pirates, they continued to wage their own private war against the French long after hostilities had officially ceased, and daring raids and bloodthirsty skirmishes across the Channel not only earned them a lot of

Unique to Fowey, the close harbour racing among the fleet of Troy one-designs is always a delight to watch

plunder, but also the nickname of *Fowey Gallants*.

The French hit back in 1457, raiding and setting fire to the town, forcing its inhabitants to take refuge in the seat of the Treffry family – Place House – the prominent large house with tall towers just behind the church. However, this attack only stimulated the activities of the Gallants, one of whom, John Wilcock, seized no less than 15 French ships in as many days, becoming a source of great embarrassment to King Edward IV, who sent a message to Fowey 'I am at peace with my brother of France'. Not impressed, the Gallants proceeded to cut off the unfortunate messenger's ears and nose, an act of defiance that resulted in considerable punishment for the town. The ringleaders were hanged, goods seized, ships distributed to other ports and the huge protective chain slung from the forts as the harbour mouth was removed. Duly chastened, the wild men of Fowey returned to more peaceful pursuits, fishing, shipbuilding, trading and, of course, smuggling . . !

THE UPPER REACHES

Deeper draught boats normally remain in the lower part of the harbour except, perhaps, when it begins to blow from the south-west for, in spite of its landlocked nature, conditions can sometimes become very uncomfortable. Perfect in so many other ways, Fowey's one major drawback is the very annoying swell that sets in off Polruan and, with a strong wind against tide in the harbour, it can at times become surprisingly rough and very rolly.

Traditionally, boats used to run upriver and anchor in Wiseman's Pool, but it is now so full of moorings that this is no longer possible. Four visitors' moorings are available here, so it is worth contacting the harbour staff for advice, otherwise proceed upstream where the river narrows above the town past the pretty hamlet of Bodinnick, keeping a lookout for Ferryside, the prominent house by the waterside where the du Maurier family were brought up, and also, mounted on the corner of the building, the figurehead of the famous Polruan schooner *Jane Slade*.

Watch out too for the Bodinnick ferry which carries cars and pedestrians across to Fowey, and make sure you pass well astern!

Beyond it, the extensive clay loading wharves appear along the west bank, a fascinating stretch of river with ships of many nationalities berthed alongside. At the height of its activity the surrounding trees were eerily wreathed in fine white dust, like a gentle fall of snow but the surrounding greenery hereabouts is now a visible manifestation of the declining export. On the opposite side of the river, beneath the high-wooded shore, you will find another 36m visitors' pontoon in this much more sheltered reach.

The other option is to continue even further to Mixtow Pill, which has excellent shelter in all weathers. Here you will find the Harbour Authority's 165m pontoon with visitors' berths along the south side. These berths are dredged to 2m LAT and fresh water taps are provided on the pontoon. An overnight berth works out at £15 for a 10m boat. The north side of the

Peaceful Penmarlam! In a wooded setting, the visitors' pontoon in Mixtow Pill provides a pleasant retreat from the busier facilities downstream

pontoon is reserved for local boats and must not be used, unless directed by the harbour staff. The pontoon is linked by a gangway to the Penmarlam Quay Boat Park, where you will find recycling bins and visitors' showers and toilets in the Portacabins a bit further up the hill. Other facilities include a 7m wide slipway and a boat hoist capable of lifting vessels of up to 8.4 tons.

The foreshore on either side of the creek is private and landing is not allowed.

The deep channel turns sharply to port at Upper Carn Point, opposite the entrance to Mixtow Pill. Particular care should be taken to look out for large ships rounding this bend. At the end of this short reach, overlooked by high woods, the docks finish and the channel turns back to the north round Wiseman Point, a wooded rocky promontory, until Wiseman's Pool, thick with moorings, comes into view.

Although the river is still navigable for small craft on a good tide as far as the country town of Lostwithiel, beyond Wiseman's Reach it dries almost completely to a mixture of sand and mudbanks. Shoal draught boats and dinghies can explore on the flood, and bilge-keelers are able to anchor and dry out off Golant, where there are a large number of drying moorings and a pleasant little village with a general store, a post office and good pub grub at the Fisherman's Arms. Also, the Riverside Restaurant at the Cormorant Hotel, Tel: 833426, has excellent seafood and a lovely view.

Golant Boat Watch office is situated here, along with a fresh water tap, rubbish bins and a public telephone by the quay.

Beyond Golant, Lerryn Creek, bearing away to the north-east, is steep-to and wooded. At Lerryn, there is a slipway and landing on the south side of the creek and the village can provide a Spar grocery/off-licence, the Ship Inn, public toilets and a phone by the head of the creek.

At St Winnow, on the way to Lostwithiel, a fine 15th century church is situated in a lovely setting close by the waters' edge, while the fascinating Barton Farm agricultural museum is nearby.

FOWEY WALKS AND BEACHES

If the weather does turn and you are stuck in Fowey for a few days, take advantage of the fine walks in the area. A guided town walk is organised by the Tourist Information Centre every Tuesday (June to September), but for something longer my favourite is the Hall Walk, which skirts a large part of the harbour. Ideally leave the dinghy in Fowey and catch the ferry to Bodinnick where the walk is signposted on the right, halfway up the steep hill leading out of the village. Far from arduous, the grassy track gently follows the contour line right round Penleath Point to the large stone memorial to Sir Arthur Quiller-Couch, where magnificent views of the harbour might possibly have inspired this fine piece of doggerel from the one time Professor of English Literature at Cambridge:

'O the Harbour of Fowey Is a beautiful spot, And it's there I enjowey To sail in a yot. . .'

From here, continue on through the woods and wild flowers above Pont Pill, and down to the hamlet of Pont with its old quay and water mill. The track then climbs another wooded hillside with more lovely views all the way back to Polruan, where a cream tea would seem to be an eminently sensible idea before catching the ferry back to Fowey where you will pass Quiller-Couch's former home, the Haven.

Another favourite is the walk to seaward of Fowey along the road to Readymoney Cove, where a track leads up on to St Catherine's Point. Pause to look at the old fortress built by Henry VIII in 1540 and the fine views into the harbour.

Above it is the curious structure that can just be seen when entering from sea. Two granite arches surmounted by a Maltese cross – looking like the top of a huge crown – is the tomb of William Rashleigh and his wife and daughter. They were descendants of Charles Rashleigh, who not only built the port of Charlestown, but also Menabilly on Gribbin Head. For many years this was the home of Daphne du Maurier and supposedly the house she immortalised as *Manderlay* in her novel *Rebecca*.

Following the coast path out towards Gribbin Head, you skirt the private grounds and woods surrounding Menabilly and, although you never actually see the elusive house, there are spectacular views of the harbour mouth, the coast, and some particularly lovely scenery around Polridmouth Cove – pronounced Pridmouth.

To visit this pleasant fair weather daytime anchorage, sound in towards the centre of the outer bay into about 2m. It is possible to proceed closer inshore with care, but there is a shallow sandbank in the centre of the inner part of the cove which has a tendency to shift! The beach has clean sand and is good for swimming,

and from here the lovely coastal path continues onwards to Polkerris if you want to make a real day of it. Alternatively, just walk as far as the splendid red and white-striped daymark to enjoy the panoramic view from beneath this silent witness to so many departures and arrivals, such as *Moonraker*'s at the end of her Pacific voyage, 40 days out from Bermuda: 'The sun soaked up the haze, and the town of Fowey was just out of sight. In an hour or two, or three or four, a breeze would come and we should sail in through the Heads into the harbour from which we had set out three years ago. What changes should we find, I wondered, and how should we take to living on the land? Would Christopher pad about the city in barefeet and bowler hat, and should we be content with creeks? My thoughts were disturbed by the sound of a vessel's engine and a boat came up that was familiar. She stopped, her sails casting their shadows upon the water. Her people welcomed us.

"Come aboard", I said, "and have some coffee" and I hurried down to start the Primus. Presently Anne looked out. "Hullo", she said, "where have they gone to?"

"They wanted to get in", said Christopher. "They've already been two nights at sea."'

The crew was Christopher Pritchard-Barrett; over half a century on, after a long lay up on the beach in Mixtow Pill and several years at the Exeter Maritime Museum before its demise, *Moonraker* came into the ownership of Christopher's son Jamie who was midway through a total rebuild in 2007, and hopefully she will soon be seen afloat again in West Country waters!

Fowey Port Guide – Area telephone code: 01726

Harbourmaster: Captain Mike Sutherland, Harbourmaster's Office, Albert Quay, Fowey, Tel: 832471 or 832472; Fax: 833738; email: FHC@foweyharbour.co.uk; website: www.foweyharbour.co.uk.

VHF: Ch 16, working Ch 12, callsigns *Fowey Harbour Radio* or *Fowey Harbour Patrol* 0800 – 2100 in season.

Mail drop: Harbour office or RFYC.

Emergency services: Lifeboat at Fowey; Brixham Coastguard.

Anchorage: Only with harbourmaster's permission off entrance to Pont Pill, clear of moorings and coaster swinging ground, or drying creeks.

Moorings/berthing: Harbour Commission short stay pontoons (up to two hours) off Albert Quay, Berrill's yard and Polruan Quay. Twenty two deep water moorings, visitors' pontoon near Pont Pill and three pontoons and fore and aft moorings within Pont Pill and in Polruan Pool. Visitors' pontoon beyond Bodinnick opposite commercial wharves. Large visitors' pontoon in Mixtow Pill with access to shore for showers and toilets at Penmarlam Quay Boat Park.

Charges: 10m boat overnight on FHC facility or at anchor £13.50. Mixtow pontoon £15.50.

Dinghy landings: Inside Albert Quay pontoon, Berrill's Yard pontoon, RFYC. Polruan Quay pontoon.

Water taxi: From Town Quay, Easter – Sept, 0800 until pub closing time daily, VHF channel 06, callsign *Fowey Water Taxi*, Tel: 07774 906730, or hail. **Marina:** None.

Phones: Near Town Quay, RFYC, Fowey Gallants SC, outside post office. **Doctor:** Fowey, Tel: 832451; Polruan, Tel: 870396. **Dentist:** Tel: 833309 or 833487.

Always bouncing 'roundabout', the doughty harbour launch, *Zebedee*!

Fowey Port Guide (Cont) – Area telephone code: 01726

There's a festive feel to Fowey's narrow main street in the summer

Hospital: Fowey Community Hospital, off Green Lane, minor injuries, Tel: 832241.

Churches: C of E.

Local weather forecast: Outside harbour office.

Fuel: Diesel only from C Toms & Son boatyard pontoon, 0815 – 1615 weekdays, 1000 – 1200 weekends, call Tel: 870232 or VHF Ch 10.

Paraffin: Upper Deck Marine, Tel: 832287.

Gas: Calor/Gaz, Upper Deck Marine, Tel: 832287.

Water: Albert Quay and Berrill's yard and Mixtow pontoon.

Tourist Information Centre: In Daphne du Maurier Centre, by the Church, Tel: 833616.

Banks/cashpoints: Open mornings only, Barclays and HSBC have cashpoints but not Lloyds TSB. Cash machine at Fowey post office and Lugger Inn, Polruan.

Post office: In main street, turn right at Albert Quay.

Internet access: WiFi broadband available in main part of harbour – visit www.myoceanwave.com. Public library, by Bodinnick Ferry car park. Pinky Murphy's café, North Street.

Rubbish: Floating skip off Pont Pill, bins ashore at Berrill's yard, Polruan Quay and Golant, all with recycling facility. Daily rubbish collection afloat mid-July to mid-September. Waste oil disposal at Berrill's yard, Brazen Island and at harbour office.

Showers/toilets: RFYC; Fowey Gallants SC; Penmarlam Quay boat park, adjoining Mixtow pontoon. Public toilets on Town Quay. Marine toilet disposal, Berrill's yard.

Launderette: None but laundry can be arranged at Caravan park, Penmarlam.

Provisions: All requirements including delicatessen. Foodstore open late and Sunday, Fowey. Mini-mart/off-licence open six days and Sunday mornings, Polruan.

Ice: Fowey Fish.

Chandler: Upper Deck Marine, Tel: 832287, and Outriggers, Tel: 833233, Admiralty Chart Agents, Albert Quay.

Repairs/hauling: C Toms & Son boatyard, Tel: 870232, Polruan; Fowey Boatyard, Passage Street, Fowey, Tel: 832194; W C Hunkin & Sons, Millpool Boatyard, Tel: 832874; Fowey Harbour Commissioners, Tel: 832471; Peter Williams, Bodinnick Boatyard, Tel: 870987; FHC Penmarlam Quay and boat park, Tel: 832471.

Drying out: By arrangement with harbourmaster.

Marine engineers: C Toms & Son, Tel: 870232; Fowey Harbour Marine Engineers, Tel: 832806, Mobile 07770 600083 or 07876 610399.

Electronic engineers: Fowey Marine Electronics, Station Road, Tel: 833101.

Sailmaker/repairs: Mitchell Sails, North Street, Fowey, Tel: 833731.

Divers: Sal Diving, Tel: 844640; Mobile 07770 598346.

Taxi: Fowey Taxi, Tel: 832676; Yeo's, Tel: 814095; Coastal Cars, Tel: 832372.

Transport: No 25 bus hourly from outside Safe Harbour pub, Tel: 0871 2002233, to main line railway station at Par (20 mins), but not all trains stop here. The 25 bus continues to St Austell (a further 25 mins), to connect with most main line trains, Tel: 08457 484950.

Yacht clubs: Royal Fowey Yacht Club, Tel: 832245, Whitford Yard, Fowey PL23 1BH; Fowey Gallants Sailing Club, Tel: 832335, Amity Court, Fowey.

Eating out: Very good selection for size of town, from bistros and restaurants to fish and chips.

Things to do: Fowey Museum and Aquarium, both in middle of town. Guided town walks every Tuesday. Good walking, Fowey and Polruan. Headland garden, Polruan open 1400 – 1800 every Thursday during season.

Special events: Daphne du Maurier Festival mid-May; Fowey Classics (traditional boat gathering) first week in August with feeder race to Falmouth Classics; Fowey Regatta/Carnival, third week in August.

Yes, it does get busy during regatta week!

Polkerris is a pleasant daytime anchorage with a popular pub

Mevagissey and St Austell Bay

Tides	HW Dover −0600 (Mevagissey and St Austell Bay)
Range	MHWS 5.5m–MHWN 4.4m, MLWN 2.2m–MLWS 0.8m
Charts	AC: 147, 148, SC5602.2 (Mevagissey only); Stanfords: CP 23; Imray: C6
Hazards	**Mevagissey:** Inner harbour dries. Black rock off North Quay (unlit). Busy fishing harbour. Dangerous to approach in onshore wind, and outer harbour very exposed in easterly gales **Charlestown:** Inner floating basin entered by narrow drying entrance and tidal lock. Dangerous in onshore winds. Drying rocks to south and east **Gorran Haven:** Shallows extend well to seaward. Cadycrowse rock east of pier (unlit). Fine weather anchorage only and dangerous in onshore wind
Harbour Speed limit	**Mevagissey:** Outer harbour and approaches five knots. Inner harbour three knots
Overnight charge	Harbour Authority alongside or on mooring £12

Mevagissey and St Austell Bay are well sheltered from the west, tidal streams are weak and depths reduce gradually. Polkerris is a small fishing cove on the eastern side of Tywardreath Bay and has a good anchorage off it in easterly winds. On passage from Fowey around Gribbin Head, the only hazard more than two cables from the shore is Cannis Rock and, once the south cardinal buoy (lit) guarding it is astern, there are no hazards more than two cables from the shore. You can safely follow the coast this distance off around the western side of the Gribbin for a couple of miles, until the houses and small harbour wall of Polkerris come into sight.

To stay afloat, anchor about three cables to the south-west of the pier in about 1.5m at Low Water. The little bay dries out completely, but boats able to take the ground can anchor inside the harbour or lie alongside the pier. It is an unspoilt little hamlet tucked snugly beneath the cliffs and trees, with a high wall along the sandy foreshore protecting it from the seas which roll in unchecked in southerly gales. At one time this was such an important fishing harbour that the whole bay, now known as St Austell Bay, was called Polkerris Bay. The pier was built in 1735 and it became a thriving centre for the catching and salting of pilchards. The old curing cellars, the largest concentration in Cornwall, can still be seen backing onto the beach – but today it is a much quieter place, little more than a cluster of houses. The Rashleigh Inn is a good pub/restaurant, and there is a café in the old lifeboat house, which was closed in 1922 when the station was transferred to Fowey.

Par, with its four conspicuous chimneys further to the north-west, is tidal. This privately-owned harbour was a busy china clay port until its closure in 2007, and of no interest to leisure sailors. Entry is only permitted in an absolute emergency, when it is approached over a large area of drying sands. Midway across the bay, on the outer edge of Par Sands, Killyvarder Rock (dries 2.4m LAT) is marked by a red beacon.

Charlestown is another former china clay port two miles south-west of Par, and is of much more interest. It has been privately owned by Square Sail Shipyard Ltd since 1993, and the inner floating basin is the home port of its fleet of square rigged sailing ships, including the *Kaskelot, Earl of Pembroke* and *Phoenix*. It is entered through a very narrow entrance and tidal lock, yet another masterful bit of engineering by John Smeaton, who built the third Eddystone lighthouse.

Charlestown has become a popular port of call for other traditional and classic sailing vessels, and the sight of them lying in the secure inner basin is an evocative step back into the past. This unspoiled 19th century harbour has been used by the BBC for episodes of the *Onedin Line*, and by several other companies for location filming.

There's always plenty to see in Charlestown. The lovely *Tern IV*, built for Claud Worth, is in the foreground

A few pleasure craft are based here and, with wind in the west, it is possible to lock into the basin one hour either side of High Water by prior arrangement with the harbourmaster, Tel: 01726 70241/67526 or VHF Ch 14, but unless this coincides with a scheduled locking for one of their vessels the charge is £25, plus £0.94 per foot per night. The cheaper alternative, in offshore winds, is to anchor just east of the piers and dinghy ashore for a visit. The harbour mouth dries completely, well beyond the outer breakwaters at Springs, but when there is sufficient water, land inside at the slip to the left of the lock gate. For further information visit the website: www.square-sail.com.

Apart from the harbour interest, the village of Charlestown has a large Shipwreck and Heritage Centre. This boasts one of the most impressive collections of shipwreck artifacts in the country, an audio visual display and life-size animated scenes guaranteed to keep the children amused. There is a café in the centre, and the post office and store, pubs and restaurants are all close by.

St Austell Bay has many fine sandy coves and beaches and, with no dangers extending more than a cable from the shore, in favourable weather it is possible to sound in and anchor off most of them. Robin's Rock, just south of Porthpean dries, and there is an isolated rock drying 0.1m a cable off Ropehaven beach.

Black Head, a bold rocky point with a grassy summit 46m high, forms the division between St Austell and Mevagissey Bays, and the fishing port of Mevagissey is two miles further to the south-west. Midway between them is the lost harbour of Pentewan, at the northern end of the long stretch of Pentewan sands, another tidal basin once approached by an artificial channel that has now completely silted up. It was built in 1826 to export clay, and was at times as busy as Charlestown. The channel was always prey to the shifting sands and, in 1862, 16 ships were trapped in the harbour for five weeks because of silting. Eventually it was the closure of the railway in 1916 that finished this port, with the last clay shipped in 1929. Ships were still able to use the harbour as late as 1940, but today the inner basins and old locks are still quite intact but completely landlocked.

MEVAGISSEY, or *Mevva* as it is referred to locally, is the best known harbour in the bay. This classic Cornish fishing port offers good shelter in the prevailing winds, but is exposed in easterlies when it can be dangerous to enter and very uncomfortable inside. It comprises an outer harbour, where fishing boat moorings take up most of the available space, and an inner harbour which dries completely and is restricted to local boats only.

It is predictably popular with holidaymakers and becomes very busy in season, but in spite of a certain

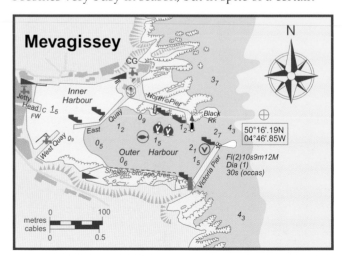

Mevagissey is a classic Cornish fishing harbour and very popular with holidaymakers

amount of commercialism it retains much of its character; slate hung pastel cottages with cement washed roofs creep up narrow alleyways to overlook the harbour, rather like a small version of Brixham. It is well worth a visit providing there is no inkling of the wind turning to the east. However, fishing is still a very important part of the town's life, with quite a large trawling and potting fleet as well as a number of trip and angling boats, so commercial activity takes precedence at all times. That said, visiting boats are very welcome as long as they are prepared to work around the port activity, and do not impede fish landing and other boat movements.

The approach is easy, with no off-lying dangers except the Gwineas rocks south of Chapel Point. Steer for the white lighthouse (Fl (2)10s 12M) on the South Pier, keeping close to it, as a shallow sandy bank (drying 0.3m LAT) extends east from the end of the North Pier, which has a 6ft wide concrete apron around its base. This covers at half tide and is marked on its southern corner by a pole with conical green topmark.

FUEL, FRESH WATER AND GAS
Diesel can be obtained from the fuel berth on the inner end of the South Pier – contact the harbour office. Fresh water is only available in cans from a tap by the harbour office or the tap on the jetty on the west side of the inner harbour, tide permitting. Calor and Camping Gaz are not easily available, so it is best to stock up in Fowey or Falmouth.

BERTHING
The outer harbour is available even at Low Water Springs, with depths over 2m alongside the inside of the outer end of the South Pier. Visitors normally berth here between the steps, rafting alongside the fishing boats, but do not leave your boat unattended in case

you have to move. Alternatively there are two visitors' fore and aft moorings between the three white buoys on the northern side of the outer harbour. Before picking them up contact the harbour office who will explain the local mooring system. Captain Hugh Bowles, the harbourmaster, listens on VHF Ch 16 and works on Ch 14, 0900 – 2100 April – Oct. His office, Tel: 01726 843305, is a clearly marked white building on the North Pier; further information will be found on www.mevagisseyharbour.co.uk.

Strengthening works on the pier completed in 1998 extended it by 4.5m and widened it by 3m. Bollards and ladders were also installed on the seaward side of the pier to provide berths in fine weather – however it should be noted that here the new piled base of the pier projects nearly a metre from the main wall Mean Low Water Springs level, so good sized fenders are necessary. The harbour office will also provide fender boards if required. Boats able to dry out can sometimes lie on Sandy Beach on the seaward side of the inner West Pier, with the harbourmaster's permission. Because of the restricted space, anchoring is not permitted and visiting boats are not allowed in the inner harbour.

Visitors can either lie on the fore and aft moorings – white buoys just inside the North Pier – or alongside the South Pier, right

Mevagissey's inner harbour dries completely and is restricted to local boats

Regardless of LOA, all visiting boats will pay £12 for an overnight stay, either alongside or on the buoys.

Mevagissey was a rough, unruly place in its heyday, renowned for smuggling activity. It was also one of the largest centres for the 18th and 19th century pilchard fishery on the south coast of Cornwall, when it would have reeked of fish as the huge landings, sometimes in excess of 30 to 40,000 fish per boat, were counted by hand.

Today you can revisit this interesting past in the excellent small museum which, close to the harbour office, is housed in a fine old wooden building dating from 1745 – once part of a boatyard. Right next to it, another real boatyard remains, where John Moore still builds beautiful traditional wooden fishing boats. There is also a fascinating aquarium run by the Harbour Trustees.

FACILITIES
(Local phone code 01726)
Although busy in summer, a wander around the town is pleasant, but the facilities are limited to a minimarket/off-licence on the St Austell road out of town (cash machine), a couple of newsagents, a fruit and vegetable shop, a chemist, a Lloyds TSB bank (0930 – 1230 Mon, Wed, Fri), and numerous gift shops. There are plenty of cafés, fish and chips, some excellent Cornish pasty shops, and no less than 10 restaurants of varying degrees of sophistication, including Portuguese at Alvorada, Tel: 842055, and seafood at Christophe's, Tel: 844888, Roovrays, Tel: 842672, and The Oyster Shell, Tel: 842174. The Kings Arms, Ship Inn and Harbour Inn all do bar meals, and there are also Chinese and pizza takeaways!

There's a small amount of chandlery available, and a marine engineer is on hand if needed – see the harbourmaster. The nearest place for petrol (again in cans) is at Pentewan, a mile away, and garden lovers should note that the famous Lost Gardens of Heligan

are within a similar distance and can be reached on foot.

Just south of Mevagissey, Porthmellon is a small cove of passing interest only, but of some significance in the history of yachting for this is where Percy Mitchell's famous boatyard was based between 1925 and 1981. Initially a builder of fishing boats, he gained a reputation for yachts during the 1930s, and was described as 'an artist in wood' by Claud Worth.

Building the boats was only half the battle, for they then had to be manoeuvered 550 yards along the road to the beach and several were even launched over the sea wall. One of these was the 28 ton *TM Windstar*, which was later owned by the Sir Philip Hunloke, King George V's sailing master and Commodore of the Royal Squadron, aboard which the Royal Family, including the young Princesses Elizabeth and Margaret, regularly cruised before and after the war.

Many other fine yachts to the design of Mylne, Harrison Butler and Laurent Giles emerged from this yard, and its fascinating history was related in *A Boatbuilder's Story*, Percy Mitchell's autobiography, which was published in 1970 shortly before he died. The yard was sold in the late 1980s and has since vanished beneath a new housing development.

Gorran Haven is an attractive fine weather anchorage, sheltered in westerly winds, with a drying small boat harbour and a gently shelving clean sandy beach. Approaching from the north, keep midway between Gwineas Rocks and the low promontory of Chapel Point, sound in and anchor two cables east of the sea wall. In settled weather bilge-keelers can dry out comfortably closer inshore.

In the village, which comprises a narrow street of old fishermen's cottages, you'll find a post office and general stores (including off-licence, newsagent, bakery, meat and vegetables), three cafés and the Llawnroc Inn. The south-west coastal path provides a lovely walk up from the beach to Dodman Point.

In offshore winds you can dry out or anchor off Gorran Haven in the lee of Dodman Point

Falmouth

Tides	HW Dover –0610
Range	MHWS 5.3m–MHWN 4.2m, MLWN 1.9m–MLWS 0.6m. HW Truro approx eight mins after HW Falmouth. Streams attain over two knots in upper reaches at Springs
Charts	AC: 32, 154, 18. SC5602.6; Stanfords: CP23; Imray: C6, WC2400.12, Y58
Waypoint	Eastern dock breakwater end 50°09'.34N 05°02'.96W
	Black Rock East Cardinal buoy 50°08'.68N 05°01'.74W
Hazards	Black Rock (lit). St Mawes Buoy/Lugo Rock (lit). Busy commercial port, beware shipping movements in vicinity of docks and upper reaches of Fal. Large areas of upper reaches dry. Beware pot and net buoys
Harbour Speed limit	Inner harbour and upper reaches above Turnaware eight knots/minimal wash. Restronguet and Mylor Creeks five knots, St Mawes eight knots/Percuil River five knots
Overnight charge	Harbour Authority Yacht Haven £20.50, visitors' mooring £12.50, at anchor £6.50. Port Pendennis Marina £26. Falmouth Marina £26. St Mawes mooring £15, at anchor £5. Mylor Yacht Harbour marina £27.50, mooring £17.50. Truro Harbour Authority pontoon, mooring or alongside Town Quay £10, at anchor £5

'Falmouth for orders' – these few words evoke so much. Although lofty spars, square yards and billowing spreads of canvas no longer grace the Western Approaches and deep laden rust streaked hulls waiting on the whims of commerce have long ceased to swing at anchor in Carrick Roads, Falmouth, by virtue of its far westerly position, is still a major port of landfall and departure for many smaller sailing vessels that now cross the lonely oceans of the world. The ensigns of many nations are a familiar and romantic sight around the harbour during the summer months. For the majority with less exotic cruising ambitions, the River Fal and its tributaries offer everything that a yachtsman might require. I must admit to a degree of bias, as this was for many years my home port, but most visitors would probably agree that it is one of the finest sailing areas in England and certainly deserves its reputation as one of the great natural harbours of the world.

APPROACHES

Flanked by St Anthony Head to the east, which is grass topped with low cliffs and a white lighthouse (Iso WR 15s 16/14M, Red Sector 004° – 022°) built in 1835, and Pendennis Point and castle nearly a mile to the west,

The Fal Estuary has a large choice of berthing options, including the popular Visitors' Yacht Haven off Falmouth's Custom House Quay. The fuel berth is on the bottom right

St Anthony lighthouse with St Mawes in the distance

the entrance is easy and can be safely negotiated in any weather, even a southerly gale. If combined with an ebb tide, however, this will not be a gentle ride! There is, however, no such thing as total perfection and, despite being deep, the entrance does have one notable hazard sited perversely right in the middle. Black Rock uncovers at half tide and is marked by a distinctive black conical beacon with an isolated danger mark (pole and two spheres) on top (Fl (2) 10s 3M). You can enter either side of Black Rock, either by the buoyed deep water channel for commercial shipping to the east, or the western channel which is quite safe for small craft, having a least depth of 6m. Do not be tempted to pass close to Black Rock, as shallows extend nearly 200m to the north and south.

Strangers arriving at night should keep to the deep water channel, which is well lit, with Black Rock BYB east cardinal buoy (Q (3) 10s) to port and Castle green conical buoy (Fl G 2.5s) to starboard. From here, steer up towards West Narrows red can (Fl (2) R 10s), but midway between them you can bear away towards the distant eastern breakwater end (Fl R 2s), leaving the Governor BYB east cardinal buoy (VQ (3) 5s) on your port hand.

Pendennis Castle, initially completed in 1543, was part of Henry VIII's massive chain of coastal defences from Milford Haven to Hull, built in response to fears of religious inspired invasion from Europe. His daughter Elizabeth then instigated the building of the large outer walls during the war with Spain, following the raiding and burning of Penzance, Newlyn and Mousehole in 1595. The awaited attack never came and Pendennis never fired its guns in anger.

The castle is preserved by English Heritage and has audio visual displays covering its history, including restored artillery from World War II sea defence fortifications, notably the impressive big guns in the Half Moon Battery. Pendennis Castle and its counterpart at St Mawes are open daily during the summer, and the walk up to the headland along

Castle Drive, with a grandstand view of the docks, estuary and Falmouth Bay, is definitely recommended.

Just below the castle ramparts, the squat modern building on the hillside is the Falmouth Coastguard Maritime Rescue Co-ordination Centre, which celebrated its 25th operational anniversary in 2007. Responsible for a sea area of over 600,000 sq miles and 250 miles of Cornish coastline, it has been regularly involved in coordinating rescues on the other side of the world thanks to satellite technology. Monitoring VHF Ch 16, the local working channels are 67, 10, 23, 73, 86 and 84, callsign *Falmouth Coastguard*.

With anchorages, moorings, berths alongside and several marinas, the Fal has a bewildering variety of options for visiting boats, but Falmouth itself does tend to be the first stop, with ample deep water well into the inner harbour. Follow the line of the northern arm of the docks, keeping a watchful eye on shipping movements in and around them, particularly when rounding the western end. This should be given a wide berth as tugs, ferries, fishing boats and sizeable ships have a nasty habit of emerging, often at speed.

Falmouth Docks, which date from around 1860, can dry dock ships up to 100,000 tons for repairs and has an important bunkering facility. Various plans to enlarge it over the years have been mooted, perhaps the most ominous, in the late 1980s, was the proposal of the unsuccessful Falmouth Container Port Company to build a major container transhipment port to the east of the docks stretching a third of the way across the entrance to the Fal!

Within the docks complex, Pendennis Shipyard specialises in the building and refit of large luxury yachts, which can often be seen lying in the wet basin at the eastern side of the docks

It has a 500-ton slip and 80-ton hoist, and is internationally renowned for its high quality work. The yard was devastated by a major fire in 1994, but re-emerged phoenix-like from the ashes within months, a triumph epitomised by the magnificent 43m schooner

Looking seaward from the Penryn River. Falmouth Marina is in the foreground, Flushing to the left, and the inner harbour and docks beyond

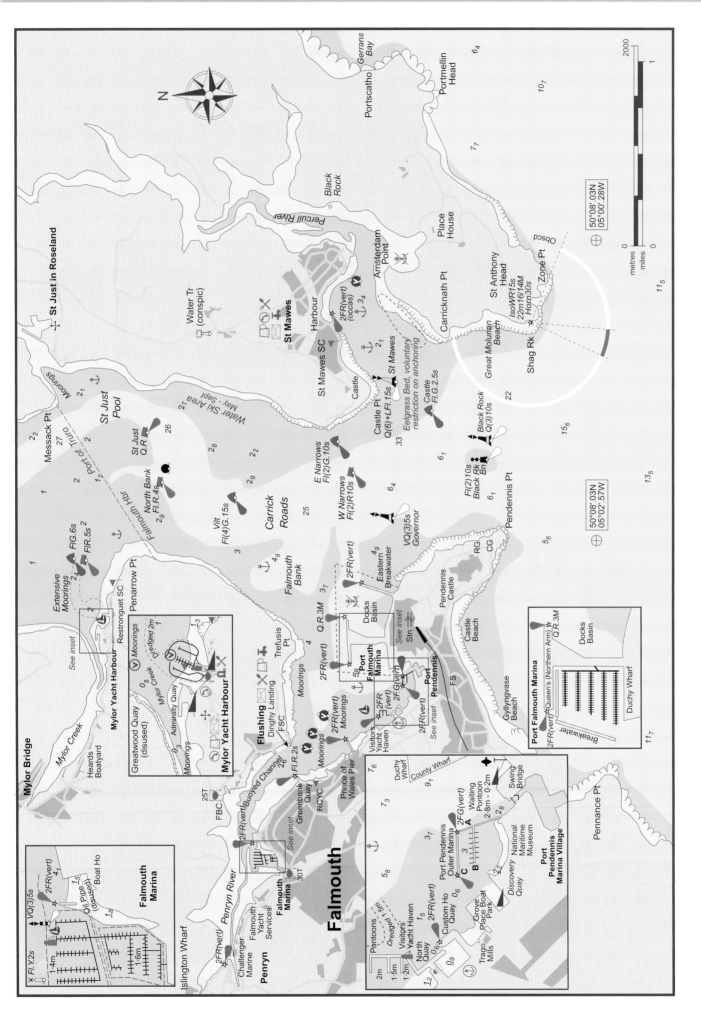

The Docks and inner harbour. Custom House Quay and FHC Visitors' Yacht Haven, left, Port Pendennis, centre, and the location of Port Falmouth Marina, right

Adela, which was launched here in 1995 and won the 1997 Atlantic Challenge race for classic yachts from New York to Falmouth.

In November 2007 planning permission was granted for the new 290-berth Port Falmouth Marina, Tel: 01326 212161; www.portfalmouthmarina.com, on the western side of the Docks, in the area between the northern Queens Jetty and Duchy Wharf. It was anticipated that the five main pontoons and finger berths would be installed in time for the summer of 2008, with a substantial 6m wide floating breakwater extending south-south-west to provide all weather protection. The marina will monitor VHF Ch 80/M, callsign *Port Falmouth Marina*, and shoreside facilities will include toilets, showers, launderette and reception office in an historic converted dockyard building, along with a 150-space car park. Located within the Docks, the security levels will be very high and visitor charges are anticipated to be on a par with other local marinas. With the former ship basin providing a depth of up to 7m LAT, a special feature of the marina will be a dedicated area for superyacht berthing with drive-on pontoons for provisioning!

FUEL, FRESH WATER AND GAS

Diesel and petrol are only available alongside at two locations on the Fal, the Falmouth Harbour Commissioners Visitors' Yacht Haven fuel berth, open 0900 – 1800 daily, and Mylor Yacht Harbour fuel berth, open 0900 – 1800 daily in May/June (and until 2000 Fri, Sat, Sun during June), 0830 – 2100 July/August, 0900 – 1900 September. Diesel is also available from the fuel berth at Falmouth Marina, open 24 hours daily.

Fresh water can be obtained alongside at the Visitors' Yacht Haven, Port Pendennis Marina, Falmouth Marina, Mylor Yacht Harbour, St Mawes, Trelissick landing pontoon and Town Quay Truro.

Calor and Camping Gaz are stocked at The Bosun's Locker Chandlery, Falmouth, Falmouth Marina and Mylor Chandlery at Mylor Yacht Harbour.

BERTHING AND MOORINGS, THE VISITORS' YACHT HAVEN

The picturesque town of Falmouth climbs in all its colourful and intriguing profusion along the hillside overlooking the mass of moorings in the inner harbour. Bear round past the western side of the docks and steer for Custom House Quay dead ahead, where you will find the main anchorage and the Falmouth Harbour Commissioners' (FHC) 100 berth Visitors' Yacht Haven. The approach channel is dredged to 1.5m and indicated by two leading marks – posts with large orange triangle topmarks, one on the end of North Quay and the other on the pontoon by the fuel barge. The northernmost corner of the Yacht Haven is lit (2FR vert), and the pontoon walkways are also illuminated.

The berths along the eastern breakwater spine are all dredged to 2.5m, the two outer western pontoon arms have 2m and the innermost 1.5m, and these are entered along the northern side of the Visitors' Yacht Haven. Keep close to the pontoons – outside the dredged area the water to the north and west of the Yacht Haven is very shallow at Mean Low Water Springs.

The approach channel to the Visitors' Yacht Haven is only dredged to 1.5m LAT. Note the leading marks

There are six different charge bands depending on LOA, an 8m to 10m boat is £19 per night, but rises to £20.50 during July and August – but it is worth noting that advantageous weekly rates are available on all the FHC berthing facilities. A week on the Yacht Haven, for example, works out at £114 for a 10m boat, £123 July/August. A short stay of up to two hours will cost £6.

The harbour office, Tel: 01326 312285 or 314379, callsign *Falmouth Harbour Radio*, monitors VHF Ch 16 and works on 12, as do its harbour patrol launches, which are usually on hand to assist during working hours when there is also a supervisor at the Yacht Haven. In addition to the fuel berth (diesel and petrol, open 0900 – 1800 daily), there are water hoses and electric points on the pontoons. WiFi internet access is also available through www.myoceanwave.com.

Yacht Haven security is good as the pontoons are accessed with a PIN number through a shoreside gate by the Yacht Haven Supervisor's office. There are rubbish/recycling bins on North Quay and, just around the corner, the Yacht Haven Amenity Centre has excellent showers, toilets and laundry facilities. Access is by a swipe card that can be obtained from the Yacht Haven supervisor or the harbour office (£5 refundable deposit).

PORT PENDENNIS MARINA AND THE MARITIME MUSEUM

Port Pendennis Marina Village lies opposite the Visitors' Yacht Haven in the south-eastern corner of the inner harbour at Challenger Quay. It is the base for Falmouth Maritime, which has been the prime mover in revitalising this part of the waterfront, notably with the £10 million awarded by the Heritage Lottery Fund in 1997 to establish a Maritime Museum and events centre on the adjoining waterfront site, now known as Discovery Quay.

A joint venture between the National Maritime Museum, Greenwich, and Falmouth Maritime Museum, the National Maritime Museum of Cornwall, which opened in March 2003, has rapidly achieved international acclaim and many awards for its imaginative displays and architecture. The distinctive landmark building, with its prominent 'lighthouse' tower, provides a permanent home for the National Maritime Museum's Small Boat Collection and is definitely a 'must visit' attraction! With a wealth of historical information, it also encompasses hands-on displays, interactive entertainment and the diverse collection of 140 boats, including many famous names such as the Dragon *Bluebottle*, raced for many years by the Duke of Edinburgh and Uffa Fox, The Dye's much travelled Wayfarer dinghy, *Wanderer*, the very first Mirror dinghy, and the converted Falmouth Quay Punt *Curlew*, in which Tim and Pauline Carr

The anchorage, Port Pendennis Marina, and Maritime Museum 'lighthouse tower'

circumnavigated and completed many voyages to high latitudes under sail alone.

Outside the museum a public piazza, the Events Square, is a regular venue for live entertainment and also real life events like Dame Ellen MacArthur's spectacular reception on 8 February 2005 after she broke the record for the fastest non-stop circumnavigation in *B&Q/Castorama*. The square is surrounded by designer stores, restaurants and coffee shops and also a Tesco Express supermarket, open 0600 – 2300 daily, with a handy cashpoint. The final phase of this major development now houses Harvey's Wharf Brasserie, Tel: 314351, and a Pizza Express, which overlook the harbour and the 70 berth all-tide Port Pendennis outer marina (minimum depth 3.5m, up to 4.2m on main walkway of outer marina). This includes approximately 40 berths for visitors alongside the outer pontoons, with a few finger berths usually available inside.

Access is around the south-west corner of the breakwater pontoons, which extend from the southern side of the entrance to Port Pendennis Inner Marina. There are lights (2FG vert) on the eastern end of the outer pontoon and equivalent red lights on the western end. Power and water are available at all berths, including 100amp 3 phase for larger yachts, as this is a popular stopover for many superyachts en route to and from the Mediterranean and Caribbean.

Port Pendennis Marina is a long-established venue for national and international sailing events, including the Atlantic Alone feeder race for the 1998 Around Alone, La Solitaire du Figaro 2000 and the International Dragon Gold Cup in 2004.

Port Pendennis inner marina is also accessible to visitors if space permits, and is a particularly safe spot if you have to leave your boat for a while. Entry is through an automatic dock gate approximately three hours either side of High Water. Call *Port Pendennis* on VHF Ch 80 or M for berthing availability in either marina, or berth on the north side of the breakwater pontoon in the approach to the gate and check in with

Port Pendennis outer marina, with Custom House Quay on left

reception, Tel: 01326 211211, which is open during normal office hours.

Onshore facilities include showers, toilets, a laundry room, car parking and even a tennis court. The marina office has a lounge for yacht crews with telephone, fax and internet access. Ideally placed for crew changes, the Falmouth Town railway station is within three minutes walk, and hire cars are available on site. There is total security throughout Port Pendennis and the only access is through PIN control gates, making it by far the safest berthing in town. The overnight berthing charge of £2.60 per metre is the same in both marinas. Short stay, two hours, is £8. The local lifeboat and RNLI base are situated adjacent to Port Pendennis.

FALMOUTH FACILITES
(Local phone code 01326)
Port Pendennis and the Visitors' Yacht Haven together provide the most convenient alongside berthing in Falmouth with pubs, restaurants, bistros and shops, all within easy walking distance. Close by, Custom House Quay, which surrounds the drying inner basin, is over 300 years old and forms an attractive focal point on the Falmouth waterfront. Here, the Chain Locker and the Quayside Inn both offer good pub food and have outdoor tables and seats on the quay overlooked by some fine old buildings, including the harbour office and the 1815 Custom House with its adjoining 'Kings Pipe', a brick chimney still used for burning contraband!

A summer ferry to St Mawes runs from Custom House Quay. To the east of the quay, beyond the large Trago Mills discount store (well worth investigating), the Harbour Commissioners have an extensive boat park and large launching slip in Grove Place, adjacent to the Falmouth Watersports Association clubhouse where visitors are welcome to use the facilities.

In Quay Hill, which leads up from North Quay, you'll find two popular bistros, the perennial Seafood Bar, Tel: 315129, and The Hut, Tel: 318229. Turn left into Arwenack Street for contemporary fare at Southside, Tel: 212122, tapas and Spanish at Bodenes,

Tel: 210759, English fare at both Clarks, Tel: 312678, and Hunkeydory Restaurant and Bar, Tel: 212997, and Indian at Balti Curries, Tel: 317905. Alternatively, turn right for steak and seafood at Two Ten 200, Tel: 210200, or Bistro de la Mer, Tel: 316509. If you head towards the opposite end of town, you will find Café No 33, Tel: 211944, Powells Cellars, Tel: 311212, Ming's Garden, Tel: 314413, serving Chinese food, and Asha, Tel: 211688, or Gurkha, Tel: 311483, offering Indian cuisine. For Italian try Da Vinci, Tel: 312277, in the High Street where you'll also find the Thai Orchid, Tel: 211028. There are a number of fast food outlets, cafés, fish and chip shops and a veritable surfeit of Cornish pasty shops – for my money Rowes still produce the best. . .

The major shops, including M&S, Woolworths, WH Smith and Boots, are strung out along the town's main street or in the area known as the Moor, which is close to Prince of Wales Pier. Here, there's a Tesco Metro supermarket, open 0700 – 2000 Mon – Sat, 1000 – 1600 Sun, and also the main post office.

Conspicuous right on the waterfront, the Bosun's Locker, Tel: 312212; www.bosunslockerchandlery.co.uk, has been trading since 1946 and is the oldest chandler in the UK. It stocks a wide range of charts and pilot books and is just minutes away from the Yacht Haven. There are also three secondhand bookshops with a good nautical selection: Bookmark, at the top of Quay Hill, Browsers in St George's Arcade or the Archway Bookshop opposite Prince of Wales Pier.

THE ANCHORAGE AND VISITORS' MOORINGS
If you decide to anchor – £6.50 a night for a 7m to 12m boat – let go just east of the Yacht Haven, clear of the quay and local moorings, but also well away from the docks, as anchoring is prohibited within a cable of the jetties. This area of water is regularly used for swinging large vessels into their berths, when the anchorage often has to be cleared. Details of impending ship movements are displayed at the Yacht Haven office and the harbour staff will give you good warning.

Depths vary between 1.5m and 2.5m, and the holding ground and shelter is good in anything except northerlies, although the wash from the ferries and pleasure boats can make it fairly lively at times and in the season it gets pretty crowded. The best place to land is on the innermost Yacht Haven pontoon, by the linking bridge to the Quay, where dinghies can be left afloat.

Finally, between Custom House Quay and Prince of Wales Pier there are seven FHC visitors' swinging moorings, R101 – R107, and between Prince of Wales Pier and Greenbank Quay there are a further 11 FHC visitors' moorings, K1 – K6, L1 – L4 and T5, all with green support buoys (marked FHC) and costing £12.50 a night for a 10m boat. They do not have pick-up buoys so have your own warps ready !

Shelter is normally good throughout the rest of the

'Climbing in all its colourful and intriguing profusion', Falmouth rises above the mass of moorings in the inner harbour. Greenbank Terrace and the Royal Cornwall Yacht Club are on the right

inner harbour except in strong easterly, northeasterly or southeasterly winds when it becomes surprisingly rough as seas build across the open fetch from the St Mawes shore. Fortunately, easterly gales are rare, particularly in summer.

Keep well clear of the Prince of Wales Pier as it is constantly busy with large trip boats and ferries to Flushing and St Mawes. There is a good dinghy landing in the boat harbour on the inner end of the pier adjacent to Market Strand, where you will find the Tourist Information Centre, Tel: 01326 312300; www.acornishriver.co.uk. This landing is also very handy for the Tesco Metro supermarket, which is a short walk away.

The Royal Cornwall Yacht Club (www.royalcornwall yachtclub.org) also has a mooring for up to 11m available at reasonable cost, marked *RCYC Visitor*, off its fine clubhouse which stands on its own quay below the elegant row of tall Regency houses along Greenbank, just upriver of the extensive Packet Quays waterfront development. The mooring can be reserved in advance through the club office, Tel: 01326 312126, or by hailing the club boatman on VHF Ch M, callsign *Club Launch*, which operates weekdays 1015 to 1300, 1400 to 1845 (later on racing evenings – Tues and Fri) and weekends 0915 – 1945 (1645 April and October). RCYC mooring rental includes use of this free taxi service. Visitors staying five nights will get the next two free of charge, and there are special rates if you wish to stay longer.

The club was established in 1871 and was originally located in the Greenbank Hotel. In 1883 it leased its present waterside premises in Greenbank House. The lease was eventually purchased by a syndicate of members in 1911 and the freehold acquired in 1945. It is open every day except Monday during the summer months and visiting yacht crews are always made very welcome. Among its many activities, every four years since 1975 it has organised the popular Azores and Back Race (AZAB). Open to single or double-handed crews, the last was in June 2007.

Facilities include showers, bar and dining room (open 1130 – 1430 and 1730 – 2300 Tues – Sat, 1200 – 1700 Sun in summer); there is a good dinghy landing and dinghy storage. Fresh water and scrubbing alongside the club quay is also possible by arrangement.

FALMOUTH PACKETS, QUAY PUNTS AND WORKING BOATS

Sir Walter Raleigh, on his way home from El Dorado in 1596, put into the Fal and found little more than a small fishing village known as Smithick, and the nearby manor house at Arwenack, home of the Killigrew family. His advice that it might make a good harbour was not then taken up, but by 1670 the Killigrews had got round to building Custom House Quay. This turned out to be a stroke of luck rather than foresight, which ultimately transformed Falmouth into a thriving seaport of major importance.

Impressed by the new quays, the post office decided to establish its Packet Service here in 1688. This fleet of fast, armed sailing ships, generally brigantines of around 200 tons, with appropriate names like *Speedy* and *Express*, were all privately owned and chartered to the Crown to carry mail, bullion and passengers, not only to Europe, but as far afield as the West Indies and the Americas, averaging a round trip of between 15 to 18 weeks. It was a tough, dangerous business,

The anchorage, Falmouth, with Working Boats and Sunbeams beating home

the valuable cargoes resulting in frequent attacks by privateers and pirates, but many owners and captains made fortunes. Around Falmouth, particularly along Greenbank and opposite, in the small village of Flushing, large elegant houses rose along the waterfront, graphic evidence of the new-found wealth, for by 1800 over 40 packet ships were based in the port.

As the first port of call for most inbound shipping, before the days of wireless, Falmouth often received the first news of dramatic events abroad – such as the death of Nelson. Ship's masters were not only anxious to notify owners of their safe arrival, but also to find the final destination orders for their cargoes, which resulted in much trade for Falmouth and led to the development of the famous Quay Punts' to service the deep-water visitors. These deep, sturdy and mostly open boats were between 25 and 32ft long and ranged the approaches to the Lizard, seeking ships before they arrived off the port. The particular rigours of the job produced a remarkably seaworthy craft, yawl rigged with a stumpy mainmast to enable them to sail in under the lower yards of the big sailing ships. Only one, named *Fat Boat*, was ever lost whilst performing her job. A worthy early proponent of recycling, she specialised in collecting the accumulated used cooking fat from the incoming ships to sell ashore, but when swamped off Black Head in 1904, she sank in seconds, leaving a greasy if not a carbon footprint!

Many of her more fortunate contemporaries – some still sailing – were eventually decked and converted to yachts, notably *Curlew* which can be seen at the Maritime Museum, and a number of yachts were built along their lines. The quay punting continued in Falmouth until the late 1990s, using a small fleet of sturdy motor launches operated by the Falmouth Licensed Watermen before it became financially unviable. The old Watermens Rest, on the quay behind Trago Mills, is now an art gallery.

The other traditional craft that originated in the estuary of the Fal are the Working Boats, the sailing oyster boats that are now unique in Europe, their freak survival resulting from the local bye-laws prohibiting the dredging with anything other than sail or oar. These are gaff cutters ranging between 20 and 32ft in length, although mostly around 28ft, and a number of these three-quarter decked boats still work the natural oyster fishery during the winter season from 1 October until 31 March, drifting down tide across the banks in the upper part of Carrick Roads and hauling their dredges by hand. During the summer they race, a tradition continued by the Falmouth Working Boat Association, formed in 1979 to preserve the unique character of the class.

Some of the wooden boats are over 100 years old, and the most famous has to be the late Toby West's *Victory*, launched in 1884. With her distinctive bright yellow hull, she was always campaigned hard by her equally colourful owner until his death in 2001. Fisherman, yachtsman and lifeboat coxwain, he was undoubtedly one of the last of Falmouth's real waterfront characters; if you want an entertaining read, try and find a second-hand copy of his autobiography *A Sailing West*. Today, in common with several of her sisters, *Victory* is owned and keenly raced by a local syndicate.

In the 1970s Mylor boatbuilder Terry Heard produced the first GRP working boat hulls and many more have followed. There have, however, been a few modern boats built in wood and even one in ferrocement. The impressive fleet numbers 20 boats at times and, with huge gaff rigs, lofty coloured topsails and long, lethal bowsprits, this is one of the most spectacular sights in Falmouth.

If you are around at the weekend, the boats, with their large open cockpits, have plenty of room for crew, and if you feel like trying it, just ask – someone will invariably take you along.

In marked contrast, the other distinctive Falmouth racing fleet, the Sunbeams, epitomises the elegance of the 20s and 30s, and the halcyon days when the mighty J-class raced in Falmouth Bay. They are classic three-quarter decked bermudian sloops with long overhangs, just under 27ft overall and immaculately maintained. This colourful fleet, established in Falmouth in 1924, is one of two in the country, the other is based at Itchenor. Originally designed in 1922 by Alfred Westmacott as a one design class for the Hamble, most of the Sunbeams were built in the Solent.

However, look out for *Milly* (V45). Crafted by Mylor Yacht Harbour's master shipwright, Brian Crockford, and launched in 1999, she was the first new Sunbeam to be built for over 20 years and the first ever to be built in Falmouth; since then two more have been built at Mylor, *Kitty* for the local fleet and *Spray* for Itchenor, maintaining the tradition that their names all end in 'y.'

Racing of every description in Falmouth is very active all year round, but Falmouth Regatta Week, during the second week of August, organised by the Port of Falmouth Sailing Association (POFSA), is the major event, beginning with the spectacular 'Falmouth Classics' weekend for traditional craft. For further details, telephone 01326 211555 or visit its website: www.falmouthweek.co.uk. It is worth noting, too, under the Falmouth harbour by-laws, during racing 'the master of a small vessel shall not permit his vessel to pass therein so as to obstruct, impede or interfere with the boat race, regatta, championship or procession. . .'

The advent of the steam ships finally removed the good fortune that Falmouth had enjoyed for over 150 years, and in 1852 the Post Office transferred the mail service to Southampton. Wireless did away with the need to call for orders, but the decline in the port was brief. The new docks were commenced in 1858; building ships, repairing them and cashing in on the new needs of the steamers for bunkers.

With the arrival of the railway in 1863, another new industry – tourism – began to emerge. In 1865 the Falmouth Hotel was the first to rise from the fields along the seafront as the holidaymakers began to arrive. Today, more than ever, they are the mainstay of the town's prosperity.

FLUSHING

Opposite Falmouth, Flushing is an attractive little village incorporating a post office and grocery with limited provisions (both closed Wednesday afternoons), two pubs which both serve good food – The Standard and Seven Stars – and also the popular Sticky Prawn Restaurant, Tel: 373734, on the quay, where the small fleet of local fishing boats land their catches.

The building on the lower New Quay is Flushing Sailing Club, which is generally only open at weekends or when evening racing is taking place. It has a bar, but no other facilities. The walk from Flushing out to Trefusis Point provides some fine views of Falmouth and the entrance to the estuary. There is a pleasant sandy beach at Kiln Quay, popular with locals, and a regular spot for barbecues. From here a delightful coastal path with more lovely views will take you all the way to Mylor Yacht Harbour, if you're in the mood for an invigorating walk!

FALMOUTH MARINA

The largest boating facility in the estuary, Falmouth Marina is about a mile further upstream, on the Penryn River beyond Greenbank Quay, which is not difficult to find as it has Greenbank Hotel in huge letters along it and a prominent sign pointing the way to Falmouth Marina!

From here on, the river becomes shallower, but the main channel has over 2m and is buoyed, with red cans to port and conical green buoys to starboard, the first red can being the only one that is lit (QR). The remaining four port hand buoys do, however, have reflective panels, which show up well with a good torch. The southern shore is particularly shallow; drying banks extend well out and are covered with oyster beds where anchoring is prohibited and you run aground at your peril.

Falmouth Marina is hidden beyond a jetty with warehouses on the port hand at Boyers Cellars, or 'Coastlines' as it is known locally, called after the coastal shipping line of the same name which acquired the jetty in 1936. It was a regular port of call for their 10 day runs between Liverpool and London. Coastal petrol tankers continued to discharge here until 1996, but now it is only used by fishing boats. Opposite, at Little Falmouth, are the slipways and large sheds of Falmouth Boat Construction Ltd (FBC), where there has been a boatyard since the early 1880s and which was the site of the first dry-dock in Falmouth.

The proposal to dredge out and build a marina in the muddy creek at Ponsharden was greeted with great local scepticism when it was first proposed in 1979, but the success of the 375-berth Falmouth Marina, Tel: 01326 316620; www.premiermarinas.com, has long since proved all the pundits wrong, and usually there are up to 50 visitors' berths available. It is always advisable to phone ahead or call *Falmouth Marina* on VHF Ch 80, to check availability, particularly if you are over 13m LOA.

It has been owned by Premier Marina Group since 1997, and the company has since undertaken a major refurbishment programme, including the acquisition of the former Port Falmouth Boat Yard adjacent to the marina in 2000. This enabled the marina to infill the old slipway and enlarge the winter storage space ashore, providing more car parking space during the summer.

The dredged approach channel affords access for boats drawing up to 1.8m at Low Water, although a certain amount of care is recommended at Low Water Springs. The isolated pontoon just beyond Boyers Cellars is private berthing for local boats with lights (2FR vert) on its northern end. Beyond it, as the arrow

The final approach to Falmouth Marina is well marked – keep the east cardinal beacon on your starboard hand

Falmouth Marina has excellent facilities for visitors in a secure and sheltered location

indicates, visitors must keep to port of the BY pole with east cardinal topmark (Fl (3) 5s) and proceed to the arrivals and fuel berth ('J' pontoon), which is clearly marked. Do not be confused by the port and starboard hand buoys just beyond the east cardinal mark; they indicate the main channel to Penryn and are not part of the marina approach channel.

Here, the berthing master will allocate a berth. If the arrivals berth is unattended you can call the office from the telephone on the pontoon. Berthing masters are usually on duty from 0700 – 1900 during the season, and there is also a night watchman providing 24 hour security who can also allocate berths. Charges are £2.60 per metre per night, with a minimum charge of £23. If you stay for a week, you will get seven days for the price of six. A short stay of up to four hours costs £1.30 per metre, with a minimum charge of £11.

The BY pole with yellow 'X' topmark (Fl Y 2s) beyond the fuel berth marks the northern and western edges of the dredged channel. At night this light should be kept open to port of the east cardinal light in the final approach.

The marina has a very friendly atmosphere and excellent facilities, comprising toilets and showers, a 24-hour launderette, Calor and Camping Gaz, fresh water at the berths, electricity and WiFi internet access. Diesel is available 24 hours – either call ahead on VHF or berth on the fuel pontoon and contact the marina office with the phone provided. Petrol can be obtained in cans from a nearby garage.

Without a doubt the focal point is the large Marine Bar and Restaurant, Tel: 313481, which overlooks the marina. Other businesses on site include Fal Chandlers, Tel: 212411, and Skywave Marine Electronics, Tel: 318314, as well as two charter operators, a car hire company, a hairdresser and a brokerage. In addition there is a 30-ton mobile hoist, a 25-ton mobile crane and full onshore repair facilities. The marina can also provide a list of approved outside contractors for engineering, rigging and most other eventualities.

Five minutes' walk away, the large Co-op Pioneer supermarket is convenient for provisioning and is open on Sundays too. There is a small convenience store/newsagent just across the road by the marina entrance, as well as Inflatable Boat Services, Tel: 313800.

The centre of Falmouth is a gentle 20 minutes walk away, with fine views of the inner harbour along elegant Greenbank. Alternatively, there are regular buses and plenty of taxis.

PENRYN

Between the marina and Penryn, a mile further upstream, the river dries almost completely. During the Middle Ages Penryn was a port of considerable importance until its trade was wrested away by the development of Falmouth and the gradual silting of the river. Following the buoyed channel, it is possible to reach Penryn Quay after half flood, but it is much used by local fishing boats and the mud is sticky and deep at Low Water. Scenically the river does not really have a lot to recommend it, although the town is architecturally very interesting. However, if you have any problems, Penryn is where you're likely to end up as most of the main marine businesses are located in the area; if you wish to avoid going upriver by boat, regular buses run from the centre of Falmouth.

Just upstream of Falmouth Marina, the long pontoon on the western shore is the departure point for the 'park and float' ferries to Custom House Quay and the Maritime Museum. Ashore, the large building is the home of Falmouth Yacht Services Boatyard, Tel: 310120, which specialises in major refit work and building Rustler, Bowman and Starlight yachts. It has a 40-ton hoist and can handle vessels of up to 70ft.

Falmouth Yacht Brokers Boatyard and Challenger Marine, which has some drying pontoon berthing available for visitors (access HW±3 hrs), are further upstream in the approach to Penryn Quay. Jubilee Wharf, just beyond the Quay, was previously a coal yard served by coasters but now it sports one of the more intriguing recent buildings, a Zero Energy eco home to a number of small local businesses with wind turbines generating its own power.

Right at the head of the creek, a number of nautical companies are situated at Islington Wharf where it is possible to dry out alongside on mud. On Commercial Road, which runs parallel to the creek, you will find the Boathouse Chandlery, SKB Sails and Robin Curnow, the outboard specialist.

ST MAWES

The real beauty of the Fal is that it can provide within its limits most of the ingredients of any enjoyable cruise – magnificent scenery, safe water for sailing and some delightful anchorages where you can find some welcome peace and quiet and escape from the crowds ashore.

Extending nearly three miles inland and almost a mile wide, Carrick Roads is a broad stretch of water surrounded by rounded hills, fields and low rocky shores. At the south-eastern end, opposite Falmouth, is the entrance to the Percuil River and St Mawes, which has only one hazard in the approach, Lugo rock, two cables south of the prominent castle (least depth 0.8m). It is marked by the YB south cardinal, St Mawes buoy (Q (6) + L Fl 15s), which should be left on your port hand when entering. The houses of the small village of St Mawes run along the northern shore, off which there are a number of local moorings, while beyond is the small boat harbour.

The St Mawes Pier & Harbour Company has 10 visitors' moorings, green buoys marked *St Mawes*, off the Quay. These are available through the harbourmaster, Captain Gary Cairns, whose office is on the Town Quay, Tel: 01326 270553. He maintains a VHF watch on Ch 16, working Ch 12, callsign *St Mawes Harbour Radio* and is often afloat in his clearly marked RIB. Charges per day, up to 10m, £15, 10m to 12m £20, 12m to 15m £30. Vessels over 15m by prior arrangement only. Alternatively, you can

anchor well clear of the moorings, but do not obstruct the fairway up to the jetty end, which is used constantly by the ferries and pleasure boats. Anchoring charges are 50p a metre for 24 hours.

Land on the large slipway or beach and keep clear of the pier. Otherwise, call the St Mawes to Place ferry on VHF Ch 12, which operates a water taxi service on request.

The Falmouth Bay & Estuaries Initiative is requesting yachtsmen to refrain from anchoring too close to the shore in the traditionally popular area along the south side of the entrance to St Mawes between Carricknath and Amsterdam Points. This is a voluntary anchoring restriction aimed to protect an eelgrass bed extending out to seaward of the Low Tide mark to a depth of 3m, but if you stay out in the deeper water there is no problem. Land on the beach by dinghy just to the west of Amsterdam Point and from here, for a pleasant walk with good views, follow the coastal footpath out to St Anthony lighthouse – as seen in the children's television series *Fraggle Rock*. This passes Carricknath and Great Molunan beaches, which can provide plenty of sand and swimming at Low Water and are popular anchorages with locals in easterly winds – sound in to a suitable depth. In northerly winds, there is a very sheltered anchorage off the beaches to the south-east of St Mawes castle.

St Mawes is a former fishing village with a particularly mild climate. Being off the main holiday track has probably resulted in its popularity for retirement and, more recently, holiday homes, which may be why it has escaped over-development and commercialism.

Built at the same time as Pendennis, St Mawes Castle is a particularly well preserved example of its type, a clover leaf formation of three immense bastions, now

In suitable weather there are several good anchorages off St Mawes

St Mawes has a number of convenient visitors' moorings just off the village

open to the public and surrounded by gardens with fine views across to Falmouth.

FACILITIES
(Local phone code 01326)
The village has a good choice of shops, including a very well stocked Spar foodstore, Barclays bank (with cashpoint) and Lloyds TSB bank, a post office/newsagent with cash machine, butcher, baker, chemist, delicatessen/fine wine shop and several cafés, including Café Chandler for 'Divine Food and Drink'. There are also several gift shops and galleries.

As well as the Old Watch House Restaurant in the square, Tel: 270279, you will find restaurants open to non-residents at The Idle Rocks Hotel, Tel: 270771, Rising Sun Hotel, Tel: 270233, Ship & Castle Hotel, Tel: 270401, St Mawes Hotel, Tel: 270266, and the Tresanton Hotel, Tel: 270055, while there is good pub fare at the popular Victory Inn. Last but not least, try the Jolly Sailor Takeway for fish and chips, jacket potatoes and other delights!

Fresh water is available alongside at the quay by arrangement with the harbourmaster, and also in cans from a tap on the quay near Lloyd's Bank. St Mawes Sailing Club, Tel: 270686; www.stmawessailing.co.uk,

overlooks the quay from above Café Chandler and visitors are welcome to use the bar and showers.

The anchorage off St Mawes is perfect in easterly winds, but exposed to the south-west, when shelter can be found up the Percuil River, around the bend past Amsterdam Point, although anchoring is difficult because of the large number of local moorings. You might just find space to anchor clear of the moorings in the bight off Place House, a peaceful spot overlooked by silent woods, but the foreshore to Mean Low Water Springs is owned by Place and the owner does not allow boats to dry out here overnight.

The Percuil River winds away inland, drying to a large extent, but shallow draught boats can follow it – the deeper water indicated by the line of moorings – with a rising tide as far as Percuil. Here it is possible to anchor clear of the moorings in mid-stream, just grounding at Low Water Springs, but do not wander anywhere close inshore above Polvarth Point as oyster beds, marked by withies, lie on both sides of the river.

This is one of those places ideal for exploration by dinghy, its quiet creeks alive with herons and other wildlife. There is excellent blackberrying late in the summer.

MYLOR YACHT HARBOUR MARINA
Leaving the narrow Percuil, do not be lulled into a false sense of security by the broad waters of Carrick Roads, for large areas are shallow at Low Water, as many have discovered to their surprise. However, the main channel is very deep, averaging 25m, and trends towards Penarrow Point, a low promontory with a prominent pillar on the western shore, then over to the eastern bank towards St Just Creek, where there are a number of moorings. At half flood there is ample water everywhere, but upstream of St Mawes Castle, St Mawes Bank extends from the shore, with a minimum

In a lovely setting, Mylor Yacht Harbour Marina is always popular. Visitors berth on the outer end of the lower breakwater pontoon

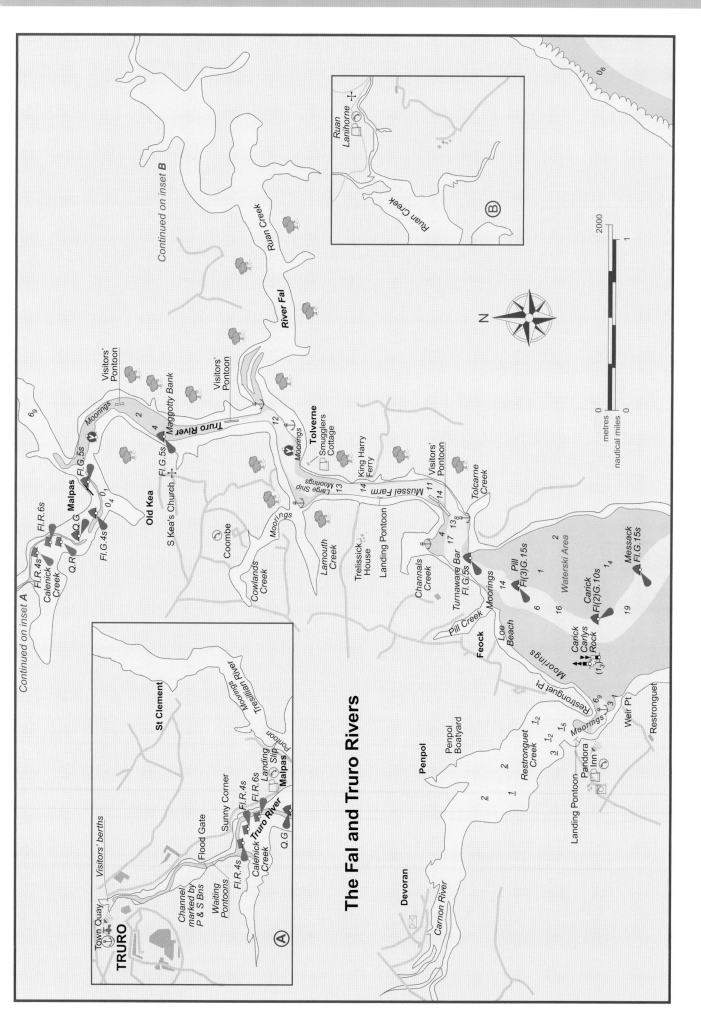

The Fal and Truro Rivers

depth of 1.2m in places.

Mylor Creek, west of Penarrow Point, is a popular base for a large number of boats which lie on extensive moorings in Mylor Pool off Mylor Yacht Harbour, but the surrounding shallows in the approaches have as little as 1.2m in places and, with Springs or a draught of over 1.5m, it is always best to wait until a couple of hours after Low Water, passing close to the North Bank red can buoy off Penarrow

Mylor Marina eastern breakwater. The people on the left are waiting for the water taxi, and the blue ketch, right, is on the fuel berth

Point. Next steer for and pass between the two smaller red can and conical green approach buoys to Mylor Pool, which mark the beginning of the dredged (2m below Chart Datum) approach channel to Mylor Yacht Harbour Marina.

Restronguet Sailing Club, a very active dinghy racing centre where Olympic sailor Ben Ainslie learned to race in Optimists, is a modern building on the foreshore, and beyond it are the houses, quays and pontoons of Mylor Yacht Harbour.

Formerly the Royal Navy's smallest dockyard, established in 1805 and base for the old wooden walled training ship *HMS Ganges*, this picturesque corner began to develop into a busy boatyard from the late 1960s. Following a change of ownership in 1997 the considerable upgrading of facilities culminated in the creation of a new marina and all tide approach channel in 2001.

There are extensive moorings on both sides of this channel, which follows the clear fairway between the moorings towards the line of heavy concrete pontoons forming the eastern breakwater arm of the marina. The entrance to the marina is around the northern end of the eastern breakwater pontoons and visitors normally berth on the inside of the eastern breakwater pontoons, rafting if required.

Mylor Yacht Harbour Marina, Tel: 01326 372121; www.mylor.com, has visitors' berths for vessels up to 22m which can be booked in advance or on arrival. There is a 24-hour listening watch, call *Mylor Yacht Harbour* on VHF channel 80 or M for berthing instructions. Swinging moorings are also available and these include a complimentary water taxi service operating from 0800 till late seven days a week during the summer from a berth adjacent to the fuel berth on the eastern side of the eastern breakwater. Both diesel and petrol are available (0900 – 1700 early season, 0830 – 2100 high season).

The overnight charge for a 10m boat, including free showers, is £27.50 alongside in the marina or £17.50 for a swinging mooring. If you stay over a week you will get a 10% discount.

There is water and power on the pontoons and WiFi internet access, with showers, toilets and a launderette ashore. The comprehensive yard facilities include a 35-ton travelift and repairs, while Marine Trak Engineers, Tel: 372121, and Simrad Marine Electronics, Tel: 374411, are also based on site.

Right on the the quayside you'll find the ever popular Ganges licensed restaurant, Tel: 374320, or try Castaways restaurant and wine bar, Tel: 377710, just next door, for tapas, seafood and lighter meals, as well as for breakfast on Fri/Sat/Sun. Both are open seven days a week. Café Mylor on the harbourside sells fresh bread, pasties and a small selection of groceries, beer and wine, or else try the well-stocked Mylor Chandlery and Rigging, Tel: 375482, which is situated in the boatyard close to the marina office. Last but definitely not least, the very friendly Mylor Yacht Club, Tel: 374391; www.myloryachtclub.org.uk, is on the quay and visitors are always welcome to use the clubhouse and bar, open evenings and weekends.

The old quays of the dockyard form a sheltered and attractive setting overlooked by the lovely church of St Mylor, where some of the gravestones are a fascinating reflection of the local maritime heritage. The Ganges Mermorial to the many boy sailors who succumbed during training provides a sombre insight into the harsh realities of the 19th century Royal Navy. It is also the peaceful resting place of packet commanders, sailors, oyster dredgermen and a luckless shipwright who died in 1770 and whose epitaph reads:

'His foot it slip and he did fall
Help Help he cries and that was all.'

The narrow entrance into Mylor Creek is overhung with trees and very congested with moorings, but widens further in, continuing for nearly a mile to the village of Mylor Bridge, an interesting excursion in the dinghy on a rising tide where there is a post office and a convenience store, The Lemon Arms pub and occasional buses to Falmouth. All of the upper part of the creek dries, and at Tregatreath on the south side you will pass Gaffers and Luggers Boatyard, where traditional shipwright work blends harmoniously with modern technology as gaff-rigged fibreglass working boats and pilot cutter replicas are built here by Martin Heard.

ST JUST

From Mylor Pool, it is tempting to head directly for Restronguet Creek just upstream – certain disaster if the tide is near Low Water, as beyond the outer moorings the extensive banks almost dry at Low Water. Instead, return to the main channel, heading for the moorings off St Just. This is a pleasant spot in an easterly wind, when Mylor inevitably suffers!

There are many local moorings, but a good anchorage, popular with locals in easterlies, can be found to the south of the entrance to the creek off the shingly beaches along the rocky shore. Be warned though – the holding can be patchy so allow plenty of scope.

The coastal footpath provides a fine walk south towards St Mawes, or north to St Just where it leads to the undoubted pride of the creek, the 13th century church. Lavishly described by Sir John Betjeman as 'to many people the most beautiful churchyard on earth', it certainly has one of the finest settings in England, nestling against the wooded hillside overlooking the peaceful creek and surrounded in Spring by a breathtaking blaze of camelias and rhododendrons. Shoal draught boats can work their way right into the creek and dry out if space permits. Land on the shingle beach at the head of the inlet that encloses a drying tidal pool, where you will find Pascoe's Boatyard nearby. Small quantities of diesel are available here, in cans, and also Calor refills.

RESTRONGUET

Near Low Water keep within the main channel, which bears north-west from St Just buoy (QR), past the conical green Messack buoy (Fl G 15s), and towards Restronguet. As you leave the main channel it becomes shallow when passing to the south of Carick Carlys Rock (north and south cardinal beacons), with little more than 0.5m, but with a couple of hours of flood you should be able to get up to the Pandora Inn, the most likely reason for a visit to the creek!

There are concentrated moorings in the deep pool at the narrow mouth of the creek off Restronguet Point, which is a low promontory with some very expensive looking properties along it, aka millionaires row, according to the locals! Here the stream runs fast through the narrows. Deep draught boats can anchor short of the moorings, east of the entrance off Weir Point. Either land on the beach and walk along the path to the pub, or take the dinghy, an easy row with the

tide, and make sure you return on the ebb. Shallower draught boats can go right up to the large pontoon off the pub and berth there around High Water but the owners do not allow boats to dry out alongside.

With its huge thatch and attractive waterside location, 'The Pan' is a very popular local watering hole which takes its name from HMS Pandora, the ship that captured the Bounty mutineers. On his return in 1790, her commander bought this 13th century inn and today it is notably yacht friendly, for not only can you find excellent food and drink, but there is also a handy shower and toilet block, a small launderette and a fresh water supply.

Restronguet Creek widens considerably above the Pandora and is fringed down to the water's edge by woods and fields. Restronguet Yacht Basin (drying) lies just upstream on the south shore, while the Penpol Boatyard is situated on the northern shore at the entrance to Penpol Creek. All of Restronguet Creek is very shallow and dries extensively, but can be explored by dinghy for over a mile as far as Devoran, a small village on the northern shore where there is a post office and general store. It was a busy port in the 1880s, exporting copper and tin, for ships were once able to berth as far inland as the Perran Wharf on the main Falmouth to Truro road. Eventually the alluvial deposits from the Carnon valley mining caused its demise, silting the river to such an extent that it is now only accessible a couple of hours either side of High Water.

THE UPPER REACHES TO TRURO

Beyond Restronguet, leave Carick Carlys Rock to port, and on a falling tide do not stray from the deep water channel, which is marked by two more conical green starboard-hand buoys, Carick (Fl(2) G 10s) and Pill (Fl (3) G 15s). The bank to the east is particularly shallow, as little as 0.2m in places at Low Water, and this is the main area of the oyster fishery in winter. Opposite, there are many moorings off Loe Beach which, comprising shingle and sand, is popular for swimming. A few visitors' moorings are sometimes available through the café, otherwise anchor off. Just above the beach, Pill Creek is a narrow wooded inlet, completely taken up by moorings.

The real upper reaches of the Fal and Truro Rivers begin at wooded Turnaware Point and its low shingle foreshore on the eastern bank. The change is dramatic as the wide expanse of Carrick Roads narrows into a deep waterway and the most attractive part of the river begins.

Keep close to the western shore, which is covered in trees and fringed with cliffs, where the notorious grounding spot, Turnaware Bar, extends north-west from the Point. It is clearly marked by a green conical buoy (Fl G 5s) which must be left to starboard. Here the streams begin to run strongly, 2 – 3 knots at Springs. A

Overlooked by the impressive edifice of Trelissick House, Channals Creek is a popular weekend anchorage for locals

small amount of commercial traffic still uses the upper reaches, such as the occasional coaster carrying building materials. The river is much used by trip boats too.

Immediately north of the buoy is Channals Creek, a popular anchorage that is well sheltered in anything except southerlies and out of the main tidal stream. All the upper reaches are under the jurisdiction of the Truro harbourmaster and visitors will be charged £5 a night for anchoring anywhere north of Turnaware Bar. Sound in off the edge of the deep channel to about 2m at Low Water. Shoal draught boats can get much closer inshore where they will ground. A fine sweep of grassland leads up from the water's edge to the impressive façade of Trelissick House, built in 1750 and now owned by the National Trust. The House is not open to the public, but the spectacular gardens featuring rhododendrons, camellias, azaleas and magnolias are open daily, 1030 – 1730, from February to October. Land at the rocky point on the east side of the bay and follow the scenic footpath along the shore through the woods.

The anchorage inside of Turnaware Point is another popular spot at weekends, particularly for picnics and barbecues. An equally good anchorage can be found nearby off diminutive Tolcarne Creek, which is overlooked by steep woods, just clear of the deep water. The first Truro Harbour Authority visitors' pontoon lies opposite; charges here, and on the other visitors' pontoons further upstream, are at a flat rate of £10 a night or £80 for 10 days, if you really want to hang around, and dues are collected by the harbourmaster's launch – make direct contact on VHF Ch 12, callsign *Carrick Three*. Truro Harbour Office uses the same channel, callsign *Carrick One*.

For many years you would have now been confronted by the Fal's biggest surprise as you round the bend into King Harry Reach. Here, in this land-locked and narrow river, surrounded by high wooded shores, there were invariably large merchant ships lying on fore and

aft moorings. The numbers varied depending on the fortunes of the international shipping trade, but at times the security and low harbour dues meant that there were often over 20 vessels laid up in the river. But one by one they all departed and now a new, and much less spectacular source of revenue fills the river, an extensive mussel farm. Do not be too distracted though, if you're sailing, the tide runs strongly and the high shores and ships make the breeze very fluky, and it's easy to get set onto this veritable cats cradle of ropes and moorings. In addition, midway along this reach is the bright blue King Harry Ferry, which runs on chains, providing a short cut for cars between Falmouth and St Mawes. There has been a ferry here since, and the current vessel was built in Falmouth Dock in 2006. Identical at both ends, ascertain which way it is running and always pass astern, and not too close!

Just downstream of the ferry, the Truro Harbour Authority landing pontoon is for local trip boats bringing visitors to Trelissick. Visitors are not permitted to berth on the outside of the pontoon but if the tide permits – there is limited depth here at Low Water – you can lie on the inside on the down-river end to take on water from the tap. If you want to land here by dinghy, leave it on the inside of the up-river end!

Next, Lamouth and Cowlands Creeks open to port, both attractive and wooded, and both drying almost as far as the moorings at their mouth, where an anchorage can be found between these and the deep water. Small craft are able to explore further on the tide, as far as the peaceful hamlets of Coombe and Cowlands, renowned for their plum orchards, where bilge-keelers can dry out on the foreshore. There's a public phone at Cowlands. Owned by the National Trust, Roundwood Quay, where the creeks meet, is a finely preserved granite quay once used for shipping minerals. There are several pleasant walks leading away from it.

The river turns sharply to the east off Tolverne Point, another regular lay up berth for large ships, and on the shore you will see the thatched Smugglers Cottage, a popular spot for visitors for nearly 100 years with trip boats running here from Falmouth. They do morning

The first of the Truro Harbour Authority visitors' pontoons is just above Turnaware

Tolverne Point and Smugglers Cottage

THA visitors' pontoon upstream of Ruan Creek

coffee, lunches and cream teas, and also have a licensed bar, although technically they are not a pub. There is a prominent landing pontoon and a number of visitors' mooring buoys, which are free to patrons of the Cottage during the day; if you decide to stay longer they cost £8 per night.

This corner has an interesting history as, during the last war, it was used as an assembly point for part of the American fleet of D-Day landing craft and was visited by General Eisenhower. The fascinating collection of photos and mementoes in the cottage are well worth seeing, in particular the *Uganda* room, devoted to the famous cruise ship and Falklands veteran that was laid up in the Fal between 1985 and 1986.

At the next junction, just above Tolverne, the rivers divide, the Fal fading away rather insignificantly into Ruan Creek, which continues to the east, and the Truro River, heading northwards.

There is a peaceful anchorage just within the entrance to Ruan Creek, off the old ruined boathouse on the north side where there is about 2m at Low Water. However, watch out for three very large abandoned mooring blocks close to the shore, marked with a yellow pole and 'X' topmark, which only begin to uncover after half tide. The south shore dries extensively, so shoal draught boats can push a bit further into the creek and dry out at Low Water beneath the dense woods along the edge of Lord Falmouth's estate.

Beyond the first bend, the creek dries completely and there is a voluntary restriction on anchoring within this Site of Special Scientific Interest, although small craft and dinghies can explore it on the tide, penetrating deep into the rural depths of Cornwall to Ruan Lanihorne, three miles away. Here there is an old quay for landing and the Kings Head pub within a five-minute walk.

Just upstream of Ruan Creek is a second Truro Harbour Authority visitors' pontoon, sections of which are constructed from recycled plastic. It is also possible to anchor anywhere along this reach out of the main

fairway, although it is busy with trip boats during the day and an anchor light is advisable at night. Beyond tiny Church Creek on the west bank, where the ruined spire of Old Kea Church rises above the trees, the Truro River becomes much shallower and the Maggotty Bank extends across the river from the eastern shore (least depth 0.7m). The channel is very narrow between the western shore and the conical green buoy (Fl G 5s) at the outer edge of the bank.

Follow the bend round to starboard past Woodbury Point, where there is an isolated white house, to a deeper pool where another Truro Harbour Authority visitors' pontoon is located. Finally, further upstream in Malpas Reach, there is one visitors' mooring suitable for up to about 7.5m LOA and another pontoon that can take vessels of the same size. Although there are many other local moorings here, beware – at Low Water Springs there is as little as 0.3m in places. The tide runs strongly, reaching a good two knots at Springs.

At Malpas, pronounced *Mope-us*, the elevated houses overlook the river, and below them is the yard of Malpas Marine and a private landing pontoon. The yard can sometimes provide a mooring for visitors if one of its permanent mooring holders is away at around £8 a day; to enquire either phone ahead, Tel: 01872 271260, or berth on the end of its pontoon, but do not leave your boat unattended as it is used by ferries to Falmouth.

For a charge of £1 a head (unless you are on one of its moorings) visitors can leave their dinghies on the pontoon, and a shower/toilet, water and diesel in cans are also available. Close by, overlooking the river, the popular Heron Inn, Tel: 01872 272773, does good food, there's a very small shop-cum-post office, a public telephone and occasional buses to Truro, which is now within walking distance, albeit not close.

Tresillian River branches to starboard and mostly dries. Truro River continues past Malpas and is well worth exploring as far as Truro. The channel, which is occasionally used by coasters, is well-marked, but do not leave Malpas any earlier than three hours before

The final approach to Truro. Sunny Corner, right, Calenick Creek, left, Lighterage Quay and flood gate, centre, with the channel meandering towards the Town Quay

HW Truro and keep in midstream, leaving the conical green buoy and private landing pontoon off the housing development at Victoria Quay to starboard.

A large bank extends west of the next long bend, so keep well towards the western shore before turning north past the first of two more conical green buoys. Beyond the second, the channel swings back to the eastern bank, high and wooded, past three port hand red cans, and then north-west again off Sunny Corner where there are always a number of boats laid-up on the beach. At the final red can, steer for the end of the Lighterage Quay, where the river narrows to about 100m wide.

Coasters occasionally berth here, and at the northern end of the quay there is a flood prevention barrage with a flood gate that normally remains open except when higher than average tides are anticipated. The gate is 12m wide and normally poses no problems, but make allowance for the fact that the tidal flow increases through this restriction. There is a waiting pontoon just downstream if the gate is closed or if you arrive too early on the tide to make Town Quay.

Beyond it is a launching slipway on the eastern, Boscawen Park, shore. Here, the river widens into a broad shallow reach, the Cathedral and houses of Truro now clearly in sight but the channel, marked by red posts with square red topmarks to port and green posts with triangular green topmarks to starboard, winds back to starboard past the playing fields, then close to the eastern bank before it swings back towards the long quay on the western bank. Following the line of this shore it narrows, with a large Tesco superstore to port, and the deepest water closest to the old warehouses

to starboard. Around the bend at Town Quay the river divides into three cul-de-sacs – berth in the port hand one, adjacent to the harbour office.

There is water here for about two hours either side of High Water; if you wish to remain longer you will dry out in soft mud, which is quite steep in places, and not the sweetest smelling at Low Water! It will cost £10 a night, and amenities include a toilet and shower on the quay, fresh water, electricity points, rubbish bins and a chemical toilet disposal facility. It is perhaps not the most prepossessing berth in the West Country, but the attractive Cathedral City of Truro, within a five-minute walk, more than makes up for this. This major shopping centre is able to provide all normal requirements, including Penrose's chandlery right on the quay, and another, Langdon's, in New Bridge Street. You will find many good pubs and restaurants, as well as a main line railway station should you need to land or pick up crew.

The famous three spires of Truro Cathedral dominate the approach to the Town Quay

Falmouth Port Guide (Cont) – Area telephone code: Falmouth 01326; Truro 01872

Harbourmasters: Falmouth: Captain Mark Sansom, Harbour Office, 44 Arwenack Street, Falmouth TR11 3JQ, Tel: 312285 or 314379; Fax: 211352; email: info@falmouthport.co.uk; website: www.falmouth port.co.uk.

Truro/Penryn: Captain Andy Brigden, Harbour Office, Town Quay, Truro, Tel: 01872 224231 or 272130; Fax: 01872 225346; email: harbouroffice@carrick.gov. uk; website: www.portof truro.co.uk.

St Mawes: Captain Gary Cairns, The Quay, St Mawes, Tel: 270553.

VHF: Falmouth, VHF Ch 16, working 12. 0800 – 1700 daily, callsign *Falmouth Harbour Radio*; St Mawes, Ch 16; 12, callsign *St Mawes Harbour Radio*; Truro, Ch 12, callsign *Carrick One*.

Mail drop: Harbour office will hold mail, also RCYC, Falmouth Marina and Mylor Yacht Harbour; Truro Harbour Office.

Emergency services: Lifeboat and inshore lifeboat at Falmouth; Falmouth Coastguard.

Anchorages: Off Custom House Quay, in harbour clear of moorings. Off St Mawes, St Just, off Restronguet, Loe Beach and in upper reaches of river. Charges apply throughout Falmouth harbour, St Mawes and upper Fal.

Moorings/berthing: FHC Visitors' Yacht Haven, North Quay, Falmouth 100 boats, max 15m LOA, up to 2.5m draught, and 18 deep water visitors' moorings. RCYC two visitors' moorings off Club. Mylor Yacht Harbour Ltd, Mylor, Nr Falmouth, Tel: 372121. Malpas Marine, Malpas, Nr Truro, Tel: 01872 271260. Truro Harbour Authority, visitors' pontoons above Turnaware, off Ruan Creek and Malpas, visitors' buoys at Malpas, drying berths alongside at Truro Town Quay.

Marinas: Port Falmouth Marina, The Docks, Falmouth, Tel: 212161; email: info@portfalmouth marina.co.uk; website: www.

portfalmouthmarina.com. Equipped with 290 berths, including visitors. VHF Ch 80/M, callsign *Port Falmouth Marina*.

Falmouth Marina, North Parade, Falmouth, Tel: 316620; Fax: 313939; email: falmouth@ premiermarinas.com; website: www.premiermarinas.com. A total of 375 berths, 50 visitors. VHF Ch 80/M, callsign *Falmouth Marina*.

Port Pendennis Marina, Tel: 211211; Fax: 311116; email: marina@portpendennis. com; website: www.port pendennis.com. A total of 70 berths, 40 visitors. VHF Ch 80/M, callsign *Port Pendennis*.

Mylor Marina, Mylor Yacht Harbour, Tel: 372121; Fax: 372120; email: enquiries@mylor.com; website: www.mylor.com. VHF Ch 80/M, callsign *Mylor Yacht Harbour*.

Charges: FHC: Yacht Haven, July/August (lower rates at other times) up to 8m £17.50, over 8m up to 10m £20.50, over 10m up to 12m £23, over 12m up to 14m £26.50, over 14m up to 16m £34. Short stay (all boats, up to two hours) £8. Swinging moorings from £8.50 (7m) to £20 (over 15m), depending on LOA; at anchor from £4.50 to £10.50 depending on LOA. Special rates for over a week.

Port Pendennis Marina £2.60 per metre per night. RCYC mooring, price on application depending on LOA. Falmouth Marina £2.60 per metre per night.

St Mawes, visitors' mooring, per night, up to 10m £15. 10m to 12m £20. 12m to 14m £30. At anchor 50p per metre per 24 hours.

Mylor Yacht Harbour, alongside in marina, £2.75 per metre per night. On mooring, £1.75 per metre per night. Special rates for longer stays.

Malpas Marine £8. Truro Harbour Authority pontoons/alongside £10, at anchor £5.

Dinghy landings: Visitors' Yacht Haven, North Quay. Fish Strand Steps, inner end of Prince of Wales Pier, RCYC. Mylor Yacht Harbour

pontoon. St Mawes, slipway and free steps.

Water taxi: If using RCYC moorings, boatman and launch, 1015 – 1845 daily in season, VHF Ch M callsign *Club Launch* (lunch 1300 – 1400). St Mawes to Place ferry operates water taxi service, call on VHF Ch 12. *Mylor water taxi* VHF Ch M, for Mylor Yacht Harbour customers. Aqua Cab fast water taxi, Tel: 07970 242258.

Phones: Nearest to Yacht Haven in Chain Locker pub or Grove Place; Port Pendennis; RCYC; Falmouth Marina; St Mawes harbour; by church at Mylor; Malpas.

Doctor: Tel: 434802.

Dentist: Tel: 314702.

Hospital: Falmouth Minor injuries Unit, Tel:434739. Nearest casualty Treliske, Truro, Tel: 01872 250000.

Churches: All denominations.

Local weather forecast: Visitors' Yacht Haven supervisor's office; Falmouth Marina office; Mylor Marina berthing office; St Mawes harbour office.

Fuel: Fuel berth on Visitors' Yacht Haven, open all year, petrol and diesel, 0900 – 1800. Falmouth Marina, diesel only, 24 hours. Mylor Yacht Harbour diesel and petrol alongside, during early season 0900 – 1800, later at weekends, 0830 – 2100 July/Aug.

Paraffin: Cox's Home Hardware, The Moor, Falmouth.

Gas: Calor/Gaz. The Bosun's Locker; Falmouth Marina; Mylor Chandlery, Mylor Yacht Harbour.

Water: Visitors' Yacht Haven; Port Pendennis Marina; Falmouth Marina; Mylor Yacht Harbour; St Mawes; Malpas; Town Quay; Truro.

Tourist Information Centre: Prince of Wales Pier, Falmouth, Tel: 312300; www.acornishriver.co.uk. St Mawes car park; City Hall, Truro.

Banks/cashpoints: All main banks in Falmouth and Truro,

with cashpoints. St Mawes, Barclays (cashpoint) and Lloyds TSB.

Post office: The Moor, Falmouth; St Mawes; Truro.

Internet access: WiFi: Falmouth inner harbour; Port Pendennis; Falmouth Marina; Mylor Marina. Public internet access: Falmouth Library; Truro Library; Q Bar internet café, The Moor, Falmouth.

Rubbish: Bins on North Quay. Bins at Falmouth Marina and Mylor Yacht Harbour; St Mawes harbour; Turnaware visitors' pontoon; Malpas; Town Quay, Truro.

Showers/toilets: Yacht Haven Amenity building; Port Pendennis Marina; RCYC; Falmouth Marina; Mylor Yacht Harbour; Pandora Inn; St Mawes SC; Malpas Boats; Town Quay, Truro. Chemical toilet disposal facility at North Quay, Mylor, Truro Town Quay, Penryn Quay.

Launderettes: Yacht Haven Amenity building; Port Pendennis Marina; Falmouth Marina; Mylor Yacht Harbour; Pandora Inn.

Provisions: All requirements in Falmouth. Number of shops open on Sundays – Tesco centre of town and also Discovery Quay, 0800 – 2300, Spar at Albany Road, 10 minutes uphill walk from harbour, and Co-op Pioneer supermarket, five minutes walk from Falmouth Marina. Most provisions also at St Mawes, good selection of basics at Mylor Yacht

Harbour, Café Mylor, seven days a week in season. All shops, Truro.

Chandlers: Bosun's Locker, Upton Slip, Falmouth, Tel: 312212; Fal Chandlers, Tel: 212411, and Skywave Marine, Tel: 318314, both at Falmouth Yacht Marina. Challenger Marine, Falmouth Road, Penryn, Tel: 377222; The Boathouse, Commercial Road, Penryn, Tel: 374177; Monsons (bonded stores) West End Ind Estate, Penryn, Tel: 373581; Mylor Chandlery and Rigging, Mylor Yacht Harbour, Tel: 375482, seven days in season; Langdon Marine Chandlers, New Bridge Street, Truro, Tel: 01872 272668; Penrose Outdoors, Town Quay, Truro, Tel: 01872 270213; Compass adjusters, Tel: 312414.

Liferaft service/repair: Inflatable Boat Services, North Parade, Tel: 313800.

Repairs/hauling: Falmouth Boat Construction Ltd, Little Falmouth Yacht Yard, Flushing, Nr Falmouth, Tel: 374309. 100-ton slipway/25-ton hoist. Pendennis Shipyard, Falmouth Docks, 80-ton hoist, Tel: 211344. Falmouth Marina Services, 30-ton hoist, Tel: 316620. Falmouth Yacht Services,

Tel: 310120, 40-ton hoist. Falmouth Yacht Brokers, Penryn, 50-ton slip, Tel: 370060. Islington Wharf Boat Yard, Penryn, Tel: 378700. Mylor Yacht Harbour, Tel: 372121, 35-ton hoist. Heard's Boatyard, Tregatreath, Nr Mylor, Falmouth, Tel: 374441. Freshwater Boatyard, St Mawes, Tel: 270443. Percuil Boatyard, Tel: 01872 580564. Pascoe's Boatyard, St Just in Roseland, Tel: 270269. Malpas Marine, Tel: 01872 271260.

Marine engineers: Challenger Marine, Penryn, Tel: 376202. Falmouth Boat Construction, Tel: 374309 – 24 hour emergency call out 0468 178746. Marine Trak, Mylor Yacht Harbour, Tel: 372121. Robin Curnow, outboards/Seagull agents, Penryn, Tel: 373438. S Caddy, Penryn, Tel: 372682. S Francis, Tel: 377122. St Mawes – David Llewellen, Tel: 07973 523320, or Andrew Cox, Tel: 07974 250533.

Electronic engineers: Skywave Marine Electronics, Tel: 318314, at Falmouth Marina. Simrad Marine Electronics, Tel: 374411, at Mylor Yacht harbour.

Sailmakers/repairs: Penrose, Upton Slip, Falmouth, Tel: 312705. SKB Sails, The Sail Loft, Commercial Road, Penryn, Tel: 372107.

Riggers: www.riggers-uk.com, the Boathouse, Commercial Road, Penryn, Tel: 374177. Challenger Marine, Tel: 377222. Falmouth Boat Construction, Flushing, Tel: 374309. Mylor Chandlery and Rigging, Tel: 375482.

Divers: Sea-Wide Services, Tel: 375095. Falmouth Divers, Tel: 374736.

Transport: Branch line to main line rail connections to London and North at Truro, Tel: 08457 484950. Daily bus and coach connections with rest of country, Traveline, Tel: 0871 2002233. Road connections to M5 via Plymouth (A38) or Bodmin (A30). Newquay Airport, 45 mins, Tel: 01345 222111.

Car hire: Europcar at Falmouth Marina, Tel: 315204; Eurodrive, Tel: 377456; Falmouth Garages, Tel: 377246.

Car parking: Several large car parks in Falmouth; Mylor Yacht Harbour; St Mawes

Quay and harbour car park.

Yacht clubs: Royal Cornwall Yacht Club, Greenbank, Falmouth, Office Tel: 312126, Bar, 311105; email: admin@royalcornwall yachtclub.org; website: www. royalcornwall yachtclub. org. Falmouth Watersports Association, Grove Place, Tel: 211223. Flushing Sailing Club, New Quay, Flushing, Nr Falmouth, Tel: 374043. Mylor Yacht Club, Mylor Yacht Harbour, Nr Falmouth, Tel: 374391. Restronguet Sailing Club, Mylor Yacht Harbour, Nr Falmouth, Tel: 374536. St Mawes Sailing Club, The Quay, St Mawes, Tel: 270686.

Eating out: No shortage of options! Seafood to curries, tapas to pasties and the rest in between.

Things to do: National Maritime Museum Cornwall; Pendennis and St Mawes Castles; good safe beaches/walks; Ships & Castles leisure pool; Pendennis Head.

Special events: Falmouth Regatta Week/Falmouth Classics, second week in August. Spectacular Working Boat and gig racing throughout summer.

Falmouth has an abundance of handy pubs and restaurants

Collecting the dues! Helford Pool looking east

Helford River

Tides	HW Dover −0615
Range	MHWS 5.3m−MHWN 4.2m, MLWN 1.9m−MLWS 0.6m. Streams attain up to two knots in river at Springs
Charts	AC: 147, SC 5603.6; Stanfords: CP23; Imray: WCP 2400.11
Waypoint	Voose North Cardinal buoy 50°05'.81N 05°06'.96W
Hazards	Gedges/August Rock, Car Croc Rock, Voose Rock (all unlit). Bar/shallows within river on north shore. Rough approach in strong easterly wind/ebb tide. Beware pot and net buoys. Large areas of upper reaches dry
Harbour Speed limit	Six knots/minimal wash in moorings
Overnight charge	Mooring Authority mooring £14

'When the east wind blows up Helford River the shining waters become troubled and disturbed, and the little waves beat angrily on the sandy shores. The short seas break above the bar at ebbtide, and the waders fly inland to the mudflats, their wings skimming the surface, and calling to one another as they go. Only the gulls remain, wheeling and crying above the foam, diving in search of food, their grey feathers glistening with the salt spray. The long rollers of the Channel, travelling from beyond Lizard Point, follow hard upon the steep seas at the river mouth and mingling with surge and wash of deep sea water comes the brown tide, swollen with the last rains and brackish from the mud, bearing on its face dead twigs and straws, and strange forgotten things, leaves too early fallen, young birds and the buds of flowers.

The open roadstead is deserted, for an east wind makes an uneasy anchorage, and but for the few houses scattered here and there above Helford Passage, and the group of bungalows about Port Navas, the river would be the same as it was in a century now forgotten, in a time that has left few memories . . .'

So begins *Frenchman's Creek*, Daphne du Maurier's bestseller that made the name of the Helford familiar to all – the haunt of the heroine Dona and hideaway for the Frenchman and his ship, *La Mouette*.

Although the numbers of yachts have certainly increased in the roadstead, her words are very true, and large areas in this gem of a river still remain untouched. Overshadowed by the busy harbour at Falmouth, commercially there was never any reason for the Helford to develop – it merely served the needs

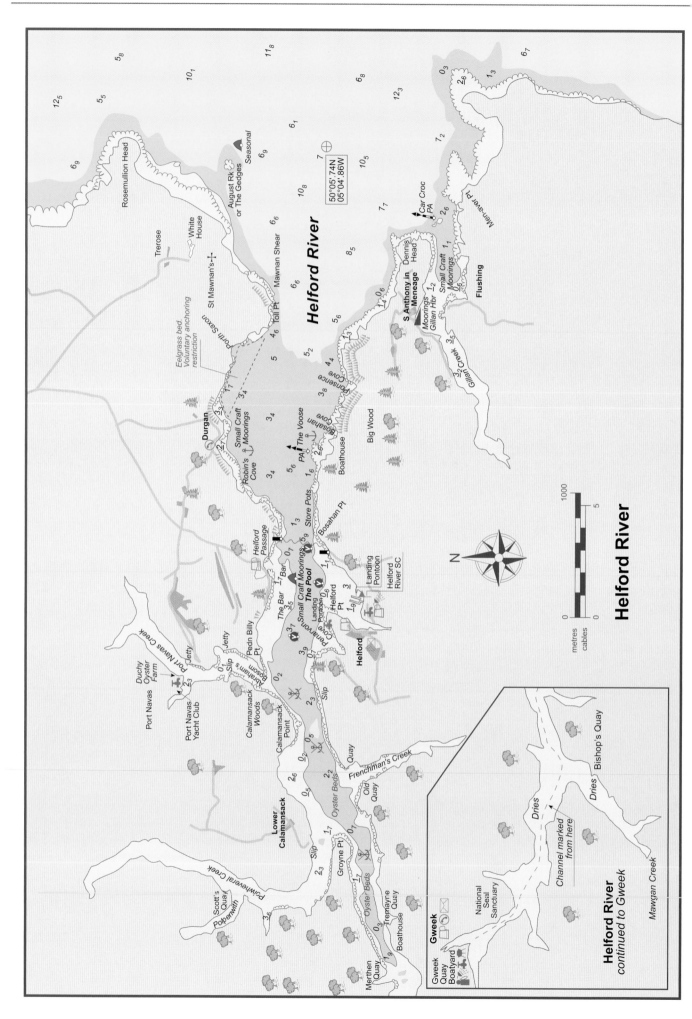

Helford River

of the surrounding farms and communities, with a few small granite quays dotted along its banks. Apart from the scattered fishing hamlets, it remained '. . . unvisited, the woods and hills untrodden, and all the drowsy beauty of midsummer that gives Helford river a strange enchantment, was never seen and never known.'

The few people that did pass along this unpopulated, silent waterway into the depths of rural Cornwall, bounded by high shores and deep mysterious woods, were mostly heading for Gweek, right at the head of navigation. As the nearest access to the inland town of Helston, this was the focal point of waterborne activity, with sailing coasters and barges slowly working their way up on the tide, bringing cargoes of coal, timber and lime and taking away granite, tin and farm produce. However, the advent of rail and motor transport and gradual silting resulted in its decline at the turn of the century, when the river slipped back into obscurity.

The other reason for the remarkable natural preservation of the inner reaches is the Duchy of Cornwall oyster fisheries. Reputedly dating back to Roman times, these extensive beds have always inhibited the spread of moorings and other commercial development. This and very limited facilities mean that today the Helford River, except in high season, can still have an almost deserted quality, a solitude that is increasingly rare and, fortunately, cherished by those who come here to seek it.

APPROACHES

At just under four miles from Pendennis Point, the Helford is a regular jaunt across the bay for many Falmouth boats, perhaps pausing to anchor off a beach or for a quick run ashore to the pub, but as the afternoon draws in, most return home. Although the entrance is well hidden away to the south-west, other boats entering and leaving will give a good indication of its position. As you close Rosemullion Head, the green conical buoy, August Rock (seasonal), to seaward of the Gedges rocks (drying 1.4m), should be left on your starboard hand before bearing round into the river mouth as it opens ahead, running due west.

There are no further hazards except very close to the shore, and depths average between 3m and 4m in the entrance. There can be a noticeable funnelling effect within the mouth when beating in, but the shelter inside is excellent in anything, except of course, easterly winds, when this is a place to avoid. Not only does Falmouth Bay and the approaches kick up a very short steep sea, but also the swell within the moorings and anchorage, particularly with wind against tide, makes for a lot of discomfort. In these conditions you are much better off in the Fal!

On the southern shore, in the approach to the Helford, the hidden entrance to Gillan Creek is easily located by the distinctive hump of Dennis Head across its mouth. This can be a delightful spot in the right conditions, but is really only of interest to shallow draught boats, as it dries for the most part and the only deep water within its mouth is almost totally taken up with moorings. Car Croc, a particularly nasty rock (dries 1m), sits almost in the middle of the entrance, marked by an east cardinal buoy, BYB, but be warned, it extends further to the south-east than might be imagined so give it a good berth, passing midway between it and the south shore when entering. Also beware of the rocks extending to seawards from Men-aver Point.

Ideally, for a first visit, arrive just after Low Water when all the hazards are easy to see, and feel your way in on the tide, anchoring clear of the local moorings off

There are various anchorages in the clear approach to the Helford, either off Durgan, right, or Ponsence Cove, centre left. Beyond, Helford Creek lies to the left of the moorings in the Pool, with Helford Passage on the right

August Rock buoy (now unlit), with the Gedges
showing on a big Spring Tide

the houses at Flushing if you can, or go further into
the creek to the picturesque hamlet and church at
St Anthony, where you will dry out, well tucked away
in this hidden corner. Here, on the shingly foreshore
is the small yard of Sailaway St Anthony, Tel: 01326
231357, which may be able to provide a mooring.
The densely-wooded creek beyond the sandy spit is
particularly attractive when the tide is in, perfect for
a dinghy trip or just a walk along the road that follows
it inland.

ANCHORAGES

Back in the main river, with wind between north and
west, there are some good sheltered anchorages just
within the entrance and remarkably there is still no
charge for anchoring! You can let go off the bight along
the northern side between Toll Point and the small
boathouse at Porth Saxon, as well as off shingly
Grebe beach further to the west. However, under the
Falmouth Bay & Estuaries conservation initiatives,
as off St Mawes, a further voluntary restriction on
anchoring in this area is now in operation to protect
another eelgrass bed. This one extends outwards from
the Low Water mark for approximately 200m, and you
should anchor outside the marker buoys.

No doubt the seahorses and other small creatures that
inhabit the eelgrass are delighted, but I have to confess
to being saddened to see yet another anchorage being
encroached on. As it's the anchors and cable that do the
damage, perhaps some visitors' moorings would be a
useful compromise?

Depending on the wind direction there are two
recommended places for anchoring, both of which will
require an anchor light and a dinghy with outboard.
Best in northerly and westerly winds, you can let
go west of Durgan, off Polgwidden Cove, or on the
southern shore east of the Voose Rocks off Bosahan
Cove or Ponsence Cove if the wind is in the south or
south-west. Both have small sandy beaches but there are
plenty of rocks in between. Locals claim that the large
house just inland from Ponsense was the *Manderley* of

Daphne du Maurier's *Rebecca*, rather than Menabilly
on Gribbin Head. Certainly, Ponsence Cove and
the tiny boathouse seem to fit the bill. One thing is
certain, there is no doubt where the inspiration for
Frenchman's Creek came from – just over a mile
upstream you can explore it for yourself!

Larger vessels should anchor anywhere between these
two areas. Anchoring is not permitted west of the Voose
on the south shore because of the fishermen's store pots
or anywhere in the inner river west of the telephone
cable in the narrows between Helford Passage and
Bosahan Point, which is clearly indicated by the warning
signs on shore. The former anchorage upriver of the
moorings in the Pool has now been taken over by the
oyster fishery and is marked by the three oyster buoys.

Durgan is a picturesque cluster of old fishermen's
cottages, partly owned by the National Trust, as is
the valley running down to the village in which the
25 exotic acres of Glendurgan Gardens are situated.
Renowned for its trees and shrubs, it was created from
1820 onwards by the well-known Fox family, Quakers
who still live here. Donated by them to the National
Trust in 1962, the gardens are open to the public from
1030 –1630 March – October. There are no facilities at
Durgan except a phone.

From here, Grebe or Porth Saxon, you can follow the
attractive coastal footpath back up over the headland
to Mawnan Church, which is set among the trees on
the cliff-top overlooking the entrance to the river.
This is a particularly lovely spot, and it is not difficult
to see why. Among the gravestones you can find
those of two eminent yachtsmen, Claud Worth, the
grandfather of modern cruising, and his son Tom, who
circumnavigated the world in 1953 aboard the Giles-
designed cutter, *Beyond*. His epitaph is particularly
succinct – 'Tom Worth, Who Sailed *Beyond*'.

THE INNER RIVER
AND THE POOL

Continuing west from the Voose, a drying rocky ledge
that has snared a surprising number of boats in spite
of its north cardinal BY buoy, as you approach the
narrows, keep just over a cable off the steep, wooded
shore leading up to Bosahan Point in order to avoid
the large cluster of fishermen's store pots, which have
a line of small red port hand marks along their outer
edge. Continue towards the large concentration of
moorings ahead, but beware the northern, starboard
side – here, shallows extend up to a cable from the
shore with not much more than 0.5m in places, and as
the houses at Helford Passage begin to appear in the
bay on the northern shore you enter the Pool where the
bulk of the Helford moorings are located. Just beyond
Helford Passage the conical green Bar buoy (seasonal)
can often be difficult to spot amongst the surrounding

Looking upstream from above Helford Passage. The area of water devoid of moorings clearly shows the extent of the Bar! The prominent white house opposite is on Helford Point

boats. Take care, however, as inshore of the buoy it dries extensively onto a sand and mud bank at Low Water Springs. Popular with locals for digging cockles, it stretches as far as the entrance to Port Navas Creek.

The Pool, nearly 15m deep in places, averages depths of about 6m and runs up the centre of the river. The entrance to Helford Creek, which dries extensively at Low Water Springs, is on the south shore between Bosahan Point and Helford Point, where there is a ferry slipway and landing pontoon.

The main fairway channel runs from just west of Bosahan Point, flanked on the south side by the fishing fleet moorings and on the north side by a line of visitors' moorings, then through the Pool with visitors' moorings on both sides, on towards the south bank as far as the oyster buoys and finally close under Penarvon Woods. This channel is frequently used at night by local fishing boats and also by Seacore Limited, the core sampling and drilling specialist, which often moves its rigs on high tides at night.

A final point of interest: all the navigational buoys in the Helford, including the August Rock buoy, are privately maintained and, although marked on the charts, there is no legal requirement for them to be in place, so beware in case they have been removed. The Helford River Navigational Aids Committee is a very worthy cause run by local yachtsmen, raising the funds to cover the cost of servicing these vital aids, which amounts to several thousand pounds a year. All river users are invited to contribute towards the cost of their upkeep and the Moorings Officer and his staff will be only too happy to accept your donation!

MOORINGS AND LANDING

In November 1884 the West Briton newspaper revealed that '. . . the beautiful Helford River has been visited this summer by an unusual number of yachts – as many as five having been at anchor there at any one time.'

Plus ça change! Today nearly all the available space in the Pool is taken up with moorings and anchoring is not permitted. However, there are usually plenty of visitors' moorings available – dark green support buoys (or any support buoy), all with dark green pick-up buoys, some of which are marked *Visitor*. Either grab one or contact the moorings officer, Simon Walker (Tel: 01326 250770), or his staff, who might be listening on VHF Channel M, callsign *Moorings Officer*. The moorings officer does not have a shoreside office but help may be available from the ferry kiosk on the beach in front of the Ferry Boat Inn at Helford Passage, if you are not able to raise him. They also monitor VHF Channel M callsign *Helford Ferry*. More often than not, though, he or his staff will be out on the water in an 18ft open white launch, and will be around to collect dues in the morning and evening. The ferry is a blue 18ft launch, or a white catamaran and their drivers are ever ready to assist.

The overnight charge (2008) for a mooring is £14 for boats up to 10m, £16 up to 11m, £17 up to 12m and £22 for boats up to 14m. Vessels over 14m can be accommodated by prior arrangement with Simon or the duty officer at £27 per night. If you are tempted to stay for a while, the seventh consecutive night is free!

In busy periods you will probably have to raft up, and the main visitors' moorings will take rafting in breezes

'Holding a strange attraction for thirsty crews', the Shipwrights Arms is in a memorable creekside setting

up to Force 6. You can either raft with friends or as directed by the duty officer.

You can drop people ashore at the ferry slipway, but do not leave dinghies here – use the pontoon just upstream. This is private, but the owner does not mind it being used as long as you leave a small donation towards its upkeep in the honesty box provided. The alternative, an hour or so after Low Water, is the large landing pontoon off the Helford River Sailing Club, the impressive Scandinavian style wooden building among the trees on the eastern side of Helford Creek.

The ferry doubles as a water taxi service; VHF Ch M callsign *Helford Ferry* or Tel: 01326 250770. This service is available to and from anywhere in the river and the cost is based on the distance travelled – although the norm is £2 per person each way, with a maximum charge of £10 per boat. Both ferries are licensed for up to 12 persons and, subject to weather, they operate from 1000 to 1800 April, May, June, September and October, and later by arrangement during July and August.

FACILITIES

Snug in its narrow drying creek, the small village of Helford is not really evident from the river, just a few houses and rooftops are visible along the shore leading out to Helford Point. If you pay the fee and land at the Helford Point pontoon, it avoids the worry of the dinghy drying out. A short walk along the point soon brings you to the Shipwrights Arms, a classic thatched waterside pub which holds a strange attraction for thirsty crews! It has a small restaurant, an outside terrace and a reputation for its summer barbecue menu, including good steaks.

Winding on above the creekside quays and boat-houses, the narrow lane squeezes past thick-walled

stone cottages, whitewashed and covered in climbing roses, their tiny gardens overflowing with flowers, the epitome of an English country idyll! Helford Village Stores & Post Office is effectively the only shop on the river and has a good selection of provisions, wines, spirits and beer, frozen meat, fresh vegetables, bread, papers and magazines.

Nearer the head of the creek, there's a public payphone. A footbridge and a shallow ford cross the stream, and the road continues past another row of equally picturesque cottages that make up the rest of Helford village. Fortunately for its residents, cars are banished to a car park on the outskirts during the summer. To reach it, continue up the hill out of the village. A short track leads down from the car park to the Helford River Sailing Club, Tel: 01326 231460; www.helfordriversc.co.uk. Visitors are welcome and the clubhouse is open from 0830 during the season for showers (£1 slotmeter) and a washing machine and dryer. Land on either one of the two impressive dinghy pontoons below the clubhouse. These dry out completely at Low Water Springs, but are normally

Small but well stocked, the Helford Village Stores & Post Office caters for most normal requirements

accessible by dinghy an hour either side of Low Water. There are hosepipes at both the inner and outer ends, but the outer hammerhead berths must be left clear at all times for boats wanting to land or take on crew or water. If you bring rubbish ashore please do not leave it in the HRSC bins but take it up to the Council car park where there is a large rubbish skip and recycling bins for bottles, cans and paper.

The popular bar is open 1200 – 1430, 1800 – 2300 every day during July and August, and a good selection of food is available at lunchtime and until 2130 in the evenings (Tel: 01326 231414 for reservations). From 21 July to 1 September, a full English breakfast is available 0900 – 1030! In May and June, the bar is open every day except Mondays. When the bar is open, the club monitors VHF channels 80 and M. A daily weather forecast and outlook are displayed in the club entrance.

On the north side of the river, being easy to reach by road from Falmouth, Helford Passage is the busiest (and that's relative!) part of the Helford River, the action mostly centred around the Ferry Boat Inn, which has a restaurant as well as bar food and often live music. There is also a payphone, a passenger ferry across to Helford Point and another pleasant coastal footpath leading to Durgan via Polgwidden Cove. Garden lovers can follow the road up the hill for just over half a mile to find the entrance to the sub-tropical Trebah Gardens, which are open daily from 1000 to 1700. Should you need to get to Falmouth, there is an hourly daytime (T4) bus service (Tel: Traveline 0871 2002233 for times), but you'll need to walk up the steep hill from where it is about another half a mile to the first major junction to reach the bus stop!

PORT NAVAS

Continuing upstream, just before you reach Pedn Billy Point and the entrance to Port Navas Creek, the large house with a small quay close to the water's edge is Bar. Built by Claud Worth in 1928 for his retirement from medical practice as an eminent eye surgeon, he lived here until his death in 1936.

Port Navas is another attractive but mostly drying wooded creek, although the eastern bank did not escape development and has a number of large expensive houses overlooking it. Just within the entrance, tucked away behind the point, the sheltered pool at Abraham's Bosom is full of moorings. Most of the creek beyond the pool is shallow, with extensive oyster beds that are clearly marked by buoys and a number of moorings, all of which dry at Low Water Springs. However, after half flood, it is possible to get up to Port Navas Yacht Club, Tel: 01326 340065; www.pnyc.co.uk, which lies in a smaller creek on the port hand side. You are able to dry out here overnight, but it is always advisable to phone ahead in case the visitors' berth is already booked. Follow a short red and green buoyed channel along the northern side of the creek, after which the mooring pontoon leads you to the marked visitors' berth, situated alongside the quay below the clubhouse. This friendly private yacht club welcomes visitors to its bar and restaurant and is open 1200 – 1430, 1845 – 2300 (last orders in restaurant 2100) daily from July to mid-September – it is advisable to make a reservation. A shower and fresh water can also be provided here.

Port Navas is a peaceful little backwater, overhung with dense woods, with just a few stone cottages overlooking the narrow creek. It does have a public

The Helford River Sailing Club has an impressive clubhouse and landing pontoons to match

From here on the oysters rule... okay!

phone box but the nearest provisions are at Constantine, a good, but pleasant half hour's walk away. Port Navas is also the home of the Duchy Oyster Farm, where nearly a million oysters are processed every year. You will find its buildings beside the main creek by following the road back towards it from the Yacht Club.

Should a sudden extravagance overcome you, it is possible to buy some of these oysters, while reflecting, as they slither down as rapidly as your bank balance, that these were once the staple diet of the poor. Mussels, too, are produced by the farm, and *moules marinieres à la Port Navas* are probably a good bet for tonight!

THE UPPER REACHES

By far the most unspoilt area of the river lies beyond the great rounded woods at Calamansack, a clear stretch of water where there are no moorings because of the extensive mussel buoys and oyster beds along both sides of the river. These are clearly marked by buoys and stakes, and anchoring is prohibited throughout the upper reaches. The deeper water lies along the south shore, which is also heavily wooded with low, steep cliffs, but just before Frenchman's Creek depths reduce considerably to little more than 1m at Low Water Springs, and half a mile further on, the river dries extensively. Yet again, this and the other creeks are ideal for the dinghy, although on a reasonable flood moderate draught boats can make it all the way to Gweek, which is accessible a couple of hours either side of High Water for up to a 2.9m draught at Springs. It is possible to dry out alongside at Gweek Quay Boatyard should you wish to stay overnight. To calculate the depth alongside the quay wall at Gweek, deduct 3m from the predicted height of High Water at Helford.

It is impossible not be drawn into the romance of Frenchman's Creek, where '. . . the trees still crowd thick and darkly to the water's edge, and the moss is succulent and green upon the little quay where Dona built her fire and looked across the flames at her lover.'

The reality is very much as it is described in the book, with glistening mud at low tide, where herons and oyster-catchers roam. As the thin trickle of the flood creeps inland again, like the yachtsman in the book, 'the sound of the blades upon the water seeming

overloud' you, too, can follow its winding course in your dinghy, past blackened tree stumps emerging like creatures from the mud, to where the dense trees close in like a tunnel, brushing the incoming tide, and the silence becomes profound. The atmosphere of Frenchman's Creek is undeniable.

At Groyne Point, just a short distance upstream, Polwheveral Creek branches off to starboard and, although just as attractive, somehow it has none of the mystery. If you are seeking some real solitude, shoal draught boats can find plenty of space to dry out round the bend beyond the moorings.

Following the flood up to Gweek, the river passes between high wooded banks with mud-fringed rocky shores most of the way. The deeper water lies in midstream. It is possible to land at Tremayne Quay, which is owned by the National Trust, from where you can follow a woodland walk. Just downstream of Mawgan Creek, the orange mooring buoy in the centre of the channel belongs to a local fishing boat, beyond which point the river dries completely at Low Water. Bishop's Quay on the south shore is private, and opposite the entrance to the creek, a large bank fills the centre of the river, the channel swinging to port around it.

Fortunately from here on it is dredged and marked with port and starboard hand buoys as it meanders from one side of the river to the other, until you reach the very narrow bottleneck with steep woods on either side just below Gweek. Once through the gap, the head of the river widens, the old coal quay lies to port, with more private quays to starboard. Gweek Quay Boatyard, Tel: 01326 221657, is straight ahead. It is usually possible to lie alongside and dry out overnight for a small charge.

This old quay will always be a nostalgic place for me, for here, back in 1973, I found my own boat, *Temptress*, laid up and neglected, and spent many long happy weekends putting her to rights and dreaming of where we would eventually sail. The atmosphere of Gweek has changed little – it is still a relaxed and peaceful place, although the yard has grown considerably, with storage ashore for over 300 boats. Visitors are welcome and services include good toilets and showers, 240 volt power at the quayside, diesel and water. Among the yard facilities are a 25-ton crane, a chandlery, an engineer and wood and GRP repairs.

In the small village close by is a well-stocked grocery store (open Sundays), a post office and a garage, where petrol is available in cans. The Gweek Inn serves pub meals, while there are also a couple of café/restaurants and occasional buses to Falmouth and Helston. The most unexpected treat that Gweek can provide, and one that children particularly adore, is the Seal Sanctuary, where injured and sick seals are looked after before being returned to the sea. It is on the north side of the creek, just downstream from the village, and opens daily during the summer.

Off the Runnel Stone buoy –
Land's End and Armed Knight rock, centre

Chapter four
The Manacles to Land's End

FAVOURABLE TIDAL STREAMS
Lizard Point:
Bound west – two hours before HW Dover
Bound east – four hours after HW Dover

PASSAGE CHARTS FOR THIS SEA AREA:
AC: 2565 Trevose Head to Dodman Point
777 Land's End to Falmouth
154 Approaches to Falmouth
1148 Isles of Scilly to Land's End
2345 Plans in South-West Cornwall is
particularly useful as it has a large scale
section covering the Lizard
SC5603 covers the area in
considerable detail
Imray: C6 Salcombe to Lizard Point
C7 Falmouth to Isles of Scilly &
Trevose Head
WCP2400.9, 2400.10
ID 4 Western Channel
Stanfords: 2 English Channel western section

SAFETY INFORMATION AND WEATHER
Falmouth Coastguard makes initial announcement on

VHF Channel 16 at 0110, 0410, 0710, 1010, 1610,
1910, 2210 Local Time, to confirm working channel
for broadcast, normally: VHF Channel 23 (Lizard),
Channel 86 (Isles of Scilly), Channel 84 (Trevose)

Bass Point NCI station Tel: 01326 290212
Penzance NCI station Tel: 01736 367063
Gwennap Head NCI station Tel: 01736 871351

WAYPOINTS
1	**Manacles (1M east of buoy)** 50°02'.80N 05°00'.35W	
2	**Black Head (2M south of headland)** 49°58'.14N 05°06'.12W	
3	**Lizard (4M south of light)** 49°53'.54N 05°12'.18W	
4	**Mountamopus (0.5M south of buoy)** 50°04'.12N 05°26'.28W	
5	**Low Lee (0.5M east of buoy)** 50°05'.56N 05°30'.61W	
6	**Runnelstone (3ca south of buoy)** 50°00'.90N 05°40'.38W	
7	**Longships (1M west of lighthouse)** 50°04'.01N 05°46'.40W	

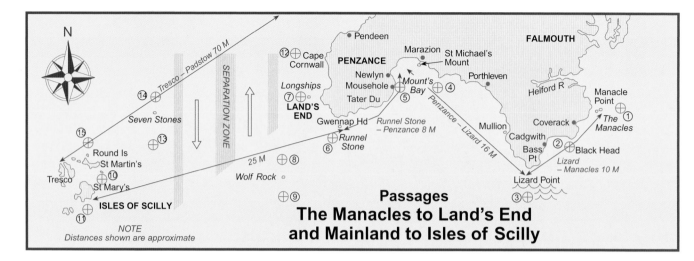

The Lizard is the most southerly point of the British Isles, a major headland and tidal gate. This point and the coast to the west of it into Mount's Bay and around Land's End has a justifiably notorious reputation and should always be treated with due respect and caution.

Composed for the greater part of precipitous granite cliffs – a long standing favourite with the rock-climbing fraternity – this inhospitable and rugged coast is open to the prevailing winds. It is an area of strong tides, and invariably suffers from the long Atlantic ground swell, not to mention concentrated shipping and no absolute harbours of refuge. But don't despair! In reasonably settled weather with an experienced crew in a well-found boat it can be explored safely, but here, more so than ever, a wary eye should be kept on the weather, with options for shelter always kept in mind.

Jack Pender, an old Mousehole fisherman, told me many years ago as I languished there in early September that 'west of the Lizard's no place for a small boat, come the end of August'. I confess to a certain youthful panic and I sailed that very night, scurrying back to Falmouth.

His words were born of a lifetime working these difficult waters and a commercial fisherman myself for several years during the 1970s, I often recalled them as we turned to run for home before the grey sea and sky piling up to the west, white crests blowing before it, and the high, dim shore to leeward suddenly vanishing in the gathering gloom. Conditions can deteriorate in a matter of hours, and a contrary tide sometimes produces large, steep and tumbling seas. It is not difficult to see how this particular coast has claimed so many ships and men over the years.

TIDES

Bound west, take full advantage of the ebb tide out of Falmouth Bay, which starts to run to the south three hours before HW Dover (three hours after HW Falmouth) and, once past the east cardinal BYB Manacle buoy, a course of 220°T will pass all offshore dangers in the approaches to the Lizard. To clear the

Manacle buoy, with Black Head in the distance

race, this course should be held until a position three miles to the south of the headland is reached. Adequate allowance should also be made for the tidal stream setting to the west, which begins about one hour before HW Dover. If bound round Land's End, because of the division of the streams into the Irish Sea and English Channel, a favourable tide can now be carried for nearly eight hours.

Bound east, unfortunately the passage is not so obliging; a vessel carrying a fair tide down the North Cornish coast and round Land's End will invariably run into a foul tide off the Lizard – from the turn of the tide at the Longships (five hours before HW Dover) only three hours of favourable tide can be carried across Mount's Bay. Once round the Lizard the ebb out of Falmouth Bay will be gathering in strength against you. Bound east from Mount's Bay to Falmouth, it is therefore advisable to arrive at the Lizard at slack water just over three and a half hours after HW Dover. Hopefully you will be sailing this spectacular section of coast in daylight and good visibility when it can be appreciated to the full. In favourable weather and settled conditions, the coastline can for the most part be followed much closer inshore.

LOWLAND POINT TO THE LIZARD

From Lowland Point, the land rises to a distinctively flat topped profile, steep-to and rocky with cliffs between 30 and 50m in height, and few off-lying dangers. It is interspersed with many attractive coves and bays, so if time permits, or if waiting for the tide, some of the smaller havens of the Lizard peninsula can provide good temporary anchorages and an interesting diversion.

Coverack, the first of these, is easily located by the conspicuous large hotel just south of the clustered houses of the village. Black Head, a mile to the south, is the next prominent feature and can easily be mistaken as Bass Point on the Lizard when approaching from the east in poor visibility. Tidal streams run up to three knots at Springs, and in strong southerly winds steep breaking seas will be encountered when wind is against tide in the vicinity. If running for Falmouth in such conditions, lay a course several miles to seaward of both Black Head and the Manacle buoy, where similar poor conditions can also be encountered.

Beyond Black Head, the coast falls back to form a wide bay, well sheltered from the west and a one time favourite haunt of the Falmouth Pilot vessels and quay punts waiting for business, and also of a Falmouth tailor's cutter, standing by to put a man aboard homeward-bound ships so that the crews could walk ashore in brand new suits! In the centre of this bay, Cadgwith nestles in a rocky cove, the houses wedged tightly at the mouth of a narrow valley. Parn Voose Cove and Church Cove, with a small landing slip, lie about a mile to the south. The present Lizard/Cadgwith lifeboat station is spectacularly sited close by in a narrow crevice in the high cliffs at Kilcobben Cove.

Special care is needed sailing inshore along this section of the coast and the large scale Admiralty Chart No 2345 or SC5603.2 is a must.

The Craggan Rocks, with less than 2m over them, lie just over half a mile south-south-east of Cadgwith, and the Voge Rock, covered by only 1.6m, lies two cables east of Church Cove. The yellow buoy further offshore marks the end of a sewer outfall. Bass Point is steep and topped by an NCI lookout, Tel: 01326 290212, with the distinctive white building of the former Lloyds signal station close by – the Spernan Shoals lie almost a mile to the east.

The notorious Vrogue Rock, only covered by 1.8m, lies four cables east-south-east of Bass Point, its position indicated by transit beacons ashore, and the passage between this rock and the shore should only be used in settled conditions. Normally, approaching from

Black Head without any diversions inshore, your course should be laid well to seaward of Bass Point. With rocks extending over half a mile to the south of the Lizard, and overfalls that are severe with wind against tide, it is advisable to give the whole area a good berth in anything but settled conditions, standing off between two and three miles. In rough weather, five miles is not unrealistic for the seas inshore can be very confused.

Tidal streams are strong – the west-going ebb can run at over three knots at Springs, the flood slightly less, and it goes without saying that a fair tide is essential for a sailing vessel with limited power. In westerly winds its full force will not be felt until clear of the Lizard, and after spells of weather from that quarter, a considerable ground swell will be encountered.

This is a headland to approach with extreme caution in poor weather or bad visibility; the long list of vessels lost in the vicinity over the years is an adequate testimony to its natural dangers. Care should also be taken to note shipping movements as they concentrate towards Land's End, as well as the activities of fishing boats, and, yet again, beware of poorly marked pot and net buoys, often without flags and half-submerged in the tide. One unusual hazard that certainly added a few grey hairs on one occasion was the sudden appearance of a totally unmarked rock nearly three miles south of the point, black, awash with breaking waves, and right ahead. The chart indicated no such horror; and several minutes of dry-mouthed panic elapsed before it dawned on me that it was an enormous basking shark, a harmless plankton-eating summer visitor to Cornish waters! The second largest fish in the world, basking sharks can grow to over 10m long and over 7 tons in weight, and were once commercially fished for their rich liver oil. Another indication of global warming, perhaps, their numbers seem to be increasing annually in these waters and in July 2007 over 460 were spotted in one day off Land's End!

The Lizard lighthouse is a prominent and distinctive long white building with two octagonal towers, the easternmost topped by its five million candlepower light (Fl 3s 26M). The first warning light on the headland, notable as the first such navigational aid in Cornwall, was established in 1619 by Sir John Killigrew amidst much local protest at the adverse effects on

Approaching the Lizard from the north-east. Bass Point is to the right

Lizard lighthouse from the south – note the basking shark in the foreground

the profits from the wrecking; significantly Killigrew himself eventually abandoned his light in favour of the more lucrative spoils from the sea!

Several other attempts to provide a lighthouse on the headland ensued during the 1700s, notably Fonnereau's twin towers with a fire in each and a cottage in between, in which an overlooker lay on a couch watching for any relaxation of the firemen's efforts; a blast on a cowhorn 'awakening them, and recalling them to their duty!' The introduction of oil lighting in 1813 put an end to such navigational uncertainty and by the end of the century both an electric light and a foghorn had been established, with a correspondingly dramatic decline in the loss of shipping.

The Boa, a rocky shoal two miles west of Lizard point, is the last offshore hazard in the vicinity and, although well covered (over 20m), it creates a lot of overfalls and even breaking seas in southwesterly gales. If the Lizard has been given a berth of three miles, as recommended, heading into Mount's Bay you should pass clear to the south of the Boa. Its location is usually easy to spot from the concentration of pot and net buoys.

LIZARD POINT TO MOUNT'S BAY
The western side of the Lizard, exposed to the full force of the Atlantic gales, is high, rugged and spectacular for the next five miles as the coast bears north-west into Mount's Bay. The tall jagged pyramid of Gull Rock and Asparagus Island, enclosing the beauty spot of Kynance Cove, are a distinctive feature, and both Rill Point and Predannack Head should be given a reasonable berth. Mullion Island will begin to open as Predannack Head is passed, and in favourable easterly conditions an anchorage can be found off the small harbour of Porth Mellin (Mullion). Although a passage exists between the island and the mainland, it is not recommended, and the approach is best made to the north of the island.

The character of the coast begins to change considerably as Mount's Bay is entered further. Beyond Pedngwinian Point, the high cliffs recede, and the long sand and shingle beach of Gunwalloe and Loe Bar stretches away northwards. Particularly vulnerable

to southerly gales, many vessels struggling to escape round the Lizard from Mount's Bay have come to grief on Loe Bar, including the frigate *HMS Anson* in 1807 when 100 men were lost in the surf trying to reach the shore. Witnessing the catastrophe, Henry Trengrouse was inspired to invent the rocket propelled line throwing apparatus, which is still used by the coastguards today.

Porthleven, at the northern end of Loe Bar, has a conspicuous clock tower by the harbour mouth and should only be approached in offshore winds and settled conditions. From here the northern shore of Mount's Bay begins to trend more to the west, with Welloe Rock (dries 0.8m) lying three miles due west of Porthleven, and the Mountamopus shoal (1.8m LAT) a mile south-west of Cudden Point.

Passing to the south of the Mountamopus YB south cardinal buoy (Q(6) +LFl 15s) marking this hazard, the distinctive pyramid of St Michael's Mount, topped by a spire and turrets, is unmistakeable, and keeping it on the starboard bow, Penzance, two miles to the west, is easy to locate, with no further hazards except the Gear rock (dries 1.8m) marked by a black and red isolated danger beacon (Fl (2) 10s) just under half a mile due south of the harbour entrance. Pass to seaward of the Gear if bound for Newlyn.

MOUNT'S BAY TO LAND'S END
Heading for Land's End or the Isles of Scilly from Penzance, you will pass to the east of the Low Lee BYB east cardinal buoy (Q(3) 10s). Departing from Newlyn, a course can be laid just over a cable from the shore inside Carn Base and Low Lee shoals past Penlee Point, with its old lifeboat house and slipway. This, and the memorial garden beside it, remain as a sad reminder of the tragic loss of the lifeboat *Solomon Browne* with its entire crew of eight on the 19 December 1981 while attending the wreck of the coaster *Union Star* near Lamorna Cove. It was the last launch from the slipway, and the replacement Penlee lifeboat is now kept afloat in Newlyn harbour.

Once past St Clement's Isle and Mousehole, the impressive grass-topped granite cliffs form a continuous line, broken only by a few tiny coves and sandy beaches such as Penberth and Porthcurno, and finally the section between Gwennap Head and Land's End is particularly precipitous.

Stay half a mile offshore until abeam of Tater Du light (Fl (3)15s 20M), when a course is best laid directly to pass just south of the Runnel Stone YB south cardinal buoy (Q(6) + LFl 15s), marking the outer end of a rocky ledge extending nearly a mile southwards from Gwennap Head, with the drying Runnel Stone at its extremity. It is not unknown for the Runnel Stone buoy to break adrift in the heavy seas that often run along this most exposed corner, and this hazardous place has been the scene of many wrecks.

There are two conical beacons inshore on Hella Point, the outer red and the inner black with a lower white band, providing a transit of 352°T over the position of the rocks. To assist you in judging distance off – when the white base of the inner beacon is also visible above the cliff top you will pass safely to the south of the hazard. This is, in any circumstance, an area to be navigated with extreme caution. Three and a half miles west of the Runnel Stone buoy, Carn Base shoals have a least depth of 9.9m which can create heavy seas in strong winds; they are marked on their south-western corner by the Carn Base YBY west cardinal buoy (Q (9) 15s).

Although the tides in Mount's Bay are weak, they rapidly gather in strength towards the Runnel Stone, probably attaining five knots at Springs, becoming increasingly unpredictable as the main tidal stream divides into the Irish Sea and English Channel.

Bound round Land's End from Mount's Bay, if you leave about one hour before HW Dover you will have a favourable tide for the next seven hours and, hopefully, soon be well on your way. As mentioned earlier, this is a very unfair tidal gate – the north-west stream begins three hours before HW Dover and runs for nearly nine hours; the east-going stream six hours before HW Dover lasting for a mere three.

The Atlantic ground swell is rarely absent for a passage 'around the Land' to the north Cornish coast. This, and the coast beyond, is an area to take very seriously. A favourable forecast is essential to attempt Land's End or the passage to the Isles of Scilly, which is covered in full detail on page 204.

THE MANACLES TO LAND'S END AT NIGHT

This passage area is well lit, although once south of the Manacle buoy (Q (3) 10s) steering 220°T, the Lizard light (Fl 3s 26M) will be obscured for the next five miles until you are a couple of miles south-east of Black Head. Inshore, Coverack and Cadgwith show only small clusters of lights. Once clear to the south of the Lizard, Tater Du lighthouse (Fl (3) 15s 20M) will be seen away to the north-west on the far side of Mount's Bay, and in the far distance to the west, Wolf Rock lighthouse (Fl 15s 16M).

This is a busy stretch of water: shipping bound to and from Land's End converges on the Lizard and fishing boats are likely to be encountered trawling at night. Their movements should be carefully observed and avoided, as should the regular Naval exercises in the area.

When entering Mount's Bay, the whole of the northern shore appears as a continuous mass of lights from Marazion to Newlyn, and it is worth noting that both the Lizard and Tater Du lights become obscured in the approach to Penzance, although by then the lighthouse on the south pier (Fl WR 5s 17/12M) should easily be visible, along with the harbour light at Newlyn (Fl 5s 9M). Other lights in the approaches to Mount's Bay are the Mountamopus buoy (Q(6)+LFl 15s) on the northern side and Low Lee buoy (Q (3) 10s) on the southern side, while Gear Rock beacon (Fl (2) 10s) is in the closer approach to Penzance.

Heading west to Land's End beyond Tater Du, the Runnel Stone buoy (Q(6) + LFl 15s) lies within the red sector of the Longships lighthouse (Fl (2) WR 10s 15/11M) and is also covered by a FR light showing 060°T to 074°T from Tater Du, so it is wisest to stand on past the buoy to westwards towards the Carn Base buoy (Q (9) 15s) until the white sector of the Longships is fully open before altering course to the north-west. Pass well to seawards of the Longships, the tide in its vicinity runs hard and is unpredictable. You are now in the Land's End inshore traffic zone and a lot more shipping is likely to be encountered.

In poor visibility, additional aids to navigation are the fog signals at the Lizard (Horn 30s), Wolf Rock (Horn 30s, Racon T 10M) and Longships (Horn 10s). In addition, the Manacle buoy has a bell and the Runnel Stone buoy a whistle.

Tater Du with Gwennap Head in the distance

Land's End from the south-east

Coverack and Cadgwith

Tides	HW Dover –0625
Charts	AC 777, SC 5603.6; Stanfords 2; Imray C6, C7
Hazards	**Coverack**: Small boat harbour dries completely. The Manacles. Isolated rocks off Dolor Point (unlit) and to north-west of harbour. Fine weather anchorage only and dangerous in onshore wind
	Cadgwith: Bow Rock (unlit) in entrance to cove. Fine weather anchorage, but dangerous in onshore wind
Overnight charge	None

COVERACK

Lying between the Manacles and Black Head, Coverack is a small, picturesque drying harbour popular with tourists and still the home to a small fleet of fishing boats, open craft used for potting and handlining and known locally as cove boats or toshers. In settled weather with offshore wind and an absence of ground swell, the bay makes a tenable anchorage, although with any indication of a shift of wind to the south-east it is no place to linger.

APPROACHES

The conspicuous large hotel to the south of the village is the easiest landmark to spot, and with the Guthen Rocks off Chynalls Point to the south and the Davas Rocks extending nearly half a mile from Lowland Point to the north end of the bay, do not attempt to cut corners. Enter on a westerly course, sounding your way in to the best anchorage in about 3m, a cable or so north-north-east of the pierhead. There is no charge for anchoring, but care should be taken

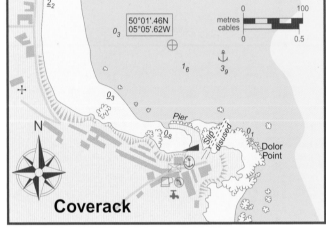

to avoid the fishermens' keep pots which fringe the bay.

The harbour, enclosed by a small, sturdy granite wall, dries to beyond the entrance with a clean, sandy bottom, but the shore immediately to the west is rocky and very foul. Although there is a minimum depth of 2.4m alongside the pier end at Mean High Water Neaps, due to the crowding of the local boats which lie on heavy rope fore and aft moorings, drying out is not really a viable proposition. Far better to anchor off and dinghy in, where you are welcome to land at the ladders on the pier or the large slipway across the head of the harbour as long as you do not hog the access. During the summer a windsurfing school operates from the western pier, and canoes can be hired, so keep a wary lookout for them!

Coverack, like so many other Cornish harbours, grew with the extensive pilchard fishery. The former salt store overlooking the harbour is now a gift shop and the Old Lifeboat House is a restaurant and fish

Coverack's small drying harbour lies between the Manacles and Black Head

Protected by a sturdy pier, Coverack is home to a small fleet of fishing boats known locally as 'toshers'. Visitors can anchor off the bay when the conditions permit

and chip takeaway. All the basic facilities are available; provisions, post office (closed Tuesday pm), several cafés, pub/hotels, including the curiously named Paris Inn, which is nothing to do with the EU or *entente cordiale*, but named after the *Paris*, an American liner stranded on the Manacles, Whitsun, 1899. Remarkably, unlike most other wrecks on the Manacles, there was no loss of life, her 800 passengers and crew were brought safely to shore by local boats and the ship was eventually refloated unscathed!

Water can be obtained from the harbourmaster, Mr PW Barker, Tel: 01326 280679, but there is no fuel.

CADGWITH

'There is a bench from which the whole of the bay can be seen where the fishermen sit in patience, and scarcely turn their eyes from the sea. It really is very exciting to hear the 'pilchard' cry for the first time; visitors rise up and leave their dinner and amusements, and every man who dwells in the village, whatever he may be doing, is called by a strange and terrible cry to come and help in the take. The boats are always ready in the bay, but the real time to see the pilchard take is by moonlight, when the fishes look like living silver.'

Cadgwith, it would seem, was popular even as far back as 1885 when this was written and, although the huge shoals of pilchards vanished in the 1930s,

the holidaymakers still descend in their droves. Nevertheless, it is still very much a working fishing community, and the traditional atmosphere of the village lingers in the tight cluster of cottages nestling snugly in a steep green valley at the head of a tiny cove. Almost too photogenic, white painted walls and heavy encrusted thatches contrast sharply with the more familiar granite cottages and the curious dark green serpentine rock that is local to the Lizard.

There is no harbour, and the fleet of small fishing boats is hauled up the shingle on wooden rollers, a daily spectacle much enjoyed by the visitors. Thumping softly, an ancient and magnificent single cylinder

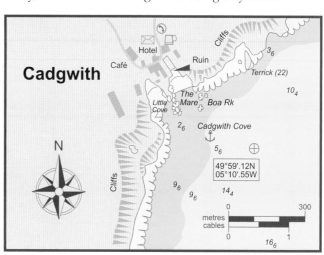

Hornsby donkey engine powers the winch, and in the cool, dark cellar where it lurks, the walls are covered with faded paintings, curling sepia photographs, all pervaded by the sweet aroma of warm oil.

A picturesque blend of thatch and granite buildings, Cadgwith is worth a visit in settled weather

APPROACHES

Well sheltered from the west, the cove should only be approached in settled weather and offshore winds, and is not recommended for an overnight stop. The houses will be spotted from offshore, forming a break in the flat line of the cliffs, and closing them you will find what is effectively two coves, split in the middle by a low rocky outcrop called the Todden. The extension of this, a group of rocks called the Mare, runs to seaward,

and it is advisable to sound in and anchor off them in about 2 – 3m. Do not proceed any further into the cove as the Bow is a dangerous rock right in the centre which covers at quarter tide, and the entrance is also in frequent use by the local boats.

Landing is easy anywhere on the shingle beach, but make sure you keep your dinghy well clear to avoid obstructing the winching operations.

There are limited provisions, a post office, the Cadgwith Cove Inn, a hotel, a café and a pleasant walk up on to the cliffs overlooking the cove, past some lovely cottages to a small black hut high on the headland. It was here that those fishermen used to sit waiting and watching, and once the cry of 'Hevva! Hevva!' sent them to sea, with the 'huers' directing the boats from this high vantage point towards the shoals by a series of special hand signals and wild shouts through a large tin megaphone.

Huers' huts can still be seen in many places along the Cornish coast, abandoned after the strange demise of the pilchard and the herring. The huge shoals that were once the livelihood of so many small villages like Cadgwith began to dwindle mysteriously in the mid 1930s, and after the war they were never found again, a phenomenon that has never really been explained, although today they are being caught in increasing quantities.

Nowadays, the fleet of cove boats works nets, pots and handlines, rock hopping along this beautiful, but at times very wild, stretch of coast.

Tucked away south of Black Head, Cadgwith lies in a small cove divided by the Todden, a rocky outcrop from which the Mare Rocks extend to seaward

In offshore winds there is a good anchorage between Mullion Island and Porth Mellin

Mullion and Porthleven

Tides	HW Dover −0635
Charts	AC: 2345, 777, SC5603.2; Stanfords: 2; Imray: C7, WCP 2400.10
Hazards	**Mullion**: Mullion Island, many rocks close inshore. Fine weather anchorage only and dangerous in onshore wind
	Porthleven: Harbour dries. Deazle rocks, Little and Great Trigg rocks (all unlit) to west and east of entrance. Dangerous to approach in onshore winds
Overnight charge	Porthleven, Harbour Authority drying alongside: £10

Although this small drying harbour three miles north-west of the Lizard is closed to fin keel boats, and no overnight stays are permitted in any craft, Mullion's spectacular location in a magnificent stretch of coast can provide a memorable overnight anchorage in offshore winds and settled weather; it can also prove useful if waiting for a fair tide eastwards round the Lizard.

APPROACHES

The approach is straightforward: both Mullion Island and the conspicuous Mullion Cove Hotel high on the cliffs above are easy to see. Although local boats use a narrow channel between the island and the mainland, it is not recommended and the northern end of the island should be given a good berth, entering the anchorage midway between it and the small Porth Mellin harbour

Porth Mellin's tiny harbour dries completely but is handy for dinghy landing

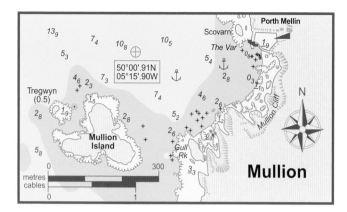

wall. This was built in 1895, a somewhat lethargic response to the disastrous loss of the cove's entire fishing fleet 50 years earlier during a freak storm. Today only a few small boats are based here, for the years have done nothing to change its exposure to the prevailing wind and sea. The harbour is now owned by the National Trust and from May to September there is a resident harbourmaster, Mr JD Foster, Tel: 01326 240222.

Although there is a temporary berth alongside the western wall (as long as it is not being used by the fishing boats), it cannot be recommended as there is frequently much surge in the harbour. The anchorage between the harbour and Mullion Island is, therefore, the only option. It is well sheltered to the north and east, with good holding on a sandy bottom in 7m midway between the harbour entrance and the northern end of the island, which is a nature reserve on which landing is not allowed.

This seems like an unusually remote anchorage, well off the normal track, but it has not always been so. RT McMullen anchored here in a northeasterly gale aboard his *Orion*, counted 64 vessels sheltering, and wrote in September 1868:

'. . I was surprised to see how regularly they were arranged according to their ability to work offshore if the wind were to fly in. The *Orion* was first in line with three pilot cutters, then came the sloops and yawls, and a brig-rigged steamship. Next schooners and ketches, then brigs and barks; those in the first division were almost still on the water, the second were rolling perceptibly, the third decidedly uneasy, and the last, having no protection at all from Mullion Island, were rolling miserably.'

MULLION FACILITIES
Dinghy ashore when the tide allows and land on the slipway at the head of the harbour, where there are just a few houses, a café, gift shop, telephone and public WC. Off the main tourist track, it is a particularly unspoilt little corner with some magnificent views and excellent walks along the cliffs in both directions. Most normal provisions are available at Mullion village, an uphill walk of just over a mile, and prominent on the clifftop above the harbour, the Mullion Cove Hotel

is open to non-residents with meals available in the bar. Owing to the potentially exposed nature of the anchorage, I would not, however, recommend leaving your boat unattended for any length of time, and do not linger with any hint of a wind shift to the south.

PORTHLEVEN
Porthleven is certainly a magnificent example of the harbour builder's art, a long protective entrance leading to a level drying basin enclosed by massive granite walls. However, its history has always been somewhat chequered and commercial success elusive. The chapter of disasters began when a group of speculators obtained an Act of Parliament in 1811, ostensibly to build a harbour of refuge. Disagreement and squabbling dogged the venture and the harbour was not completed until six years later, surviving for another six before it was devastated by a storm, a fact that did little to encourage ship-owners to use it.

Although it was rebuilt and greatly improved in the mid-1800s, the fundamental problem has always been that the narrow entrance faces right into the prevailing southwesterlies, frequently rendering it unapproachable and forcing its closure with large baulks of timber in heavy weather. Few winters seem to pass without spectacular photographs of huge seas breaking over the seafront appearing on the front pages of the national press!

Today, Porthleven is mostly used by pleasure craft and a dwindling fleet of small fishing boats. However, as with all the other smaller harbours of the Lizard, with offshore winds and settled summer conditions, it makes another interesting place to visit off the regular cruising track, and a feasible overnight stop, providing you don't mind drying out.

APPROACHES
The harbour mouth lies at the northern end of Loe Bar, the long shingle beach that begins just over two miles north of Mullion Island. The houses on the hillside are easily visible on the cliffs, and the south pier, with its prominent clock tower at the landward end, should be closed on a bearing of 045°T.

The harbour dries right to the entrance at Mean Low Water Springs, but is accessible from half-tide onwards. If waiting for water, anchor in the outer entrance to the harbour or pick up one of the six moorings, where average draught boats will lie afloat except at low Springs. Care must be taken to avoid the submerged Little Trigg rocks off the pier end, though there are no further hazards once past the old lifeboat house on the north shore.

Pass through the outer entrance and into the inner basin where the local boats mostly lie on fore and aft moorings on heavy ground chains running north-south up the harbour. Visitors should berth inside

Porthleven harbour should be approached with care in settled offshore weather; the darker area in the foreground, left, shows the extent of the extent of Great Trigg Rock

the entrance on the East Quay and seek out the harbourmaster, Mr Phil Ward, if he has not already spotted you. His office is at the head of the harbour and he will advise on the most suitable berth. Overnight charges start from £10 for a 10m boat.

There is no VHF watch and all vessels should call ahead on Tel: 01326 574270 or Mobile 07971 278551 to arrange a berth. The South Quay is used by the local fishing boats and should be avoided. The crane at its outer end is used for lowering the timber baulks when bad weather is imminent.

PORTHLEVEN FACILITIES

Another popular place with holidaymakers, Porthleven provides a curious contrast of old fishermen's cottages and converted net stores, and a long row of typically bold Victorian semi-detached houses that completely dominate the entrance. All normal facilities are available: a post office, the well-stocked Porthleven supermarket (open 0800 – 2200 daily), banks and a launderette. Water and fuel can be obtained locally; ask at the harbour office.

Porthleven's eating places consist of cafés, pubs and restaurants, including the inevitable Ship Inn, overlooking the harbour entrance, and the

Harbour Inn on the east side of the inner harbour.

To stretch the legs, head east along the great shingle sweep of Loe Bar as far as Loe Pool, a large freshwater lake formed when the bar sealed off the estuary of the Cober, a river once navigable as far inland as Helston. It is part of the large Penrose Estate, now owned by the National Trust, and there are some delightful walks through the woods along its banks.

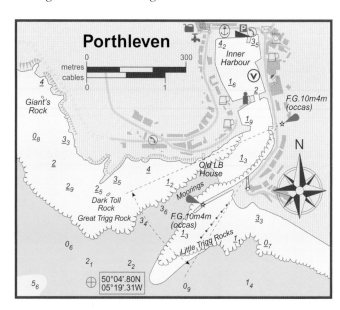

Penzance

Tides	HW Dover –0635
Range	MHWS 5.6m–MHWN 4.4m, MLWN 2.0m–MLWS 0.8m. Tidal dock gate manned every tide from two hours before to one hour after High Water
Charts	AC: 2345, SC5603.7; Stanfords: 2; Imray: C7
Waypoint	South Pier Head 50°07'.06N 05°31'.68W
Hazards	Gear Rock (lit). Outer harbour dries, tidal wet dock. Harbour approach very dangerous in strong southerly weather. Pot and net buoys in Mount's Bay. Keep clear if *RMS Scillonian* or other commercial shipping are entering or leaving
Harbour Speed limit	Five knots
Overnight charge	Harbour Authority, alongside, £17.50

When McMullen put into Penzance in 1868, it was still in its busy commercial heyday and he moaned bitterly about the state of the quays, '. . .which are allowed by the Corporation to be in so offensive a state, encumbered with coal dust that nothing short of real distress will drive me into the nasty harbour again.'

The coal has long vanished from the quays of Penzance but so, too, has most of the waterborne trade. Now a busy centre for tourism, the town grew around the export of tin, reaching its peak in the mid-1800s when nearly half of the minerals mined in Cornwall passed through the port, stacked in 300lb ingots on the quayside for shipment to places as far afield as Russia and Italy.

A major centre for the export of salt herring and mackerel, there are records of a thriving trading and fishing village here as early as 1300, but the major extensions to form the present day harbour were made in 1745–72 when the Albert Pier was built, with further improvements during the 19th century. The dry dock was constructed in 1814 and is still operational today.

Penzance was also home to the first lifeboat in Cornwall in 1803, but this was discontinued in 1917 and the lifeboat is now based in Newlyn. Until the late 1980s this was the westernmost Trinity House buoy depot and the distinctive buildings can be seen on the west side of the wet dock, on the far side of the road.

The outer harbour dries almost completely at LAT and is given over to a large number of local moorings on fore and aft trots. Visitors normally use the wet dock, which is only accessible for two hours before High Water until one hour after High Water and entered through a hydraulic gate. Here there is ample berthing for up to 50 yachts, afloat at all times in total protection.

The outer harbour at Penzance mostly dries but visitors can lie afloat and secure in the wet dock, bottom left, which is accessed through a tidal gate

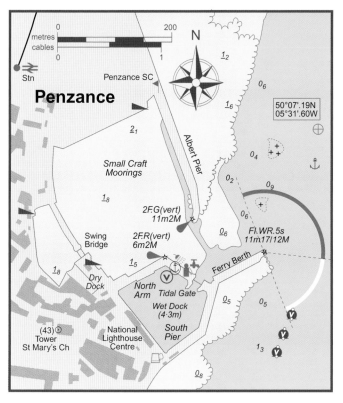

The basin is still used by a small amount of commercial traffic, including the Isles of Scilly cargo vessel *Gry Maritha,* which makes three trips a week to the islands. It is also used by fishing boats and has become popular for refits and repair work. By arrangement, boats can be left unattended without worry for a few days or longer, making it an ideal base to explore West Cornwall and the rugged Land's End peninsula, with good bus services and cars for hire.

There are ambitious proposals (2008) for a major redevelopment and enlargement of Penzance harbour, to include an upgraded ferry terminal, dry-dock repair facility, and a 200-berth marina with all-tide and improved weather access. As a regeneration project that would hopefully qualify for Objective 1 funding, this is still in the initial consultation stage but if this and the proposed 'Port Penlee' 195-berth MDL marina development in the old Penlee quarry between Newlyn and Mousehole were to happen, it would definitely have a significant impact on the viability of Mount's Bay as a generally more appealing cruising destination!

APPROACHES

Approaching from the east, pass to the south of the south cardinal YB Mountamopus buoy

(Q(6)+LFl 15s) marking a 1.8m shoal, holding the unmistakeable bulk of St Michael's Mount on your starboard bow. The conspicuous tower of St Mary's Church provides a good landmark to locate Penzance. In the approach from the south-west, Gear Rock (dries 1.8m) lies just over 800m, almost due south of the harbour entrance, and is marked by an isolated danger beacon (Fl (2) 10s). Penzance Harbour lighthouse, a white tower, displays a red and white sectored light (Fl WR 5s, white 268 – 345°T 17M; red 159 – 268°T 12M). The white sector safely clears Gear Rock and, if approaching from the east cardinal BYB Low Lee buoy (Q (3) 10s), steer a northeasterly course until the white sector opens. There are vertical lights displayed from the harbourmaster's office by the north side of the dock gate to indicate whether it is open or closed: three vertical red = closed; three vertical green = open.

Penzance should not be considered as a harbour of refuge in bad weather. Although it is safely accessible in winds from the south-west to north, heavy breaking seas can build up in the shallowing approaches, often breaking over the south pier and making the whole entrance highly dangerous in winds from the east through to the south. In these conditions Newlyn is the only place to consider. Approach with extreme caution and as near to High Water as possible.

During the season there are at least six yellow visitors' buoys laid 150m due south of Penzance lighthouse in about 2m LAT, which can either be used to await entry into the tidal basin or for an overnight stop in settled weather and offshore winds. A temporary small craft anchorage can be found just over 350m north-north-east of the end of the Albert Pier, in about 1.2m LAT, or further offshore, depending on your draught, ensuring that you are clear of the fairway into the harbour entrance. Alternatively anchor 350m due south of the south pier head, clear of the visitors' moorings.

Visitors waiting to enter the wet dock can use the convenient moorings off the pierhead

Penzance wet dock. The harbour office is adjacent to the closed tidal gate

The harbour office monitors VHF Ch 16 during office hours and works on Ch 12, callsign *Penzance Harbour Radio*. It is also manned HW–2 to HW+1 when the tidal dock is open. Although the outer harbour is full of moorings, with the harbourmaster's permission it is possible to dry out alongside the Albert Pier where Penzance Sailing Club is based.

If waiting for the tide, the alternative to mooring or anchoring off is lying on the inside of the South Pier in the berth used by the Isles of Scilly ferry, *RMS Scillonian III*, which is normally empty Monday to Friday from 0930 to 1830, and Saturdays (summer) from 1400 to 1830. At Low Water, keep close to the south pier as the water shoals rapidly on the northern side of the entrance, but between the convenient ladder halfway along the wall and the lighthouse, a depth of 1.8m will be found, even at LAT. You can lie alongside the large floating fenders – be warned, though, if you clamber onto them they roll instantly and you'll end up swimming. Check in with the harbour office once berthed and do not leave the boat totally unattended or

Rafting is inevitable in high season

obstruct the stone steps by the entrance to the wet basin as this is in constant use by local fishing trip boats.

The dock gate is manned two hours before High Water every tide, day and night, and opens soon afterwards. Once in the basin, the berthing master will allocate a berth, charges are £1.75 per metre per day, with every third day free, providing someone remains aboard the vessel. There are special weekly rates available for unattended vessels should you have need to leave your boat.

You will be given an access code to the toilets and showers (£1 slotmeter), situated beneath the harbour office in the end of the large white building nearest to the lock gate.

FUEL, FRESH WATER AND GAS

Small quantities of diesel can be obtained alongside or in cans by arrangement with the berthing master. Petrol can only be acquired in cans from the garage near the railway station. Fresh water is available alongside by hose. Calor and Gaz refills can be bought from nearby Penwith Marine Services.

FACILITIES
(Local phone code 01736)

Penzance is a popular tourist centre, as well as a busy and interesting old market town with many fine buildings. This is the largest town in the far west and just about all normal requirements will be found. The main shopping centre, the curiously named Market Jew Street, derived its name from the Cornish *Marghas de Yow* meaning 'Thursday Market' and climbs up the hillside past the main post office and a Co-op Pioneer supermarket towards the impressive granite Market House, with its ionic columns and domed roof, which also houses the Lloyds TSB Bank. In front of it is a statue of Penzance's famous son, Sir Humphrey Davy, best known for his invention of the miner's safety lamp.

Chapel Street, leading back down from the top of Market Jew Street towards St Mary's church and the harbour, has a number of fine listed buildings, many of them gift shops, and also the bizarre Egyptian House, restored by the Landmark Trust. Near the top, at the junction with Parade Street, there's another handy Co-op supermarket, open 0800 – 2200. Close to the station, on the road out of town, the launderette is open 0900 – 1930 seven days a week.

The wide choice of options for eating ashore include several good pubs close to hand, notably the Turks Head, Dolphin, Dock Inn and the Admiral Benbow, all of which serve food. With over 30 pubs in total, there are plenty more to choose from as you get deeper into the town. Restaurants within easy reach include the Boatshed, Tel: 366746, and the Waterside Meadery, Tel: 364424. Heading towards the centre of town, you'll find a host of others, including Harris's,

Tel: 364408, for seafood, tapas at Bar Coco, Tel: 350222, and fine views of Mount's Bay from the Abbey, Tel: 330680. Most other tastes are amply catered for with Italian, Indian, Chinese, Thai and a very good choice of fish and chips!

During the last week in June, the town bursts into colourful activity with the Golowan Festival, celebrating ancient Celtic traditions with music, dance, street theatre and fireworks.

If time permits, a trip inland to the north coast or Land's End is well worth the effort, and there are regular bus services to St Michael's Mount if you decide against a visit by sea.

Should the weather scupper your plans to sail to the Isles of Scilly, you could always console yourself with a day trip to the islands, Tel: 0845 710 5555; www. ios-travel.co.uk. As well as the *Scillonian's* daily sailings there are also frequent helicopter flights from nearby Penzance Heliport, Tel: 363871; website: www. scillyhelicopter.co.uk.

The small town museum is located centrally in the Penlee Memorial Park. Apart from historical accounts and old photographs of the harbour, it is also the home of the town's permanent collection of the Newlyn Painting School. This provides a romanticised glimpse of the town's final years as a simple working

No problem with finding food or drink in Penzance; there are over 30 pubs for starters!

port, before Brunel's Great Western Railway wiped out the isolation of the far west and the first large hotels began to rise along the new promenade at the shingly head of the bay. There's nothing like a bit of nostalgia; conveniently, we tend to forget all that coal dust!

Penzance Port Guide – Area telephone code: 01736

Harbourmaster: Mr Neil Clark, Harbour Office, North Arm, Penzance Harbour, Penzance, TR18 4AH, Tel: 366113; Fax: 366114. Open 0900 – 1300 and 1400 – 1800 Mon – Fri.

VHF: Ch 16, working Ch 12, callsign *Penzance Harbour Radio* (office hours and HW–2 to HW+1).

Mail Drop: Harbour office.

Emergency services: Lifeboat at Newlyn. Falmouth Coastguard.

Anchorages: In fair weather 350m east-north-east of Albert Pier, clear of fairway or similar distance due south of South Pier.

Mooring/berthing: Six visitors' buoys off South Pier. Tidal wet dock (maintained depth 4.3m) entry two hours before to one hour after local High Water. Pick up mooring, anchor off or berth inside South Pier if Isles of Scilly ferry berth available when waiting to enter.

Dinghy landings: Steps on inside of Albert Pier.

Marinas: None.

Charges: £1.75 per metre per day. Every third day free providing boat is attended.

Phones: Nearest public phone on promenade.

Doctor: Tel: 363340 or 363866.

Hospital: West Cornwall Hospital, Tel: 362382.

Churches: All denominations.

Local weather forecast: Harbour office.

Fuel: Diesel by arrangement with berthing master. Petrol in cans from garage.

Gas: Calor/Gaz from Penzance Marine Services, Wharf Road, Tel: 361081.

Water: See berthing master.

Tourist Information Centre: At railway station, Tel: 362207.

Banks/cashpoints: All main banks, all with cashpoints.

Post office: Market Jew St.

Internet access: Public library, Morrab Road.

Rubbish: Red bins on both quays.

Showers/toilets: Under harbour office, coded entry lock. £1 slotmeter.

Launderette: Near railway station.

Provisions: All normal shops. Co-op in Market Jew Street. Tesco superstore on main road out of town or Morrison superstore at Long Rock, both bus or taxi ride away. All supermarkets are open on Sundays.

Chandler: Small selection at Penwith Marine Services, Tel: 361081, or see Newlyn Port Guide on page 193.

Repairs: Drying out by arrangement with harbourmaster.

Marine engineers: R&D Engineering, Tel: 360253; Mounts Bay Engineering, Tel: 363095; Penwith Marine Services, Tel: 361081.

Electronic engineers: MJ Marine, Tel: 330200, or see Newlyn Port Guide on page 193.

Sailmakers: Lodey Sails, Tel: 719359, at Long Rock, taxi/bus ride.

Transport: Main line rail terminus to London and the north, Tel: 08457 484950. Buses, Tel: 01209 719988. Ferry service to Scilly, Tel: 0845 710 5555. Helicopter service to Scilly, Tel: 363871.

Car hire: Europcar, Tel: 360356, at railway station. Enterprise, Tel: 332000. Tucker, Tel: 362980.

Bike hire: The Cycle Centre, Tel: 351671.

Taxi: Tel: 330864, 350666 or 366166.

Car parking: Large car park adjoining inner harbour.

Yacht Clubs: Penzance Sailing Club, Albert Pier, Tel: 364989.

Eating out: Excellent choice of pubs and restaurants.

Things to do: Penzance Town Museum; trips to Land's End or St Michael's Mount; Golowan Festival last week in June.

If space is available, visitors can only use the inner pontoons in Newlyn for an overnight stay with the harbourmaster's permission

Newlyn

Tides	HW Dover −0635
Range	MHWS 5.6m–MHWN 4.4m, MLWN 2.0m–MLWS 0.8m.
	Main harbour dredged to 2.4m LAT
Charts	AC: 2345, SC5603.7; Stanfords: 2, SC23; Imray: C7 WCP2400.10
Waypoint	South Pier Head 50°06'.18N 05°32'.57W
Hazards	Low Lee Rock (lit). Gear Rock (lit). Busy fishing harbour, beware vessels in narrow entrance. Approach dangerous in strong southerly weather, heavy swell sets across entrance. Many pot and net buoys in Mount's Bay
Harbour Speed limit	Three knots
Overnight charge	Harbour Authority alongside: £18

According to the plaque on a house overlooking the harbour, Newlyn, not Plymouth, was the last port of call in England for the *Mayflower* and her intrepid crew before setting out on her voyage to the New World. Recent research reveals that she berthed on the Old Quay on the 16 August 1620 to take on water, as Plymouth's supply was tainted with fever and cholera. Apart from that brief unsung moment in history, Newlyn's abiding claim to fame has always been as a busy fishing port, alive with colour, boats and activity, and you walk the streets at your peril as large articulated refrigerated lorries, fork lift trucks and spraying hoses create an assault on all sides!

In contrast with its declining neighbour Penzance, Newlyn saw considerable commercial expansion during the 1980s following the opening of the central Mary Williams pier, and is now the largest fish landing port in England and Wales, with around 9,500 tons of fish landed annually representing a value of approximately £20m.

The port is dredged to an average depth of 2.4m LAT and is accessible at all states of the tide, providing the only real harbour of refuge in Mount's Bay. However, in strong southerly or southeasterly winds, a heavy sea builds up in the shoaling water at the head of the bay, particularly at Low Water, causing a significant run across the harbour entrance.

This should be carefully considered if heading for shelter, and entry is best attempted as close to High Water as possible.

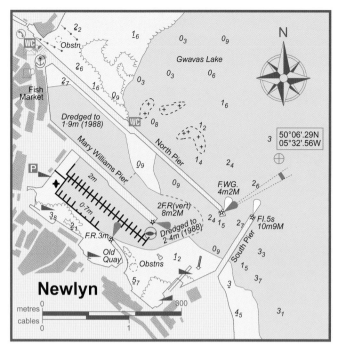

Gwavas Lake

North Pier

50°06'.29N
05°32'.56W

F.WG.
4m2M

2F.R(vert)
8m2M

Fl.5s
10m9M

Dredged to
2.4m (1988)

F.R.3m

Old
Quay

Obstns

South Pier

Newlyn

metres

cables

Fish
Market

Dredged to
1·9m (1988)

Mary Williams Pier

Obstn

APPROACHES
Approaching from the east, the run across Mount's
Bay is straightforward, passing to the south of the
Mountamopus YB south cardinal buoy (Q(6)+LFl 15s)
and well clear of Gear Rock (Fl (2) 10s), three-quarters
of a mile to the north-east of the harbour entrance,
which dries 1.8m and is marked by an isolated danger
beacon. From the west, Low Lee shoal, least depth
1.5m LAT, is marked by the Low Lee BY east cardinal

buoy (Q(3) 10s), but Carn Base shoal, three cables to the
north-west is unmarked, has a least depth of 1.8m and
breaks in heavy weather.

However, once St Clement's Island, off Mousehole,
is abeam, a course should be held just over a cable
from the shore. This will lead inside all the shoals,
past Penlee Point with its former lifeboat house, from
where the white lighthouse on the end of the south pier
(Fl 5s vis: 253° – 336°T) is easy to spot against the town,
which rises up the hillside overlooking the harbour.
The entrance is 47m wide and the northern side has
a FWG sectored light (green 238° – 248°T). The only
other hazard to consider, particularly at night, is the
significant amount of pots along this stretch of coast
and also the large numbers of small craft that will be
found working them. As always, fishing craft restricted
by gear should be given a generous berth and your
intentions made obvious at an early stage.

BERTHING AND ANCHORAGE
In offshore winds, it is possible to anchor 200m south-
south-east of the harbour entrance, sounding in to about
3m, or alternatively, a similar distance to the north-east
in Gwavas Lake. Owing to the frequency of fishing boat
movements and the intensity of the background lights
on the shore, a very good riding light is essential.

Newlyn is a busy commercial harbour with no
dedicated facilities for visitors. In contrast to Penzance,
its main attraction is obviously the all-tide access, which

One of the busiest fishing ports in the West Country, Newlyn has all tide access but should be approached
with caution in strong winds with an easterly component

is particularly useful if you are on passage and wanting to make the most of the tides or intent on an early start. However, the creation of a large, newly-dredged area, with pontoons and finger berthing to the south-west of Mary Williams pier in 2006 has since been a source of confusion for visitors due to the initially incorrect perception among many that this was a new marina. In actual fact, the project was specifically funded with a European Fisheries Grant to upgrade the berthing facilities for the local commercial fishing fleet, and not as a facility for pleasure craft. This has inevitably led to some ill-feeling among local fishermen returning from sea to find them filling up with visiting boats. To clarify the situation for potential visitors to Newlyn, it remains exactly the same as it was prior to the installation of the new pontoons and **visiting pleasure craft can only be accommodated for an overnight stay if space is available**. There is no provision for long stay berthing – the wet dock in Penzance is the nearest place where a vessel can be left unattended for any length of time – and preference will be given to fishing boats at all times. It is therefore absolutely essential that you contact Newlyn Harbourmaster, Mr Andrew Munson, on VHF Ch 16/12 or Tel: 01736 362523 to check availability before entering the harbour. He is always very helpful and will endeavour to find you a berth!

If a pontoon berth is allocated, the north-east side is dredged to 2m LAT and can accommodate vessels up to 15m long at £27 per night. The south-west side is dredged to Chart Datum and can accommodate vessels up to 10m at £18 per night. If pontoon berths are not available, as previously, and, again, *if space is available*, visitors will have to lie alongside the fishing boats on the west side of the Mary Williams pier, which tends to be occupied by local vessels that are laid up for refits or repairs. There is less movement here in contrast to the continual comings and goings elsewhere in the harbour, where the fleet lands daily. As well as breast lines to your neighbour, bow and stern lines should be taken ashore if intending to stay overnight and, with the boats often five or six deep, this will involve quite a scramble. Someone will usually appear to take your dues in the late afternoon. Alternatively, make your way to the harbour office, which is at the head of the harbour by the north pier alongside the fish-merchants' offices.

As in all busy fishing harbours, remember that commercial activity takes absolute precedence over pleasure. Sailing and anchoring is prohibited anywhere in the harbour except in an emergency.

FUEL, FRESH WATER AND GAS

Diesel can be obtained by arrangement with the harbourmaster. Petrol is only available in cans from the local garage. Calor Gas and Camping Gaz can be acquired through the harbourmaster, while fresh water is available from taps on the new pontoons.

As a working port, fishing vessels have berthing precedence at all times in Newlyn

FACILITIES
(Local phone code 01736)
The town, although small, provides most necessary provisions, catering as it does for the fishing fleet. There is a Co-op supermarket (with cash machine) close to the harbour, open 0800 – 2200 daily including Sundays, as well as a butcher, a newsagent and a Barclays bank that is open 1000 – 1230 Mon – Fri (cashpoint planned for 2008). There are two chandlers, and anything unobtainable in Newlyn can usually be found in Penzance, a pleasant walk along the promenade, or accessible by bus every 15 minutes.

Showers can be found at the Royal National Mission to Deep Sea Fishermen or, alternatively, you can use the Harbour Authority shower (£1 slotmeter) near the fishmarket – the key is available from the security office, which is in the tower on the Mary Williams Pier.

This part of Cornwall has a long tradition of popularity with artists, in particular the famous Newlyn School of the 1890s, whose realistic paintings have enjoyed a great resurgence of interest with fishing and fisherfolk one of its central themes. Today's cultural diversion is provided by the Newlyn Art Gallery on the seafront, with regular local and visiting exhibitions. The lively Newlyn Fish Festival takes place at the end of August.

Gastronomic diversion is well catered for, with several fishermen's cafés, the China Garden takeaway, Tel: 367483, and Aunty May's Pasty Co for a superlative lunchtime pasty and *very* fresh fish and chips! There are plenty of good pubs with food, the Tolcarne, Star and Swordfish near the harbour head, while the Red Lion and Fisherman's Arms overlook the harbour on the Mousehole road where you'll also find The Smuggler's seafood restaurant, Tel: 331501. Pizza Patio, a wine bar/restaurant, is by the bridge on the Penzance road or for something completely different, try the Meadery, Tel: 365375.

NEWLYN AND FISHING

Newlyn is a bustling working town, its fishmarket central to its life. Early risers, providing they keep out of the way of the very serious business in hand, can spend a fascinating hour or two watching the landings and daily auction which starts at around seven in the morning, Monday to Saturday.

The old town, a pleasant meandering sort of place, climbs up the hillside in tight rows of sturdy granite cottages, sheltered courtyards and narrow alleyways. It has been a fishing harbour since medieval times and the magnificent remains of the original pier, a gently curving wall of huge granite blocks, weathered and mottled with orange lichens, can still be seen forming part of the small inner basin beneath the cliff on the west side of the harbour.

The present harbour, built between 1866 and 1888, was the centre of the huge mackerel and pilchard fishery and scene of the infamous riots in 1896 when the devout local fishermen ran amok, angered by visiting east coast boats landing fish on Sundays. Hurling their catches back into the sea, the bloody disturbance that ensued was only eventually put down by military intervention.

Renowned for their speed and sea-keeping ability, the magnificent 30-50ft double-ended luggers that once filled these west Cornish ports have mostly vanished, but the restored Mount's Bay mackerel driver *Children's Friend* PZ101 is now based in the port, while the 111-year old St Ives pilchard driver *Ripple* SS19 was relaunched in October 2007 after a four year restoration right beside the harbour. She had fished out of St Ives until December 1933 when she was almost written off by a fire on board, but fortunately the hulk was repaired and converted into a 'Gentleman's motor yacht' in 1936, and for 50 years she was based on the Helford. Now the oldest boat on the UK fishing registry, she carries the same name and number as when she was launched in 1896 and will remain based in Newlyn as part of the West Cornwall Lugger Industry Trust's project to create a fishing heritage centre.

The *Barnabas*, another fine example of a St Ives lugger owned by the Maritime Trust, is based in Falmouth where she can often be seen sailing during the summer months.

The present fishing fleet has grown considerably in recent years and ranges from large beam trawlers and scallopers that venture as far afield as the North Sea and Irish Sea, to the smaller pot, net and mackerel boats that work the tricky inshore waters round Land's End.

Newlyn Port Guide – Area telephone code: 01736

Harbourmaster: Mr Andrew Munson, Harbour Office, Newlyn, TR18 5HW, Tel: 362523. Office hours 0800 – 1700 Mon – Fri.

VHF: Ch 16, working Chs 12 and 9, callsign *Newlyn Harbour*, office hours only.

Mail Drop: c/o Harbour office.

Emergency Services: Lifeboat at Newlyn; Falmouth Coastguard.

Anchorages: In fair weather to north-east or south-east of harbour entrance clear of approaches. No anchoring within harbour.

Mooring/berthing: Only if space is available by arrangement with the harbourmaster, either on pontoons or alongside fishing boats, both on west side of Mary Williams pier.

Charges: Per night, up to 8m £12; 8m up to 12m £18; 12m and over £27. Fifty per cent surcharge for multihulls.

Phones: By harbour office.

Doctor: Tel: 363340.

Hospital: Tel: 362382.

Churches: All denominations.

Local weather forecast: At harbour office.

Fuel: Ask at harbour office for diesel. Petrol in cans from garage.

Gas: Ask at harbour office.

Water: Taps on pontoons.

Banks/cashpoints: Barclays 1000 – 1230 Mon – Fri. Cashpoints planned for 2008. Cash machine in Co-op. All banks in Penzance have cashpoints.

Post office: By harbour office.

Internet access: Public Library, Morrab Road, Penzance.

Rubbish: Bins on quays.

Showers/toilets: Royal National Mission to Deep Sea Fishermen, North Pier. Showers near fishmarket. Public toilets on quay.

Launderette: Nearest in Penzance.

Provisions: Co-op Supermarket (open 0800 – 2200 daily inc Sundays), butcher, newsagent.

Chandler: Cosalt, Harbour Road, Tel: 363094. South

West Nets, Harbour Road, Tel: 360254.

Repairs: Large slip for commercial craft. Drying out by arrangement with harbourmaster.

Marine engineers: Mount's Bay Engineering, North Pier, Tel: 363095. See also Penzance Port Guide on p189.

Electronic engineers: Mannel Marine, Tel: 333655; Selex Communications Ltd, Tel: 361320.

Sailmakers: Lodey Sails, Tel: 719359, at Long Rock,

near Marazion, taxi/bus ride away.

Transport: Buses to Penzance. Mainline rail terminus at Penzance.

Car hire/taxi: See harbourmaster.

Car parking: Near fishmarket.

Eating out: Pub food, bistros, fish and chips and excellent pasties.

Things to do: Newlyn Fish Festival, late August Bank Holiday; Newlyn Art gallery; pleasant walk along coastal bike trail to Mousehole.

The *Mayflower*'s last port? The old harbour, Newlyn

St Michael's Mount and Mousehole

Providing an interesting alternative to the larger Mount's Bay ports of Penzance and Newlyn, St Michael's Mount and the old fishing harbour of Mousehole are well worth a visit if conditions permit. Both have small harbours which dry completely at LAT, but are normally accessible after half flood.

ST MICHAEL'S MOUNT

There is no problem identifying St Michael's Mount, Cornwall's own mini version of the famous Mont St Michel in Normandy, for this dramatic tidal island rises into a distinctive 90m pyramid in the north-eastern corner of Mount's Bay, topped by a fairy tale castle at its summit. The St Aubyn family have lived here since the mid-1600s. They continue to do so, but the island was presented to the National Trust in 1954 by the present Lord St Levan. During the summer months, the Mount and parts of the castle buildings are open to the public on weekdays, 1000 – 1700; there is a charge for admission.

Historically, the tiny harbour on the northern side of the Mount was once the most important in Mount's Bay. This major centre for the export of tin was chronicled by the Romans in the first century BC, when the ore was brought overland from the mines on the north coast to avoid the treacherous journey around Land's End.

A Benedictine monastery was established here in 1135, making it an important place of pilgrimage, but this was dissolved by Henry VIII during the Reformation and during the Civil War the Royalists held the Mount for four years, a vital siege as the fortress was an ideal place for the import and stockpiling of arms and ammunition brought in from France.

In 1727 the modest harbour was rebuilt and extended, and by the early 1800s it had prospered considerably,

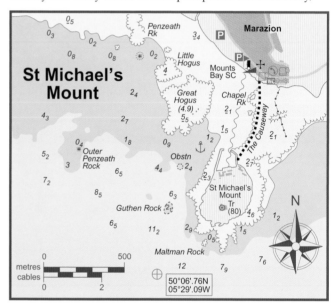

The spectacular island of St Michael's Mount is linked to the mainland by a Low Tide causeway. The best anchorage is between Great Hogus Reef, the dark patch, top left, and the western harbour wall

with over 50 houses on the island and a population of about 300. As you will see from the many pictures and prints if you visit the castle, large numbers of vessels regularly lay here, anchored in the bay or crammed into the tiny harbour, discharging timber from Scandinavia, coal and salt, before loading the return cargoes of copper, tin and cured fish that were exported in considerable quantities all over Europe. It was, however, the new harbour at Penzance that eventually sealed the fate of the Mount and by the turn of the century it had lost all the trade to its larger rival.

Overlooked by the fairy tale castle, visitors able to take the ground can dry out on clean sand in the harbour

APPROACHES AND ANCHORAGE

The best anchorage for a visit to the Mount is just to the north-west of the harbour entrance, or it is possible to lie alongside in the harbour where you will dry out on hard sand. The approaches have a number of rocks and shoals and should only be considered in fine weather, offshore winds and a rising tide. Do not attempt it at night, and under no circumstances should an approach ever be made to the east and north of the Mount where there are extensive rocky shoals.

From Penzance keep offshore to avoid the reefs across the head of the bay; Western Cressar Rocks and Ryeman Rocks are both marked by a YB south cardinal beacon and a course towards the southern extremity of the Mount will clear both these and the Outer Penzeath Rock, awash LAT and unmarked.

Closing the Mount, approach on a northeasterly course, keeping a good 300m from its steep western side to avoid Guthen Rocks, a shoal patch with just over 2m LAT, due west of the castle. Sound in towards the anchorage where about 2m will be found at Low Water, over a firm sandy bottom between the Great Hogus reef, which dries 4.9m, and the western pier end.

After half-tide, the harbour is accessible to average draught boats – stay a reasonable distance from the pier heads and beware of the constant stream of ferry boats. Known locally as 'hobblers', they operate continuously from the steps on both sides of the entrance as soon as the tide covers the causeway and should not be obstructed in any way. Berth between the ladders on the western wall and report to Keith Murch, the

harbourmaster, whose office is on the opposite side of the harbour; if you can't find him immediately don't worry – he is also the island's postman and is probably dealing with the mail! A charge of about £10 will be made for an overnight stay.

ST MICHAEL'S MOUNT FACILITIES

Today, the Mount is the focal point of a very different kind of industry – tourism – and at times is almost overrun by the hordes of holidaymakers streaming, with a wary eye on the tide, like the Israelites along the causeway from Marazion, or packing the small ferries that run during the summer months when the tide is in. In spite of it, the small harbour, with its simple row of neatly restored cottages, is well worth a visit.

Despite the dire warning that the climb to the castle 'should not be attempted by those suffering from any kind of heart condition', it is not as steep as it looks and provides spectacular panoramic views across Mount's Bay. In the evening, when the crowds have gone, this is once again, for a few brief hours, a peaceful and tranquil place.

The Sail Loft Restaurant and Island Café are both open during the day for lunches and cream teas, as well as a harbourside gift shop. The harbourmaster can fill a container of water if you're desperate. No fuel or gas is available.

Over in Marazion you will find a convenience store/newsagent and off-licence, with cash machine and mobile phone top-up, another cash machine in the post office, a baker, plenty of cafés and a fish and chip shop. Among the several pubs are the Godolphin Arms, where the Gig bar looks out across the water to the Mount, the Kings Arms or the Fire Engine Inn on the outskirts.

MOUSEHOLE

Mousehole is in many ways similar to St Michael's Mount, for this is another picturesque honey pot around which the tourists swarm. Available from half tide, this small, oval harbour, with massive granite boulder walls, is the epitome of a Cornish fishing village, though its heyday during the mackerel and pilchard fishery is long past. The residue of the fishing fleet once based here is now kept in Newlyn, but a few local pot, net and angling boats can be seen lying on fore and aft trots along with a number of small pleasure craft.

From mid-October until the end of March, the harbour mouth is closed completely with heavy wood baulks and few winters pass without some damage to the seemingly impregnable walls as the southeasterly gales roll into Mount's Bay. Privately administered by its own Harbour Commissioners, the unfortunate dominance of car parking beside the harbour and on the quays does pay for its upkeep, and the small charge for visiting yachts contributes to it too. In suitable conditions, the harbour provides a worthwhile diversion for an overnight stay or just a daytime visit.

APPROACHES AND ANCHORAGE

Approaching across Mount's Bay, the houses of Mousehole climbing the hillside are easy to spot to the south of Newlyn, although St Clement's Isle, a low rocky outcrop with a small obelisk on its highest point just east of the harbour mouth, will be lost against the land until much closer.

Approaching from the south, from Penzer Point the island is much easier to see as it lies clear of the land. You can anchor south of a line between the obelisk on St Clement's Island and the harbour entrance, taking care to avoid the submarine power cable running between the north-west side of the island and the mainland shore, which is used to light the tableau that is erected on the island at Christmas.

If you are merely waiting on the tide, let go to the south-west of Shag Rock.

Although local fishing boats regularly use the inshore passage to the north of the island, there are rocks on both sides and a very narrow channel at Low Water. Strangers should always use the approach from the south of the island, which is far wider and safer, and enter mid-way between the island and the shore. Beware Tom Kneebone ledge (least depth 0.9m LAT) 100m south of the obelisk – do not cut the corner, but enter on a northwesterly course, midway between the island and the south pier head before turning in towards the harbour entrance as it begins to open.

Closer inshore, about 100m south and slightly east of the entrance, isolated Chimney Rock dries 2.3m, but the biggest hazard is probably the many pot buoys around the island and along the shore – be particularly wary in the approach and, if remaining at anchor overnight, a riding light is essential.

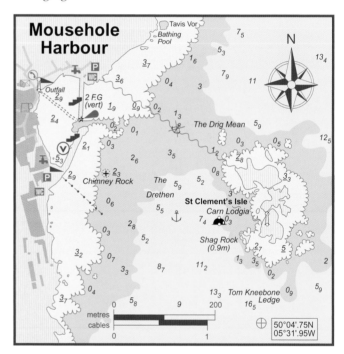

Approaching Mousehole and Mount's Bay from the south, the harbour wall is in the centre, St Clement's Isle lies on the right, with Penzance appearing beyond

Mousehole dries completely to a firm sandy bottom. Visitors should berth alongside the far South Pier, clear of the steps

BERTHING

After half-tide you will find plenty of water inside the harbour. A depth gauge to 10ft is attached to the end of the North Quay, while there are also a number of horizontal concrete ledges on the outer corner of the northern wall, and if only the top three are showing there will be a good 8ft inside the outer ends of the harbour walls.

Visitors should berth on the South Pier where you can dry out alongside on a firm sandy bottom, but keep clear of the stone steps as these are used by the local boats for landing fish and crews. Bilge-keelers intending to dry out should not attempt to anchor among the fore and aft moorings for local boats that fill the centre of the harbour without the harbourmaster's permission. As there is no harbour office, the harbourmaster, Mr Paul Gilchrist, Tel: 01736 731644, is usually around in the early evening to collect the dues – a flat rate of £10 a night (£12 for multihulls). He can also point you in the direction of the water tap at the inner end of the quay, while a public toilet is located in the car park. No fuel or gas is available.

Mousehole is a bustling, colourful place where visitors bravely compete with the traffic trying to squeeze through the narrow streets. Its unique charm has not only survived the onslaught of recent years, but also considerable mayhem in the Middle Ages when the village, then the most important port in Cornwall, was raided and burnt to the ground by marauding Spaniards in 1595, and Keigwin House, with its splendid granite pillared porch, now tucked away in the back streets, was one of the few buildings to survive. Mousehole also enjoys a certain fame today as the home of Dolly Pentreath who died in 1777, reputedly the last person to speak Cornish as her native tongue, and a commemorative plaque can be found on the wall of her cottage close by the harbour. Perhaps she would have been able to provide the answer (although presumably few of us would have been able to understand it . . .) to the village's curious name, for which there seems to be no definitive explanation. Remember, though, that it is always pronounced as *Mowzull* and never, never as *Mouse Hole*!

After Dolly Pentreath, Tom Bawcock is probably the other most celebrated former inhabitant, and Tom Bawcock's Eve on 23 December recalls the time when this fabled local fisherman put to sea in desperation after weeks of gales, returning with a fine catch of seven different kinds of fish to provide Christmas feast for the starving village. Hopefully you will not be visiting by sea at this time of year – not only will you find the storm baulks in place, but you will also be confronted by the infamous Starry Gazy Pie, a delectable creation with the heads of the seven varieties of fish poking through its crust!

MOUSEHOLE FACILITIES

Starry Gazy apart, the majority of other basic provisions are available in the village shop: fresh bread, most groceries, off-licence, newspapers and phone top up.

Looking seaward, the distant St Michael's Mount is framed in the harbour mouth

You will also find a post office in the village. With several cafés, a good fish and chip shop and the Ship Inn which, in spite of the tourism, has managed to retain a distinctively village pub atmosphere, there is no shortage of places to eat. In addition, there is also a small, reasonably priced restaurant adjoining the Ship, Tel: 01736 731234, along with two other restaurants in the village – No 2 Fore Street and The Cornish Range, Tel: 01736 731488, which, situated near the post office, offers a seafood menu. Alternatively, the Old Coastguard Hotel, Tel: 01736 731222, on the Newlyn Road out of the village provides meals for non-residents and has fine views of Mount's Bay.

Almost everything else is obtainable in Penzance, to which there is a regular bus service. The more energetic can hire bikes just outside the village on the Newlyn Road and follow the new bike trail running along the coast through the remains of the old Penlee Quarry workings. Whether you need to work up an appetite or not, the fine walk along the cliffs to the south of the village towards Penzer Point and the beautifully named Lamorna Cove should not be missed. The Wink pub can provide refreshment en route. Children will also be fascinated by the Wild Bird Hospital on Raginnis Hill, on the south side of the village.

Mousehole, like many of its counterparts in Cornwall, has a famous male voice choir. If you are lucky you may hear soft Cornish voices drifting in a strangely haunting harmony across the natural arena of the harbour into the gathering twilight around the bay, for sometimes they assemble on the quayside on balmy summer's evenings. It will be one of those evocative moments that you, like me, will probably never forget!

Mousehole is the epitome of a Cornish fishing village. There is a good anchorage in settled weather just off the harbour entrance if you do not wish to dry out inside

The islands looking east over Tresco and Bryher to St Mary's.
St Martin's is on the left

Chapter five
The Isles of Scilly

Tides	HW Dover –0630
Range	St Mary's MHWS 5.7m–MHWN 4.3m, MLWN 2.0m–MLWS 0.7m.
	See special note (6) on tides at end of this section
Charts	AC: 34, 883, 1148, 2565. SC5603; Stanfords: 2; Imray: C7
Waypoints	See Mainland to The Isles of Scilly, pages 204 and 209
Hazards	Many unmarked rocks and shallow ledges, large areas between islands dry.
	No harbours offering all weather security
Harbour Speed limit	St Mary's harbour three knots. Tresco New Grimsby Sound six knots
Overnight charge	St Mary's Harbour Authority mooring £15.
	Tresco Estate mooring £15, at anchor £5. Tean Sound Hotel mooring £10

'A straggling collection of barren rocks, wonderfully broken up, narrow strips of land bordered with marvellously white gleaming beaches, rocky hills covered with heath and gorse, intersected by ravines running down to the loveliest little bays, piles and piles of strangely weird grey, lichen covered rocks, little dales where bask a few isolated cottages festooned with mesembryantheums and giant geraniums sheltered by a few tangled tamarisks . . .'

Frank Cowper, on his first visit to the Isles of Scilly in 1892, was clearly impressed by what he had found; over a century on, his appraisal still holds good.

Set in water of breathtaking clarity, this tantalising archipelago of 48 islands, some little more than glorified rocks, extends over an area of approximately 45 square miles between 21 and 31 miles west-south-west of Land's End. Only six islands are inhabited, St Mary's, St Martin's, Tresco, Bryher, St Agnes and

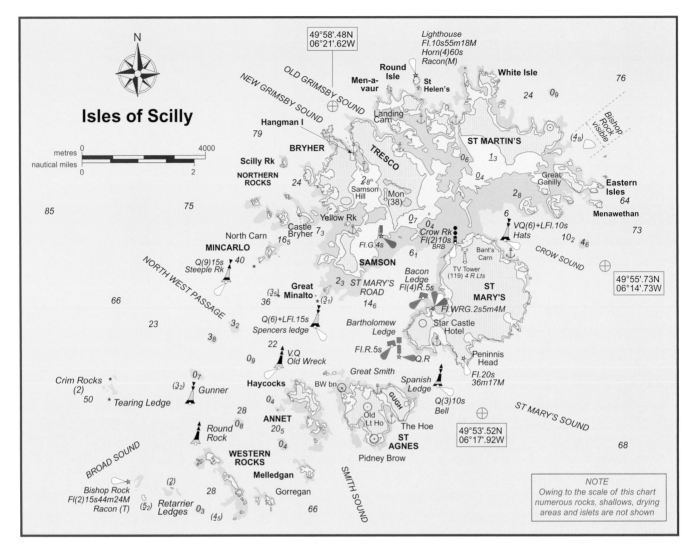

Isles of Scilly

49°58'.48N
06°21'.62W

Lighthouse
Fl.10s55m18M
Horn(4)60s
Racon(M)

Round
Isle

Men-a-
vaur

St
Helen's

White Isle

76

OLD GRIMSBY SOUND

NEW GRIMSBY SOUND

Landing
Carn

ST MARTIN'S

24   0₉

Bishop
Rock
visible

Hangman I
79

BRYHER

TRESCO

0₆   1₃

(4₈)

Scilly Rk

NORTHERN
ROCKS   24

Samson
Hill

28°

Mon
(38)

0₄

Great
Ganilly

Eastern
Isles
64

Menawethan

metres   0   4000
nautical miles
0   2

Yellow Rk

2₈

85   75

Castle
Bryher 7₃

0₇   0₄
Crow Rk
Fl(2)10s
BRB

6

VQ(6)+LFl.10s
Hats   10₂ 4₆   73

North Carn   16₅

MINCARLO

Fl.G.4s

6₁

Bant's
Carn

CROW SOUND

49°55'.73N
06°14'.73W

Q(9)15s
Steeple Rk   40

2₃   ST MARY'S
ROAD

SAMSON

Bacon
Ledge
Fl(4)R.5s

TV Tower
(119) 4 R Lts

ST
MARY'S

NORTH WEST PASSAGE

66   (3₅)
36   Great
Minalto

23

Q(6)+LFl.15s
Spencers ledge

3₂

3₈

(3₁)

14₆

Fl.WRG.2s5m4M

Star Castle
Hotel

Bartholomew
Ledge

22   V.Q
Old Wreck

0₉

Fl.R.5s

Great Smith

Q.R

Peninnis
Head

Fl.20s
36m17M

Crim Rocks
(2)
50

(3₂)   0₇
Gunner

Haycocks

BW bn

Spanish
Ledge

* Tearing Ledge

0₄

Q(3)10s
Bell

ST MARY'S SOUND

28

0₈

ANNET
20₅

GUGH

Old
Lt Ho

The Hoe

49°53'.52N
06°17'.92W

68

BROAD SOUND

Round
Rock

0₄

ST
AGNES

WESTERN
ROCKS

Pidney Brow

SMITH SOUND

Melledgan

Bishop Rock
Fl(2)15s44m24M
Racon (T)

(2)
28

(5₂)

Retarrier
Ledges   0₃

Gorregan

0₄   (4₅)

66

NOTE
Owing to the scale of this chart
numerous rocks, shallows, drying
areas and islets are not shown

Gugh. Of the rest, 18 are described by the Admiralty Channel Pilot as 'being capable of bearing grass, the remainder are barren'.

Their warm oceanic climate prompted the Romans to name the area *Sillinae Insulae*, meaning Sun Isles, from which Scilly now derives its name. This is something of a moot point, for although many loosely refer to the islands as the Scillies – and I have been guilty of this – the locals let it be known that they prefer their archipelago to be called the Isles of Scilly or just plain Scilly. Nor do they take kindly to being described as Cornish – they are Scillonians, most definitely, and proud of it!

In fine and settled weather it is hard to believe that you are still so close to mainland Britain. It is easy to imagine, if momentarily, that you are in a far more exotic location, given a few more palm trees in addition to those that already flourish here. However, such delights are, alas, not always so lightly enjoyed! As a cruising ground the Isles of Scilly can have a definite downside. It is not an area to be trifled with, and a clear understanding of the potential problems will go a long way to ensuring a successful visit.

The first consideration is getting there. It will involve an offshore passage of over 20 miles, admittedly not

a great distance, but one that takes you out into the Atlantic and a particularly exposed sea area renowned for sudden changes of weather and poor visibility. With strong tides, shipping, including the Land's End Traffic Separation Scheme (TSS), and the rarely absent Atlantic ground swell, this is no place for the inexperienced. Even for the experienced, it can be a very unpleasant stretch of water to get caught out in.

The second consideration is Scilly itself. Apart from the obvious dangers of any group of islands strewn with rocks, most unmarked, large areas of shallow water and strong and often unpredictable localised tidal streams and races, it also lacks a harbour or anchorage that can be considered secure in all weather. As each anchorage is only safe in certain combinations of wind and sea, any amount of time spent in the islands will inevitably involve shifting as the weather changes, often in deteriorating conditions.

Once among the islands, distances are not great, usually only a matter of a few miles, but the problems of riding out bad weather have been greatly exacerbated by the demands made on the available anchorages by the ever increasing numbers of visiting yachts, particularly during August when large numbers of French boats arrive.

The third consideration is the relative lack of facilities for visiting yachts compared with the mainland. Although there are now visitors' moorings in St Mary's Pool, New Grimsby Sound, Old Grimsby Sound and Tean Sound, overnight berthing alongside and afloat is not available anywhere in the islands, and in most other places you will have to anchor. Simple enough, one might think, but the holding ground in the majority of places is of fairly indifferent quality, either fine loose sand, sand covered with weed or weed covered rocks.

It is also worth noting that **anchoring is no longer allowed anywhere within St Mary's Harbour Limits**, here you must use the visitors' moorings which fill up quickly at the height of the season or, alternatively, dry out alongside the inner end of the quay where there are a limited number of berths.

Finally, owners of deeper draught boats should be aware of one other little mentioned factor which can at times seriously detract from full enjoyment of Scilly – the all-pervading Atlantic ground swell which manages to creep into most of the normal mooring and anchorage areas. Usually it is most prevalent towards High Water and ironically when the wind is at its lightest – calm weather does not necessarily mean a calm sea in Scilly! In my opinion the ideal craft for exploration of these waters will either have bilge keels, a lifting keel or moderate enough draught to be able to edge close inshore and,

if necessary, dry out on legs for then the options for a more relaxing stay increase considerably.

However, the object of all this is not to deter, although this is often the reaction on first perusal of the large scale chart. The hazards seem myriad and the pilotage overly complicated, not least the abundance of transits which are traditionally associated with Scilly as leading and clearing lines for passages and hazards. For many, these can prove confusing, particularly on first arrival when the topography is itself bewildering enough. The 307°T leading line to clear the Spanish and Bartholomew Ledges in St Mary's sound, 'North Carn on Mincarlo in line with south side of Great Minalto', is a typical example, as Great Minalto, in spite of its name, is actually a much smaller rock than Mincarlo!

The leading lines are not critical to navigation. They are an aid as long as you can identify them, but often the visibility is such that the more distant marks are indistinguishable.

Transits are also useful to gauge any tidal set across your course, but if you do decide to try using them, leave nothing to chance. Many rocks have a tendency to look similar – once you believe you have identified your leading marks, check that they tally with the heading on the compass – remembering that all bearings are **True from Seaward** and will need to be corrected for magnetic variation. If in any doubt, don't panic, concentrate instead on making your approach in the

There are many delightful anchorages, depending on the weather. St Helen's Pool in ideal conditions!

normal fashion using any other visible criteria you have at your disposal.

The choice of anchorages I have described is limited to those most likely to be used during a first visit, and I am also assuming that most readers will be approaching from the mainland. The western side of the islands has by far the greater number of isolated offshore hazards and in my opinion it should be avoided, certainly by newcomers to the area. For this reason the western approaches through Broad Sound, Smith Sound and the North West Passage are deliberately not covered in any great detail – see 'Scilly from North Cornish Coast on page 209'. If you're desperate to see the Western Rocks at close quarters there is much to recommend a trip in one of the local pleasure boats!

There are, of course, numerous other possible anchorages and more intricate passages requiring suitable weather and local knowledge that might appeal to the more adventurous or those who have already explored the more familiar places. However, my only intention here is to try and ensure a safe and pleasant stay in these waters. To this end, my own pointers for a first and, hopefully, trouble free visit to the islands would be summarised as follows:

1. Have a well found boat with a reliable engine, a crew of adequate strength and experience and, absolutely essential, up-to-date editions of Admiralty charts 883 (Isles of Scilly, St Mary's and the principal off-islands) and 34 (Isles of Scilly), which includes useful tidal charts for the islands, or its excellent Small Craft Folio 5603 (Falmouth to Padstow including the Isles of Scilly).

The chartlets accompanying this text are simplified and much detail has been omitted to assist clarity. They must therefore not be used for navigation. Familiarise yourself with the layout of the area in advance. Although the pilotage seems complicated it is, for the most part, more straightforward after you have got your initial bearings. Once you have arrived make

every effort to identify and memorise salient features – it is surprising how quickly you begin to feel more at home.

The clarity of the water enables the rare treat of eyeball navigation and a good lookout will be able to spot the majority of dangers long before you hit them. Most of the rocks are covered with long growths of bright green weed that are usually visible on or near the surface at anything other than High Water.

2. Ideally, choose a spell of fine settled weather, with Neap tides, and arrive in daylight with ample time in hand to find a suitable berth. Do not be tempted to make a dash for the islands if there is any hint of deteriorating weather in the offing. You are far better off remaining on the mainland.

3. Try to visit the islands in June or July. If possible avoid August when they are at their busiest and the weather has a tendency to be less settled.

4. Have a more than adequate amount of ground tackle on board to cope with all eventualities. Most boats will normally have a CQR, Bruce or Danforth as their main anchor, but here you cannot afford to skimp on the size of your kedge(s). With the poor holding and fine sand in many anchorages, I have found that my CQR does not always perform at its normal best and most local boatmen seem to favour a good-sized Fisherman or Danforth. I would recommend one of each in addition to your normal ground tackle, with ample chain and warp of adequate weight.

Be sure you know how to use it all! Lower your anchor until you feel it touch the ground, go astern and slowly veer the chain to lay it out along the bottom, allowing at least three times the anticipated depth at High Water (five times the depth if using chain and warp). Belay the cable, go astern gently at first to ensure that the anchor bites, then increase the power to test the hold. If you feel the chain whilst doing this, you can tell if the anchor is biting – or not! If the chain or warp jumps and loses tension it has definitely not taken. Don't take a chance, but start again. There is much sense in the old maxim that it is better to be safe than sorry and I invariably lay a kedge. Certainly, if you are leaving your vessel unattended for any length of time this is definitely recommended.

5. Keep a careful watch on the weather and be constantly aware of any potential changes, particularly from the direction to which the wind is most likely to shift. Accordingly, choose your anchorage not only with regard to the prevailing conditions, but also to what might happen within the next 12 hours. Before settling in overnight, be certain that you will be able to leave in the dark by working out an exit course to steer – at all

Pilot gigs and anchoring are both synonymous with Scilly

states of the tide! Always have an alternative anchorage in mind before you need to find one.

In addition to the normal BBC shipping forecasts, Radio Cornwall shipping and inshore forecasts can be obtained in Scilly on FM 96.0. Following an announcement on VHF Ch 16 indicating which listening channel to select, Falmouth Coastguard repeats inshore or shipping forecasts for Scilly on VHF Ch 86 every three hours, commencing at 0110 Local Time.

If there is a serious likelihood of bad weather in the offing, and the timing permits, do not overlook the possibility of making a speedy return to the mainland before its onset. Remember that Mount's Bay can be dangerous to approach in heavy weather from the south-east and south and that the tidal dock at Penzance is only accessible from two hours before to one hour after local High Water.

6. Once in the islands, don't hurry. Take life at a gentler pace and don't take chances, least of all with the tide. The tidal streams are very unpredictable in the close proximity to the islands and for short periods they can often attain much greater strength than indicated in the Admiralty chartlets and Pilot. Predicted tidal heights are particularly susceptible to the atmospheric pressure – during prolonged spells of high pressure they can sometimes be almost a metre less than anticipated, and remember, too, that the range of nearly 6m at Springs will considerably reduce the amount of space in many anchorages. Conversely, with just a 2.3m range at Neaps, there is a lot more water available.

However, if you plan your moves on a rising tide, ideally after half flood, most of the trickier, shallower passages can be tackled with impunity. Try them once the ebb has set in and you've no one to blame except yourself when things go wrong!

Following the local trip boats is not recommended – their skippers know these waters intimately, many of their short cuts pass rocks within a hair's breadth and they seem able to skim over the shallows on little more

These boats all have serious work to do, so do not get in their way!

than a heavy dew. Be particularly wary of the large Bryher ferry, *Firethorn*; in spite of her size, she draws little more than 2ft!

7. Do not impede local boatmen, fishermen or other commercial craft; they are earning a living, you are there for fun, and they do not take kindly to finding yachts lying on their moorings when they return after a hard day's work, or blocking the quay steps when trying to embark or disembark passengers. If you are in any doubt – ask! Be wary of the large jet boats that increasingly provide much of the inter-island communication – they can create a large wash particularly at close quarters.

8. Water is a valuable commodity in Scilly, so aim to leave the mainland with full tanks. As food and booze (which is all freighted in by sea or air) is inevitably more expensive, it is also worth stocking up before you leave. Gas refills are only obtainable on St Mary's, so make sure you always have a spare!

9. A number of the uninhabited islands are important bird breeding areas. The following are closed to visitors between 15 April and 20 August: Annet, The Western Rocks, Crebewethan, Gorregan, Melledgan, Rosevear, Norrard Rocks, Castle Bryher, Illiswillgig, Maiden Bower, Mincarlo, Scilly Rock, Stony Island, Green Island (off Samson) and Men-a-vaur.

In addition Tean is closed on a voluntary basis between 15 April and 20 July, when ringed plovers and terns are nesting, and certain areas of other islands have clearly marked nesting sites, such as the southern end of Gugh which visitors are asked to avoid. Nesting and territorial birds, particularly gulls, can be extremely aggressive. They will attempt to ward off intruders with alarming swoops to the head that are potentially injurious and definitely frightening for smaller children and timid souls like me!

10. Beware pot buoys! They will be encountered both in the outer approaches and anywhere among the islands. With such a wide selection to choose from, wreck diving is also very popular and you should give any boat flying international code flag 'A' (vertical white with blue swallow tail) a wide berth.

As Cowper concluded: 'A stay of a few days in these bewildering islands should afford most people a good deal of pleasure. There is perpetual variety. Every rock and bay and hill offers some new view, and the contemplation of this decomposing heap of stones in the midst of the ever-vexed Atlantic must arouse a wondering curiosity, if not an enthusiastic admiration. . .'

Mainland to The Isles of Scilly

Always a cheering sight – *RMS Scillonian III* heading for the islands, with the Longships to the extreme left and Land's End to the right

Scilly from the South Cornish Coast

(For safety information, charts and passage chart see: The Manacles to Land's End, pages 175 & 176)

WAYPOINTS

1   Manacles (1M east of buoy)
    50°02'.80N 05°00'.35W

3   Lizard (4M south of light)
    49°53'.54N 05°12'.18W

6   Runnel Stone (3ca south of buoy)
    50°00'.90N 05°40'.38W

8   Wolf Rock (1.5M north of lighthouse)
    49°58'.24N 05°48'.58W

9   Wolf Rock (1.5M south of lighthouse)
    49°55'.22N 05°48'.54W

10 Crow Sound approach
    (9ca south of Menawethan Island)
    49°55'.73N 06°14'.73W

    Hats south cardinal buoy (Crow Sound)
    49°56'.21N 06°17'.14W

11 St Mary's Sound approach
    (7ca south-south-east of Peninnis Head)
    49°53'.52N 06°17'.92W

    Spanish Ledge east cardinal buoy
    (St Mary's Sound)
    49°53'.94N 06°18'.86W

Given a well-found boat, suitable weather and preparation, the passage from the English mainland should pose no major problem. Given unsuitable weather it should not even be contemplated. On a clear day, from the high ground of Land's End, the islands are often visible but with the daymark on St Martin's rising to a mere 56m and the highest ground on St Mary's 48m, they normally do not begin to show from sea level until about 12 miles distant – often it will be a lot less. As you sail ever further away from the land and, it seems, far out into the Atlantic, the doubts do not take long to crowd in – it is always worth remembering that one tends to anticipate a landfall a lot sooner than it usually appears.

The sight of the all-white ferry *RMS Scillonian III* helps to dispel a bit of unease – she sails a direct course from the Runnel Stone to St Mary's, leaving Penzance Monday to Friday at 0915, and returning from St Mary's at 1630. Saturday sailings vary depending on the time of year, but from early June to the end of August the ship leaves Penzance at 1100 and returns from St Mary's at 1500. Additional Sunday sailings only occur during August. Subject to the tide and weather, she makes her island approach and departure either through Crow Sound or St Mary's Sound.

Wolf Rock lighthouse provides a useful check on your course. Land's End can be seen in the distance on the right

The frequent British International helicopters are direct flights from Penzance to St Mary's or Tresco, and the Skybus flights to St Mary's are from Land's End and Newquay Airports, on the North Cornish coast. In the season, the odds are also very much in favour of there being many other pleasure craft bound in either direction: returning from Scilly in mid-August 2007 at one point I had over 20 sails in sight, quite a few powerboats and four ships!

GPS will doubtless do much to boost the confidence but, as always, a conventional and regular DR plot should be maintained at all times. Radar will hopefully confirm the island's existence from afar and the Racons on Wolf Rock (Morse 'T' 10M), Bishop Rock (Morse 'T' 18M), Round Island (Morse 'M' 10M) and Seven Stones (Morse 'O' 15M) should prove invaluable.

In the event of fog, a sudden reduction in visibility or an unexpected deterioration in the weather, the option of aborting the passage and returning to a mainland port should never be overlooked, however frustrating it might seem. In any of these conditions, an approach to Scilly is risky at the very least and potentially extremely dangerous. With so many offlying rocks and unpredictable tidal streams, the fog signals should be regarded as a warning to stay well clear of the islands and not an invitation to attempt an approach: Round Island (Horn (4) 60s), Wolf Rock (Horn 30s), Longships (Horn 10s), Seven Stones (Horn (3) 60s) – do not confuse with Round Island), Spanish Ledge buoy (bell), Runnel Stone (whistle) and Tater Du (Horn (2) 30s).

Do not be tempted to run for the islands in heavy weather in anticipation of finding shelter: the overfalls and heavy seas in the approaches during gale force conditions, particularly with wind against tide, could in themselves easily overwhelm small craft. Should

you find yourself in trouble, all rescues in this area are co-ordinated by Falmouth MRCC VHF Ch 16 callsign *Falmouth Coastguard* (working Ch 67, MSI broadcasts on Ch 86). Lifeboats are based at Newlyn, Sennen, St Ives and St Mary's.

A clear spell of settled anticyclonic weather would seem to be the ideal, for then the odds are in favour of a good easterly breeze to whisk you out to the west. However, in such conditions, fine weather haze is more than likely to be prevailing and the visibility often much diminished.

Given the low-lying nature of the islands, there is much to be said for a night passage, timed to arrive soon after daybreak, for this busy stretch of water is well lit with the Runnel Stone south cardinal buoy (Q(6) + LFl 15s), Carn Base west cardinal buoy (Q (9) 15s) and the lighthouses at Tater Du (Fl (3) 15s 20M), Wolf Rock (Fl 15s 16M), Longships (Fl WR 10s W15/R11M), Seven Stones Light float (Fl (3) 30s 23M), Round Island (Fl 10s 18M), Peninnis Light (Fl 20s 17M) and Bishop Rock (Fl (2) 15s 24M) – all of which should be visible long before you would normally pick up any detail in daylight.

Although a night entry into the islands is not recommended for a first time visit, with due care it is quite feasible now that most of the buoys and navigation marks are lit. St Mary's Sound is the best option, using Peninnis lighthouse (Fl 20s 17M), Spanish Ledge buoy (Q (3) 10s), Bartholomew Ledge beacon (QR), North Bartholomew buoy (Fl R 5s), Bacon Ledge buoy (Fl (4) R 5s), the leading marks into St Mary's Pool, lower (Iso RW (vert) 2s), upper (Oc WR (vert) 10s), and the (Fl RWG 2s) sectored light on the outer end of St Mary's harbour wall. If the tide permits a night entry through Crow Sound is also now possible since the

Closing Scilly from the north-east, about six miles off. St Martin's is to the right, St Mary's to the left, Tresco in centre

Approaching St Mary's Sound, with St Agnes to the left – note the old lighthouse – and Peninnis Head to the right

Hats buoy (VQ(6) + L Fl 10s) became lit in 2006, along with Crow Rock (Fl (2) 10s).

Bound for Scilly from the South Cornish coast, you will most probably be making the passage direct from Falmouth or the Helford, a distance of just under 60 miles to St Mary's, or from Mount's Bay where it is about 36 miles from Newlyn to St Mary's. In both cases the timing will invariably revolve around the tidal considerations, and the need to arrive in the islands in daylight.

FALMOUTH BAY TO ST MARY'S

To carry a fair tide south and west from Falmouth Bay around the tidal gate of the Lizard, it is best to leave at about three hours after HW Falmouth (three hours before HW Dover). This will then ensure a fair tide for the next six hours which should get you well across Mount's Bay and hopefully clear of the mainland (see The Manacles to Land's End – page 175).

The rhumb line course of 270°T from a point about three miles south of the Lizard to Peninnis Head, at the entrance to Saint Mary's Sound, is a distance of 43 miles and will take you two miles south of Wolf Rock, which lies seven miles south-west of the Runnel Stone, providing a useful check on the tidal set.

Wolf Rock lighthouse is a slender grey granite column with a helipad and it can often prove difficult to spot, particularly if it has the morning sun upon it. Give the lighthouse a berth of at least a mile for, although the rock only covers a small area, it creates strong tidal eddies and heavy overfalls immediately to the west in bad weather. Traditionally, the Wolf earned it curious name from its voracious appetite for passing ships, and the first attempt to mark it in 1791 was a drole reflection of this. A 20ft iron mast was erected on the rock by Lieutenant Henry Smith, topped with a replica of wolf's head, its open jaws forming a sound box that produced a hideous wail as the wind blew through. As predicted, it vanished in the first winter storms and it was not until 1840 that a 46ft high stone beacon was erected by the Trinity House engineer,

James Walker, who later masterminded the present lighthouse, a magnificent feat of engineering standing 110ft above Mean High Water.

Although begun in 1862 using pre-formed interlocking granite blocks shipped from Penzance, the structure was not completed until July 1869 and was brought into service on 1 January 1870. Always regarded as one of the most difficult lights to relieve, in 1973 it became the first offshore light to be fitted with a helipad. In common with most offshore lighthouses, it is now unmanned.

West of the Wolf you will encounter large vessels emerging from the Land's End Traffic Separation Scheme (TSS). The northbound traffic lane begins four miles west of the Longships, the southbound lane half-a-mile east of the Seven Stones light float. Both lanes are three miles wide with a two-mile wide separation zone, and are marked on Admiralty charts 1148 and 2565. As with all TSS, you must cross the traffic lane on a heading as near as practicable at right angles to the general direction of traffic flow. This means that you must keep your vessel in full profile to the oncoming shipping with your fore and aft line at right angles to the traffic and not your track through the water. You must also cross the TSS as rapidly as possible; if your speed is less than three knots over the ground, motor.

In good visibility the islands will begin to appear as a seemingly arbitrary jumble of jagged humps along the horizon, very confusing at first and bearing little resemblance to what you are probably expecting. Initially you are only seeing the highest ground – closer-to they take on a more identifiable shape, but remain confusing as the overlapping effect makes them appear as one continuous land mass rather than separate islands. However, once you begin to identify the conspicuous landmarks, things rapidly slip into place.

The red and white horizontal striped daymark is on the north-east corner of St Martin's and should not be confused with the all-white lighthouse on Round Island, at the north-west corner of the islands. The pyramid-shaped island of Hanjague, just east of

The daymark, St Martin's

St Martin's, is also very distinctive, particularly in early morning sunlight. This and the rest of the Eastern Isles soon begin to detach themselves.

St Mary's is most easily identified by the tall television mast (FR vert) and the greater amount of visible greenery and trees. Approaching from the east, the sight of a prominent white lighthouse seemingly at the southern end of St Mary's can be confusing. This is not Peninnis light (a much more diminutive structure), but the old lighthouse on St Agnes immediately to the west of St Mary's. From this approach the two islands look as if they are one.

There are two main entry channels into St Mary's Road when approaching from the east – the northernmost via Crow Sound requires sufficient rise of tide as you will have to pass over Crow Bar (least depth 1m). This and the other shallows in the area tend to deter most first timers who generally opt for the deeper and better marked southern entrance through St Mary's Sound.

ENTRY THROUGH ST MARY'S SOUND
St Mary's Sound lies between St Mary's and Gugh/ St Agnes. Although nearly a mile wide, the navigable area is restricted by two groups of rocky shoals along its southern flank, the Spanish Ledges (least depth 0.9m) and the Bartholomew Ledges (least depth 0.6m), which effectively reduces the width of the sound to under two cables in places. Approaching from seaward, the entrance to the Sound is marked to port by the Spanish Ledges BYB east cardinal buoy (Q (3)10s) and to starboard by the small iron lighthouse structure on Peninnis Head (Fl 20s), which is fringed by low cliffs with distinctive and sculptural rock formations.

There is plenty of depth in the approach and in the sound, but care should be taken if arriving near High Water to avoid the Gilstone (dries 4.0m), which lies four cables due east of Peninnis light. When the rock is submerged, if there is any sea running, both it and the Gilstone Ledges further inshore are normally visible from the seas surging and breaking around them. Keeping all of Menawethan (the easternmost of the Eastern Isles) well open of Newfoundland Point, the easternmost extreme of St Mary's, you will pass to seaward of the Gilstone. Turn into the Sound once Peninnis Light is bearing just north of west. Immediately west of Peninnis Inner Head, the entrance to Porth Cressa is easy to identify – a long, wide inlet, with a sandy beach and houses at its head and, if the weather is favourable, many boats anchored within.

From here the long straight line of the Garrison fortifications mirrors the line of low cliffs forming the coast. Close inshore, the Woolpack YB south cardinal beacon marking the Woolpack Rock (dries 0.6m) should be left on your starboard hand. The red Bartholomew Ledges beacon (QR) identifies these dangerous rocks (least depth 0.8m) at the inner end of St Mary's Sound – leave this and the North Bartholomew red can buoy (Fl R 5s) on your port hand before curving gently northwards into St Mary's Road.

If there is much ground swell from the west, as there invariably is, the sight of the sea breaking on the Bartholomew Ledges can be intimidating and, with a wind of any strength from the east or south-east against the tide, a surprisingly nasty sea can build up in St Mary's Sound. The ingoing (north-west) tidal stream

Peninnis Head, with yachts anchored in Porth Cressa emerging on the left

The inner end of St Mary's Sound – Bartholomew Ledges beacon, left, and Woolpack beacon off headland, right

begins at HW Dover –0310; the outgoing (south-east) stream begins at HW Dover +0245 and attains a Spring rate of nearly two knots and about three-quarters of a knot at Neaps.

In quiet conditions there are no further hazards from the North Bartholomew buoy as long as you keep at least a couple of cables off the south and west side of St Mary's. Although Woodcock Ledge is covered 2.7m, in common with most of the other submerged rocky ledges in the islands it can be a serious problem if there is any ground sea running, when the depth can be much reduced in the troughs, and dangerous if the seas are breaking. To safely avoid the Woodcock Ledge, keep further out into St Mary's Road and do not begin to turn towards St Mary's Harbour until the anchorage is well open and you can see the inner end of the quay (see St Mary's Pool, approach from south, page 215).

ENTRY THROUGH CROW SOUND

Crow Sound lies between the north-eastern shore of St Mary's and south-west of the Eastern Isles. Although wide at its mouth, any approach is conditional on having sufficient rise of tide to pass over Crow Bar, which dries between 0.7m and 0.5m over much of its length, but has a narrow channel (least depth 0.8m) between its southern end and Bar Point on St Mary's. Watermill Cove, on the northern side of St Mary's, is a handy anchorage to wait for the tide.

When approaching from the east, if there is a sea running do not cut the corner past the Eastern Isles, but hold well to the south to avoid the shallower waters of the Ridge and Trinity Rocks. These can

often kick up uncomfortable seas and they break heavily in bad weather.

With the north-east going tidal stream, which begins HW Dover +0500, a race develops across the entrance to Crow Sound for a couple of hours and this can extend up to two miles offshore. In reasonable weather this seldom presents a problem, but with a strong wind against tide it can be dangerous to small craft. Races also form to the east of the Eastern Isles, off Menawethan and Hanjague.

Within Crow Sound, the streams are much weaker, rarely exceeding one knot at Springs, running (north-west) into the Sound for three hours from HW Dover –0100, then out of the Sound (east-south-east) for eight hours, beginning HW Dover +0200.

Once the Eastern Isles are well abeam on your starboard hand, you should be able to spot the Hats YB south cardinal buoy (VQ(6)+L Fl 10s) about a cable east-north-east of Innisidgen, a low and jagged peninsula which rises to a distinctive conical rocky point. Pass just south of the Hats buoy, but do not edge too close to Innisidgen as there are a couple of offlying rocks (both drying 1.3m). Instead, maintain a course parallel to the shore until the Crow Rock isolated danger beacon (Fl (2)10s) is well open of Bar Point, a long sandy beach backed by dunes and higher ground covered in trees.

You are now looking south-west down the full length of St Mary's Roads: Tresco, wooded and fringed with a long white sandy beach lies to starboard and in the far distance the two rounded green hills of Samson should be easy to spot. South Hill is the left hand of the two, and once Crow Rock beacon is centred on this you have the line of the deepest water over the bar. Crow Rock is steep-to and can be passed on either side; from here on the depths begin to increase noticeably as you enter St Mary's Road. If beating, beware of the Pots (dries 1.8m) and Round Rock (dries 1.5m), which lie nearly half-a-mile off the southern shore of Tresco. When covered, they can be avoided by either holding Crow Rock beacon on a back bearing of 029°T, or ahead by keeping the old lighthouse on St Agnes in transit with Steval, the low island on the distant westernmost point of St Mary's, to give a course of 209°T.

Entering Crow Sound from the east. Hats buoy is to the right and Innisidgen to the left, with Tresco beyond

Crow Rock beacon almost in transit with the summit of South Hill on Samson, left

PASSAGE FROM MOUNT'S BAY

A departure from Mount's Bay has the advantage of not having to worry about the tidal gate of the Lizard. However, to maximise on the tide, it is probably best to push the foul tide out of Mount's Bay for an hour or so by leaving about three hours before HW Dover. By the time you reach the Runnel Stone it should be setting well to the south-west, and then west for the next four hours, giving you a good shove on your way until two hours after HW Dover, when it will be running northwards.

To be able to depart at this time, you will have to be lying in Newlyn or moored or anchored off Penzance, Mousehole or St Michael's Mount as the tidal dock at Penzance does not open until two hours before local High Water (HW Dover –0635). If you leave then you will have a foul tide for the next three hours and a strong tide setting you south for a further three.

Scilly from the North Cornish Coast

WAYPOINTS

12   Cape Cornwall (2.5M west of chimney)
50°07'.62N 05°46'.43W
Longships (1M west of lighthouse)
50°04'.01N 05°46'.40W
13   Seven Stones (5M south of light float)
49°58'.61N 06°04'.33W
Seven Stones light float:
50°03'.65N 06°04'.37W
14   Seven Stones (4M north of light float)
50°07'.57N 06°04'.38W
15   Round Island (4ca north of northern tip)
49°59'.21N 06°19'.38W
New Grimsby approach (1M north-north-west of Hangman Island)
49°58'.48N 06°21'.62W

Eastern Isles (5½ca east of Menawethan Island)
49°56'.70N 06°13'.84W
Crow Sound approach
(9ca south of Menawethan Island)
49°55'.73N 06°14'.73W

From the North Cornish coast, Padstow or St Ives are probable points of departure, aiming for a landfall on the north-western side of the islands, most probably New Grimsby Sound (see Tresco pages 228–230 for approach and entry directions). It is about 70m from Padstow to New Grimsby, and slightly more to St Mary's. From St Ives the distance is about 40 miles.

If you are lying in the tidal basin at Padstow, you can conveniently leave about an hour after local High Water (HW Dover –0550) and you should then carry a fair tide along the length of the North Cornish coast and beyond for the next seven hours, after which it will become north-going from two hours after HW Dover.

From St Ives Bay, again leave an hour or so after local High Water (HW Dover –0605) and you will have at least six hours mostly favourable tide. From Cape Cornwall the direction of the prevailing wind will most likely dictate your course to the islands and whether you will pass to the north or south of the Seven Stones, a large group of dangerous rocky ledges (drying up to 2.9m) nearly a square mile in extent 14 miles west of the Longships and seven miles north-east of Round Island.

They are marked by a 12m high unmanned red light float (Fl (3) 30s 23M), anchored two miles to

Round Island lighthouse

Scilly approach from the north. Round Island, centre, with Men-a-Vaur to the right. White Island can be seen in the distance to the left

the north-east. This can provide a good check on the tidal set, although it is a lot less easy to spot than the lightship that formerly marked this reef, which attained international notoriety after the Torrey Canyon disaster in 1967. Whether bound north or south, the whole area should be given a suitably wide berth.

As with the passage from the south coast, you will have to traverse the Land's End TSS, and my preferred route is to hold closer to the coast and make a departure from the mainland a couple of miles north of the Longships, with a course to pass well south of the Seven Stones and a landfall on the north-east side of the islands. Here, depending on the prevailing weather conditions, you can make the final decision on whether to enter by way of Crow Sound or St Mary's Sound, or northabouts by New Grimsby Sound or the North West Passage.

NORTH WEST PASSAGE, BROAD SOUND AND SMITH SOUND

As most visitors will be arriving from the Cornish mainland, these westernmost approaches are the least likely to be used and, due to the number of off-lying dangers and strong tidal streams, they are best avoided by newcomers to the area. If they are to be attempted, good visibility and weather are essential.

The North West Passage, previously known as the North Channel on older charts, leads you in to the west of Bryher and Samson and the Northern Rocks, which have the smaller islands of Maiden Bower and Mincarlo at their extremity. In recent years this passage has been much improved with the strategically located Steeple Rock YBY west cardinal buoy (Q (9) 15s) marking this dangerous and isolated hazard, which almost dries LAT

just over a mile south-west of Mincarlo, and Spencers Ledge YB south cardinal buoy (Q (6) + LFl 15s) at the south-western extreme of the rocky ledges extending from Samson and Great Minalto. Once past the buoy, you have a clear run across to St Mary's, as long as you make due allowance to steer up clear of Woodcock Ledge as you close the island. This approach from the north-west is made on 127°T, and the black and white beacon on the islet of Tins Walbert (just off the northern shore of St Agnes), in line with old St Agnes lighthouse, provides a useful transit.

The far western approach through Broad Sound is made just over a quarter of a mile to the north of Bishop Rock lighthouse on a course of 059°T. It is probably the least enticing of all the routes into the islands, heavy overfalls occur in bad weather over the whole area north and south of the Bishop Rock lighthouse and numerous unmarked rocks and ledges, some just awash at LAT, create large areas of breaking seas in heavy weather or ground swell. The transit of 'the summit of Great Ganilly island just open to north of Bants Carn on St Mary's' is extremely difficult to make out at this distance. Care must also be taken to allow for the tidal streams setting across your course. Round Rock BY north cardinal buoy will be left well over on your starboard hand to clear the northern end of the Western Rocks, with the Gunner YB south cardinal buoy to port. Both provide a good check on the tide, which sets strongly across your track. You must then steer just to the north of the Old Wreck BY north cardinal buoy (VQ), from where it is a clear run into St Mary's Road.

Smith Sound, though deep, is narrow and fringed by many unmarked rocky shoals, making it a poor substitute for St Mary's Sound if approaching from the south. It should only be used with local knowledge.

Approach to New Grimsby from the north-west. Cromwell Castle, the moorings and Hangman Island are all in sight

St Mary's harbour, late season, with most of the visitors' moorings vacant just left of centre. Porth Cressa is to the upper right with Hugh Town in between. Newford Island is on the bottom left

St Mary's

Tides	HW Dover –0630
Range	St Mary 's MHWS 5.7m–MHWN 4.3m, MLWN 2.0m–MLWS 0.7m
Charts	AC: 34, 883, 1148, 2565, SC5603; Stanfords: 2; Imray: C7
Waypoints	See Mainland to The Isles of Scilly, page 204
Hazards	Pool and Bacon Ledges (lit). The Cow (unlit). No harbour offering all-weather shelter. Very busy in season
Harbour speed limit	Three knots
Overnight charge	St Mary's Harbour Authority mooring £15

The largest and most fertile of the Isles of Scilly, St Mary's is also the most populated, its inhabitants variously dependent on farming, fishing, ship husbandry, pilotage and most recently, tourism. A blend of sheltered wooded and marshy valleys, tight clusters of daffodil fields surrounded by high evergreen windbreak hedges and invigorating areas of bleaker, more windswept heathland, the island is criss-crossed with many deep-hedged roads. Although it would seem impossible to get lost in such a small area, the virtual lack of signposts makes inland forays very interesting!

The coastal footpath is one of the best ways to explore, the views are splendid and for 10 gentle miles it meanders past secluded coves, fine sandy beaches (frequently empty even in the height of summer), some memorable cliff and rock formations and a

number of outstanding ancient burial chambers.

Old Town was the capital until Hugh Town began to develop after Star Castle and the garrison were built between 1593 and 1594 on the peninsula known as the Hue. This was part of Queen Elizabeth's continuing development of the chain of coastal fortifications begun by her father Henry VIII in anticipation of a Spanish invasion.

Scilly became an important Royalist outpost during the Civil War. Prince Charles, later Charles II, was billeted in Star Castle for nearly six weeks during March and April 1646, while his escape route to the Low Countries was planned via the Channel Isles. In 1667, after 118 years of military occupation, the army abandoned Scilly and the bemused inhabitants lapsed rapidly back into their hand-to-mouth existence of

Approaching the quay. The visitors' berths are on the inner end, extreme left

fishing, farming, smuggling and reaping the heaven-sent rewards, as the increasing amount of shipping resulted in ever greater numbers of shipwrecks. Between 1745 and 1796, 750 men died in the seas off Scilly from this cause alone.

The bay to the west of Hugh Town offered scant shelter and the Old Quay was built in 1601 to facilitate landing and give some extra protection to coasting vessels which dried out on the beach to discharge their cargoes. When Cowper visited the island in 1893, he commented on the need for a better breakwater linking the shore to the outlying Rat Island, in those days home to 'an infectious diseases hospital containing eight beds'. The New Quay was built just after the turn of the century, not only linking Rat Island to the shore, but extending to seaward beyond, making it accessible at any state of the tide.

St Mary's has long been the base for the mainland link with the off-islands. In 1920 the islanders formed their own Isles of Scilly Steamship Company, and in 1926 the first *Scillonian* was built. Today the *RMS Scillonian III* continues the tradition of carrying visitors, vital supplies and the mail. Additional cargo to the islands is shipped into St Mary's by the Steamship Company's other vessel, the blue hulled *Gry Maritha*, from where it is distributed by smaller craft to the off-islands.

Visitors can arrive either by sea or air, but once in the islands, the colourful fleet of large open motor boats belonging to the members of the St Mary's Boatmen's Association becomes the primary form of transport. The Association was formed in 1958 and most of these sturdy waterborne charabancs were built prior to, during, or just after WWII, all of which are skipper owned, with each skipper being born and bred on St Mary's. The lack of a wheelhouse is no macho indulgence – their very special brand of eyeball navigation precludes any such interference with vision! Increasingly though, custom-built steel ferries and high speed jet-powered RIBs have been coming into service on the island links.

ST MARY'S, VISITORS' MOORINGS, BERTHING AND ANCHORAGES

Most first time visitors to Scilly in their own boats tend to make St Mary's their first port of call not least because the island possesses the only artificial harbour of any size in the islands and the knowledge that there are visitors' moorings in St Mary's Pool. However, there are several factors that can sometimes combine to make this option less attractive than it might initially appear.

Hugh Town – St Mary's Harbour – is first and foremost a commercial port, privately administered by the Duchy of Cornwall, which has owned the Isles of Scilly since 1337. It is the only shopping centre of any size within the islands, the only place where fuel and water are available alongside, and home to the largest selection of pubs and restaurants! The facilities are often stretched to the limit by the ever increasing annual influx of visiting craft and at the height of the season the moorings are usually very crowded – several thousand yachts visit the port annually!

The demands on the near-sacred ground of the Quay are particularly heavy – the outer end is used daily by the *RMS Scillonian III* between 1145 and 1630, and the various steps along its length are very busy prior to the 1015 and 1400 trip boat departures, and during the late afternoon when the boats return to disembark their passengers.

The quay is also much used by local fishing boats and off-island supply boats; neither their skippers, the boatmen or the harbour staff take kindly to finding it or the steps impeded by yachts. However, at the inner end of the quay there are now three visitors' berths which dry out on a firm sandy bottom, with adjacent power, water and access ladders. Only one fin keel vessel is allowed in each berth, but bilge-keelers can raft along side each other. They have proved very popular, providing there is not too much prevailing surge. When making your approach, it is useful to know that the depth at these inner berths is 1m less

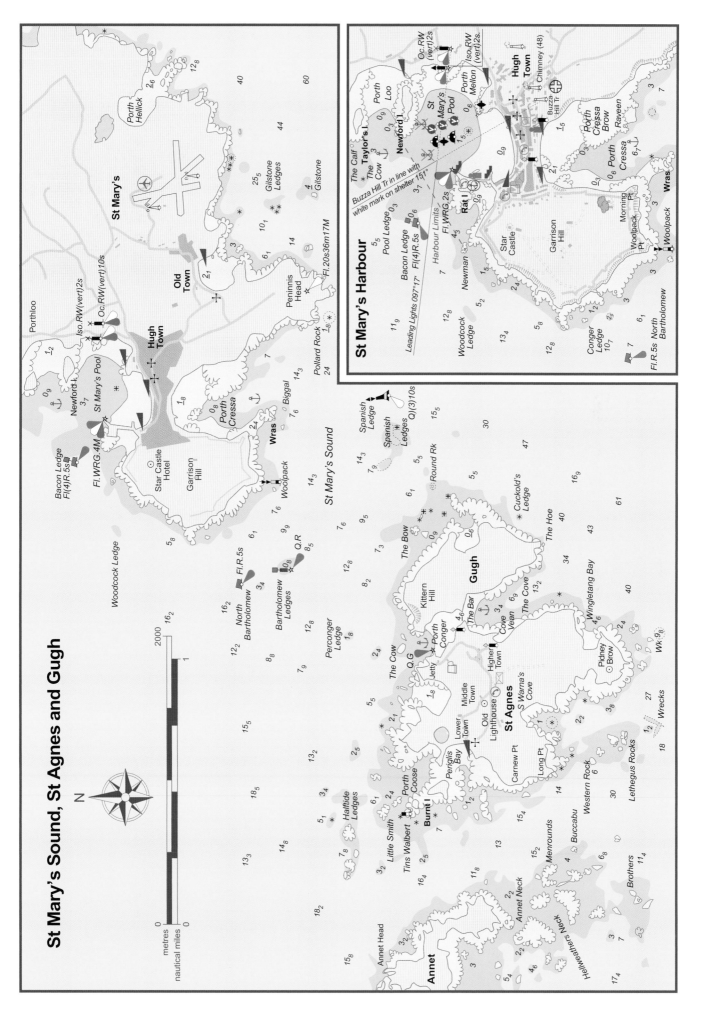

St Mary's Sound, St Agnes and Gugh

St Mary's Harbour

No anchoring is allowed in St Mary's Pool – the visitors' moorings are packed together and very exposed to the north-west. The *Scillonian* is in her daytime berth

than the depth showing on the gauge at the outer end of the pier head.

Normally, when the outer end of the pier is free of commercial activity, boats are allowed alongside between 0830 (0945 Saturdays) and 1130, or from 1630 to 1700 to take on water and fuel (diesel and petrol). Here again, there is but one simple rule of thumb to keep everyone happy – ask before you make any attempt to berth alongside – either contact the harbour office on VHF Ch 16, 14, callsign *St Mary's Harbour*, or hail the harbour staff who are usually evident somewhere on the quay and will always do their best to help.

The second problem is the harbour itself, which does not always guarantee the shelter or comfort that most visitors are probably anticipating.

The large inner part is shallow and dries as far as middle steps on the quay at Springs. The remaining area of water sheltered by the quay is entirely taken up with local moorings. None of these are to be used by visitors, even temporarily, and you should keep well clear of them – many have very long floating pick-up warps just waiting to ensnare the unwary.

The 38 orange and yellow visitors' moorings lie further to seaward in St Mary's Pool in six trots arranged with the 10 largest and deepest for vessels up to 18m to seaward in 2.1m LAT, and the remaining 28 for vessels up to 12m further inshore, with depths gradually reducing to 1.5m LAT. They have substantial pick-up strops and are more than heavy enough to hold most normal sized yachts in gale force conditions, although the degree of onboard comfort will leave much to be desired! At the height of the season, if there is not too much wind or swell, you will probably have to raft up.

Visitor mooring charges, per night, are £15 up to 12.18m and £20 for 12.19m to 18.27m – if you decided to linger and pay for three nights in advance the fourth night is FREE, a concession that does not apply to vessels over 18.28m, for which there is limited mooring availability at £30 per night, or to those using the drying quayside berths, which cost £20 per night regardless of size. A short stay – up to half a day – costs £8. The harbour staff will usually be out to collect dues in the morning.

Anchoring is not permitted anywhere within St Mary's Harbour Limits, an imaginary line extending from the outer end of Newman Rock (lies to west of quay head) north-east to the westernmost point of Newford Island. This is clearly shown on Admiralty Chart 883. There is also a speed limit of 3 knots throughout the harbour.

The nearest anchorage is off Porth Loo between Newford Island and Taylors Island, sounding well in to a suitable depth. If you lie too far to seaward you will find yourself not overly popular and subject to much wash from local boats coming through the fairway from the North Passage. If you anchor anywhere to the south-west of Newford, to seaward of the life-boat mooring or the large red Customs buoy, you will be in the ship turning ground and the *Scillonian*'s track when she uses the Crow Sound approach and the harbour patrol will move you on pretty swiftly!

Porth Loo and the visitors' moorings are well sheltered from north-east through east to south but this part of the harbour is very exposed to winds with a westerly component, particularly northwesterlies. It is also uncomfortable if there is any ground swell running from the west or south-west, as there frequently is. The anchorage in Porth Cressa, on the south side of Hugh Town, is then the most popular alternative, with shelter in winds from west through north to east. Watermill Cove, on the northern side of the island, provides excellent shelter from south through to west and is a particularly good retreat in strong southwesterlies, but here you are well removed from any facilities. The good news though – there are no charges for anchoring in Porth Cressa, Porth Loo, Watermill Cove or anywhere else along St Mary's indented shores!

The anchorage off Porth Loo is well sheltered in easterly weather

The 38 substantial visitors' moorings in St Mary's Pool are always popular

when there is a forest of masts in the anchorage that lies immediately to seaward.

At night, the lower leading mark displays an Iso RW (vert) 2s light, and the upper leading mark an Oc WR (vert) 10s light. At the outer end of New Quay, the white sector (vis 100° – 130°) of the Fl RWG 2s sectored light gives a clear passage past Bacon Ledge (Fl R 5s) if approaching from the north-west.

ST MARY'S POOL, APPROACH FROM SOUTH

The direct approach from St Mary's Roads is partially encumbered to the west by the rocky shallows of the adjoining Pool and Bacon Ledges (least depth 0.3m), marked by the Bacon Ledge red can buoy (Fl (4) R 5s). Here again, if there is any ground sea running, the potential danger of this hazard is much enhanced by the surge and seas breaking upon it. If the seas are breaking white on Newford Island and the shore to the north of St Mary's Pool, the moorings will be very uncomfortable and you should seek an alternative. Even if you are only intending to go alongside for water or fuel, you will encounter an uneasy surge along the quay.

The South Passage is straightforward and as long as you leave the Bacon Ledge buoy several good boat lengths on your port hand you can begin to turn in toward the harbour once the two sandy beaches of Porth Thomas and Porth Mellon are open of the outer end of the quay wall – the visitors' moorings and lifeboat mooring will now be clearly in sight and you can head directly for them.

Amazingly, it was not until 2000 that the Bacon Ledge was finally marked by the buoy, prior to that the leading marks were the only navigational aid to clear this hazard and, although they are now less critical than previously, it is still worth including them just in case the buoy is off station for some reason. Porth Thomas and Porth Mellon are separated by a scrub covered headland with a rocky foreshore, and careful scrutiny (binoculars are a definite help) will reveal the two leading marks, the lower, a post with large orange triangle topmark, and the upper, on the higher ground of Mount Flagon, a post with large orange 'X' topmark, just to the right of a prominent bungalow. These give a leading line of 097°T. They are not the easiest marks to pick out from a distance, particularly in poor light or if the morning sun is behind them. The lower one is particularly elusive

ST MARY'S POOL, APPROACH FROM NORTH

Approaching from the north, particular care should be taken to avoid the Cow, an isolated rock (dries 0.6m) 1.5 cables west of Taylor's Island, over which seas of any significant size will break. The leading line of 151°T between the Cow and the Bacon Ledge, known locally as the Middle Passage, has the Buzza Tower as the upper mark, which is prominent and easy to spot on the skyline, whereas the lower mark, a white-painted beach shelter with a white stripe on the roof by the Town Beach, is much harder to see.

There is a third approach into St Mary's Pool known as the North Passage, inshore of the Cow and to seaward of the Calf Rock (dries 1.8m) off Taylor's Island, using a white-painted mark on the eastern end of the Old (inner) Quay and a white-painted window on the triangular-shaped roof behind it. Unless you have seen these marks at close quarters and know exactly where and what you are looking for, I would not recommend the north passage for strangers – given the small distance saved, it is far easier to use the middle passage.

St Mary's Pool – Middle Passage leading marks, Buzza Tower with the white stripe on the beach shelter roof

For boats able to dry out, the inner end of St Mary's Quay provides the only berths in the islands where you can lie alongside overnight

FUEL, FRESH WATER AND GAS

Diesel and petrol can be obtained alongside at the outer end of the pier between 0830 (0945 Saturdays) and 1130, or from 1630 to 1700 by arrangement with Sibleys, Tel: 422431, and the harbour staff. Otherwise you can fill cans in Sibleys depot behind the Harbourside Hotel. Here oil, battery charging etc are also available, 0800 – 1200, 1300 – 1700 Mon – Fri and 0800 – 1200 Saturdays. Tide, and harbour office permitting, call VHF Ch 16/14 – water is available from the hoses at the inner quay visitors' berths, where you will probably have to raft temporarily alongside boats if the berths are already taken. There is also a public tap outside the harbour office. Larger quantities of water can be provided at the outer end of the quay by arrangement with the harbour office. Calor and Camping Gaz refills can be obtained from Island Home Hardware in the centre of town, while Sibleys has Camping Gaz refills at its depot on the quay.

ST MARY'S FACILITIES

As the only town in Scilly, Hugh Town, though small, is a busy, bustling place during the season, and even more so when the *Scillonian III* makes her daily appearance and the quay becomes a frantic mass of activity!

You can either land and leave your dinghy (on a good long painter) at the clearly marked steps by the inner end of the quay or, alternatively, anywhere on the beaches. This is often a far better ploy as the steps can become very crowded and dinghies can suffer if there is any surge.

Situated beneath the harbour office, the Harbour

Authority's showers (£1 slotmeter) are in four self-contained cubicles and open 24 hours daily. There are also adjoining WC facilities. Weather forecasts are displayed on the board outside the office while rubbish skips and a public payphone are located on the quay. The Rat Island Sail Loft is based here behind the Harbourside Hotel.

Wireless Internet is available in the harbour; call Tel: 07745 952707 to arrange connection. Alternatively, internet access can be found at the Public Library in Buzza Street, the Tourist Information Centre, The Boatshed Bistro, Tregarthwens Hotel and WiFi at the Deli!

It is but a short walk along the quay and past the Mermaid Inn to find all normal provisions within easy reach of Hugh Street, the main centre. Early closing is Wednesday, although most shops remain open during the season, including Sundays. They also tend to open earlier than on the mainland, usually between 0800 and 0830. The post office's hours are 0815 – 1630, but it closes at 1215 on Saturdays. The two banks – Barclays and Lloyds TSB – are open weekdays 0900 – 1600. Note that only Lloyds TSB has a cashpoint facility, although the Co-op supermarket, open 0800 – 2200 Mon – Sat and 1000 – 1600 Sundays, does offer a cashback facility.

Shops include two butchers – as well as meat Griffins also sells a good selection of seafood and vegetables – a newsagent, chemists, hardware store, nautical books/charts, several gift shops and a good mix of cafés, including a delicatessen/café with WiFi access. The pubs sporting appropriately nautical names – The Atlantic Inn, Bishop and Wolf, and the Mermaid

The dinghy parking area is clearly marked – it can get crowded at times!

– all do food, along with a variety of other places to eat, many of which specialise in local produce and seafood: try the Pilots Gig Restaurant, Tel: 422654, the Galley, Tel: 422602, Chez Michel, Tel: 422871, or the Blues Restaurant, Tel: 422221. Just out of town, The Boatshed Bistro, Tel: 423881, is right on the beach at Porth Mellon and Juliet's Garden Restaurant, Tel: 422228, on the road climbing up from Porth Loo, has great views over the harbour. Hotels like Tregarthens, Tel: 422540, or the Star Castle, Tel: 422317, are also open to non-residents.

Beyond the Isles of Scilly Steamship Office in Hugh Street, turn right into the Thorofare and behind the blue door opposite the RNLI shop you will find Southard Engineering, which also had the best stock of chandlery in the islands. Island Home Hardware in Garrison Lane is the only place in the islands where Calor refills can be obtained. Camping Gaz is also sold here as well as at Sibleys on the quay.

The Tourist Information Centre, Tel: 422536, is located in the main street next to Barclays bank.

Follow the footpath around the head of Porth Cressa beach past the public WC and you will come to that other cruising essential, the launderette, which does service washes only, 0900 – 1300 and 1330 – 1700 Mon – Sat. Alternatively Sibleys, which owns the launderette, can pick up and deliver your washing from the quay. Sibleys filling station is next door.

Heading out along the Strand around the east side of the harbour, you'll find St Mary's bike hire. From here, continue onwards and over the hill behind the lifeboat station, and you will eventually reach the Porth Mellon industrial estate, which might seem to be an unappealing sort of place until you enter the portals of the Porthmellon Stores. This unquestionably has the best selection of fresh vegetables and fruit

on the islands and much else to offer in the way of provisions, including frozen meat, beer and wines. If this is your only destination, it is far quicker to land on Porth Mellon beach from the anchorage. Nike Marine Engineering is also based on the estate. Right on Porth Mellon beach, in spite of the name, you'll also find the Rat Island Boatyard, which can undertake repairs, marine engineering and also rigging.

There is a fairly limited choice of things to do ashore, apart from the shopping and walks. In Church Street you will find the excellent local museum with the fully-rigged gig *Klondyke* as its centrepiece; those less inclined to use their legs and partial to the eccentric can opt for one of the entertaining guided bus tours of the island, but undoubtedly the best spectacle is the summer evening gig racing. Women crews race on Wednesdays, men on Fridays, usually starting at 2000 on the far side of St Mary's Roads off Nut Rock, and finishing off the end of the New Quay, which is an excellent vantage point. However, to get really close to the action, join one of the many trip boats which follow the race. Packed to the gunwales with screaming and fanatical supporters, this is one Scilly experience that you will never forget!

These elegant and racy clinker rowing boats are on average between 28 and 32ft long, with a beam of about 5ft. Once unique to Scilly, they evolved during the last century to take pilots off to ships, either from the land or towed behind the larger sailing pilot cutters for use as boarding boats in the open sea. Their fine turn of speed meant that they were inevitably used for less lawful activities. In an attempt to reduce the amount of smuggling, the number of oars was limited to six by the Customs, whose boats they would otherwise outrun. Nevertheless, they regularly rowed and sailed (with a fair wind they could set a lugsail and small leg o' mutton mizzen) across to Brittany to collect contraband. Their handiness and the skill of their crews was also crucial to the other major activity in

Most shopping essentials are on hand in Hugh Town along with a good choice of pubs

In northerly weather, Porth Cressa is a popular and free alternative to St Mary's, although much of the eastern side is encumbered by shallows and drying rocks

Scilly, saving life and salvage from shipwrecks.

The revival of interest in these fascinating craft began in the 1950s when the Newquay Rowing Club bought most of the surviving gigs in Scilly, including the oldest in existence *Newquay*, built in 1812, refurbished them and began to race them. This generated new enthusiasm for racing in Scilly, some of the boats were returned to the islands and new ones built, spurred on with annual visits by Newquay crews.

In 1986 the Cornish Pilot Gig Association was formed and led by prolific Fal-based gig builder, Ralph Bird, who finally built his 29th and last gig in 2007 before retiring. The sport has snowballed dramatically over the last 10 years or so. New gigs and dedicated crews, both male and female, have emerged from just about every Cornish port, there are nearly 30 clubs in the West Country and over 100 gigs, with a hotly contested calendar of racing events all around the coast. The highpoint, the World Pilot Gig Championship, is held in Scilly every Spring.

PORTH CRESSA

When the weather permits – wind in the north-west, north or east and no ground swell from the south – Porth Cressa can be a more relaxing alternative to St Mary's pool. However, although sheltered in westerly winds, if there is much swell it can become uncomfortable, particularly around High Water. Convenient for the town and free of any commercial

activity, this is inevitably a popular anchorage and it does get overcrowded at times. If you are lying at the seaward end of the bay, it is a good dinghy ride to get ashore at High Water on the sandy beach at the head of the bay, or a scramble through rocks and weed at Low Water.

Be warned though – with any hint of a wind shift to the south-west, south or south-east, or a sudden onset of swell from this direction, do not linger. Porth Cressa can become untenable more rapidly than you might predict, so seek an alternative anchorage at the earliest opportunity.

PORTH CRESSA, APPROACH AND ANCHORAGE
Although the entrance to Porth Cressa opens immediately west of Peninnis Inner Head, if approaching from the east, care must be taken to avoid Pollard Rock (dries 1.8m) 100m due south of Inner Head, and it is best to hold on more to the west before steering up towards the Wras, the isolated rocky island on the western side of the entrance. If approaching from the west, keep well to the south of the Woolpack beacon to avoid a rock which dries 0.6m just under a cable south-west of the Wras. Biggal Rock (2.4m) is a visible outlyer just south of the Wras and, once this is abeam to port, you can begin a gradual turn into the bay.

The appearance of Porth Cressa is very deceptive at High Water – there are extensive drying rocks all along the eastern side, the head of the bay, and the area between the Wras and Morning Point dries completely on big tides. If possible, a Low Water approach has much to recommend it as all the hazards will then be evident, notably Fennel Rock (dries 1.8m), which lies at the north-eastern corner of the large drying rocky base of the Wras. Approach with care, keeping the Wras about 100m on your port hand and steering about north-north-west. Ahead Raveen, a 4.6m rocky islet, marks the outer edge of Porth Cressa Brow (dries up to 4.9m) on the east side of the bay; once this is abeam on your starboard hand, you can begin to sound for an anchorage, with the depth beyond this point rapidly reducing from 6m or 7m to between 3m and 2m. Brow Breeze Rocks, which dry 0.3m, extend across most of the head of the bay.

Although a number of underwater cables are indicated on the Admiralty chart, these are well covered and not normally a problem.

The bottom is mostly fine sand and the holding once again is indifferent. I would not leave a boat unattended here on a single anchor for any length of time except in the very calmest of weather.

WATERMILL COVE

This remote and pleasant anchorage at the northern end of St Mary's, just east of Innisidgen (see Crow Sound and St Martin's chartlet on page 235), is often almost deserted. It is an option if you are seeking somewhere less crowded, and is also handy when waiting for sufficient tide to cross Crow Bar. Its greatest value, however, is as a bolt hole in strong southwesterly weather when St Mary's Pool becomes very uncomfortable and Porth Cressa potentially dangerous.

In common with all anchorages in Scilly, Watermill has its limitations and, in winds of any strength from much north of west, can become uncomfortable once the western reef covers, unless you are of shallow enough draught to tuck right inshore. However, if there has been a blow from the south-west followed by the normal predictable wind veering to the north-west, it is not difficult to run back down under the lee of the eastern side of the island to the shelter of Porth Cressa, providing there is not too much swell from the south.

Although sheltered in southerly winds, swell will tend to work its way in from the east, particularly around High Water, making it uncomfortable. Once the wind shifts anywhere from south-east

through east to north-west, the cove becomes untenable and dangerous. The coastal footpath to the west leads to the dunes and broad sandy beach at Bar Point, passing the Innisidgen burial chambers en route. The footpath to the east leads to the delightful beach at Pelistry Bay. Do not swim here when the sandy spit to Tolls Island is covered, as there are dangerous rip currents.

Watermill Cove has a fine sandy beach at Low Water, and from here it is a pleasant and easy 45-minute walk to Hugh Town. The best route is to take the footpath from the beach to the lane, turn right at the head of the lane, continue past the duck ponds and follow the road up hill to Telegraph (public pay phone), then first right once you have passed Telegraph tower. This leads down to Porth Loo – whence follow a sandy footpath across the head of Porth Thomas and Porth Mellon beach and join the main road into town. Should you intend to return laden with provisions, the Community Bus will deliver you part of the way or, alternatively, there are plenty of taxis.

WATERMILL COVE, APPROACH AND ANCHORAGE

If approaching from the south or east, keep well to seaward to avoid the outlying rocks off Toll's Island and, if nearing towards Low Water, be wary of the outlying rock shown on the Admiralty chart as just awash LAT, well to seaward in the centre of the cove.

The cove is most easily located by the prominent pine trees on the fern-covered hill overlooking the western side. Do not turn inshore until you have the sandy beach at its head on a southwesterly heading, but remember that at High Water Springs the beach is entirely covered. Alternatively, turn in once the distinctive sheer profile of Carn Wethers headland on the easternmost end of St Martin's is just open to the east of the conical island of Gt Ganinick to give a back bearing of 027°T.

Watermill Cove provides good shelter in winds from the south-west, a sandy beach at Low Tide and fine views of the Eastern Isles

Beware when approaching Watermill Cove from the west – the drying reef off Block House Point, left, extends much further than you might expect

Take particular care when approaching from the west. Keep up towards Hats YB south cardinal buoy and do not cut the corner off Block House Point, as the drying reef here extends much further to the north-east than you might imagine. Keep at least a cable offshore until the head of the cove is well open and you are onto the Carn Wethers back bearing. Nose your way in from here into a suitable depth – if you keep the highest, outer point of Innisidgen just open of the rocky islet off Block House Point, you should have between 5m and 3m at LAT.

Here the bottom is mostly sand and weed with some rock, so the holding is reasonably good. Closer inshore is a clear band of sand leading into the beach, fringed by weed-covered rocks. Although the shelter improves closer to the shore, the rocks limit the swinging room.

Avoid the wide south-eastern part of the bay, which is not only rocky but shallow almost as far to seawards as the small boat moorings in the south-eastern corner. Here there are some boat stores, an old gig house and small slipway which has a ingenious low tide, sandy approach channel dug through the rocks. Do not obstruct it though, as several locals keep dinghies here to access their boats moored in the cove.

Hugh Town, St Mary's Port Guide – Area telephone code: 01720

Harbourmaster: Captain Glenn Covell, Harbour Office, The Quay, Hugh Town, St Mary's, Isles of Scilly, Tel: 422768. Open 0800 – 1700 daily.

VHF: Ch 16; 14. Callsign St Mary's Harbour, office hours.

Mail drop: c/o Harbour office only by arrangement with harbourmaster.

Emergency services: Lifeboat in St Mary's. Falmouth Coastguard.

Anchorages: Porth Loo, Porth Cressa or Watermill Cove, depending on weather. Anchoring is not allowed anywhere within St Mary's Harbour limits.

Mooring/berthing: There are 38 visitors' moorings in outer harbour. Three drying berths alongside inner end of quay.

Dinghy landings: Where indicated at inner steps on quay. On beaches.

Marina: None.

Charges: On visitors' mooring, between £15 and £20 per night depending on size up to max 18.28m. Larger vessels,

limited mooring availability at £30 per night. Drying berths alongside quay £20 per night.

Phones: Public phone on quay and others in town.

Doctor: Health Clinic, Tel: 422628.

Dentist: At St Mary's Hospital, Tel: 422694.

Hospital: Tel: 422392.

Churches: C of E, RC and Methodist in Hugh Town.

Local weather forecast: Daily forecast, maps and outlook on board outside harbour office and at Tourist Information Centre.

Fuel: Sibleys, Tel: 422431, will provide diesel aboard alongside quay by prior arrangement with harbourmaster (0830 – 1130 Mon – Fri, 0930 – 1200 Sat). Otherwise petrol and diesel in cans from Sibleys depot on the quay or filling station at Porth Cressa.

Water: Available alongside from hoses on inner end of quay or in cans from tap outside harbour office.

Gas: Calor/gaz from Island

Home Hardware, Garrison Lane, Tel: 422388. Gaz from Sibleys depot on quay.

Tourist Information Centre: Hugh Street, Tel: 422536.

Banks/cashpoints: Lloyds TSB (cashpoint) and Barclays in Hugh Street. Cashback facility at Co-op supermarket, Douglas Chemists, and at several pubs and restaurants.

Post office: Hugh Street.

Internet access: Wireless Internet in harbour; call Tel: 07745 952707 to arrange connection. WiFi at the Deli. Landline access at the Public Library in Buzza Street, the Tourist Information Centre, The Boatshed Bistro, Tregarthwens Hotel.

Rubbish: Bins on quay.

Showers/toilets: Toilets and showers are situated beneath harbour office.

Launderette: Porth Cressa or contact Sibleys on the quay

Provisions: Most normal requirements available. Co-op supermarket open 0800 – 1000 daily, 1000 – 1600 Sundays.

Chandlers: Southard Engineering, Tel: 422539.

Repairs: Ask at harbour office.

Marine engineers: Southard Engineering, Tel: 422539; Nike Engineering, Tel: 422991; Rat Island Boatyard, Porth Mellon, Tel: 423399.

Electronic engineers: None.

Sail repairs: Rat Island Sail Loft, Tel: 423311.

Riggers: Rat Island Boatyard, Tel: 423399.

Transport: Daily ferries from St Mary's to Penzance (inc Sundays during August) and Skybus air connections to Land's End and Newquay airports, Tel: 0845 710 5555. British International Helicopter Service to Penzance, Tel: 01736 363871. Mainline rail connections at Penzance, Tel: 08457 484950.

Car hire: None.

Eating out: Good selection from fish and chips to pubs, restaurants and bistros.

Things to do: Museum; excellent walks and beaches; gig racing every Wednesday and Friday evening.

St Agnes and Gugh

Tides	HW Dover –0630
Range	St Mary's MHWS 5.7m–MHWN 4.3m, MLWN 2.0m–MLWS 0.7m
Charts	AC: 34, 883, 1148, 2565. SC5603; Stanfords: 2; Imray: C7
Waypoints	See Mainland to The Isles Scilly, page 204
Hazards	Many unmarked rocks and shallow ledges, Perconger Ledge, Cuckold's Ledge, Halftide Ledges, The Cow (all unlit). No harbour offering all weather security
Overnight charge	None

'With this Mark you run in amongst many rocks terrible to behold . . .' still serves as a warning to those who have the good fortune to spot the old lighthouse on St Agnes from afar. Closer to, it is rarely long out of sight, standing proud on the low summit of this gentle island, as it justly deserves, for this was the earliest offshore light to be established by Trinity House. The coal braziers were fired up for the first time on 30 October 1680. They, and the Argand lights that succeeded them, continued to burn bright until 1911 when the lighthouse was deemed redundant after Peninnis Head light was built. Despite the tower and its keeper's house now being a private home leased from Trinity House, it is still responsible for keeping this important navigational daymark gleaming white.

Although St Agnes and Gugh outwardly display similar physical characteristics to the rest of the inhabited islands, there is one fundamental underlying difference – they were never joined to the others, which were originally a single land mass until the sea levels rose during the Bronze Age. Leaving the waters of Scilly shallow and rock strewn, this gave rise to the legend that these are the last remaining fragments of the lost land of Lyonnesse, which once supposedly extended far west of Land's End. Even today it is theoretically possible, on big Spring tides (although in practice you would not have enough time), to make a Low Water circuit of most of the islands on foot, crossing via Crow Bar to Tresco and St Martin's, and across New Grimsby Sound to Bryher and Samson.

The inhabitants of St Agnes and Gugh form the most southwesterly community in the British Isles and, like the rest of the islands, their livelihood today is dependent on the tourist industry and a small amount of fishing, but sadly, due to the inroads of cheap foreign imports, increasingly less on the traditional flower farming. A century ago, the men of St Agnes were renowned worldwide as among the

The Turks Head pub overlooks the anchorage in Porth Conger, but it's time to be leaving as the wind hooks round to the north-west

A fine overview of the tidal bar between St Agnes, top, and Gugh, with anchored boats in the Cove and an empty Porth Conger, right

finest pilots in Scilly, capable of navigating ships from the western approaches as far north as Glasgow or as far east as Bremen.

This compact and attractive island is easy to explore in little more than a couple of hours. Its central part is a dense and intimate patchwork of flower fields surrounded by high windbreak hedges, in marked contrast to the open moorland of Wingletang Down to the south. Here, in an inlet on the rocky and boulder strewn coast, you might just find terracotta beads from a wrecked Venetian trader in the sands surrounding Beady Pool.

Castella Down lies to the west and here the Troy Town stone maze will catch your eye. Laid out in 1729 on the low clifftop by the bored son of the lighthouse keeper, it provides an impressive if chilling foreground to a very different kind of maze – the off-lying rocks bordering Smith Sound, Annet, the Western Rocks and the distant finger of Bishop Rock lighthouse.

This light was built between 1852 and 1858 by Nicholas and James Douglass to the design of James Walker, and the team of workmen were billetted on the small island of Rosevear, where the remains of their cottages can be seen. Standing in one of the most exposed locations in the world, in 1874 the lighthouse was hit by such heavy seas that the lenses were

broken, the structure was felt to 'reel and stagger', and the upper gallery was filled with sand! By 1887 the foundations had undergone major strengthening and the height increased by 40ft to 167ft (50.9m), making it the tallest lighthouse in Britain. In spite of this, in heavy gales, much of it is frequently hidden by the mountainous seas.

Periglis Bay, on the north-west corner of the island, provides a small natural but drying harbour for local boats, protected by Burnt Island and overlooked by the church and old lifeboat house which closed in 1920. To seaward of Burnt Island, there is a prominent BW beacon on the islet of Tins Walbert, one of the leading marks for the North West Passage.

Apart from two houses more reminiscent of somewhere on the eastern seaboard of Maine, the island of Gugh is virtually featureless. It is connected to St Agnes by a sand bar (except at High Water Springs) and is a heathy, heathery place with many rocky outcrops and several important megalithic remains, including the Old Man of Gugh, a 9ft standing stone, and Obadiah's Barrow. Today, some of the island's present inhabitants are likely to make a more immediate impression, as the southern end is home to a large colony of very aggressive gulls during the nesting season in early summer.

There are two possible anchorages depending on the direction of the prevailing wind and sea – the sand bar connecting Gugh to St Agnes normally separates them. This dries to about 4.6m and covers at Springs when there is a noticeable tidal stream from north to south through the inlet, making bathing dangerous.

Porth Conger on the northern side of the bar is sheltered from north-east through south to west, but exposed once the wind edges any further north. The Cove on the southern side is well-sheltered from west through north to north-east, except around High Water if the bar is covered, when fresh northerlies and north-westerlies can create quite a bit of chop. Although nominally sheltered from southwesterly and easterly winds, any swell will make itself increasingly felt, particularly towards High Water. In the onset of winds from the south or south-east, get out as soon as possible.

PORTH CONGER, APPROACHES AND ANCHORAGE

Approaching from the east, keep to the north of Spanish Ledges until the Bow (10m), an isolated island off the eastern side of Gugh, is abeam when it is safe to steer across for Kittern Rock (17m) on the northern end of Gugh. Keep about 100m off the rock and steer for the northern end of the Cow (St Agnes), leaving it several boat lengths to port to avoid the ledge extending to the north-west, before bearing round into Porth Conger and making an approach midway between Gugh and St Agnes. There is a short cut used by local boats in the narrow passage between the Cow, the Calf (St Agnes) (dries 1.2m) and the shore, which is best avoided by strangers.

Approaching from St Mary's, keep well to the west of the Bartholomew Ledges buoy and the North Bartholomew shoal, which breaks heavily if there is any sea running. So too does the Perconger Ledge (least depth 1.8m). If the visibility is good, the best plan is to use the leading line for St Mary's Roads – the daymark on St Martin's over the top of Creeb Island – until you can see the gap opening between Gugh and St Agnes. In the distance the Hakestone (2m) should be visible beyond the sand bar – if you keep this more or less on the centre of the bar it will give you a clear line in.

The deepest water lies north of the end of the jetty.

Sound into a suitable depth and anchor well clear of the few local moorings and the approach to the jetty, which is in regular use. Close to the St Agnes shore there is a rocky patch, otherwise the bottom is clean fine sand, although the holding is indifferent. South of the jetty, in what looks to be the ideal and most sheltered place to anchor, depths reduce rapidly and much of this flat sandy area dries at Springs, making it ideal for bilge-keelers or those with legs.

In a major project to upgrade landing facilities in the islands, St Agnes Quay, Church Quay and Anneka's Quay on Bryher and Higher Town Quay, St Martin's, all underwent a big makeover during the summer and autumn of 2007. St Agnes Quay was extended by 10m and widened by six, and given a new face and non-slip surface, plus additional strengthening on its western side. There is a light (QG) at its outer end.

THE COVE, APPROACH AND ANCHORAGE

The approach to the Cove will invariably be made from the east or north-east. If arriving from St Mary's, the safest bet is to exit St Mary's Sound to the north-east of Spanish Ledge buoy, and then steer south until Pidney Brow, the 13m hill on the southern end of St Agnes, is just open of the Hoe, the prominent rock on the southern tip of Gugh. This line keeps you in clear deep water past Cuckolds Ledge (dries 1.4m).

As you close the Hoe, which is steep-to, keep a couple of boat lengths to seaward and, once the Cove opens and you have the distant lump of the Cow lined up on the centre of the sand bar, you can steer straight up into the anchorage, leaving the Hakestone (2m) 50m or so on your starboard hand. The only real hazard in the approach is the Little Hakestone (dries 3m) on the south-western corner of the entrance – as long as you keep up to the Hakestone this is not a problem, the entrance is over 300m wide and there is plenty of room.

Chock-a-block! The Cove is always popular in westerly weather

In clear calm weather and once you have got your local bearings, it is possible to take a short cut to the south-west of the Spanish Ledges by using the transit of Steval, the islet off the westernmost extreme of St Mary's, in transit with Hangman Island in New Grimsby Sound. This gives a back bearing of 344°T and takes you close to Round Rock (dries 1.2m) and the Brow Ledge which extends east from Gugh. Do not be tempted to cut the corner, but keep on this course until Pidney Brow is well open of the Hoe.

There will invariably be other boats at anchor in the Cove, so sound in towards the head of the inlet and select a suitable spot. The depths reduce gently the further north you proceed, with a mostly sand and weed bottom and reasonable holding. Ideally let go somewhere along the centre line of the inlet as the shoreline is very rocky on both sides (but easy to spot by the weed), except across the head of the bay where the bar forms a fine sandy beach that is excellent for swimming. The bar should be avoided when covered as the current can run hard across it.

Avoid Cove Vean – the inlet on the western side – which is rocky and dries almost to its mouth on big tides. Although the Admiralty chart shows a number of underwater cables running out of the Cove, they are well buried and will not present a problem.

ST AGNES FACILITIES

The essential thing to know before you even set sail for St Agnes is that no water or fuel can be obtained on the island so make sure you have ample before you set off!

If anchored in Porth Conger, do not leave dinghies tied alongside the jetty, which is busy with pleasure boats late into the evening, but land on the sandy beach/old slip immediately below the Turk's Head pub, Tel: 01720 422434. A particularly convivial watering hole where bar food, including excellent home-made pasties and evening meals, is available, this pub was originally the Custom's Boat and Watch House which, according to the Isles of Scilly museum, 'has changed its purpose into a more customer friendly-use'! Close by, the island's 131-year old gig *Shah* lives in a gig house beside the road when the locals are not out racing her.

Anchored in the Cove, land by the St Agnes end of the Bar where the footpath leads up to join the concrete road. Turn right for the pub, or turn left and you will climb the gentle hill past Covean Garden Café, which is open for morning coffee, lunches and teas, and you will eventually reach the well-stocked post office, general store and off-licence, Tel: 01720 422364, which can cater for most normal requirements, including vegetables and frozen meat. There is not usually a surplus of bread, but if you are lingering here for a while they will order this (and anything else you might need including local pasties and newspapers) from St Mary's on a daily basis.

Continuing along the road towards the old lighthouse, you will come to a public phone box; alternatively, you can also find a payphone in the Turk's Head as well as further on in the old Coastguard Cottages, complete with its intriguing 'mistake', a lookout tower that faces inland! Here Coastguards Café serves lunches and teas. If you carry on along an increasingly rougher track, you will eventually reach the campsite at the delightfully named Troytown Farm, where fresh milk, dairy produce and island-reared beef can be purchased.

Looking across the Cove to Gugh. St Agnes can also provide some lovely coastal walks as well as a memorable anchorage!

Looking seaward, the dramatic entrance to New Grimsby Sound, Tresco, is guarded by Cromwell's iconic castle

Tresco, Bryher and Samson

Tides	HW Dover −0630
Range	St Mary's MHWS 5.7m–MHWN 4.3m, MLWN 2.0m–MLWS 0.7m
Charts	AC: 34, 883, 1148, 2565. SC5603; Stanfords: 2; Imray: C7
Waypoints	See Mainland to The Isles of Scilly, page 209
Hazards	Many unmarked rocks and shallow ledges, large areas between islands dry. No harbour offering all weather security
Harbour Speed limit	Tresco, New Grimsby Sound, six knots, dead slow in moorings
Overnight charge	Tresco Estate mooring £15, at anchor £5

Those seeking expensive works of art, bottles of claret, exotic shrubs and flowers, or merely an attractive and sheltered anchorage need look no further than Tresco. The second largest island in Scilly, it is private and unique in that it is leased from the Duchy of Cornwall by the Dorrien-Smith family, the descendants of Augustus Smith, a Herefordshire land owner who took over the administration of the islands in 1834. Assuming the title of Lord Proprietor of all Scilly, his beneficial dictatorship lasted a remarkable 38 years until his death in 1872 and transformed their prosperity.

Based on Tresco, he built the house known as Tresco Abbey as his main residence and immediately began to establish the Abbey Gardens for which the island is internationally renowned. Today, the 17 acres of south facing terraces are a botanist's paradise, with sub-tropical plants from all over the world flourishing in this unique outdoor location. Crew members less

interested in flora can ponder sagely on the collection of ship's figureheads and memorabilia salvaged from local shipwrecks housed in the Valhalla museum within the gardens.

On a wider scale, Smith did much to enhance the general well-being of the inhabitants and eventually managed to virtually wipe out the rampant smuggling to establish a well-ordered society. A fervent believer in education, he introduced the first compulsory schooling in the United Kingdom, established five shipbuilding yards and created a new industry – the cultivation of early flowers and potatoes – which have long been one of the commercial mainstays of the Isles of Scilly.

Tresco's economy today is based on the hyper-efficient management of tourism, and it even sports its own heliport with direct flights from Penzance.

Although there is still a small amount of farming, the majority of the old workers' cottages are now

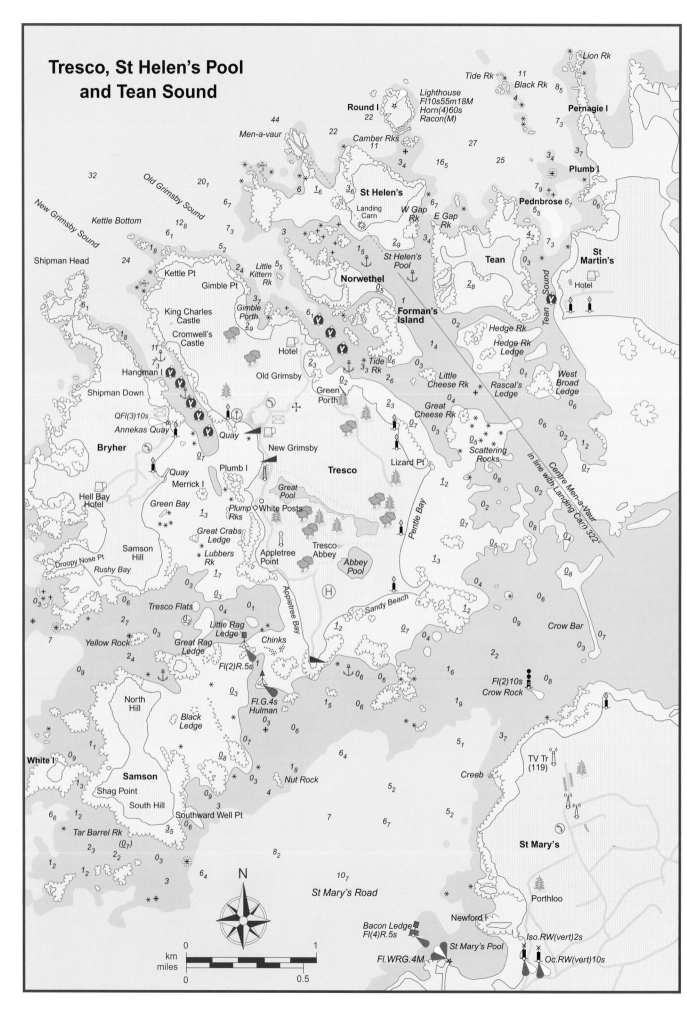

Tresco, St Helen's Pool and Tean Sound

Lion Rk

Tide Rk   11   Black Rk   8₅

Round I   22
Lighthouse
Fl10s55m18M
Horn(4)60s
Racon(M)

Pernagie I

44
Men-a-vaur   22   Camber Rks   11
27

34   16₅   25   3₄   3₇

32   20₁   Plumb I

Old Grimsby Sound   St Helen's   7₉   7₃   0₆
6₇   1₆   3₆   Landing   Pednbrose   6₇
New Grimsby Sound   Kettle Bottom   12₈   7₃   Carn   W Gap   E Gap   5₅
Shipman Head   24   6₁   5₂   Rk   Rk   St Martin's
18   Kettle Pt   2₄   Little   5₅   1₅   St Helen's   2₉   3₄   4₂   7₃   Hotel
Gimble Pt   Kittern   Pool   Tean   0₃   Tean Sound
King Charles   Rk   Norwethel   2₈
Castle   3₇   6₁   0₅   Hedge Rk
Gimble   2₉   1   Forman's   0₂   Hedge Rk
Cromwell's   Porth   Island   Ledge
Castle   Hotel   2₃   1₄   Little   West
11   Old Grimsby   0₆   Cheese Rk   Rascal's   Broad
Hangman I   3   0₂   Tide   3₃   0₃   0₁   Ledge   Ledge
Shipman Down   Green   3₃ Rk   2₆   Great   0₄   0₆
QFl(3)10s   Porth   2₃   Cheese Rk   0₇   0₆   0₂   1₂
Annekas Quay   Quay   0₂   0₇   0₃   0₅   0₇
Bryher   New Grimsby   Lizard Pt   Scattering   0₈   0₂
0₇   Tresco   1₂   Rocks   0₂
Plumb I   0₅
Merrick I   Great   0₇
Quay   Pool   0₈   0₄
Hell Bay   Green Bay   1₃   White Posts   Pentle Bay   1₃   0₈
Hotel   Plump   0₅   Crow Bar   0₇
Samson   Rks   Great Crabs   Tresco   1₂   0₈   0₃
Hill   Ledge   Abbey   Abbey   0₄
Droopy Nose Pt   Lubbers   Appletree   Pool   0₆
Rushy Bay   Rk   Point   1₃   0₆
1₇   (H)
0₃   0₃   Sandy Beach   1₂
Tresco Flats   0₄   0₁   Crow Bar   0₇
0₃   0₂   Little Rag   Chinks   1₂   0₇   0₄   0₃
Yellow Rock   2₇   Ledge   0₉   2₂
0₃   Great Rag   Fl(2)10s   0₈
2₄   Ledge   Crow Rock
7   Fl(2)R.5s   1   0₃   1₆
0₉   North   Fl.G.4s   1₅   0₆   1₉
Hill   Hulman   0₃   5₁   3₇
Black   0₃   0₆   TV Tr
Ledge   0₇   (119)
White I   0₉   1₈   6₄   Creek
1₁   Nut Rock   5₂
Samson   0₃   4   5₂
1₃   Shag Point   0₉   3   8₂   St Mary's
South Hill   0₆   7   6₇
6₆   1₂   Southward Well Pt   Porthloo
Tar Barrel Rk   3₅
(0₇)   0₆   Newford I
1₂   2₃   2₂   0₃   6₄   Bacon Ledge   Iso.RW(vert)2s
1₂   1₂   3   Fl(4)R.5s   Oc.RW(vert)10s
N   St Mary's Road   St Mary's Pool
Fl.WRG.4M

Centre Men-a-Vaur in line with Landing Carn 322°

km
miles
0   0.5   1

Tresco looking east to St Mary's: Old Grimsby Sound, left, with New Grimsby Sound, Bryher and Shipman Head to the right. Note the seas breaking on Kettle Bottom Ledge

converted into up-market self-catering holiday homes and timeshare properties, the latest of which, 'The Flying Boat Club' complex on the seafront by the farm beach, was completed in 2007. It takes its name from the old seaplane slipway in this corner of the bay built during the First World War when Tresco was used as a base for flying boats. This colourful medley of smart holiday homes enjoys spectacular views over New Grimsby and Bryher along with an indoor swimming pool, gym, tennis courts and members' clubhouse! On the eastern side of the island, overlooking Old Grimsby, the luxurious Island Hotel was the first prestigious development on the island and this, too, would not look out of place in a Caribbean setting.

Apart from tractors and golf buggies, Tresco is blissfully car free, although the few miles of road seem at times to be positively overrun by small children on hired bicycles, of which there are nearly 300! It is, however, a quite intriguing island of two very distinct halves, both physically and spiritually.

The south-eastern end is low lying, heavily wooded in the vicinity of the Abbey Gardens and has two large reed-fringed lakes, Great Pool and Abbey Pool, and a shoreline of magnificent white sandy beaches. The cottage-lined road that climbs the gentle hill between New Grimsby on the west side, Dolphin Town in the centre and Old Grimsby on the east forms a natural divide.

North of this, delightful walks along the coastal footpath soon take you back to nature in the raw, the untouched, windswept expanse of rock-strewn heathland, gorse and heather of Castle Down, named after the gaunt granite remains of King Charles Castle. Built between 1550 and 1554, this was superseded in 1652 by Cromwell's Castle, which was better positioned to protect the entrance to New Grimsby.

Walking the rugged cliff top around the north-eastern end of the island, you can search for, and hopefully find, the island's best hidden attraction – the cave at Piper's Hole. It was, until recently, much easier to find as there was a steel ladder leading down into a gully where the narrow, rock-encumbered entrance lies. The ladder has now been removed, but those who explore beyond the entrance will find that the cave eventually opens into a much larger inner chamber where there is a shallow pool, its bottom composed of a horribly glutinous clay. A torch, some candles and a complete lack of claustrophobia are essential for the successful completion of this expedition!

For the visiting yachtsman, Tresco is best known for having the most protected anchorage in Scilly – New Grimsby Sound – which lies between the western side of the island and Bryher. This long narrow passage is for the most part little more than a couple of cables wide and much of it is now taken up with the Tresco Estate's 24 visitors' moorings. In high season the demand for these is always heavy and the remaining anchorage space inevitably crowded, as it is the ideal base from which to explore both Tresco and Bryher.

New Grimsby Sound is perfectly sheltered in winds from south-west to west and north-east through to south-east. Although safe, in strong winds from the north, particularly northwesterlies, and strong southerlies, it can become very uncomfortable and rough with wind against tide, particularly at Springs. Nor too is it entirely devoid of swell and, like just about every other anchorage in the islands, it can be quite rolly at times.

Old Grimsby Sound on the eastern side of the island is the best alternative anchorage on Tresco and, although shallower and more exposed, in fine weather it is often quieter and less crowded. The Tresco Estate has seven visitors' moorings here. Depending on your position, there is good shelter in all except easterly wind directions, but it is prone to swell in northerlies. Due to the many unlit hazards, neither New Grimsby nor Old Grimsby should be approached in darkness by strangers.

NEW GRIMSBY SOUND, APPROACH FROM NORTH

Given favourable weather, the easiest approach to New Grimsby Sound is from seaward, by way of Round Island and the northern side of the islands. The soundings drop away fast and there are no offshore hazards more than a few cables from the main land masses, although if there is much wind or ground sea running from the west or south-west, the sight of seas breaking heavily along the rocky north-western shores can be somewhat daunting. The tidal streams generally run at up to two knots at Springs (and reputedly over four knots close inshore off Round Island), creating confused seas with wind against tide for several miles to seaward. Close to the entrance to the sound, overfalls can occur off Kettle Bottom Ledge from three to four hours after HW Dover.

Once Round Island is well on your port quarter, with the rounded humpback of St Helen's Island and the distinctive summits of Men-a-vaur abeam, hold a southwesterly course about a quarter of a mile from the shore and the northernmost point on Bryher, Shipman Head, will appear as a long, undulating and rocky promontory on your port bow.

This forms the western side of the entrance to New Grimsby Sound, so keep your distance off until you can see clearly into the Sound and can identify the two prominent marks within: Cromwell's Castle, a flat-topped rounded stone tower is on the eastern side of the entrance, and the pyramid-shaped bulk of Hangman Island (16m) lies slightly further into the Sound on the western side.

Though relatively narrow, the entrance to the Sound is deep and easy to enter as long as due care is taken to avoid Kettle Bottom Ledge (dries 3.2m), which extends two cables to the north-west of Tresco, forming a trap for the unwary who try to cut the corner. Normally, if there is any hint of ground sea, it is easy enough to spot from the ominous surge over it.

Once the steep western side of Hangman Island is

bearing about 157°T, it is safe to steer inshore, but make due allowance for the tide which sets across the entrance in excess of two knots at Springs, running east at HW Dover +0115 and west HW Dover −0510. Shipman Head is steep-to, and it pays to keep up to this side of the entrance before easing midway between Cromwell's Castle and Hangman Island in the final approach.

NEW GRIMSBY SOUND, VISITORS' MOORINGS AND ANCHORAGES

Immediately south of Cromwell's Castle there is a deep water anchorage with mainly sandy bottom, where depths range between 7m and 11m. Here two large yellow visitors' moorings can take vessels between 18.3m and 24.4m at £30 per night. Once Hangman Island is abeam, the depths rapidly reduce to between 3m and 4m. On the Tresco shore there is a prominent rocky outcrop, beyond which the rest of the 22 red visitors' moorings extend southwards along the eastern side of the sound. If there is no indication that they have been reserved and you are happy to pay the £15 overnight charge, just pick one up – they are all good for up to 15 tons, maximum 15.2m (50ft), no rafting permitted, and do not have pick-up strops. Most visitors are tempted to linger on Tresco, even more so when they discover that they will get the third night free if they pay for two nights in advance! Should you wish to try and reserve a mooring in advance, you can contact the affable harbourmaster, Henry Birch, on Tel: 01720 422792 or mobile 07778 601237. Normally he will be out to collect your dues in the late afternoon.

If you prefer to anchor, either let go to the north of the moorings, clear of them along the Bryher side of the channel, or further to the south, but here you must take care – beyond the cluster of private moorings the depths reduce rapidly and there is little more than than 0.5m abeam of New Grimsby Quay. The overnight charge for anchoring is £5.

There are also two underwater power cables, clearly marked on both the Tresco and Bryher shores by triangular yellow boards which must be avoided. Shallow draught boats can work their way closer inshore and anchor, although they will not be able to dry out as this is not permitted on Tresco except with the harbourmaster's prior agreement. Anchoring is prohibited inshore of a line from the end of the quay southwards to Plumb Island, as the quay is in constant use with trip boats and ferries and their approach must not be impeded. For this reason visitors are not allowed to lie alongside the quay except in very special circumstances with the harbourmaster's permission. All dinghies must be left on the sandy beach – you will find yourself very unpopular if you leave them alongside the quay or any of the steps.

If there are many boats at anchor, the restricted swinging room and convoluted tidal streams can

With good shelter from most wind directions, New Grimsby Sound has plenty of deep water moorings for visitors. Hangman Rock and Bryher are to the right

cause problems. At Springs they run at up to two knots from one hour before local Low Water to one hour after Low Water (HW Dover –0140 to +0140), and the flow is intriguing as the direction changes four times every 12 hours: south-east from HW Dover –0010, north-west from HW Dover +0125, south-east from HW Dover +0415 and north-west again from HW Dover –0340.

NEW GRIMSBY SOUND, APPROACH FROM SOUTH ACROSS TRESCO FLATS

The shallow southern approach to New Grimsby Sound from St Mary's Road is across Tresco Flats, an extensive area of drying sands, which seems complicated and almost daunting at first glance. However, as long as you do not attempt it on a falling tide and preferably wait until after half flood, it should not present a problem for boats of average draught. At Mean High Water Springs you should easily carry 5m over the Flats or about 3.3m at Mean High Water Neaps. For boats drawing no more than 1.2m this approach can be made with care from about two hours after Low Water, although deeper draught boats should wait at least until half flood.

When approaching from the direction of St Mary's, leave through the south passage and steer 340°T across St Mary's Road. The island of Samson, with its twin rounded hills, lies well away on your port bow, with Bryher beyond and the larger wooded bulk of Tresco, with its long sandy beaches, on your starboard bow.

The isolated Nut Rock (1.5m) is a useful and fairly visible outlier to the Tresco channel – leave this a couple of boat lengths to port. From here the Hulman Beacon, a rather spindly looking iron perch with a green triangular topmark (Fl G 4s), will be visible on your starboard bow – steer a course to leave this a good 30m on your starboard hand as the rocks extend well beyond the perch. On your port bow the Little Rag Ledge Beacon is another flimsy affair, topped with a red-painted radar reflector (Fl (2) R 5s). Do not steer directly for this as the beacon lies on the northern – far – side of Little Rag Ledge (dries 1.3m) so hold your course north-east beyond the Hulman, taking care not to stray too far to starboard to avoid the isolated patch of the Chinks Rocks (dry 1.3m). Keep a good 100m east of Little Rag Ledge beacon until it begins to come abeam to port.

It sounds and looks more complicated than it really is, particularly if you keep a good lookout and proceed with due caution. The water is disturbingly clear and as long as the light is good you will not only be able to see the darker areas of weed over the rocks and the clean sand beneath your keel, but even the crabs running around upon it!

Tresco's Appletree Bay, the long sandy beach backed by dunes on your starboard hand, is a popular daytime anchorage when the weather permits, but it should be noted that yachts are not allowed to anchor within 150 yards of the beach, and in no circumstances are they allowed to dry out on the beach as this is in the direct line of the helicopter flight path into Tresco heliport. Any yacht that is considered to constitute a danger to the helicopter will be towed away!

Once Little Rag Ledge Beacon is abeam and there is enough rise of tide, you can proceed directly across Tresco Flats. This large sandy spit dries up to 1.7m in places and extends nearly a mile westwards from Appletree Point at the northern end of Appletree Bay. In the far distance you should now be able to spot two distinctive rocky islands in mid channel – the left hand one, Merrick Island, is the lowest (2.6m), while Plumb Island (7m) is on the right. Further beyond, the pyramid-shaped profile of Hangman Island (16m) is quite unmistakeable. Keep Merrick in front of Hangman, on about 340°T, and you will avoid the rocky ledges closer inshore off Appletree Point.

However, if you are doubtful whether you have sufficient depth over the Flats, deeper water will be found by swinging more to the west once you are past

Tresco Flats from Samson Hill on Bryher. The dog-leg between Hulman Beacon, centre, and spindly Little Rag Ledge Beacon, left, is very evident. St Mary's is in the distance

Little Rag Ledge beacon. Ahead, Samson Hill on the south end of Bryher has two small summits; steer for the left hand one on about 302°T for just over a mile. Further away on your port hand, Yellow Rock is a small rocky islet midway between Samson and Bryher – once you have this abeam and bearing about 230°T, you can turn north-east. In good visibility the top of the distant Bishop Rock lighthouse over the right hand side of Yellow Rock gives a good idea of when to turn and the line of the deepest water. The bottom is all sand so if you touch on a rising tide you will come to no harm.

Little Rag Ledge beacon, New Grimsby moorings in distance and Cromwell's Castle, left

The only real hazard is the isolated Lubbers Rock (dries 1.7m), which should be left on your port hand. Two white posts have now been located in Cliff Field on the Tresco shore to provide a transit to clear Lubbers Rock – once they are in line follow the transit which will also keep you well clear of the Bryher side of the channel that is fringed by Little Crab Ledge (dries 2.4m) and Great Crab Ledge (dries 5.3m, just covers at High Water) – normally some of it can be seen as a cluster of rock heads. On the Tresco side, Plump Rocks, which dry 2.2m, are the only potential hazard. Once you have the small white-gabled building on the inner end of New Grimsby Quay just open of Plumb Island, you will be clear of Plump rocks and can then head up midway between Plumb Island and Merrick Island. With Merrick Island abeam, head straight for the lower end of the moorings to avoid the only other hazard on the Bryher side of the channel, Queens Ledge (dries 2.5m).

OLD GRIMSBY SOUND APPROACH, VISITORS' MOORINGS AND ANCHORAGES

With suitable weather and a quiet sea, the easiest approach to this alternative Tresco anchorage is, again, from seaward. Ideally, aim to make your approach soon after Low Water when most of the hazards will be easy to spot. Do not cut the corner off the isolated rounded rocky island known as Golden Ball if approaching from the north-east as there are several isolated off-lying rocks. As with New Grimsby, hold a course of a mile to seaward until you can see clearly into the Sound – the island of Norwethal on the eastern side is a good mark, as it has a very distinctive flat-topped rock formation at its highest point – and make your approach following the line of the Tresco shore, giving due allowance for the tide which can set strongly across the entrance.

For a first visit I would suggest visiting New Grimsby to begin with, and reconnoitering the entrance to Old Grimsby from the land. It is then but a short hop around the northern end of Tresco, taking care, of course, to avoid Kettle Bottom.

Once inside the entrance to the sound, Little Kittern Rock (dries 1.9m) is the biggest hazard and lies on your port hand opposite the entrance to Gimble Porth, the sandy bay on your starboard hand, which can provide a pleasant temporary anchorage in the north-eastern corner. Merchant's Point is the rocky headland at the southern end of Gimble Porth – aim to pass 30m or so off this and maintain this offing. In the distance, on your starboard bow, the prominent ruined blockhouse overlooking the southern end of Green Porth will soon be in sight on a grassy headland, with the long sandy beach and dunes of Green Porth running round to the small pier that separates it from Raven's Porth. Once this is open to starboard, you can anchor anywhere in mid-channel clear of the seven visitors' moorings (no pick-up strops), where there are depths of just over 3m, with a sandy/weedy bottom. As in New Grimsby, the moorings cost £15 a night and it will cost £5 a night to anchor, but you will not be visited by the harbourmaster – here an honesty payment is requested

Old Grimsby Sound and visitors' moorings, looking east. The boats on the right are anchored off Green Porth, with Blockhouse Point's gleaming sand beyond

which can be made at the Island Hotel, to coincide perhaps with suitable refreshment in the Terrace Bar!

The tidal stream can be strong here, up to two knots at Springs, running south-east through the sound for eight hours beginning HW Dover –0210, and north-west for the remaining four hours.

Shallower draught boats are able to edge out of the tide and closer into Green Porth where there is generally better shelter and less swell, but no anchoring is permitted anywhere inside of a line drawn from Long Point to Blockhouse Point and take care to avoid the underwater cable which is indicated by the sign at the head of the beach and runs out of the bay to the south of the quay. Leave your dinghy either on the beach or the quay; the long causeway at the northern end of Raven's Porth belongs to the hotel, is private and should not be used for landing.

If continuing further south, take care once Trafford Rock is abeam as the isolated trap of Tide Rock (dries 1.4m) lurks 100m to the south-south-west. To avoid it, bear over towards Block House Point once Middle Ledge is abeam.

PASSAGE FROM OLD GRIMSBY TO ST MARY'S ROAD

With sufficient rise of tide it is possible to exit Old Grimsby to the south and into St Mary's Road by following the Tresco shoreline beyond Block House Point. Cooks Rock (dries 4.3m), which lies about 150m due east of the point, is the only hazard. From here keep about 250m from the dunes backing the white sandy beaches until you are past Rushy Point, which has a post with a diamond-shaped yellow sign marking an underwater cable and, maintaining a similar offing,

continue to Lizard Point, keeping a wary lookout for Tree Ledge (dries 3.7m) on your port hand.

From here you should be able to see Crow Rock beacon and beyond, on St Mary's skyline, the high television tower. Keep these in transit to give a course of 160°30'T and hold this until Skirt Island, at the south end of Pentle Bay, the long sandy beach on Tresco, is bearing just south of west. At this point Cones Rocks (drying 0.8m and 0.6m) will be close ahead and with some careful eyeball navigation you should be able to detour slightly more to the east to get past and clear into the main channel at Crow Beacon. From Crow Beacon, bear away for St Mary's, keeping Steval and the old lighthouse on St Agnes in transit, to give a course of 208°T.

TRESCO FACILITIES

Tresco Estate, and in particular its harbourmaster, Henry Birch, do everything they can to assist the visiting yachtsman in the friendly and helpful manner that has always been their hallmark. Water containers

Always a cheery wave – the affable Henry Birch!

The New Inn, Tresco, where you will find good food,
a drink and a shower if you need one!

can be filled free of charge from the tap by the waiting
room on the Quay, where there are also public toilets.
Rubbish should be left in bags in the trailer behind
the building.

The harbour road leads past the Gallery Tresco,
which specialises in contemporary artwork mostly
by Cornish artists, to the bustling New Inn, Tel: 01720
422844, the island's only pub, where the atmospheric
Driftwood Bar was built with prime pitchpine planks
washed ashore during the winter of 1993. It is full of
photographs and memorabilia, boasts an interesting
selection of real ales and a good choice of bar meals.
Alternatively, you can choose from the extensive menu
in the quieter restaurant or the Pavillion extension.
Showers are also available (£1) – enquire at the bar.

If you continue along the shoreside road past the
Flying Boat Club development you will find Tresco
Stores, Tel: 01720 422806, which is open daily 0900
– 1800 Mon – Fri, 0900 – 1730 Sat, 1000 – 1300 Sun.
Without a doubt it's the most sophisticated shop of its
kind in the islands, but also one of the most expensive
too! There's a large and impressive delicatessen, locally-
reared meats, both fresh and frozen, and excellent
fruit and vegetables, including island-grown produce.
The choice of wines is equally memorable, there's a
wide selection of freshly baked bread, newspapers
and magazines and also the post office (0930 – 1600
weekdays, except 0930 – 1230 Wednesdays). The bike
hire shop is next door.

The Tresco Estate Office (0900 – 1700 weekdays, 0900
– 1400 Saturdays) is opposite the Tresco Stores. Ask
here for diesel and petrol, which can be obtained in
cans, or for laundry which can be done the same day
if you deliver it to them before 1200; they will also dry
washing if required.

From the Estate Office it's an easy 20-minute walk to
the Abbey Gardens (open 1000 – 1600 daily, moderate
admission charge). Here there is also a Visitor Centre
with a licensed café, history room and gift shop.

Continue up the road beyond the New Inn and a
brisk five to 10-minute walk brings you to Old Grimsby,

passing St Nicholas' C of E church en route. The
luxurious Island Hotel, Tel: 01720 422883, overlooks
the north-western side of Old Grimsby Harbour
and its Terrace Bar is open to non-residents for lunch
and cream teas. Depending on how full the hotel is,
dinner is often a possibility, but it is essential to make
a reservation.

BRYHER

Bryher is the smallest of the inhabited islands and has
a sleepy charm all of its own, much enhanced by the
interesting topography which gives the island its name,
being Celtic for 'place of hills'. Fishing, flower growing
and, increasingly, the tourist trade are the mainstay of
the small population, but with limited accommodation
ashore, it remains one of the least visited of the islands.

Like Tresco, it is an island of contrasts. Rushy Bay on
the southern tip is a delightful white sandy beach with
good bathing, the coastal footpath along the western
side of the island provides a panoramic if somewhat
chilling view of the Norrard rocks stretching away to the
west, while a foray over the tight turf of Shipman Down
affords a spectacular view of the aptly named Hell Bay,
and a wild rock-strewn path out towards Shipman Head.

Watch Hill, one of the highest points in Scilly, was
formerly used as a lookout for shipwrecks and has
some of the best views in the islands.

BRYHER, GREEN BAY ANCHORAGE

From the shoal draught yachtsman's perspective,
Bryher is best known for Green Bay, an attractive and
very popular drying anchorage with excellent shelter
from the south-south-west through to the north, and
probably one of the most secure places you will find
in bad weather.

The easiest approach is immediately to the north
of Merrick Island and south of Halftide bar, a higher
bank which dries 2.8m. Keep up more towards the
northern side of the bay and sound your way into a
suitable spot where you will dry out on a mostly flat
sandy bottom. Take care to avoid the drying Brow
Ledge and Three Brothers Rocks, which lie closer
inshore towards the southern corner of the bay. If
you land on the beach where the sandy track joins it
and turn left you will find Dan Bennett's boatyard,
Tel: 422411, mobile: 07979 393206, tucked away in the
bushes beneath the shelter of Samson Hill. He can
provide a shower (£2) and a laundry service. You can
use the rubbish bins and fill cans from the water tap,
for which he requests a small donation towards the
fund for a new Community Hall on Bryher. He also
has a limited amount of chandlery on site.

It is well worth continuing along the coastal footpath
for a short distance and then bearing off up the track
to the summit of Samson Hill to enjoy the great view
across Tresco Flats, New Grimsby and Bryher itself.

BRYHER FACILITIES

The promise of the grandly-named settlement known as the Town belies the reality, for this is little more than a hamlet where you will find the Vine Café and a public telephone box. Though limited, the facilities on Bryher are surprisingly good, not least the Bryher Post Office and Stores (open 0900 – 1800 daily, 1000 – 1500 Sun in season). Renowned for Mrs Bushell's superb home-baked pies, bread and pasties, no cruise to Scilly is complete without sampling them! The international code flags S-H-O-P make it easy to spot from the anchorage.

If you can dry out, Green Bay, Bryher, offers the best all-round shelter in the islands in a lovely setting. Note the extent of the drying rocks on the right

You can land in Kitchen Porth, or on the beach further to the south, but keep clear of the jetty on Bar Point, which is in more or less constant use. This unassuming structure is probably the most famous jetty in the UK – its high speed construction was witnessed by thousands of television viewers in 1990 when it was built as one of the many frantic challenges faced by Anneka Rice. It has done sterling service ever since and as part of the jetty improvements it was due to be extensively rebuilt and extended a further 12m in late 2007! There is a light (Q Fl (3) 10s) at its outer end.

The Fraggle Rock Bar, Tel: 01720 422222, Scilly's smallest pub, is open throughout the day with a good choice of lunches and evening meals (reservations essential) that are served both indoors and alfresco when the weather permits. Upstairs an attractive coffee bar with a splendid view also provides internet access.

Alternatively, follow the road up the hill until you come to the Vine Café, Tel: 423168, open for lunches

and cream teas as well as a set menu evening meal. Here again reservations are essential, preferably the day before. Continuing onwards, follow the signposts over to the Hell Bay Hotel, Tel: 01720 422947, in its spectacular setting on the western side of the island, with memorable views out over the western rocks. Here meals are available, either in the bar or the full works *à la carte* in the dining room.

There is no fuel available on Bryher. However, limited chandlery, rigging and mechanical repairs can be obtained from Blue Boats, Tel: 01720 423095, on the foreshore and a good marine engineer, Steve Hulands aka Bryher Marine, Tel: 01720 423047 or mobile 07786 235107, is also on hand.

SAMSON

Today, barren Samson is the largest of the uninhabited islands, its sole residents aggressive gulls and timid black rabbits. Burial cairns and ruined cottages are the only remaining evidence of the people who lived here, latterly in abject poverty, until the 1850s when Augustus Smith removed them to the larger islands and consigned Samson to cattle grazing and, briefly, a deer park. This proved a failure when the deer discovered they could wade across at Low Water to enjoy the lusher delights of Tresco!

The best landing is on the fine sandy beach at Bar Point on the north-eastern corner, where it is possible to anchor in settled weather midway between Puffin Island and Bar Point in about 1m, making a careful approach from Yellow Rock. This is very exposed at High Water and is not somewhere I would recommend for anything more than a daytime stop.

Self-sufficiency Bryher style!

St Martin's, Tean and St Helen's Pool

Tides	HW Dover –0630
Range	St Mary's MHWS 5.7m–MHWN 4.3m, MLWN 2.0m–MLWS 0.7m
Charts	AC: 34, 883, 1148, 2565. SC5603, Stanfords: 2, Imray: C7
Waypoints	See Mainland to The Isles of Scilly, pages 204 & 209
Hazards	Many unmarked rocks and shallow ledges, large areas between islands dry. No harbour offering all weather security
Overnight charge	Tean Sound Hotel mooring £10

The north and north-eastern side of the Isles of Scilly is much less developed and less visited. St Martin's has a small population, both Tean (pronounced *Tee-Ann*) and St Helen's are uninhabited, so for those seeking a quieter anchorage there are several possibilities, although the pilotage is more demanding.

ST MARTIN'S

Surrounded by extensive shallows and drying sands along its southern side and exposed rock-encumbered bays along its northern coast, the long narrow island of St Martin's has few anchorages suitable for deeper draught boats, with the exception of Tean Sound. Fin keel boats of moderate draught will just be able to lie afloat at Neaps in Higher Town Bay, whilst for those able to dry out comfortably the choice is marginally better, although very dependent on the prevailing weather. Although the bays on the northern side of the island look enticing, the numerous rocky ledges make this an area that should only be explored with extreme caution in settled weather – all of which is a shame, as the island is very attractive.

A backbone ridge of granite forms a distinct division along its length – the northern side is wild heathland edged with some deep cliffbound coves, in marked contrast to the fields and softer agricultural scenery of its gently sloping southern flank, with an atmosphere in many ways reminiscent of rural Brittany, an impression that is further enhanced by the presence of the St Martin's Vineyard and Winery, which overlooks Higher Town Bay. Established in 1996, it produced its first vintage in 2000, a medium dry white, and the vineyard offers tours and tastings throughout the summer 1030 – 1600 daily. There is a small visitor centre and farm shop.

From the holidaymaker's point of view, the magnificent sandy beaches are the main attraction, and the island has also acquired something of a reputation for arts and crafts in recent years, with several galleries and holiday sketching, painting and even paper-making

There's a magnificent beach at Higher Town Bay, St Martin's, but the anchorage is limited to boats of moderate draught or those able to take the ground

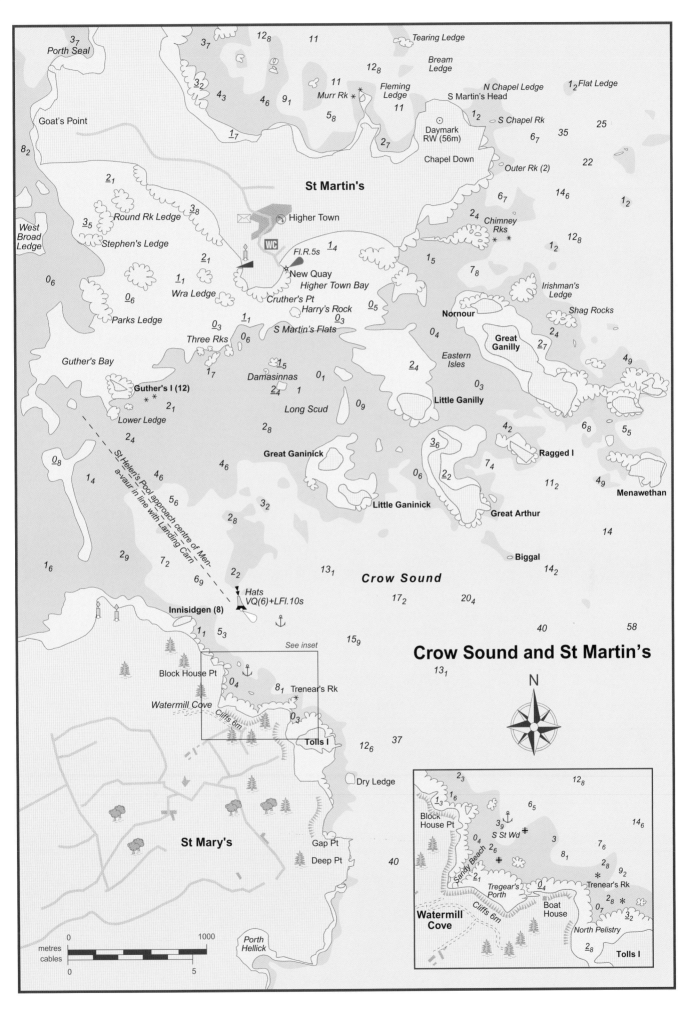

Porth Seal

3_7

3_7

12_8

11

Tearing Ledge

Bream Ledge

12_8

3_2

11

Fleming Ledge

N Chapel Ledge

1_2 Flat Ledge

4_3

4_6

9_1

Murr Rk *

S Martin's Head

1_2

S Chapel Rk

25

Goat's Point

5_8

11

6_7

35

2_7

Daymark RW (56m)

1_2

8_2

Chapel Down

Outer Rk (2)

22

2_1

St Martin's

6_7

14_6

1_2

3_8

2_4

Chimney Rks

West Broad Ledge

3_5

Round Rk Ledge

* *

1_2

12_8

Stephen's Ledge

2_1

Fl.R.5s

1_4

1_5

1_2

0_6

1_1

New Quay

7_8

Irishman's Ledge

0_6

Wra Ledge

Higher Town Bay

Cruther's Pt

Shag Rocks

Parks Ledge

0_3

1_1

Harry's Rock

0_5

Nornour

2_4

0_6

S Martin's Flats

0_3

Great Ganilly

2_7

Three Rks

0_4

Guther's Bay

1_5

4_9

1_7

Damasinnas

0_1

Eastern Isles

2_4

1

2_4

Guther's I (12)

0_3

* *

2_1

Long Scud

Little Ganilly

6_8

5_5

Lower Ledge

0_9

4_2

2_4

0_8

Great Ganinick

3_6

Ragged I

1_4

4_6

7_4

11_2

4_9

5_6

0_6

2_2

Menawethan

3_2

Little Ganinick

Great Arthur

14

2_8

2_9

7_2

2_2

13_1

Crow Sound

Biggal

14_2

1_6

6_9

Innisidgen (8)

Hats
VQ(6)+LFl.10s

17_2

20_4

1_1

5_3

40

58

See inset

15_9

Crow Sound and St Martin's

Block House Pt

13_1

Watermill Cove

0_4

8_1 Trenear's Rk

Cliffs 6m

0_3

Tolls I

12_6

37

Dry Ledge

St Mary's

Gap Pt

Deep Pt

40

Porth Hellick

Inset (Watermill Cove):

2_3

12_8

1_3 1_6

6_5

Block House Pt

3_9

S St Wd

14_6

0_4

3

7_6

2_6

8_1

2_1

2_8 9_2

Sandy Beach

Tregear's Porth

0_4

Trenear's Rk

Watermill Cove

Cliffs 6m

Boat House

2_8 *

0_7

3_2

North Pelistry

2_8

Tolls I

Scale:

metres 0 ... 1000

cables 0 ... 5

ST MARTIN'S, TEAN AND ST HELEN'S POOL

There are seven deep water visitors' moorings in Tean Sound off the white sands at St Martin's on the Isle Hotel

courses. The sailor, however, knows the island best for the splendid rocket-shaped red and white striped daymark, which stands 56m above sea level at the summit of Chapel Down, the north-eastern corner of the island. This was erected in 1687 by Thomas Ekin (the date inscribed on the tower is, curiously, incorrect) and it is well worth walking up to for the views from this bracing and expansive vantage point.

ST MARTIN'S, NORTHERN APPROACH TO TEAN SOUND

Tean Sound is a narrow but mostly deep passage between the western end of St Martin's and the deserted neighbouring island of Tean. It can be entered from seaward at any state of the tide, but the approaches require considerable care as they are fringed with rocky ledges, and I would only recommend it in fair weather, good visibility and with an absence of swell. If there is a heavy ground sea running from the west or north-west, seas can break heavily across the approach, particularly between Pednbrose and Pernagie, making it potentially very dangerous.

Ideally, try to time your arrival fairly soon after Low Water when most of the off-lying hazards will be visible, notably Black Rock (6m) and its associated ledges which extend northwards to Deep Ledges (least depth 0.6m) and southwards to South Ledge (dries 1.4m). Together they form a line of reefs nearly a mile in length, but it is possible to enter either east or west of this hazard depending on the direction of your approach.

From the east, give all of the northern shore of St Martin's and White Island a reasonable berth until you have Lion Rock (8m) abeam to port. Keep a good 100m off this and its associated rocks and gradually ease round onto a heading of 180.3°T. This course can be confirmed by keeping the tall television tower on the distant skyline of St Mary's just open of Goat's Point, the western-most point on St Martin's.

Once Pernagie Island (9m) is on your port quarter, you should edge more to port towards Plumb Island (13m) and its cluster of smaller islets to make sure you avoid Rough Ledge (dries 1.4m). This lies almost midway between Plumb Island and Pednbrose (12m), the prominent island immediately to the north of Tean which forms the western side of Tean Sound.

Keep about 100m off Tinkler's Point and about 50m off Goat's Point on St Martin's to avoid Thongyore Ledge, a nasty rocky shoal (dries 1.4m) on the starboard side of the channel.

From the west or north, keep up towards Round Island, taking care to avoid the Eastward Ledge (dries 2.9m) a cable to the north-north-east of the island. From here identify Babs Carn, a rocky bluff on the west side of St Martin's, which is easy to spot, and the small flat island of Pednbean (1.8m) which lies to the east of Pednbrose. This is more difficult to identify from afar, but Pednbean in transit with Babs Carn on 154°T gives you the best approach line, leading midway between Pednbrose and the Corner Rock (least depth 0.3m). Once you have Pednbrose abeam, steer more to port towards Tinkler's Point and the centre of Tean Sound.

ST MARTIN'S, TEAN SOUND MOORINGS AND ANCHORAGE

The deepest water in the anchorage is taken up with seven moorings belonging to the St Martin's on the Isle Hotel, Tel: 01720 422092, callsign *Santa Marta* VHF Ch 16 or 12. Visitors are welcome to use these free of charge if they book for dinner at the hotel, otherwise a charge of £10 per night will be made. Its good value Round Island Bar and Bistro, open daily for lunch 1230 – 1400 and supper 1800 – 2100, Tues – Sun, has fast become one of the most popular eating places in the islands. Moving up a notch, the gourmet Tean Restaurant on the first floor has stunning views across Tean and an even wider reputation, with a recommendation for a 2007/2008 Michelin Star. The Hotel can also provide visiting crews with showers and a tap for water containers, if you ask at reception.

Alternatively, anchor in the centre of the channel to the north or south of the moorings depending on the wind direction, but keep well clear of the end of the quay which is in regular use. Depending on your position, shelter can be found in winds from most directions except the north, and it can be exposed in southerly winds at High Water. At Springs the tide runs at up to two knots in the narrows, which often creates uncomfortable conditions with wind against tide and a risk of dragging as the bottom is mostly rocky, so a two anchor moor is definitely recommended.

In easterly or southerly winds, an alternative anchorage can be found off Porth Seal, between Plumb Island and Tinkler's Point. There are sandy patches, but also boulders and heavy kelp closer inshore and it is advisable to use a trip line.

ST MARTIN'S, SOUTH APPROACH TO TEAN SOUND

This approach to Tean Sound lacks any good transits, but is easier than it looks on the chart. Once you have had a bit of practice it is a good exercise in eyeball navigation – provided you have reasonably good light.

Make the approach at about half flood and steer 005°T from Crow Rock beacon until Broad Ledge (dries between 4.3m and 5.3m) is on your starboard beam. From here leave West Broad Ledge (dries 2.5m, but beware 0.7m outlier on eastern side) to port and John Martin's Ledge (dries 3.9m) to starboard, then steer up for the moorings in the centre of Tean Sound. Even if covered, both rocky ledges will be easy to spot from the weed over them.

ST MARTIN'S, APPROACH TO HIGHER TOWN BAY ANCHORAGE

Higher Town bay is sheltered from west through north to north-east and, although there are a few groups of rocks, with due care it is relatively easy to approach from Crow Sound, ideally after half flood.

If you have sufficient water over Crow Bar you can use the useful stern transit, keeping the Crow beacon in line with the middle of the distant jagged backbone of the Haycocks rocks on the northern end of Annet, which should give you a heading of about 048°T. This

No, it's not Antigua! The stunning view from the Hotel across Tean Sound visitors' moorings to Tresco

will take you well clear to the south of the distinctive Guther's Island with its twin flat-topped rocks and rocky outliers, leaving the three Damasinnas (known locally as the Sinners) Rocks (drying between 2.4m and 1.5m) on your starboard hand and the Three Rocks Ledges (drying between 0.9m and 0.7m) to port. Here again, a good lookout on the foredeck will be able to spot both these hazards from the large amount of weed clinging to them.

As you draw abeam of Cruther's Point and the small landing quay, wait until you have the two boathouses on the dunes behind the beach open of the end of the quay before turning inshore – this will clear the last remaining hazard, the isolated Harry's Rock (dries 1.2m) a cable south-east of the quay.

Anchor anywhere in the western end of the bay, but keep clear of the approach to the quay which is used by the ferries. Do not leave dinghies tied to the quay, but you can land anywhere on the beach. This was the last of the local quays to be upgraded in 2007/08, with new facing, widening and reinforcement. There is a Fl R 5s light at the outer end.

ST MARTIN'S FACILITIES

Do not be misled by the enticing prospect of three towns, for here again these are little more than hamlets – Higher Town in the centre, Lower Town at the western end and Middle Town in between!

Lower Town is where you'll find the popular Seven Stones pub, Tel: 423560, which serves bar meals and is open for evening meals 1930 – 2100. Middle Town has little more to offer than a public phone box. There is a surprise, though, at the Fire Station just before you reach Higher Town, for in the room at the back you will find a small heritage centre and a computer for public internet access! Higher Town Post Office Stores and Off-licence (open 0900 – 1730 daily, closed for lunch, open 0900 – 1000 on Sundays) has a reasonable selection of tinned food, frozen produce, gifts and books, and fresh food. Just along the road, St Martin's remarkable bakery offers an excellent choice of fresh organic bread and other delights, pastries, pies and tarts. The bakery now supplies most of the other islands too and if you're inspired to learn all about baking, it even runs special Holiday Baking Courses during the winter! Other facilities include a public phone, tea room and bistro crafts/gift shop.

No fuel is available on the island.

ST HELEN'S POOL AND TEAN

St Helen's Pool is an open roadstead fringed by Tean, St Helen's Island and Tresco. At one time this was the favoured bolt hole for larger vessels when St Mary's Roads became uncomfortable. On St Helen's Island there is a legacy from the days of sail; the small ruined building, dating from 1756 and known as the pest house, was once an isolation hospital for disease-ridden seamen. St Elidius' hermitage, the oldest Christian building in Scilly, and a small complex of excavated church buildings dating from the eighth to 12th century will be found nearby. Behind them a steep path leads to the heathery summit of the island from where there are spectacular views of St Helen's Pool, the lighthouse on Round Island and Men-a-vaur.

Tean was inhabited until the latter part of the 18th century and was a centre for burning kelp for fertiliser. The remains of the few small cottages can still be found on the southern foreshore. The island is voluntarily closed between 15 April and 20 July when ringed plovers are nesting.

The total lack of facilities and sheer isolation of St Helen's Pool are its main attractions, making it a quieter alternative to the more popular anchorages. At Low Water, when the extensive reefs of Golden Ball Brow are uncovered to the north-west, they form a perfect natural breakwater and the virtually landlocked shelter in St Helen's Pool is excellent. At the top of the tide, however, if there is any swell, you are likely to feel it and it will pay to look around for a more comfortable berth further to the south, either east of Foreman's Island or west of Old Man, depending on the wind direction.

The tide through the Pool follows much the same pattern as in Old Grimsby, running south-east at up to two knots Springs for nearly eight hours, beginning HW Dover –0040 then turning north-west for four hours.

There is, however, plenty of depth, usually ample room and the holding is good. Although you will certainly feel fully exposed to the force of the wind in a blow, it will not generate a great deal of sea and this, in many ways, is as safe as any anchorage in Scilly in such conditions.

For boats able to creep closer inshore and dry out comfortably, West and East Porth on the southern side of Tean provide excellent shelter and a fine sandy beach.

ST HELEN'S POOL, APPROACHES AND ANCHORAGES

St Helen's Pool can be approached from several directions. Firstly, from Crow Sound, which is shallow

East Porth, Tean, is quiet, well sheltered and just perfect for bilge keels!

but straightforward with sufficient rise of tide; or from Old Grimsby, again, shallow but easy with a rising tide; from St Mary's Sound towards High Water; and from seaward from the north through the passage known as St Helen's Gap.

St Helen's Gap is deep enough in itself, but the inner shallow bank between it and the Pool means that you will again need sufficient rise of tide. The tide runs strongly across this approach and it is both narrow (about 300m wide) and flanked by rocky ledges, which leaves little room for mistakes.

Personally I would recommend one of the 'overland' approaches for a first visit, you can then reconnoitre St Helen's Gap for future reference, or perhaps for leaving this way, particularly if you climb to the summit of St Helen's Island to take in the view (definitely best at Low Water), when you will be able to clearly see St Helen's Gap, and the narrow (100m) passage out to the north between the West (0.9m) and East (2.3m) Gap Rocks. Although both are visible at High Water, ledges extend beyond them for some distance, particularly to the north of the East Gap Rock.

ST HELEN'S POOL, APPROACH FROM CROW SOUND

The most straightforward approach to St Helen's Pool is from the south-east, from the Hats buoy in Crow Sound. Looking northwards, in the far distance, to the left of the gently rounded summit of St Helen's Island,

Approach to St Helen's Pool from Crow Sound, the rocky Landing Carn centred on Men-a-vaur's distinctive peaks

St Helen's Pool is a remote and classic Scilly anchorage that cannot be bettered in weather like this

Rock (dries 0.6m) and Diamond Ledge will be left close to port, so keep a good lookout. You will then pass midway between Little Pentle Ledge (dries 2.8m) and West Craggyellis Ledge (dries 0.8m). Both will be covered, but Great Pentle Rock (1.7m), at the western end of the Pentle Ledge, gives you a good indication of when you have passed these hazards.

Once Lizard Point on Tresco is abeam, keep slightly to port to avoid Tea Ledge (dries 3.7m), on which the weed should be visible, and then gradually bear round to starboard leaving Great Cheese Rock to starboard, Little Cheese Rock on your port hand and thence straight into the anchorage.

the unmistakeable pointed rocky summits of Men-a-vaur are the marks you now need – get the Landing Carn, a prominent lump of rock on the western end of St Helen's, in line with the gap between the two highest summits on Men-a-vaur on a bearing of 322°T. This will take you well past the distinctive Guther's Island, and more important, Higher Ledge (dries 4.0m), which should just still be showing, and holding this 322°T transit will take you safely into the anchorage, passing between the Chinks Rocks (awash LAT) and Hunters Lump (dries 0.9m). This is the narrowest part of the approach, so proceed slowly with a lookout on the bow.

Once the impressive bulk of Hedge Island is abeam you are entering the Pool, which extends for nearly a mile, with depths varying between 2.5m and 7m. If you intend to anchor close to St Helen's Island, beware the sandy spit (dries 2.9m) which hooks round to the south and west from the island, and sound in until the pest house ruin on the shore is bearing about north-east.

ST HELEN'S POOL,
APPROACH FROM OLD GRIMSBY

This is a simple bit of eyeball navigation, ideally undertaken from half flood onwards. It is easiest if you pass south of Lump of Clay Ledge (dries 1.4m) and leave Little Cheese Rock several boat lengths to port before heading up towards St Helen's. Little Cheese (0.7m) is visible even at High Water and when covered, the surrounding ledges are easy to spot from the weed on them.

ST HELEN'S POOL,
APPROACH FROM ST MARY'S SOUND

This is more demanding and uses the same marks described in the southern exit from Old Grimsby – St Mary's Old Telegraph tower in transit with Crow Rock Beacon, 162°T as a back bearing. On this the Cones

ST HELEN'S POOL, NORTHERN
APPROACH THROUGH GAP ROCKS

Approaching from seaward keep up to Round Island, leaving it 200 – 300m to starboard, and then steer to leave Didleys Point, the eastern end of St Helen's, about 100m to starboard. The Gap Rocks should be clearly visible from here – steer to leave the West Gap Rock on your starboard hand until you are almost abeam of the East Gap Rock, at which point you should ease more to port, passing midway between the two. Keep this course to the south-south-west and do not be tempted to haul round too rapidly into the Pool or you will fall foul of the sand spit (dries 2.9m), which extends a good 200m from the island shore.

THE EASTERN ISLES

With calm weather and good visibility, Admiralty chart 883 and considerable care, the more adventurous can make an interesting foray amongst the Eastern Isles. They offer a number of temporary daytime anchorages, depending on the prevailing conditions, and the chance of seeing a few seals along the way, particularly in the vicinity of Menawethan. It is, however, not an area I would recommend for an overnight stop other than in exceptionally settled weather.

The easiest approach is south of Biggal and to the east of Ragged Island, keeping over to the west side of Great Ganilly. There are several passage graves on the Arthurs, but Nornour is probably the most interesting of these now deserted islands for here, along the southern edge of the island, you will find the impressive excavated Bronze Age settlement for which the island is famous.

Isles of Scilly – Anchorages at a glance

Wind from	Shelter options	Comment
North	St Mary's Pool	Reasonable, if closer inshore
	Porth Cressa	Very good
	New Grimsby	Good, but prone to swell
	Old Grimsby	Good
	St Helen's Pool	Good in lee of St Helen's
	The Cove	Very good, except when bar covered at High Water
North-east	St Mary's Pool	Very good
	Porth Cressa	Very good
	New Grimsby	Very good
	Old Grimsby	Good, but prone to swell at High Water
	Porth Conger	Good, if well in
	The Cove	Good
	St Helen's Pool	Good in lee of Old Man
	Tean Sound	Good at south end
East	St Mary's Pool	Very good
	Porth Cressa	Very good
	Porth Conger	Very good
	The Cove	Good
South-east	St Mary's Pool	Very good
	New Grimsby	Good
	Porth Conger	Very good, except at High Water if bar covered
	Tean Sound	Good at northern end
South	St Mary's Pool	Very good
	Watermill Cove	Very good, but possible swell around High Water
	Porth Conger	Very good except at High Water if bar covered
	Old Grimsby	Good
	New Grimsby	Good, except near High Water, wind against tide
	St Helen's Pool	Good
South-west	New Grimsby	Good, particularly at north end
	Old Grimsby	Very good
	Watermill Cove	Very good, but possible swell at High Water unless well in
	Porth Conger	Very good
	The Cove	Good, if well in, but subject to swell
	St Helen's Pool	Good
West	New Grimsby	Very good
	Old Grimsby	Very good
	Watermill Cove	Very good, if well in
	Porth Cressa	Good, if well in, but subject to swell at High Water
	Porth Conger	Reasonable, if well in
	The Cove	Very good
	Tean Sound	Good
	St Helen's Pool	Good in lee of Norwethal
North-west	Porth Cressa	Very good
	The Cove	Very good
	Old Grimsby	Good, if well in
	St Helen's Pool	Good, but swell likely around High Water. Best towards south end of pool

Land's End looking north to Cape Cornwall. The Brisons are on the left

Chapter six
Land's End to Pentire Point

FAVOURABLE TIDAL STREAMS
Land's End
Bound west/north: One hour after HW Dover
Bound south/east: hours before HW Dover

PASSAGE CHARTS
AC: 2565 St Agnes Head to Dodman Point
          1148 Isles of Scilly to Land's End
          1149 Pendeen to Trevose Head
          1156 Trevose Head to Hartland Point
          1168 Harbours on the North Coast
          of Cornwall
          SC5603 is particularly useful
Imray: C7 Falmouth to Isles of Scilly &
          Trevose Head
          C58 Trevose Head to Bull Point
Stanfords: 2

SAFETY INFORMATION AND WEATHER
Falmouth Coastguard makes initial announcement
on VHF Channel 16 at 0110, 0410, 0710, 1010, 1610,
1910, 2210 Local Time, to confirm working channel for
broadcast, normally VHF Channel 84.

Cape Cornwall NCI station Tel: 01736 787890
St Ives NCI station Tel: 01736 799398
Stepper Point NCI station Tel: 07810 898041

WAYPOINTS
1	**Longships (1M west of lighthouse)**	
	50°04'.01N 05°46'.40W	
2	**Cape Cornwall**	
	(2.5M west of chimney)	
	50°07'.62N 05°46'.43W	
3	**Pendeen**	
	(1.5M north-west of lighthouse)	
	50°10'.98N 05°42'.02W	
	St Ives (West Pier head)	
	50°12'.78N 05 28'.73W	
	Stones buoy	
	50°15'·64N 05 25'.47W	
	Newquay (North Pier head)	
	50°25'.08N 05°05'.19W	
4	**Trevose Head**	
	(2M west of lighthouse)	
	50°32'.96N 05°05'.33W	
	Padstow (just off St Saviour's Point)	
	50°32'.75N 04°55'.92W	

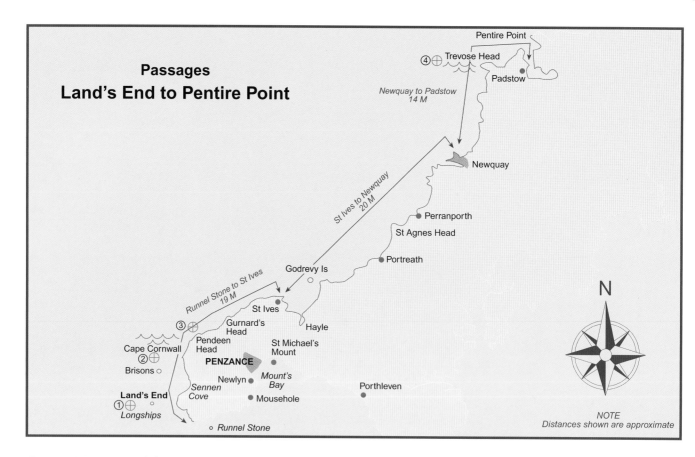

Passages
Land's End to Pentire Point

Pentire Point
④ ⊕ Trevose Head
Padstow
Newquay to Padstow
14 M

Newquay

St Ives to Newquay
20 M

Perranporth
St Agnes Head
Portreath

Godrevy Is
St Ives
Runnel Stone to St Ives
19 M
Gurnard's Head
Hayle
Pendeen Head
St Michael's Mount
Cape Cornwall
② ⊕
PENZANCE
Brisons ○
Newlyn
Mount's Bay
Sennen Cove
Porthleven
Land's End
① ⊕
Mousehole
Longships
○ *Runnel Stone*

N

NOTE
Distances shown are approximate

③ ⊕

As a cruising ground there is, sadly, little to recommend the North Cornish coast. In the prevailing southwesterly winds it presents an exposed and rugged lee shore with just a few drying harbours that cannot be guaranteed as places of refuge – an unwholesome combination and a natural deterrent for pleasure boating. Rounding Land's End and bound up the Irish Sea, your course will soon take you well away from the coast, an offing that you should endeavour to maintain.

Although there is little real cruising potential on this dangerous stretch of coast, it has become increasingly used by yachts on passage to and from South Wales and the Bristol Channel to the Isles of Scilly and the West Country during the summer months. Most would, I'm sure, agree that it is an area they try to pass through as quickly as possible, waiting for the right conditions, and completing it in one leg. However, there will obviously be occasions when circumstances dictate a need to put in somewhere, or when in very settled weather and an offshore wind, a little bit of cruising can be contemplated, and it is for this reason that this short passage section is included.

LAND'S END TO ST IVES BAY

Land's End, the most westerly point in England, is not a particularly distinctive headland, being somewhat lost against the rest of this noble stretch of pinkish grey granite cliffs which rise to over 70m along one of the most rugged sections of coast in southern England. The prominent white Land's End Hotel and other buildings are all part of the privately-owned Land's End tourist complex, and further to the north the famous First and Last House in England is high on the cliff top.

A mile offshore, and guarded by the grey, lonely finger of the prominent Longships lighthouse (Fl (2) WR 10s W15/R13M) topped with its precarious helicopter landing pad, this infamous reef has claimed many ships. The tidal streams are strong and unpredictable in its vicinity; although the north-going flood begins one hour after HW Dover, it does not turn north-east along the north Cornish coast until two hours later, attaining over two knots at Springs. Five hours before HW Dover, the ebb begins to run south-west back along the coast.

In daylight, settled conditions, good visibility and an absence of ground swell, the inshore passage between the Longships and the mainland can sometimes provide a useful short cut. Pass a quarter of a mile to seaward of Land's End, from where the Brisons, two conspicuous rocky islands to the north, provide the best transit. The highest point of the highest island (27m) should be kept just open to the west of the highest point of the low island (22m), a bearing of 001°T. Kettle's Bottom, forming the inshore, easternmost extremity of the Longships rocks, dries 5.2m, and Shark's Fin, the most northerly reef, dries 3.2m. With jagged rocks and breaking water to seaward, even on a fine day this is an uncomfortable stretch of water where you will feel little inclined to linger!

On the normal passage to the west of the Longships, give the whole area a good berth, and bound up the coast maintain a course well north of east for just over a mile to clear the Shark's Fin. At night, the north-

The Longships looking east to Land's End with seas breaking on Kettle's Bottom, centre. The inshore passage lies between this rock and the mainland

eastern red sector of the Longships covers all hazards along this section of coast and should not be entered until Pendeen lighthouse opens up.

The large sandy sweep of Whitesand Bay forms a break in the cliffs, and the village and tiny harbour of Sennen Cove will be seen at its southern end with its lifeboat house, the most southwesterly station in England. It was here in 1794/95 that Samuel Wyatt, the Trinity House architect, assembled, numbered and shipped the granite blocks to Carn Bras Rock to build the first Longships lighthouse, which was replaced in 1873 with the present structure by Sir James Douglass.

The keepers were often stranded here during winter storms and in 1966 it was one of the first lighthouses to receive much needed supplies by helicopter, the lantern house windows padded out with mattresses in case the rotors touched!

There is a fair weather anchorage in offshore winds just off Sennen village, inside the Cowloe Rocks, but this is very exposed and cannot be recommended. Passing to the north of the Brisons the tidal streams run strongly past Cape Cornwall, a distinctive, cone-shaped headland, uniquely, the only cape in England. Topped by a conspicuous ruined chimney, this is one of the first indications of the extensive mining operations that once covered this stretch of coast. For the next 10 miles, the cliffs are dotted with old pumping houses, chimneys and other buildings, from which the underground workings extended far beneath the sea bed, in places

well over a mile out into the Atlantic. Cape Cornwall also has an NCI lookout, Tel: 01736 787890.

The Vyneck is an isolated rock three cables north-west of Cape Cornwall – from here on a course a mile to seaward will clear all hazards except the overfalls which extend westwards from Pendeen Head, a bold headland. On it, the squat white lighthouse of Pendeen Watch (Fl (4) 15s 16M) looks out over the Wra, or Three Stone Oar, a group of small rocky islands just under a half mile offshore.

The coast follows a northeasterly direction from here on, a continuous unbroken line of impenetrable granite cliffs which have long been one of the major sea cliff climbing centres in England. Along it, and in the approaches to St Ives Bay, a good lookout should be kept for pot and net buoys; in spite of the exposure of this coast, it is much worked by local boats.

ST IVES BAY TO TREVOSE HEAD

The drying fishing harbour of St Ives is tucked in behind St Ives Head at the south-western corner of this four mile-wide bay. There are drying moorings for visitors within the harbour; deeper draught vessels can anchor off in suitable offshore weather. An NCI station is located on St Ives Head, Tel: 01736 799398; www.nci-stives.org, which has a useful webcam for visual appraisal of prevailing wind and sea conditions.

The rest of St Ives Bay is backed by the long sandy beach and extensive dunes of Hayle Towans, which stretch away to its far northern end where the lighthouse (Fl WR 10s W12M R9M) on Godrevy Island lies close inshore. Built in 1859, this was always a controversial siting for it gives little indication of the notorious reef, the Stones, which extends nearly a mile to the north-west of the island. A lightship or lighthouse on the outermost rock was the favoured option, but was turned down because of the cost. An area of strong currents and drying rocks, many awash at High Water, their outer limit is marked today by the Stones BY north cardinal buoy (Q) and the area is covered by the red sector of the Godrevy light 101° – 145°T.

The Longships inshore passage marks: Brisons high summit just open of low summit

The Sound, the inshore passage between Godrevy and the Stones, is half a mile wide and not recommended without local knowledge as there are overfalls, particularly with wind against tide, and the additional hazard of numerous pot buoys – this is no place to be caught with a fouled propeller if motoring. Pass well to seaward of the whole area.

Bound north from St Ives Bay, the flood begins about two hours after HW Dover (two hours after local Low Water). **Bound south**, ideally leave around local High Water, which will entail pushing the tide for the first hour, but will ensure a fair tide around Land's End and into Mount's Bay.

From the Stones buoy it is just over 17 miles to the next possible drying harbour at Newquay, along an impressive but unwelcoming stretch of coast; mostly high, crumbling cliffs, averaging between 40 and 75m in height. Along them there are numerous sandy coves and bays, such as Porthtowan and Perranporth, holiday resorts particularly popular with surfers thanks to the almost perpetual ground swell which produces ideal conditions for the sport. Numerous small rocky islets lie close inshore, but with the exception of Bawden Rocks, two small islands a mile north of St Agnes' Head, there are no off-lying dangers.

Unless heading for Newquay, the direct course to Trevose Head, just over 22 miles to the north-east, takes you safely two to three miles offshore. Inland, higher ground runs parallel to the coast, and a conspicuous feature is the large obelisk on the skyline south-east of Portreath.

Trevose Head lighthouse (Fl 7.5s 21M) is a prominent white tower on a precipitous headland with two large rocky islets, the Bull and Quies, nearly a mile to

Trevose Head from the west, with Stepper Point, centre, and Pentire Point in the distance

seaward. There is an inshore passage between them and the coast, but this should not be used without local knowledge and again the tide runs hard here. Give the islets and the headland a wide berth. From here Padstow Bay begins to open, with Pentire Point forming its distant northern extremity just over five miles away.

With no possible shelter in winds between south-west and north-east throughout this passage area, if the weather deteriorates and a blow looks likely, particularly from the south-west, the advice in the Admiralty Pilot 'to seek a good offing' is probably as sensible as you will get. Padstow is the only place where complete shelter will be found **once you are inside the harbour**. However, this is tidal and only accessible two hours either side of High Water, and the Camel estuary on which it lies is approached over a bar that becomes very dangerous in strong onshore weather.

A decision to run for Padstow in deteriorating conditions should be considered very carefully, with particular regard to the state of the tide, aiming to arrive between half-flood and High Water. With any ground swell, once the ebb commences, the shallow waters of Padstow Bay become very hazardous and unapproachable in strong winds from the north-west. The Stepper Point NCI station, Tel: 07810 898041, overlooks the approach to the estuary and can always be contacted 0900 – 1800 in season for details of current weather and sea state.

In fog or poor visibility, additional aids to navigation along this section of coast are the Longships (Horn 10s), Pendeen (Horn 20s), Stones Buoy (Whistle) and Trevose Head (Horn (2) 30s).

Godrevy lighthouse, the inspiration for Virginia Woolf's novel *To the lighthouse*

With surf breaking on Porthmeor Sands, St Ives' drying harbour is well tucked in behind St Ives Head. The Hayle estuary can be seen in the far distance

ST IVES AND NEWQUAY

Tides	HW Dover–0605
Charts	AC: 1168, SC 5603.4, 5603.5; Imray: C7
Hazards	**St Ives**: Harbour dries, exposed in onshore winds. Hoe Rock and starboard hand buoy to the north-east (both unlit), Carracks Rocks to south-east (unlit)
	Newquay: Harbour dries. Listrey Rock in northern approach
Overnight charge	**St Ives**: Harbour Authority mooring £16.16
	Newquay: Drying alongside £16.

From a distance St Ives Head looks like an island and, when entering the bay, this should be given a good berth to avoid Carn Everis Rocks on its northern side, which dry 3m, and Hoe Rock on its north-eastern side, which dries 1.8m. In the closer approach, an unlit conical green starboard hand buoy marks the end of the ruined outer pier. Smeatons Pier, which forms the eastern protective arm of the harbour, has a prominent but disused white lighthouse at its outer end. At night the pier head is marked by 2 FG vert lights; this and the shorter west pier (2FR vert) enclose a harbour which dries completely at LAT, but is normally accessible after half flood. It has a firm sandy bottom and there is a fleet of quite large fishing and trip boats based here during

the summer months which lie on heavy fore and aft drying moorings or alongside the quay while landing their catch or picking up people. Shelter is good in southerly and westerly weather, but anything further north can send a considerable sea into the bay and causes a heavy swell within the harbour.

In favourable conditions, anchor about 100m south-east of the harbour entrance in about 3m, but watch out for the large number of buoys marking keep pots towards Porthminster beach.

Due to the increase in fishing boat activity and landing, it is no longer possible to berth overnight inside the outer end of Smeatons Pier, but High Water permitting, deep keel boats can berth here temporarily,

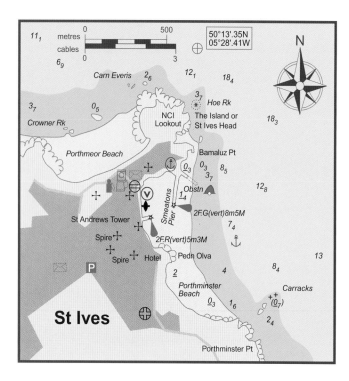

over a dangerous bar and tricky entrance channel through a large expanse of drying sands, it is not recommended for visitors. There are currently (2008) ongoing plans to regenerate and develop the harbour.

NEWQUAY

In fair weather and offshore winds, Newquay is a pleasant small drying harbour that is feasible for an overnight stop. Midway between it and Godrevy, St Agnes' Head is prominent, 91m high, with steep cliffs, while inland the isolated St Agnes' Hill (200m) is covered in heather and gorse and surmounted by a beacon. This was another site of intensive tin mining activity in the 1800s, and several conspicuous ruins can be seen along the shore. Just north of St Agnes' Head, Trevaunance Cove was but one small port exporting tin and copper – it was frequently rebuilt between 1700 and 1920 as gales swept away the massive granite walls.

Closing the land from the south, East and West Pentire Points form the entrance of the Gannel, a silted-up river mouth creating a fine sandy beach, and Fistral Bay, renowned for surfing, leads up to Towan Head, the entrance to Newquay Bay, which has the large Atlantic Hotel prominent on its highest point.

Although there are no off-lying dangers, overfalls occur up to half a mile off Towan Head, and it is wise to give it a reasonable berth before turning into the bay, when the eastern extremities of Newquay's extensive hotels and houses will come into view along the skyline right down to the cliff-backed beaches. The harbour lies in the south-western corner of the town, hidden behind a headland, east-north-east of which the Listrey Rocks, least depth 0.5m and 1.2m, lie 300m offshore. Keep well out into the bay before heading in towards the harbour walls as they come into view.

The whole of the inner part of the bay dries at Low Water Springs and the harbour is normally only accessible for average draught boats three hours either side of Local High Water (HW Dover –0604). If waiting for the tide, anchor off in the bay, which is well sheltered from the south and west. The entrance is 23m wide between the north and south quays, and the isolated jetty in the centre of the harbour dates from 1870 when it was originally linked to the shore with a wooden bridge carrying a railway track, which came down to the harbour through a tunnel to facilitate the loading of copper ore and china clay brought overland by rail from Par.

There were once four shipbuilding yards around Newquay and, at the height of its prosperity in the mid-1800s, nearly 150 trading vessels were owned in the port. The last cargo of clay was exported in 1921 and the last inward cargo (manure!) was discharged by the ketch *Hobah* in 1922.

Visitors normally berth alongside the inner end of the south quay, where there is a clean, hard sandy bottom,

if space is available, for short stays to replenish stores or in emergencies. However, bilge-keelers or boats able to take the bottom are well catered for, with six drying visitors' moorings in the harbour just off the prominent Woolworths store on the waterfront. The charge is £16.16 per night. The harbourmaster, Mr Steve Bassett, will help with any problems.

His office is on the pier, Tel: 01736 795018, and he normally works on VHF Channel 12, although VHF Channel 16 is also usually monitored when the harbour office is open. Fresh water is available on the piers, while Calor and Camping Gaz can be had from the Fishermen's Co-operative. Diesel is readily available in cans but the nearest petrol is just over a mile away.

During the season the town reels under the assault of tourists, its picturesque narrow streets and alleyways, harbour and wide sandy Porthmeor Beach on the seaward side of St Ives Head providing all the essentials of a seaside holiday. In spite of a certain amount of inevitable commercialism, the town retains much of its unique atmosphere, a factor that has made it a popular haunt of artists for many years, even more so with the arrival of the Tate Art Gallery's western outpost in a landmark building overlooking Porthmeor.

All other normal requirements can be found, such as banks, post office and provisions, and there are many cafés, pubs and restaurants. A very handy toilet and public shower block is in the car park just behind the harbour front. There are road and main line rail connections. A lifeboat is stationed at St Ives, launched on a trailer across the beach.

St Ives Bay stretches away to the north-east, backed by the extensive sand dunes and beach of Hayle Towans. Hayle, in the south-eastern corner, is a run-down, tidal harbour used by a few local fishing boats. Approached and you will dry clear of the local fishing boats lying on fore and aft moorings in the middle of the harbour, which suffers from a surge if there is much swell.

Harbourmaster Captain Derek Aunger is very helpful and is usually around 0830 – 1700 in the summer. His office is on the south pier, Tel: 01637 872809. Charges are £1.60 per metre per night, and water and diesel are available from him on request. Public toilets are close by, as is the licensed clubhouse of the Newquay Rowing Club where temporary membership is available, thus saving the trek up into town for a pint! These dedicated enthusiasts own several beautifully restored Scilly pilot gigs, including the oldest one still afloat, *Newquay*, built in 1812.

Newquay is one of the largest holiday resorts in Cornwall and, dubbed 'the Surfing Capital of Britain', its lively main centre is a short walk from the busy harbour. All normal requirements are here, including post office, banks, provisions, launderettes, and many pubs, cafés and restaurants. It has road, rail and air connections.

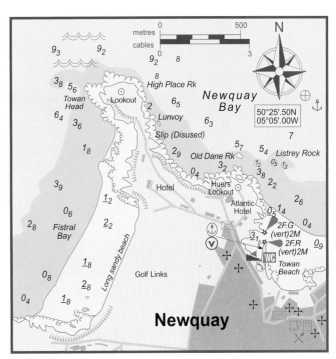

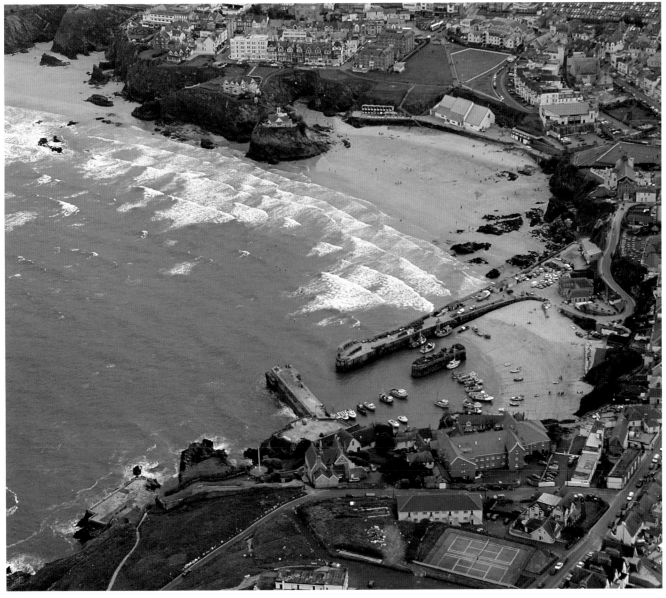

A visit to Newquay's small drying harbour should only be considered in settled offshore conditions

PADSTOW

Tides	HW Dover−0550
Range	MHWS 7.7m–MHWN 5.5m, MLWN 2.6m–MLWS 0.8m
Charts	AC: 1168, SC: 5603.5. Imray: C7, C58
Waypoint	North Pier End 50°32'.51N 04°56'.17W
Hazards	Gulland, Newland, Gurley, Chimney and Roscarrock Rocks (all unlit). Pot buoys to seaward. Wreck west of Stepper Point (unlit). Doom Bar and much of river and outer harbour dries. Buoyed channel (lit) but liable to change. Approach can be dangerous in onshore wind and sea. Busy tidal fishing port.
Harbour Speed limit	Five knots
Overnight charge	Harbour Authority, at anchor or alongside £15.

It is 13 miles from Newquay to the mouth of the River Camel, and Padstow lies two miles upstream. The Camel is a most attractive estuary, a spectacular area of golden drying sands, with a shoreline of low cliffs, fine sandy beaches and rolling dunes providing some lovely walks.

In 1989, as part of a flood prevention scheme, a hydraulic bottom-hinged gate was installed in the entrance of the formerly drying inner harbour at Padstow, making it possible to lie afloat here, and this has not only resulted in a steady increase in visiting pleasure craft, but also ongoing improvement to shoreside facilities.

However, the mouth of the river is restricted by the Doom Bar, a large sandbank drying at Low Water, and during strong onshore winds or heavy seas this lives up to its melancholy name, particularly around Low Water when the sea can break right across the entrance – conditions that are not always obvious from seaward. With care though, the River Camel is not difficult to enter in daylight and yachts of normal draught will have ample water from half-flood onwards.

The approach at night is relatively straightforward once you have located Stepper Point light (L Fl W 10s), not always easy at first as it is only 12m above sea level and has a range of just four miles. Note, however, that the shore lights of Trebetherick and Polzeath on the eastern side of the entrance are by far the most dominant feature from seaward and should not be mistaken for the lights of Padstow, which are far less visible and do not really begin to emerge until you are well into the river.

Flanked by clean yellow sand, the final approach to Padstow is clearly visible on the right. Visitors lie afloat in the inner harbour, which is accessible two hours either side of High Water

The attractive Camel estuary looking seaward – the Doom Bar is just beginning to uncover, left. Newland Island can be seen in the centre of the picture, with Pentire Point on the right

APPROACHES

The approach from the north or south is unmistakable. Trevose Head, four miles to the west, is a steep 80m high headland, which rises above the surrounding hinterland, giving it the appearance from a distance of being a separate island. In addition, the Bull and Quies, prominent large rocks, lie a mile to the west.

Trevose lighthouse is on the north-western corner of the headland and dates from 1847; Padstow lifeboat house is on the north-eastern side of the headland in Mother Ivey's Bay, re-sited here in 1967 after the original station at Hawkers Cove inside the mouth of the estuary fell prey to the encroachment of the Doom Bar. This bar, according to local legend, was created by a mermaid, shot by a local man who thought she was a fish. Cursing him with her dying breath, she threw up a handful of sand which turned into the Doom Bar, vowing that 'henceforth the harbour should be desolate!'

Tidal streams run strongly off Trevose – over two knots at Springs – particularly between the rocks and the headland and you should keep to seaward of the Quies before heading up into Padstow Bay, passing inside Gulland Rock, a prominent rocky island 28m high, where, again, the stream can run strongly.

Beware of several isolated hazards further inshore; Gurley Rock (least depth 3m) and Chimney Rock (2.3m) are not normally a problem to boats of average draught, but worth remembering near Low Water, particularly if there is any ground swell running. Stepper Point, a bold and rounded grassy headland, footed with cliffs, forms the south side of the river mouth and is easily identified by the large stone daymark, like a truncated factory chimney. There is an NCI lookout, Tel: 07810 898041, high up at its eastern extremity, and almost at sea level the harbour approach light on an iron pillar (L Fl 10s 4M).

Three cables west-north-west of the daymark there is a dangerous wreck, almost awash at Low Water, so

give the headland a wide berth and head up towards Pentire Point, another bold headland forming the north-eastern arm of the bay, with the distinctive island of Newland, a pyramid 35m high, half a mile to the north-west. Approaching from the north, it is best to keep well to seaward of Newland, as Roscarrock, a rock with least depth of 0.8m, lurks three cables west of Rumps Point, the north-eastern corner of Pentire. The brig *Maria Asumpta* was disastrously wrecked here in May 1995.

THE RIVER CAMEL TO PADSTOW

Enter the river on a flood tide, ideally no earlier than three hours before Local High Water (HW Dover –0550) and do not attempt it in any ground swell from the north-west, or if breaking water can be seen.

The Doom Bar, a large expanse of drying sand, fills the south-western corner of the river mouth, and opposite, the houses of Trebetherick sprawl along the low cliffs. These are fringed with rocky ledges, and the

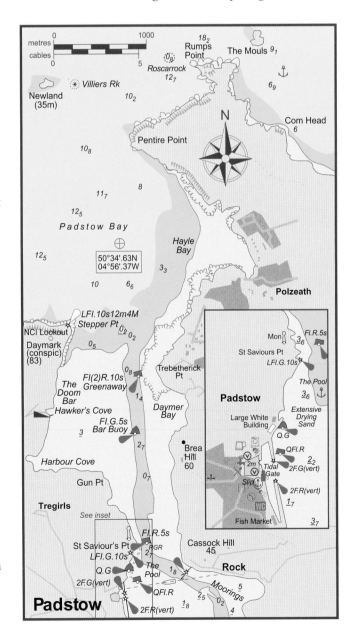

Padstow outer harbour approach at Low Water – note the proximity to the shore. The Pool lies beyond

channel between them and the sands runs due south, with the western end of Pentire Point providing a useful back bearing.

Depths reduce quickly from 3m to a least depth of 0.8m two cables north of the first channel buoy, Greenaway, a red port hand can (Fl (2) R l0s), while Doom Bar, two cables further south, is a conical green starboard hand buoy (Fl G 5s). At Low Water the channel is a cable wide and depths vary between 2m and 0.4m as far as St Saviour's Point, known locally as *Ship-me-pumps*, a quarter of a mile downstream of the harbour.

A prominent monument stands on this rocky headland and a red and green middle ground buoy (Fl R 5s) abeam of it, where the channel divides. The main channel to the harbour lies to starboard of the buoy, while the river bears away towards the village of Rock on the eastern shore. Just south of the buoy, there is the Pool, with an average depth of 3m and a number of local moorings in it. It is possible to anchor clear of them, if waiting for sufficient water to get into the Inner harbour, although at Springs the tide can run hard, between four and five knots at times, on both the flood and ebb.

A large area of drying sandbanks fills the centre of the river and the narrow approach channel to Padstow also dries almost completely at Springs. Hold tight to the western shore and leave the green beacon with triangular topmark (Fl G 10s) close on your starboard hand. Pass the green Kettle Rock buoy (QG) to starboard and just short of the harbour entrance leave the red Town Bar can (QR) to port. The outer pier ends are marked with 2FR vert and 2FG vert port and starboard lights.

Proceed under power and watch out for fishing boats under way, particularly in the harbour mouth, where the main stream runs strongly at right angles to the entrance. South Dock, the commercial harbour, lies immediately to port, a long narrow, drying basin, but yacht borne visitors should continue straight ahead through the tidal gate into the Inner Harbour, which is open two hours either side of High Water, day and night, weekends and Bank Holidays. The maximum depth within the harbour is usually maintained at three metres, although more water can be retained to accommodate deeper draught boats if the berthing master is informed on arrival. Visitor charges (the same whether you anchor in the river or lie alongside) are £1.50 per metre per night.

The harbour office (open 0800 – 1700 weekdays, and two hours before and after High Water, every tide) is close by on South Quay and incorporates an amenity block housing showers, toilets and a laundry with 24-hour access by pin code/keypad. The showers are included in your berthing fee and the laundry is operated by pre-pay tokens available from the harbour office. You should try to report by VHF before arrival, or as soon as you have berthed. Visitors are requested not to leave vessels unattended for any length of time without first consulting the harbourmaster.

The Harbour Commission sometimes has visitors' moorings available in the river for vessels up to 12m. To check either call Padstow Harbour (VHF Ch 16, 12, during office hours) or telephone ahead for availability.

FUEL, FRESH WATER AND GAS

Diesel is available alongside South Pier when the tide permits, otherwise both diesel and petrol can be obtained in cans if you leave them outside the harbour office at 0900 or 1600. Fresh water is available on the

Once inside Padstow's inner harbour, visitors lie afloat and secure in attractive and colourful surroundings

inner harbour berths. Calor and Camping Gaz can also be acquired through the harbour office – leave your empty cylinder at the same times as for the fuel pick up.

PADSTOW FACILITIES

A small, unspoilt town, with attractive and colourful old buildings lining the quayside, Padstow is inevitably popular with holidaymakers but has managed to avoid much of the overt commercialism of some of the other north Cornish resorts.

Formerly a vital port for north Cornwall, exporting tin, copper, slate, granite, china clay and grain, and importing coal, salt and timber, it was also important as a shipbuilding centre. By the beginning of this century, however, commercial trade had dwindled steadily with the silting of the Doom Bar and the advent of road and rail transport, and it would seem that the mermaid's wish had been fulfilled, for little more than a small fishing fleet remained. However, in recent years this has grown considerably, evidence of the resurgence in prosperity. Pot and net boats land vast quantities of shellfish here, as a look in the sizeable wet tanks on the Fish Quay will reveal, and large beam trawlers also work out of the port. Coasters occasionally discharge cargoes of fertiliser and roadstone and the resident sand dredger, *Sandsnipe*, lands about 100,000 tons a year, mostly for agricultural use.

The prominent red brick building on the north side of the harbour was formerly a warehouse – today it houses the Tourist Information Centre and additional visitors'

showers, toilets and a laundry, accessed 24 hours by the same pin code. All the berths in the inner harbour have access to water and electricity (£1 and £5 card meters). Close by in the town centre you will find HSBC, Lloyds TSB and Barclays banks, all with cashpoints, provisions, including a Spar (open late and on Sundays), Steins Delicatessen and a Tesco supermarket on the outskirts of the town, with a regular courtesy bus from the harbour (see harbour office for times). Chandlery can be ordered through the harbour office.

As a popular holiday town, there is an abundance of quayside cafés, no shortage of pubs, notably the London Inn, Old Custom House and Old Ship, all of which have good pub menus, and a number of restaurants catering for all tastes and prices, including the celebrated Seafood Restaurant, Tel: 532700, owned by the well-known television chef and author Rick Stein. Inevitably, here, reservations well in advance are essential. Rick Stein's Café offers simpler, cheaper fare or, alternatively, try Margots, an informal bistro, Tel: 533441, R Bar for tapas, burgers and seafood, Rojanos, Tel: 532796, for pizza/pasta, or last but not least, a choice of good fish and chip shops!

The walks out towards Stepper Point and beyond are a delightful way to work up an appetite or thirst, with an abundance of fine sandy beaches en route. Alternatively, head inland and explore the Camel Trail, which follows the course of the old railway line to Wadebridge, beyond which Padstow was linked to the main rail network until it fell victim to Dr Beeching's

Padstow's outer harbour and the spectacular sands of the Camel

axe in 1966. It's an attractive and gentle riverside walk as long as you are prepared to run the gauntlet of the myriad of cyclists! If you'd rather join them than be at their mercy, bikes can be hired at the beginning of the trail.

However, much of the pleasure boating activity in the estuary, particularly dinghy sailing, is centred on Rock, on the opposite shore. Here there are several deeper pools and a large number of local moorings as well as some drying Harbour Commission moorings also available for visitors, athough these tend to be hired on a weekly basis for people holidaying in the area. Rock is a much quieter little village, with many holiday

homes, and is linked to Padstow by the Harbour Commissioners Black Tor pedestrian ferry, which runs continuously between 0800 and 1950. If you are lying in the Pool, the ferry can be hailed to take you ashore.

Rock Sailing Club has a fine clubhouse, an old converted grain warehouse on the quay with excellent facilities. Visitors are welcome to use the bar and showers, and snack meals are also available. The sand dunes and clean beaches running seaward from Rock towards Brea Hill are most attractive, and those seeking a longer walk should head out through Trebetherick and Polzeath to the distant heights of Pentire Point, with its fine views of the estuary and the rugged coast beyond.

The Camel, once a busy waterway, is still navigable on a good tide as far as Wadebridge, about five miles inland where yachts can dry out alongside Commissioner's Quay. However, this definitely needs some local knowledge or reconaissance in the dinghy, as the channel is tortuous and unmarked.

Padstow Port Guide - Area telephone code: 01841

Harbourmaster: Captain Rob Atkinson, Harbour Office, Padstow, PL28 8AQ, Tel: 532239; Fax: 533346. Open 0800 – 1700, Mon – Fri. Email: padstowharbour@btconnect.com; website: www.padstow-harbour.co.uk.

VHF: Ch 16, working 12, callsign *Padstow Harbour*, office hours and two hours either side of High Water.

Mail drop: c/o Harbour Office.

Emergency services: Lifeboat at Trevose Head. Falmouth Coastguard.

Anchorages: The Pool, a quarter mile downstream of Padstow. Drying, clear of moorings at Rock.

Moorings/berthing: Inner harbour, afloat at all times, access through tidal gate two hours either side of Local High Water, day and night, weekends and Bank Holidays. Harbour Commission moorings in river

sometimes available on application.

Charges: £1.50 per metre per night.

Water taxi: Regular ferry Padstow to Rock will pick up from boats in the Pool.

Marina: None.

Phones: On quay.

Doctor: Tel: 532346.

Hospital: Treliske, Truro, Tel: 01872 250000.

Churches: All denominations.

Local weather forecast: Harbour office.

Fuel: Harbourmaster can arrange diesel and petrol in cans. Diesel alongside seaward side of South Pier when tide permits.

Gas: Calor/Gaz from harbour office.

Water: On quay.

Tourist Information Centre: Red brick building, north side of harbour, Tel: 533449.

Banks/cashpoints: Barclays,

Lloyds TSB and HSBC all have cashpoints.

Post office: Duke Street.

Internet access: Public Library, Market Strand.

Rubbish: Bins on quay.

Showers/toilets: In harbour office, and red brick building, North Quay. Public toilets on quay. Toilets/showers, Rock Sailing Club.

Launderette: In harbour office and red brick building, North Quay.

Provisions: Most normal requirements. Spar open until 2130 and Sundays. Courtesy bus to Tesco on outskirts of town.

Chandler: Limited selection at Rigmarine, South Quay, Tel: 532657. Harbour office can usually assist.

Repairs: Chapman & Hewitt, Tel: 01208 813487; GB Smith & Son, Tel: 01208 862815.

Marine engineers: GB Smith & Son, Tel: 01208 862815.

Electronic engineers: Marconi Marine, Tel: 01326 312855.

Transport: Western Greyhound bus service 555, Tel: 01637 871871, hourly connection with mainline railway at Bodmin Parkway, Tel: 08457 484950. Newquay airport, Tel: 01637 860551, flights to London and other UK destinations.

Taxis: Padstow Cabs, Tel: 532384, Aacorn Cabs, Tel: 532903.

Car parking: Large car park on South Quay.

Yacht Club: Rock Sailing Club, The Quay, Rock, Wadebridge PL27 6LB, Tel: 01208 862431.

Eating out: Good pubs, cafés and restaurants in both Padstow and Rock.

Things to do: Local museum in Padstow. Guided tours of Prideaux Place (stately home). Excellent beaches, swimming and walking.